THE ODD MAN OUT

THE ODD MAN OUT

THE FASCINATING STORY OF RON SAUNDERS' REIGN AT ASTON VILLA

GRAHAM DENTON

pitch

First published by Pitch Publishing, 2017

Pitch Publishing
A2 Yeoman Gate
Yeoman Way
Worthing
Sussex
BN13 3QZ
www.pitchpublishing.co.uk
info@pitchpublishing.co.uk

A CIP catalogue record is available for this book
from the British Library.

ISBN 978-1-78531-283-0

Typesetting and origination by Pitch Publishing

Printed and bound in Great Britain by TJ International

Contents

'Villa have been a great club,
are still a great club, and
always will be a great club.'

Fred Rinder, Aston Villa
chairman, 1936

Acknowledgements

FOR helping guide *The Odd Man Out* in the right direction, I would like to express my gratitude to Paul and Jane Camillin at Pitch Publishing, Derek Hammond and Gareth Davis, as well as to Duncan Olner of Olner Design Limited. Researching this book involved many long, painstaking but very enjoyable hours poring over numerous sources. A big thank you for the information they provided is due to every single person whose words I had the pleasure of reading. *Aston Villa: The Complete Record* by Rob Bishop and Frank Holt was a constant and particularly useful reference point throughout. Rob Bishop also warrants huge appreciation for reading my manuscript and making many beneficial suggestions.The views and opinions of so many ex-players, managers, coaches and journalists have been invaluable in my painting a more rounded picture and I'm extremely grateful for that. Wherever possible, credit is given in the text to the books from which I've quoted. Throughout the writing process, the encouragement of my wife Dianna and my most loyal supporter James Carter was a much welcome rock. Lastly, I am especially indebted to two former Villa players, John Deehan and Gordon Smith, for taking the time to reply to my communications. Shortly after our correspondence, Gordon Smith passed away and this book is dedicated to his memory, as well as to all the Villans who've gone before and all those still to come.

Introduction

'I'm the odd man out; the one who, as a youngster, had no burning ambitions about becoming a professional footballer and scoring the winning goal at Wembley... by the time I was 24 or 25, I had become obsessed with the idea of managing a professional club and making my mark on that side of the game.'

Ron Saunders' Aston Villa Scrapbook

SOMEONE on a Facebook page celebrating 'football nostalgia' had uploaded a photo of Ron Saunders. In it, holding aloft the League Cup trophy his Aston Villa side had just won, Saunders played host to a cheery grin that spread from ear to ear. The picture, one poster commented, had clearly 'been Photoshopped'. Why? Because Saunders looked happy! Witty as it may have been, it was a typical observation about the manager. With what ATV commentator Hugh Johns once called 'his gloomy face' and sometimes glowering expression, Saunders was persistently caricatured for his joylessness, the only Scouser in the world without a sense of humour. He 'did come over as a miserable old git', another online contributor added.

In *Best, Pelé and a Half-time Bovril* by Andrew Smart, the author describes Saunders as 'a hard man, taciturn, rarely seen with a smile'. It is another archetypal image. Mention the name and it almost instantly summons a flurry of similar epithets: *Sergeant major Saunders, Mister 110 per cent, The Iron Man.* Stock encapsulations are bandied about. He was a 'tough guy', a 'no-nonsense character', a 'strict disciplinarian'. Very few are meant to be complimentary. Such was the impression of the Birkenhead-born boss as a sourpuss, when the fledgling football fanzine *When Saturday Comes* first set up in 1986, the editorial in its initial issue posited as one of the questions it sought to answer, 'Does anybody in football actually like Ron Saunders?'

With his penchant on matchdays for sporting a long, leather coat (and often matching black gloves), Saunders appeared to be soccer's answer to *The Sweeney*'s Jack Regan or, possessing a passing resemblance to Bob Hoskins in *The Long Good Friday*, seemed more East End gangster than football boss. Cynics were certain he wore it simply to look even more sinister! The general belief was that he had a personality to match. 'Saunders,' wrote Richard Whitehead in *The Soul of Aston Villa in 50 Moments*, with a touch of exaggeration for amusing effect, 'was just about the scariest man in the game, able to turn players, journalists and possibly even members of his own family into quivering wrecks with just one hard stare.'

Whenever lists are compiled of the top British football bosses of all time, cast-iron certainties to be heading the queue are Sir Matt Busby, Bill Shankly, Bob Paisley, Don Revie, Brian Clough, Sir Alf Ramsey, Jock Stein, Bill Nicholson, Herbert Chapman and the most successful club manager of the modern era, Sir Alex Ferguson. You'll seldom, if ever, find Saunders keeping them company. In fact, in a 2009 poll of the '50 greatest managers in British football history' run by the *Daily Mail*, he only registered with the various contributors at a lowly number 43. One place above him was Jim Smith. 'A manager who could make ordinary players do great things,' Smart also writes of him. He remains, however, rarely anything more than a figure in the background.

Of course, there are enough related tales about him to give them some credence, but the abiding public perception of Saunders as a tyrant who mishandled his players, upset his coaching staff and fought with members of the boardroom has undoubtedly overshadowed his achievements. While, in terms of actual silverware, the trophies his teams won were relatively few, Saunders' accomplishments were nonetheless significant and deserving of recognition. Certainly they were far more than many of his managerial peers.

BBC sports broadcaster Pat Murphy wrote in the *Birmingham Post* in 2006, 'If any journalist manages to unpick that lock, the memoirs of Ron Saunders would be fascinating.' Fascinating, yes. But as with any memoir they would only show one side of the coin. Besides, Saunders' famous reticence when it comes to talking about himself means those memoirs will never see the printer's ink. *The Odd Man Out* – the title taken from a description Saunders gave to himself – isn't an out-and-out biography. It's primarily the story of Saunders' time at Aston Villa and the relationship he and the football club shared during a period in which Saunders enjoyed – if that is the correct word – his greatest success. It's a story worth telling. Ron Saunders may not have been one of its main protagonists but without his presence the portrait of English football in the 1970s and 1980s would undoubtedly be much, much less.

Revolutions

AT three o'clock that Saturday afternoon, had the ten bells tolled in the tower of the town's 'crooked spire' barely half a mile away, not a soul at Saltergate would have heard a sound. The home of Chesterfield FC, one of the oldest grounds in the Football League, was playing host to one of its oldest members, Aston Villa. Most of them coming from the West Midlands, 16,689 – more than double the Derbyshire club's usual gate – were there. Close to kick-off, spilling in their dozens on to the sloping pitch, the Villa fans had forced a call for calm from the team's manager Vic Crowe. Urging them to cease their surges, it took a megaphone to get his message over. Their fervour was understandable. The date was 15 August 1970. It was the opening day of the 1970/71 season. It was also the first time in their 96-year history that Aston Villa were competing in the third tier of English football.

Those 96 years had been punctuated with many triumphal moments. Villa, one of the founding fathers of the Football League, were the most successful club of the late Victorian and Edwardian eras, becoming the first to win the championship six times including the 'Double' triumph of 1897. Not since 1910, though, had they registered a league title and the years when they'd enjoyed an unprecedented 'Golden Age' and, in the words of *The Times'* Geoffrey Green, 'the claret and blue shirt was the most respected and feared in the land' were fading fast into obscurity. 'Aston Villa. All that is good in the game is captured in that magical world-famous name: goals, glory in the FA Cup and league, players who have become legends, vast baying crowds in the cauldron of Villa Park,' wrote one scribe. 'The tragedy about the club is that it all happened in the past.'

Once described in the 1934 edition of *The Football Encyclopaedia* as 'the outstanding professional organisation of the world', the Birmingham club were now English football's fallen giants. Villa, according to Green, had 'slipped down the depths'.

Such a plummet was the culmination of decades of steady decline. After numerous disappointing post-war seasons, an FA Cup win in 1957 for a seventh and record-breaking time – a controversial 2-1 victory secured by two Peter McParland goals in five second-half minutes putting paid to Busby's Babes' prospects of becoming the first team to achieve the 'Double' since Villa themselves managed it 60 years earlier – promised a genuine revival in the Midlanders' fortunes. Instead, it marked the start of a rot that, two seasons later, saw the club condemned to Second Division football for only the second time. Less than nine years on and Villa had become, Peter Morris wrote in *Charles Buchan's Football Monthly*, 'no more than seedy "has-beens" trapped in the wrong half of the Second Division with the unfashionables'.

Cup-winning manager and former Villa favourite Eric Houghton, ex-Sheffield United boss Joe Mercer (despite moulding together a highly gifted, youthful side christened 'Mercer's Minors' that won promotion as well as the inaugural League Cup), and Dick Taylor had all paid the price for failing to halt the deterioration. In 1966/67, 'with the worst side in their long history' according to Morris, Villa lost 24 of their 42 matches, won just three league games after the turn of the year and on 6 May, following a 4-2 home defeat by Everton, were condemned to relegation back to the second tier. By the time Southampton hammered a final day nail in Villa's coffin – 6-2 at The Dell – Taylor had been shown the door.

The day he departed, Taylor issued the board with the warning, 'You must get around and find out more about what's going on at other clubs before it's too late.' Under the chairmanship of Norman Smith, a former school headmaster in his mid-60s, the five-man Villa board (three other members of which were septuagenarians) had entirely failed to keep abreast of their contemporaries. Smith, who now worked for the local council, didn't even own a car.

Rising wages and transfer fees – a consequence of the 1961 abolition of the maximum wage limit and the old 'retain and transfer' system – had necessitated clubs to source new methods of generating income. While their rivals explored original commercial avenues and recognised the need to promote their clubs in ways that would appeal to the existing support and attract entirely new fan bases, Villa had been left out-of-step.

The club's traditional motto was 'Prepared', but the board couldn't have been more ill-equipped. Ensnared by old-fashioned values, Smith and co., well-meaning as they were, ran Aston Villa like league clubs were run in the 1920s and 30s. It was, said Scottish full-back Charlie Aitken, one of Mercer's bright young things, comparable to 'a corner shop'. Neither a scouting network nor an effective coaching structure had been developed. Villa's best players had been allowed to leave and so inferior were the replacements that Peter Morris wrote, 'Villa Park, long denigrated in Birmingham as the "Hall of Memory", has also become a tomb of unknown warriors.'

In desperate financial straits, with debt spinning out of control, bold action was patently required. Unfortunately, Smith and his cohorts didn't share the same clarity of vision. As Taylor's replacement, former Burnley player Tommy Cummings was brought in. It was another misguided act. A qualified coach with a strong reputation, having led Mansfield Town to promotion from the Fourth Division in 1963, Cummings was hardly the high pedigree manager needed to steer the club upwards. The task was beyond him. Villa ended a turbulent campaign in 16th.

Eighteen games into the following season, with just two wins and 11 points to their name, they sat right at the foot of the table. How, asked Morris, had it come to this? That while the likes of Manchester United and Spurs had 'marched forward to new dimensions of high success', Villa had 'slipped just as steadily downward'. Morris was in little doubt. 'Complacency? Muddle-headed policies? Diminished financial resources? Inability to find good players? All have something to do with it.' The bulk of the blame, though, he apportioned to the ageing directors.

On 9 November 1968, forever subsequently referred to as 'Black Saturday', a 1-0 home defeat to Preston North End (the winner an own goal by Villa centre-half Fred Turnbull) proved to be the tipping point. In the final minutes of the match, between 800 and 1,000 angry fans assembled in the Villa Park paddock, venting their venom towards the directors sitting in the main stand. Chants and banners demanding 'The Board Must Go' were accompanied by boos and slow hand-clapping. Several mounted police advanced to quell a sit-down protest. The demonstration, the *Sunday Mercury* reported, was described by the police's Chief Superintendent Arthur Brannigan as the 'most violent' witnessed at the ground. Later that evening, more than 200 youths stood en masse on the steps outside the *Mercury* offices in Birmingham city centre, echoing their calls for the board to quit, before being dispersed by police on foot and motorcycle. Inevitably, it was Cummings who paid the heaviest price. Two days later, after just 16 months in office, Cummings took the bullet along with his assistant Malcolm Musgrove, with Villa's trainer Arthur Cox put in temporary charge.

The revolutionary air that had been prevalent in Paris earlier in the year had at last reached B6. After voting with their feet, the restless natives were now up in arms. A threat to withdraw their support by a splinter group of fans was issued. Assurances were demanded that the board resign by the start of the next season. Smith kept denying any financial difficulties but, with the announcement that re-capitalisation of the club had been discussed and the directors were 'considering concessions', it was obvious that a crisis existed. Essentially, Aston Villa was now up for grabs and a takeover bid imminent. The board's position was untenable.

As results continued to nosedive and numbers through the turnstiles dried up – on 7 December, 12,747, an all-time Saturday low for Villa Park, watched a goalless draw with Charlton – speculation about potential new owners gathered pace. Various offers of assistance were forthcoming, with rival consortiums expressing an interest in assuming control. Finally, on 16 December, news was released: a proposal by a group, the Birmingham Industrial Trust, led by wealthy London financier Pat Matthews, was accepted. A buy-out of the existing Villa directors' 800 shares at £60 for each £5 share signalled a behind-the-scenes revolution and a whole new regime was swiftly convened, with only Bob MacKay, recruited just a few months earlier, retained from the deposed board.

Harry Kartz, owner of a string of racehorses and Harry Parkes, a Villa full-back from the club's post-war years, whose Birmingham-based sports goods business had made him a wealthy man, were brought in. For chairman, Matthews had but one man in mind: Doug Ellis, a Cheshire-born businessman who'd been so successful in pioneering the package holiday with his Birmingham-based travel company, he was a millionaire by 40. Though a self-confessed Villa fan who claimed he'd first seen them play in April 1948, Ellis's three years spent as a Birmingham City director didn't exactly enamour him to large sections of the Villa support. Gratitude that their beloved club now had in place some possible saviours was, however, the overriding emotion.

'I am not unaware of the formidable task I have before me,' the new chairman declared. One of his first jobs was to fill the empty hotseat. Two days later, he did so with the exuberant figure of Tommy Docherty. The charismatic Scot who'd won his managerial spurs at Chelsea between 1962 and 1967 was renowned for his hard-fighting personality. If anyone was brave enough to take on the challenge of leading Aston Villa, it was Docherty. 'I'd love to stay at Villa Park for the rest of my career,' he stated in his opening gambit, 'but in football who can tell?' Longevity and

Docherty weren't two words that went together. His previous tenancy at QPR had lasted all of 29 days.

He wasted little time in imposing himself. Within a week, Brian Tiler arrived from another of Docherty's former clubs, Rotherham United – in February 1968 Docherty's Rotherham side had dumped Villa from the FA Cup at Villa Park – and was instantly made captain. Under their new manager's charge, Villa won their first five games, the fifth a sweet 2-1 FA Cup victory over Docherty's last employers from Loftus Road. 'To call Tommy Docherty rumbustious is like calling a tornado a gust of wind,' one journalist wrote. Docherty breezed into Villa Park and players and fans alike were swept up by his enthusiasm.

Buoyed by a newborn sense of purpose, the club's latent support resurfaced; 41,250 watched a Boxing Day clash with Cardiff. At January's end, nearly 60,000 at Villa Park witnessed a 2-1 beating of Southampton in an FA Cup fourth-round replay. Bottom of the division with only 15 points from 23 games when Docherty arrived, by the season's finish Villa were in 18th, staving off what had seemed like a nailed-on relegation.

The financial problems were still considerable. In debt to the tune of £182,000, with no money in the bank when Ellis took over, Villa remained on the edge of disaster. Ellis had inherited a club he later described as being 'low in morale and spirit and bereft of ideas'. The ground was dilapidated, glass was broken, wooden doors and windowsills were rotting. There was graffiti everywhere. Aston Villa had become, Graham McColl wrote in *The Hamlyn Illustrated History of Aston Villa, 1874–1998*, 'a down-at-heel aristocrat, forced to struggle for survival in sometimes seedy surroundings'. The situation was, in Ellis's words, 'so bad as to be indescribable'.

A long, hard economy drive had to be undertaken. 'A once proud club,' journalist Ian Johnson put it, 'suffered the humiliation of having to hold out the begging bowl.' They launched a massive appeal for public support. Companies were asked to provide services gratis. Fans were invited to send in money for shares, sold at £5 each, which they would eventually be issued. Ellis and his staff, using the boardroom as an office, were opening an average of 200 letters a day.

To those who couldn't afford a £5 share, Villa, in conjunction with the *Birmingham Mail*, asked for a pound to be donated, if people could. No fewer than 2,000 responded and were each presented with a parchment scroll in recognition of their support. By April 1969 the share issue, the club's first since 1896, was subscribed to the tune of £205,835. In Villa's hour of need, help seemed to come from every quarter. 'We got barrels of beer off Ansells and buns from a cake shop and asked the tradesmen, plumbers, painters, decorators to bring all their gear,' recalled Ellis.

A commercial manager, Eric Woodward, was persuaded to return from the States to organise a new set-up. Fundraising became a fine art. Off the pitch, lights were switched off to save money. Staff wore overcoats just to keep warm. The club, Ellis said, 'wouldn't spend a penny if a half-penny would do.' The price of season tickets rose by 60 per cent. It all saw much-needed revenue pour in.

In the summer of 1969, with money raised from the shares, Docherty entered the transfer market, wheeling and dealing with typical gusto. Southend's Ian 'Chico' Hamilton – first acquainted with Docherty at Stamford Bridge – was happy to reunite with his former boss. Midfielder Pat McMahon, Jock Stein's first post-Lisbon signing, joined on a free from Celtic. Most significantly, in July, Docherty pulled off the sensational double signing of brothers Bruce and Neil Rioch from Luton Town for a combined total of £110,000. The acquisition of Bruce Rioch, 21 and a rising star coveted by many, was viewed as a major coup. His £100,000 fee – inconceivable only months previously – was the first such sum to be paid by a Second Division club. 'The only way we got him,' Ellis later said, 'was to convince his mother, who was a Tommy Docherty fan.' The common consensus was that Villa, now the most expensively constructed side in the division, would be on the up and up.

All three made their debuts in the opening league game – against Ron Saunders' Norwich City side. But when the Canaries came away from Villa Park 1-0 victors, all the pre-season optimism seemed to vanish in that one afternoon. Instead of a road upwards, the signposts clearly pointed towards a season of struggle. Villa took ten games to register a win, 3-2 at home to Hull City. The patient was still ailing and even a massive blood transfusion – £275,000 was spent on new players – looked to have had little effect. Harry Kartz would later say, 'Tommy Docherty brought the place back to life. He had personality.' The media-savvy manager 'lifted morale and spirit and changed the outlook overnight,' Ellis reflected, 'because he had such a magnetic appeal in the eyes of the public.' But the disease infecting the club had gnawed at its very bones and was still spreading.

There was to be no miracle cure. By mid-November 1969, Docherty had tried 27 different players in the first team. Villa were 21st in the table and in dire trouble. Arguments broke out over contracts and discipline. Docherty made enemies in both the boardroom and the dressing room, with senior players feeling he treated them unfairly. They were no longer performing for him. All that initial sunlight had now been clouded. By the turn of the year, Villa had gained only three more victories. Hoping for a new morning, the supporters had suffered another false dawn.

Nonetheless, Docherty remained a firm favourite. Dissent and disgruntlement was aimed primarily at Doug Ellis. The loud cries for him to leave, he ignored. In the week before Christmas, after Watford won 2-0 at Villa Park, the Villa chairman convened a marathon board meeting. The manager was given the time-honoured vote of confidence but the writing was on the wall in bold lettering. Docherty, in one writer's words, had been 'feted like a Roman Emperor by fans grateful for the way he had restored Villa's self-respect'. Now the assassins were plotting behind his back.

When, shortly after an FA Cup third-round replay exit to Charlton, Villa suffered a humiliating 5-3 defeat at home to Portsmouth – another once-great club struggling near the bottom – Docherty's doom was sealed. Villa's first league game of the decade had left them nestled at the very foot of the division. During the match the Holte End had chorused, 'Walsall, Walsall, here we come.' Whether it was gallows humour or a cry of resignation didn't really matter: either way, no one was laughing. Two days later, Ellis announced, with regret, that Docherty's stormy, controversial 13-month tenure in B6 was over. He'd been in charge for just 397 days. According to *Rothman's*, Docherty was number 712 on the list of managers who'd lost their jobs since the war. Football management sure was a precarious profession.

Ellis, Docherty would later say, 'has claret and blue blood in his veins'. It had turned icy cold. Recalling how Ellis had initially said he was right behind his manager, Docherty quipped, 'I told him I'd sooner have him in front of me, where I could see him.' The board, Docherty felt, acted too hastily in dismissing him. Lifting the club from the pit of despair into which it had fallen had still been possible. The timing of Docherty's sacking was thought ill-judged by others, too. With just 16 games to salvage Villa's pride if not their Second Division status, the new incumbent in the hotseat had a thankless task.

The man handed it was former Villa wing-half and captain Vic Crowe. Welsh-born but raised in the Birmingham suburb of Handsworth from the age of two, Crowe had established himself in the Villa team when Danny Blanchflower vacated the right-half berth in 1954. He missed the 1957 FA Cup Final due to injury but captained the side to the Second Division title in 1960 and League Cup Final success in 1961. The chalk to Docherty's cheese, the quiet, thoughtful Crowe had been coaching for three years with Atlanta Chiefs in the States when Villa's call came and together with newly appointed first team trainer Ron Wylie (Eric Houghton's last signing as Villa manager), they instilled a fresh competitive mentality into the ranks.

The February signing of experienced centre-forward Andy Lochhead from Leicester would prove a key acquisition. But it was all too little too late. In March, after just one win in Crowe's first 11 games, Villa were still marooned at the bottom and, despite beating both Middlesbrough and Sheffield United in their final two fixtures, the battle had already been lost.

Docherty, with typical frankness, opined that, although it was a 'tragedy' that his former club were relegated, 'I will back them to bounce back. *Then* watch them go!' Any betting man would surely have done likewise. Crowe, however, was under no illusions. 'This is going to be a tough, demanding season,' he said on the eve of the historic campaign, 'and we will need all-out professionalism to get through in the manner we are hoping for.'

After only two minutes of that opening day game at Saltergate, Pat McMahon fired Villa into the lead. Two Bruce Rioch thunderbolts ensured a 3-2 victory. Further journeys to unfamiliar destinations – Wrexham, Reading and Fulham – had the Villa faithful referencing their British atlases but rewarded with witnessing vital wins. Despite the blow of losing Rioch at the end of August to an injury that later necessitated cartilage operations on both knees, the early signs were positive. Villa kept pace with the frontrunners and, with attendances at Villa Park averaging around 28,000, their supporters had every reason to suppose that their travels to strange outposts would soon be at an end.

Towards the end of January 1971 Villa were top of the table. They also had a League Cup Final to look forward to. In Christmas week, before more than 62,000 fans packed tight into Villa Park, the Third Division underdogs claimed a memorable semi-final second-leg victory over First Division Manchester United. A goal down on the night to a Brian Kidd strike and trailing 2-1 on aggregate, Villa bagged a place at Wembley with two headed goals from McMahon and Lochhead, delivering a knockout blow to a United side fielding Best, Charlton, Law et al. For United boss Wilf McGuinness, it was one punch too many. Less than a week later, McGuinness was sacked and Sir Matt Busby was back in charge at Old Trafford.

At Villa Park, there was, wrote Ian Johnson in the *Sports Argus*, 'an air of quiet authority generated by Vic Crowe'. In tandem with the tactically astute Wylie, within the space of less than 12 months they'd engineered an amazing transformation.

In the final, making a mockery of the gap between themselves and a Spurs side boasting internationals such as Jennings, Mullery, Gilzean, Chivers and Peters and riding high in the First Division, Villa produced so dominant a performance they might well have pulled off a shock win. Had fortune been kinder – Lochhead's too-soft shot towards an empty net was swept away by the back-pedalling Steve Perryman and Ian Hamilton saw a long-range effort clip the Tottenham crossbar – they would have.

While Villa bemoaned their luck, Spurs rode theirs and two late strikes in the 78th and 82nd minutes by England striker Chivers gave them their expected if undeserved victory. With what *The People*'s Maurice Smith termed a 'bitter, tantalising failure' in the famous old stadium, Crowe's side endeared itself completely to the hearts of the football public. More importantly, it reminded them that a dormant giant was, if not exactly flexing any muscles, at least stretching its limbs once more.

Alas, it soon started nodding again. The cup run, while providing a huge financial boost to the club – helping towards a record profit of £84,452 – brought a distraction to the players; amid the glamour and the glory they became blinkered to the more earthy demands of Third Division life. No longer able to raise their game against opponents all too keen to lift theirs, there were too many Davids for Goliath to conquer.

In the lead-up to the final Villa had headed the table by two points. The week before, they lost 3-1 at Bury to lie second. In the six matches following their Wembley appearance, though, only five points were mustered and just 15 from the final 18 games. Villa's promotion push faltered and ultimately fell away. Fourth spot, seven points off the top two of Preston ('The Invincibles' of the Football League's early days) and Fulham was all they had to settle for by the season's end.

Yet the shoots of recovery were showing. It wasn't long before they flowered in the most spectacular fashion. Crowe bought well. After Geoff Vowden, added in the spring from Birmingham, Bristol Rovers' Ray Graydon arrived, Crowe so determined to bag the fast, incisive winger he was willing to let his captain Brian Godfrey go in the opposite direction. When, in November, £35,000 for West Brom keeper Jimmy Cumbes further strengthened Crowe's hand, the spine of a title-winning team was in place. 'The strange, half-believable life they were leading in the Third Division underworld,' as Peter Morris put it, 'was not fated to last long.' With Rioch the midfield's cultured and competitive heart and the tall, balding Lochhead piloting the frontline, an almost unstoppable Villa dictated the pace throughout the 1971/72 campaign, romping away as runaway champions with a record 70 points.

An astonishing 32 league victories were racked up. Villa failed to score in only five of their 46 league fixtures. When, despite the presence of BBC's *Match of the Day* cameras, 48,110 watched their vital top-of-the-table encounter with Bournemouth (a game Villa won 2-1), it set a new Third Division attendance high. More than a million people in all watched Villa's home matches, with the average home gate 31,952. Football correspondent Geoffrey Green celebrated the unwavering support in an article entitled 'Over the Claret and Blue Rainbow'. 'The old cry of the Villa is being heard again ringing round Villa Park,' he wrote, and added, 'What has been abundantly revealed it that the soil of Birmingham is ripe for sowing and that the long tradition of loyalty to Aston Villa still lives on.'

At the following home game, on 12 February 1972, Villa banked record receipts of over £35,000 when Pelé's Santos appeared in an 'International Friendly', with fans among the 54,437 crowd scaling floodlight pylons or clambering on to the scoreboards to see a Pat McMahon header and Graydon's penalty, after Rioch had been upended, give the home side a morale-boosting 2-1 win.

Forty-eight hours later those profits went towards the £70,000 fee laid out for 24-year-old Ian Ross, a useful all-rounder who'd had many a run-out with Liverpool. It said much for Villa's renaissance that the Glasgow-born Ross, witness to the Santos game and suitably enthused by the club's ambition and fanaticism of its followers, wasn't fazed by dropping down two divisions to join the Midlanders. Ross, ignoring all Bill Shankly's last-minute attempts to persuade the player to remain at Anfield, was convinced that Villa would soon be back among the elite. Shankly, too, was confident of better things to come. 'Son, in ten years' time, there will be a super league,' the Liverpool boss told the departing Ross, 'and you can be sure Aston Villa will be in it.'

On transfer deadline day in March, Crowe also brought in Luton Town centre-half Chris Nicholl, with the initial £75,000 rising to £90,000 if Villa secured promotion. They did. Nicholl, who'd already helped the two Towns, Halifax and Luton, in his first season at each club to achieve promotion, now completed a notable hat-trick. On Saturday 29 April, needing only a point from the home game with Torquay to confirm the title, Villa swept aside the Devon club 5-1 and the boom of 'champions, champions' echoed around all four sides of Villa Park.

The highlight of an emphatic victory was a scintillating debut by youngster Brian Little who'd first appeared for the senior side in October 1971, coming on as a substitute against Blackburn Rovers. Handed his full debut against Torquay, the sharp, elf-like striker responded by netting once and setting up two. Four days earlier the 18-year-old with the nickname 'Superboy' had stolen the show, scoring twice at Anfield as Villa became the first Third Division club to win the FA Youth Cup, with a 5-2 aggregate triumph over Liverpool. The feeling was that Villa had unearthed someone genuinely special.

Running parallel to the transfer activity, a policy of homegrown youth (set in place by Tommy Docherty and Peter Doherty three years previously) as part of the overall blueprint, was producing a wealth of exciting talents. Nurtured under the guidance of Frank Upton, Little, John Gidman, Bobby McDonald and Jimmy Brown were all blossoming within the system. 'To actually go into the Third Division was to us almost the end of the world,' Doug Ellis would say, 'but we knew it would only be a matter of time before the young players would come through.'

On 5 May, Villa's adventure in the third tier ended against the same club with which it began, Ian Ross's first goal in claret and blue putting the final stamp on the triumphant season in a 1-0 home win over Chesterfield. Even the news that arch-rivals Birmingham City had satisfied a seven-year itch to return to the top flight, winning promotion with a late-season push – they'd also reached the FA Cup semi-final before losing to eventual winners Leeds – couldn't deflate Villa's spirits. 'After a period of crisis when ageing hands were prised from the tiller and a younger generation took over,' wrote Geoffrey Green, Villa, under the driving chairmanship of Ellis and the managership of Vic Crowe – 'realists whose eyes were not grown misty by heroic deeds of the past' – were 'on the rise again.'

In *The Official Football League Yearbook 1972/73*, Crowe, deservedly named the Third Division Manager of the Year, was hailed by Peter Fay as the man who had 'restored that age-old pride' to an ailing club. 'The flame-haired Welshman with the Black Country accent,' Fay declared, 'is the new messiah of Villa Park.' Irrespective of how miraculous Crowe's feats were, 'the staid old club with the red brick image, the massive ground and the unique support' were now seen as being very much 'back in business'.

Having 'successfully rid the club of the cobwebs of failure', Crowe was fully expected to lead the club ever upwards. His recruitment continued. In the close season, Alun Evans, like Ross before him, left Liverpool, the ex-Wolves striker who'd become the country's first £100,000 teenager when joining the Merseysiders from Molineux in September 1968, returning to the Midlands for £72,000.

Evans made his debut (substituting Lochhead) as Villa pitted their wits against top-flight opposition on 5 August in the Charity Shield. With both champions Derby County and FA Cup holders Leeds United declining to take part, the curtain-raiser to the new season was contested at Villa Park between Crowe's side and Manchester City, who'd finished fourth in the First Division. In a 1-0 defeat to a Francis Lee penalty, Villa showed they weren't that far away from being ready to compete at the highest level. 'Our aim,' Crowe announced, 'is to regain our First Division status for 1974 – the club's centenary year.'

One defeat in their first ten games was an impressive start. But, plagued by infuriating inconsistency, Villa failed to make good on their early promise. Players lost form. The new attacking spearhead, Evans and Lochhead, lacked any edge. Even Mr Reliability, Rioch, the club captain and fans' favourite, looked out of sorts and found himself the victim of terrace dissatisfaction. He wasn't the only one singled out. A 3-0 defeat at home to league leaders Burnley saw a rousing chorus of 'Crowe Must Go' ring out from a large portion of the crowd. At the season's conclusion Villa were in third spot, but it was highly misleading; champions Burnley and second-placed QPR were, in truth, streets ahead in both the table and in talent. Twelve months later, the Football League introduced the three-up and three-down regulation. It was perhaps a blessing that Villa had missed out – they clearly weren't yet equipped for top-flight football.

Crowe reiterated his hope that Villa could celebrate its 100th birthday in grand style. 'The club and our thousands of faithful supporters,' he said, 'certainly couldn't wish for a better present.' Aware that the weight of its tradition was a burden the club was still bearing, Crowe added, 'Tradition is all right if it is kept in its proper place. But it mustn't dominate the progress of the club or hinder it. And I think we have overcome the problem.'

During the summer, he spent again. Lochhead, sold to Oldham, was replaced by Northern Irish centre-forward Sammy Morgan. The much-travelled Welshman Trevor Hockey bolstered the midfield. Villa entered 1973/74 as one of the firm favourites to go up. They never really justified the tag. Although unbeaten in their first seven league games, just two of them were victories and, while form picked up, it was only briefly; from early November Villa embarked on a disastrous run, winning just one of 15 league games, including a club record 12 without victory. By the start of the following March, they were fifth-bottom.

A notable 2-0 success over Arsenal in an FA Cup fourth-round replay – the Gunners, finalists in the previous two seasons, succumbing to goals by Evans and Morgan before 47,821 at Villa Park after a 1-1 draw at Highbury – gave notice of what Crowe's side were capable of. But against Second Division opposition they were simply unable to replicate it. When First Division high-flyers Burnley knocked out Villa in the cup's next round, it marked the final appearance for Bruce Rioch.

Citing his desire for top-flight football and his belief that Villa wouldn't be playing it 'for a couple of years at the earliest', Rioch headed to Derby County for £200,000. 'I would love to keep my best players and have unlimited funds,' Crowe said, but with a reported transfer budget of only £65,000, Derby's offer was just too good to refuse. The young, ambitious Rioch had seen a much brighter future on the horizon and must have felt totally validated the following season when, as an ever-present in Dave Mackay's side, he helped the Rams become league champions for the second time in four years.

Ironically, with the loss of arguably their most influential player, Villa's best run – one defeat in nine matches – followed soon after. That defeat, 3-1 at home to West Brom on 2 March, 100 years to the month since Villa's first-ever fixture, was an afternoon on which hooliganism – so common a feature of 1970s football – stamped its foot over the headlines again as fans from both sides rushed each other, such ugliness emblematic of the mood now pervading Villa Park.

Four more defeats in their last six fixtures, including two at home, meant a 14th-place finish and the end of the road for Crowe. A week after the final game – a 1-1 draw at Orient – Crowe and his assistant, Wylie, were handed their P45s and scanning the Situations Vacant ads. According to Peter Morris in *Aston Villa: The First 100 Years*, 'Out on the park, Villa teams had been disturbingly short of flair. There was no recognisable style to their play, no panache, no hint of something just around the corner. Despite certain individual skills and the promise of youth, the team looked mediocre. And mediocrity is just what Villa cannot afford – not when there is so much potential at stake.'

Like Docherty before him, Crowe believed he could have turned things around. Such was his self-conviction, the day before his dismissal Crowe had declined an offer to take over the Welsh national team. But Crowe wasn't the right man for Ellis. Geoffrey Green had written, 'Aston Villa's real place of course is among the elite. Tradition demands it.' More to the point, the board demanded it, too. The club appeared to have headed into a cul-de-sac. Ellis, who, according to Chris Nicholl, 'wanted it all now', wasn't prepared to let them stand still. Although the *Evening Mail* front-page headline read, 'Villa Sensation: Crowe Sacked', it was hardly unexpected.

It had become, Peter Morris stated, 'depressingly apparent that the Crowe–Wylie tandem had achieved as much as it was ever going to'. In Crowe's opinion, though, there was far more than poor performances behind his sacking. Ellis's dislike of the manager's 'attitude' was, Crowe felt, a chief contributing factor. There was also a sense that the fall-out from further boardroom battles in 1972 – when Ellis had regained his chair just 43 days after losing it to Jim Hartley – was still affecting the club. The Villa directors, to Crowe's mind, remained divided as to the direction the club was going.

While Docherty was the figurehead of the revolution, Crowe had carried the flag and made much greater advances. Yet, as in 1968, Villa were now a struggling side in the lower reaches of the Second Division watched by ever-dwindling crowds and, like then, were searching for a new manager. 'Before Villa can make any real progress,' Morris wrote, 'they must get back to the First Division.' The man charged with the responsibility of guiding them there had a gargantuan task ahead of him.

The Odd Man Out

AT the end of the 1971/72 season, as Vic Crowe's Aston Villa were re-writing the Third Division record books, Norwich City were penning a whole new chapter in their own 70-year history. On the night of 24 April 1972, the Norfolk club, formed in 1902 by local schoolmaster Joseph Cowper Nutchey, won 2-1 at Orient to clinch their elevation to English football's upper echelons for the very first time. Five days later, on a rainy Saturday afternoon at Watford, they secured the Second Division title with a point in a 1-1 draw.

Not since 1958/59 when Norwich, then a Division Three South team, took some noteworthy scalps on the way to an FA Cup semi-final before losing to Luton Town after a replay, had the town experienced such footballing euphoria. Ten years after Ipswich Town, guided by a pre-knighthood Alf Ramsey, had upset all the odds to become the league champions, East Anglia, for so long a soccer outpost, now had two teams in the top tier. Someone should tell the Ministry of Transport, wrote Eric Nicholls in the July 1972 issue of *Goal*, 'Norwich is now very firmly on the map. A guy named Ron Saunders has seen to that.'

Largely unfancied at the season's start – two mid-table finishes in 1969/70 and 1970/71 giving little indication of any future glory – Norwich had triumphed, wrote Bob Baldwin in *The Official Football League Yearbook 1972/73*, due to 'the quietly-efficient managerial technique' of their boss. Mustering together a good blend of experience and youth, Saunders – 'a blunt Northerner brought up in the bleak surrounds of Merseyside', wrote Baldwin – reinforced his first team pool with burly young forward David Cross from struggling Rochdale, Partick Thistle's pacy striker Jim Bone and Fourth Division Lincoln City's utility man Phil Hubbard as the Canaries became a team 'which, although lacking individual stars, set the Second Division alight with all-round effort, method and consistency...

probably the greatest ingredient needed for success at any level in the game.' Saunders' infectious enthusiasm played its part, too. 'He never believes he is beaten,' said Scottish striker Ken Foggo.

After a mid-September 3-2 win over Oxford, Norwich headed the table and, but for two short spells when Millwall edged above them, there they remained until the season's end. While Freddie Goodwin at second-placed Birmingham City, with their star strike force trio of Trevor Francis and the two Bobs, Latchford and Hatton, garnered far more headlines, Saunders, named Bell's Scotch Whisky Second Division Manager of the Year, had proved himself hugely adept at working best with relatively unknown, workaday pros. His side may have been criticised for winning more through toil than talent, but Saunders took it as a compliment: 'In a way, this shows great credit on the players,' he said, 'in that any individual shortcomings were offset by discipline and hard work.'

Discipline and hard work. Over his three-year tenure at Carrow Road these two terms became synonymous with the manager's style. From day one of his reign, Saunders developed a reputation for valuing physical exertion far more than footballing ability. It was well-earned. The strict fitness regime Saunders inflicted upon his charges was notorious. As Anglia Television presenter Gerry Harrison put it, Saunders 'became the terror of the Trowse training ground'. A reconstruction job was under way and the players paid the price.

Local reporter Keith Skipper, in his book *Confessions of a Norfolk Newshound*, writes that Saunders put them 'through a training mangle that wrung out enough sweat to sink the River End'. Daily slogs up and down Mousehold Heath were a feature of matchday preparation. Mousehold, an area of heathland and woodland on the city's outskirts, was home to Britannia Barracks that had once served as an Initial Training Centre for recruits during World War Two. Now its testing slopes played host to a squad of exhausted footballers as Saunders exposed them to his punishing, 'commando-style' routines. If City's footballers weren't the most skilful, they could definitely be the most durable.

As muscles ached, stomachs also heaved. Centre-forward Peter Silvester, Saunders' first signing for the Norfolk club, claimed that the manager 'wasn't happy if at least four of us weren't sick'. Two hundred press-ups a day was not uncommon practice. Sticks were jumped over while carrying weights. Saunders, unstinting in his demands, 'got the last pint of blood out of us' said goalkeeper Kevin Keelan. Roy Waller, the regular radio presenter on BBC Radio Norfolk reporting on Norwich City, felt that the City boss occasionally exceeded limits. 'Sometimes he

[Saunders] took it to extremes,' Waller wrote in his autobiography, *Waller's World,* 'for example, by making the players head medicine balls, which would not be allowed these days.' In Skipper's view, Saunders 'plotted a deliberate course towards some kind of ogre figure he deemed necessary to shake up the weak-hearted', and 'his methods built on a parade-ground mentality have to remain open to question'.

Saunders' resemblance to a fierce physical education instructor was, Waller believed, 'an image he [Saunders] rather enjoyed; certainly he did very little to dispel it'. As though to emphasise the benefit of such exercise, the supremely-toned Saunders, a fitness fanatic and body builder as a player, led by example, stripping off his shirt and pounding up and down the steep Mousehold slopes alongside his players. The sight of Saunders bare-chested on the training ground was not unusual.

Keith Skipper, whose residence at *Eastern Evening News* coincided with Saunders' arrival at the club, felt that the City manager 'nailed up his working man's creed immediately on booking in at Carrow Road during the summer of 1969. Our first proper conversation, him stripped to the waist and flexing muscles and me fiddling with a loose tie and mopping anxious brow, made it clear what sort of relationship he wanted. "I don't expect you to keep going on about past glories, especially that FA Cup run ten years ago. That's history. I'm here to write a new chapter of success, and I'll do it my way."'

Saunders' way didn't involve kowtowing to traditions. 'The only thing that matters is the future,' he liked to say. He just wasn't interested in the old image of the club. 'On The Ball, City!', considered the world's oldest football song and sung as an integral part of the Carrow Road matchday experience, was quickly dismissed as a dirge. Norwich songs of any sort only commanded indifference. When hearing 'The Canaries', crooned by the City squad backed by The Chic Applin Band to mark the Second Division championship victory, Saunders' initial remark to Johnny Cleveland, the song's co-writer, was not an appraisal but, 'How much do we earn out of it?'

It was also during his Carrow Road occupancy that Saunders' profound mistrust of the press first revealed itself. Wary of journalists who focussed on the negative about the game in general – 'It's easier to knock something than to praise it and bad news makes better headlines,' he once said – Saunders had a particular loathing of those who, he thought, sought to sway public opinion rather than reflect it. Skipper contended that Saunders 'should have accepted an automatic right for sports reporters to honestly reflect their own opinions and the feelings of thousands of spectators'.

However, it only made the manager more determined to throw 'a fiercely protective shield around his charges, especially as complaints hardened over an ultra-caution approach to away fixtures.' Whether it were brickbats or backslaps, Saunders buffeted their efforts, however objective or fair. 'At times,' Skipper said, 'that meant the manager resented any sort of outside judgement on what he was striving to achieve on thin resources.'

Disagreeing with Saunders publicly wasn't tolerated. Skipper made the mistake of criticising Peter Silvester in an article headlined, 'For Pete's Sake, Goals Must Come!' A heated debate took place on the team bus between Saunders and Skipper and when the reporter refused to apologise he 'took the clear hint to disembark at Newmarket'. Being thrown off the team bus and left stranded, often at away grounds, was nothing new to local journalists. 'A reporter who felt he might upset Ron by what he said or wrote,' Waller penned, 'would take the return train fare with him as insurance for getting home.'

The ever-defensive Saunders seemed sensitive to any perceived slur. 'He despised what he saw as smart-alec replies,' Skipper said, 'or any kind of droll observation at the expense of his tactics or personnel.' Undermine Saunders' authority and you were treated unceremoniously. Once, when Skipper telephoned the club to check a fact for a story and was put through to the office, the reporter made a remark about the manager's team selection. The voice at the other end abruptly said, 'This is Ron Saunders, and I do not care what you think!' Saunders slammed down the phone. The Norwich manager eventually banished Skipper from the boardroom after home matches and refused him access to both players and officials.

The image of an uncompromising character was one Saunders had carved out through most of his playing career. That career began close to home. The son of a coal-heaver, born just across the Mersey from Liverpool, Saunders had earned a certain repute in local football for his exploits as a raw teenage forward but left grammar school, aged 16, fully expecting to become a trainee cost accountant with a nearby tobacco company.

It was Everton, managed by former player Cliff Britton, who first spotted his untapped potential. Initially signing two-year amateur terms, then – following the completion of his two-year spell of National Service in the army – on a full-time basis, Saunders joined the Goodison club just as they'd endured a catastrophic start to the decade, dropping out of the top flight for only the second time in their history. Two points clear of the relegation zone at the end of the 1950/51 season, on the last day Everton suffered a 6-0 trouncing by Sheffield Wednesday. On the same afternoon fellow strugglers Chelsea beat Bolton Wanderers 4-0 and Everton were demoted on goal average. Wednesday's six goals weren't sufficient to spare them the same fate.

In the second tier, forced by the board's refusal to fund any new big-money signings, Britton blooded youth into the squad. After a seventh-place finish in 1951/52, the following season Everton struggled to a lowly 16th. Saunders, though, understudying for first-choice centre-forward Dave Hickson, still found opportunities weren't forthcoming. Even when the goalscoring Hickson, whose robust style earned him the affectionate nickname of 'The Cannonball Kid', left at the end of 1954/55 for a brief, unsettled spell in the Midlands that brought only 12 games with Aston Villa, Saunders was still unable to make a breakthrough. The following summer, he was released by the club. In five years he only appeared on three occasions for the Everton first team, failing to find the net on any of them.

Already capped by England at youth level, Saunders remained highly rated. Several clubs – Derby, Cardiff and Bournemouth, as well as his boyhood favourites Tranmere – were either linked with or made overtures towards the youngster. Recently married and discovering he could actually earn more as a part-timer, Saunders took the plunge to play instead at Southern League side Tonbridge. For the 23-year-old, swapping the School of Science for an education at much less hallowed halls wasn't a backward step, just a different path to where he eventually wanted to be.

Signed by Doug Hunt, Saunders made an enormous impact at non-league level. In 1956/57 he bagged a club record-equalling 39 goals, including four hat-tricks, his keen eye for goal immediately attracting admiring glances from a number of league clubs. After only a year during which, by his own account, 'I turned my hand to anything going' to earn a little extra income, in May 1957 Saunders was on the move.

Although Everton still retained his registration, both they and Tonbridge had failed to notify the authorities of such, and Gillingham boss Archie Clark stepped in, the Priestfield club agreeing to pay Tonbridge a minimal fee – £800 – as well as stage a fixture between the two sides. Saunders snapped up the opportunity. Playing up front alongside former England amateur international Jim Fletcher and ex-Arsenal frontman Don Rossiter, a disappointing 1-0 debut defeat at home to Brighton & Hove Albion was soon forgotten; only a week later, Saunders notched his first Gills goal at Southampton. Even though part of a struggling side that eventually finished third bottom of Division Three South, the powerfully built marksman, contributing 24 league and cup goals, was easily the club's leading scorer. Five of those came one glorious November afternoon when Saunders scored half of the Kent team's goals in a club record 10-1 FA Cup first-round victory against Eastern Counties League side Gorleston. Only a missed penalty denied him a double hat-trick.

Inevitably, the bigger clubs came knocking. In September 1958, Freddie Cox, boss of First Division Portsmouth, made a bid. Moving to Fratton Park in an £8,000 deal, Saunders became the first-ever player to be transferred from the Fourth to the First Division (the new national Third and Fourth Divisions having been created from the old Third Divisions North and South). The stocky forward soon discovered his scoring touch. Having failed to find the net in a 2-2 draw with Chelsea on his debut, after replacing young Irish striker Derek Dougan, the following week Saunders was on the mark in a 2-1 win at West Brom and, though a dismal season ended with rock bottom Portsmouth dropping out of the top flight for the first time in 32 years, Saunders was the team's outstanding figure with 24 goals in all competitions, a commendable return in such a difficult campaign.

The following season proved no less arduous. Despite their forward's 16 goals, Portsmouth struggled once more, only just winning the relegation dogfight. In 1960/61, though, that battle was lost. Saunders' talent for converting chances – he netted 20 times in only 33 starts – was all in vain as Portsmouth fell through the trapdoor and landed in English football's third tier after a 37-year absence.

In April 1961, too late to stave off the drop, George Smith had taken over the managerial reins. Always direct and often outspoken, Smith was a noted disciplinarian, known for his rigorous training routines. Having spent much of the early period of World War Two as a PT instructor at Aldershot as well as on troop ships, when he received his discharge papers at the war's end, Smith had reached the rank of sergeant major. His strong team ethic and tough man-management technique galvanised the dispirited south-coast club. With some inspired signings – wingers Tony Barton and Dave Dodson, in particular – the 1961/62 season saw Pompey bounce back up at the first attempt.

Under the captaincy of the 37-year-old and seemingly ageless Jimmy Dickinson, Portsmouth stormed to the summit, looking title contenders from the opening day in August until a 5-0 thrashing of Bristol City at Fratton Park in March. Despite a dip in form following that victory, a vital 2-1 win over Watford on Easter Monday 1962, in which Saunders got both, secured the club's promotion. A win and a draw later and the Division Three trophy was safely in the silverware cabinet. With 26 goals to his name, Saunders led the revival from the front.

The prolific Scouser's goal threat, together with his bravery and willing, made him a priceless asset. Back in the Second Division, he flourished further, 19 goals coming in 40 games. Though the majority of those were unspectacular, many merely tap-ins, Saunders' knack for being in the right spot in the penalty box was unerring. What he lacked in stature, he more than compensated for with strength. Defenders found him a real handful, difficult to knock off the ball, dangerous in the air and accurate with either foot. The following campaign, Saunders exceeded all that had gone before; including three hat-tricks, two of which came in consecutive matches against Newcastle and Leyton Orient, he found the net a remarkable 33 times. 'Ron the tantaliser! Ron the superb! Ron the genius! Pompey's pin-up boy is the toast of the ancient port!' was how a cartoon of the time hailed him. The season proved to be a pinnacle in Saunders' Fratton Park career.

Just three games – and another three goals – into the 1964/65 campaign, Smith took the controversial decision to sell him, unwilling to meet his star forward's demands for a rise in his weekly wage to £35. Third Division Watford, with Bill McGarry in command, swooped. For a £15,000 fee, Vicarage Road became the next stop on Saunders' travels. He had been Portsmouth's top scorer for six consecutive seasons. It was as Portsmouth struggled to safety in his absence that the seeds of Saunders' ambition to become a football manager first began to sprout. Just four months into Saunders' Watford career, McGarry left to join Ipswich Town, whom he would take into the First Division. Saunders threw his own hat into the ring as a potential replacement. 'I decided I might as well try my luck,' he wrote in *Ron Saunders' Aston Villa Scrapbook*.

But a young player-manager with no experience of running a club wasn't what Watford wanted. They plumped instead for Ken Furphy. It soon became apparent that Saunders, now 32, didn't figure in Furphy's plans as a player. When Charlton Athletic boss Bob Stokoe offered a fee of £10,000 for Saunders' services, the hard-shooting forward was on his way again. The move to the capital was to be the last of his playing career. In 1967, after two years at The Valley, Saunders decided to hang up his boots. He already knew it was into management that he wanted to venture. It wasn't simply the next logical step; the desire had long been simmering. 'I had been quietly nursing the idea for the best part of ten years,' Saunders wrote, 'and I felt that I had become equipped not only to handle players, but to help them.' In April 1967, having failed to land jobs at Shrewsbury and Brighton, the 34-year-old was gifted his chance.

The 1966/67 season had been a disappointing one for Yeovil Town. Early results were poor and the team slipped to 14th place in the Southern League. Supporters became restless and demands were made for the introduction of fresh blood both on and off the field. Early in December five second-half goals were conceded at Guildford City, who won 6-1 to inflict Yeovil's biggest league defeat since 1957.

On 23 January, the club's directors decided not to renew manager Joe McDonald's contract. McDonald carried on until mid-March, before Doug Hunt (Saunders' ex-boss at Tonbridge) took over caretaking duties, but when Saunders applied for the position, the first step on a managerial odyssey was his. On 17 April 1967, Saunders' appointment was confirmed. The wheel had turned full circle: back in the Southern League where his playing days began, Saunders was happy to start on the lower rungs knowing that a move up the ladder would only be a matter of time. 'I had seen sufficient of the game at all levels to believe that I could do as well as anyone else,' he wrote, 'and better than most, as a manager myself.'

Brian Clough, then experiencing the deprivations of life as manager of Fourth Division Hartlepools United, stated, 'The ideal place for a manager to start a career would be as high in the league as possible. Because the higher the club the better the players, and that is what a manager needs most. Good, skilful players.' Saunders wasn't afforded such a luxury. It was a tough apprenticeship. Yeovil had a staff of one part-timer. Saunders wasn't just managing a team full of amateurs to perform on the pitch; he was virtually doing every job off it as well.

Yet though Yeovil's on-field fortunes failed to revive considerably – reaching the FA Cup first round, where they were beaten by Third Division Oxford United, being the brightest spot – Saunders' thoroughness shone through. His meticulous preparation – highlighted by a knowledge of legalisation, rules and contracts – hugely impressed the Somerset club's board (chaired by the football commentator Brian Moore). Knowledge, Saunders understood, was a weapon fundamental to any manager's armoury.

At the end of the season, limited to £250 per week for wages, he set about building a new team. Four signings – Ken Jones, Chris Weller, Kenny Thompson and Trevor Allen – fired up public interest. By the end of September, Yeovil were second behind Barnet, their only defeat a 2-1 loss at Hereford. Home gates averaged 3,050 and membership of the supporters' club had risen to over 1,500. It didn't last. By December,

Yeovil had slumped to a mid-table position and, while the New Year saw a small improvement, an 8-2 defeat at Cheltenham on 10 February was a crushing blow. At the season's end, with gates below the 1,600 mark, they were 12th on 44 points, 13 behind eventual champions Chelmsford City. Despite success in the Floodlight League and reaching the final of the Somerset Professional Cup (losing 4-0 on aggregate to Bath City), it had been an underwhelming campaign.

Saunders continued to change his playing staff. In the opening weeks of 1968/69, the Huish Park supporters had more to cheer about. Results picked up. In October, the club splashed out a record fee of £3,000 for Bristol Rovers' Dick Plumb. The following month saw them reach the FA Cup first round again, unluckily losing 2-1 at Weymouth. At one point Yeovil topped the Southern League table.

Saunders' feats were impressive enough for Second Division strugglers Oxford United, then seeking a new manager after Arthur Turner's move upstairs to general manager, to make advances. Saunders was eager to grasp his chance. Though slipping and breaking an ankle while running up and down the Huish terraces just two days before meeting his prospective new employers, Saunders, undaunted and unwilling to display what might possibly be perceived as a sign of weakness, removed the plaster cast and, ignoring all discomfort, proceeded with his interview at the Manor Ground. It did the trick. Saunders became the first manager to move from non-league football to a Second Division club, officially taking up his new post on 1 March 1969, his salary more than doubling to £80 a week. When he returned to Yeovil to pack his bags, the plaster cast went back on.

Multitasking in Somerset, Saunders went to the city of dreaming spires expected to work a minor miracle. Oxford, with only 18 points from 33 matches, sat bottom of the Second Division and were staring relegation full-on. It was a massive challenge, but one the rookie boss was ready to meet. 'I've always enjoyed wakening up in a morning with the knowledge that there are problems to be solved,' he later said, 'and that seemed one of the best reasons of all for taking the job at Oxford.' Saunders more than solved them. Taking 15 points from the last 12 games – the safety target Saunders had set – Oxford, Third Division champions in 1967/68, clung tight to a lifeline and hauled themselves clear. The salvage job Saunders performed saw his stock rise considerably, drawing attention from clubs up above. Among them were fellow Second Division side Norwich City, now managerless after Lol Morgan, in charge for the previous three seasons, had failed to scale the hoped-for heights.

In Saunders, Norwich's chairman Geoffrey Watling earmarked someone who, Edward Couzens-Lake wrote in *Norwich City FC: The Seventies*, 'was ambitious and focussed, a disciplinarian who would stop at nothing to meet his goals'. In short, he was just what the club needed. When Norwich came calling that summer, despite some initial reservations (he turned down their first approach), Saunders felt ready to answer. In July 1969, signing a four-year contract, he became City's seventh manager in 12 years, and certainly their highest paid.

The 37-year-old arrived in Norfolk with the clearest brief: take the Canaries up to join the elite of English football. He told the players it would take him three years to do so, and he was right. Promotion was, he said, 'reward for all the hard work put in by everyone at the club'. For all his exacting methods, Saunders had won the respect of his players. It had been earned, not demanded. 'And that is the sign,' wrote Eric Nicholls in the July issue of *Goal*, 'of a man destined for great things.'

On the eve of City's inaugural top-flight campaign, Saunders' blueprint couldn't have been more black and white. His players had ability, character and backbone and, he told *Goal* magazine, 'With these three things, you have got a chance of success.' Their fitness, however, was their chief advantage. Norwich were so fit they ran teams off the park. Getting the ball forward quickly, the backline would move upfield, too. With all the running they were forced into, the opposition forwards exhausted themselves trying to keep onside and barely had the energy to attack. Quizzed by Gerry Harrison on what the advantages of Norwich's style would be in the First Division, Saunders cited Leeds United – 'probably the most criticised side over the last ten years and yet they're the most successful' – as a comparison. 'Every side of any consequence has got a style,' he said, 'has got a method, has got a lot of discipline in the side.' Saunders was convinced Norwich's would help them prosper. The prospect of managing at the highest level didn't daunt him one bit. 'I think the last time I was frightened,' he told Harrison with a smile, 'was when I was at the dentist at about seven years old.'

What Norwich had achieved under Saunders was, in Harrison's view, 'the biggest leap in their history'. A manager who, to Keith Skipper's mind, 'banked on sweat and dedication rather than the cheque book', Saunders had performed what Harrison considered a 'one man revolution'. He chose, for the most part, to persevere with the tried and trusted troopers who'd served him so successfully.

His faith was rewarded. A 1-1 draw in their opening game at home to Everton – Jimmy Bone claiming the club's first goal in the First Division

– was followed three days later by a trip down the A140 to nearest rivals Ipswich where they recorded a historic 2-1 victory, Bone again on the scoresheet.

Despite a 3-0 defeat at Maine Road in their next game, over the next few weeks City continued in fine fettle. Reigning champions Derby, Stoke, Arsenal and Spurs were all beaten at Carrow Road. Liverpool, who would go on to win the title, were held 1-1. There were away triumphs at Palace and Leicester. On 18 November, following another Carrow Road victory, 2-0 over West Bromwich Albion, the Canaries were perched in sixth just five points behind Bill Shankly's league leaders. Life for the team in yellow and green was looking distinctly peachy. On the Tuesday after the win over the Baggies, Saunders saw his side dismiss Arsenal from the League Cup, 3-0 at Highbury. But what ensued was a calamitous sequence of results that had them dropping perilously down the table and battling for First Division survival. From 25 November, after a 4-1 defeat at Birmingham City, Norwich didn't win another league match until 14 April 1973. On 7 April, a 1-0 loss at Old Trafford, in Denis Law's last game for the home side, left Norwich bottom.

Two successive 1-0 wins – at home to Chelsea and away at The Hawthorns (City completing the double over relegation rivals West Brom with a solitary goal by Cross) – proved priceless. Norwich's fate was now in their own hands. Four days later, after a 3-0 defeat at Wolves the previous night, a nervous crowd of 36,922 at Carrow Road saw goals by Colin Suggett (a recent signing from West Brom) and an injury-time winner by David Stringer edge City past Crystal Palace 2-1 and secure their safety, the result condemning the Londoners to the drop after four difficult seasons in the top division. The following evening West Brom, 2-1 losers at home to Manchester City, joined Palace through the trapdoor.

In the midst of their alarming slide, Saunders guided City to the League Cup Final, and their first Wembley appearance, meeting Bill Nicholson's Tottenham Hotspur on Saturday 3 March 1973. En route to the final, Norwich, having already seen off Arsenal in the quarter-finals, won a semi-final with Chelsea (following a replayed second leg after fog at Carrow Road put a halt to the first game). Hopes of claiming a hat-trick of scalps from the capital, however, were extremely slim. Without a win in any of their previous 12 league matches, Norwich headed into the final on the back of five straight defeats. To make matters worse, just ten days before the game, City had sold their star forward Jimmy Bone, the Scottish striker the sacrificial lamb in a part-exchange for Sheffield United's Trevor Hockey.

The League Cup, with entry into European competition the prize for the victors, was now regarded far more favourably than in its initial years. City, then a Second Division side, had actually won the competition in its second year, beating Rochdale 3-1 over two legs, but Spurs, as against Villa two years before, were clear favourites. With both sides largely cancelling each other out, it was a dour, physical contest devoid of sparkle. Norwich had the occasional scoring opportunity – though perhaps the best, a header from captain Forbes that cleared Jennings' bar, didn't arrive until the last minute – but it was Spurs who claimed the one, important strike. In the 73rd minute, a long throw from Chivers was helped on by Peters and when a defensive clearance only reached the edge of the Norwich penalty area, Ralph Coates – a first-half replacement after John Pratt had twisted his left leg – rifled home a low shot past Kevin Keelan to secure the silverware. The Londoners maintained their record of having won every final they'd played at Wembley.

Despite Saunders' post-match assessment that 'the goal came against the run of play when we were getting on top', there was no disguising the fact that the 'fantastic occasion' he'd told his players to enjoy had passed them by. While Spurs had booked another ticket into Europe, City were faced with the prospect of a nerve-tingling battle to preserve their First Division status.

Ultimately it was won, but further trials and tribulations weren't very far away. Two days before Norwich's opening fixture of the 1973/74 campaign – a 3-1 defeat at Wolves – Geoffrey Watling announced his resignation after nearly 17 years in the chairman's role. Watling's replacement was Arthur South. South, like Watling's father, was a former Lord Mayor of Norwich, and had joined the Norwich board in the late 1950s around the same time as his predecessor. South, renowned as a forthright, straight-talking man, somewhat ominously laid down a mark, making it known that frank discussions with Saunders were inevitable, as South, as with the City manager, also had a 'hard streak'. The portents for a fractious relationship were clear.

Saunders, he later wrote, 'had been there four years, worked damned hard, and achieved a great deal' but the moment Watling, a close ally, relinquished the chair, the convivial relations Saunders had enjoyed were replaced by potentially combustible dealings with his successor.

An explosion wasn't long in coming. The date that detonated it was 17 November. That Saturday, as Norwich prepared to host Everton, the home side had won just two of their first 15 league games and were again struggling near the foot of the table. Saunders' position was rumoured to be under increasing scrutiny, especially from South. Earlier that week, four days after a 2-0 loss at Stoke, David Cross was surprisingly sold to Coventry City. It was a move sanctioned by South. Desperate for a win against Billy Bingham's Toffees, Norwich instead produced probably their worst performance under Saunders' stewardship.

Despite going behind – albeit through a McLaughlin own goal – the visitors hit back in style, scoring three, their third put into his own net by the unfortunate Forbes. The goal was the cue for large numbers of disgruntled home supporters to hurl cushions on to the Carrow Road pitch, but the atmosphere on the terraces was nothing to the hostilities that reportedly took place, post-match, in the club boardroom.

Less than an hour after the final whistle, an extremely heated exchange – 'an angry scene' according to *The Times*' Geoffrey Green – was said to have taken place between manager and chairman, at the end of which Saunders thrust a scribbled letter of resignation at South. Exactly what was said – or shouted – was unknown, but the consequence was clear: Ron Saunders had quit as manager of Norwich City Football Club. In an unwinnable clash of two wilful personalities, the unstoppable force had met the immovable object and clearly there was no way forward.

Only three months into South's tenure, Saunders was walking through the exit door. He didn't even stop to say goodbye. Later that evening, *Match of the Day*'s Jimmy Hill claimed that South had confirmed that he had indeed received a letter from Saunders but had yet to examine its contents. Hill, with Saunders 'laughing out loud' as he watched his TV screen, dared the City chairman to take a peep. It didn't matter; Saunders' mind was made up in that dramatic confrontation and there would be no backing down. Norwich, wrote Green the following Monday, 'again find themselves in the shadows, made even darker' by Saunders' departure. He'd been in charge for a little under four-and-a-half years.

Saunders may, as Keith Skipper wrote, have 'regarded briar patches as inevitable before the chance came to sniff the roses', but the end had, chiefly, justified the means. Aged just 41, he was still considered an outstanding young manager who, Roy Waller believed, couldn't be blamed for leaving Carrow Road, albeit acrimoniously. 'He moved on to better himself,' Waller wrote. Just five days later, that betterment had, seemingly, happened, Saunders accepting an offer from one of the country's biggest clubs. His destination? Maine Road, Manchester.

A Tale of Two Cities

IN 1971/72, with Malcolm Allison in full control of all footballing matters for the first time after Joe Mercer had been 'demoted' upstairs, Manchester City finished the season fourth in the First Division, level on points with second-placed Leeds United and Liverpool in third, though with an inferior goal difference, and one point behind champions Derby County.

In March, City had been four points clear at the top when Allison, the epitome of champagne and showiness, decided that Rodney Marsh, signed from QPR for £200,000, could be Maine Road's answer to George Best and exactly what City needed as the championship drew to its climax. It proved a crucial error. Marsh's failure to integrate into the near-rotation system that Allison employed and successfully link with the likes of Mike Summerbee and Francis Lee saw City stagger towards the line, eventually missing out on a title whose winning had looked to be almost a formality.

The following campaign, with Mercer now managing Coventry City, the Maine Road club started poorly, exiting the UEFA Cup to Valencia, being dumped out of the League Cup by Fourth Division Bury and struggling in the bottom half of the division by September's end. The next few months saw little upturn and in March 1973, with Allison declaring his relationship with players he could no longer motivate had soured, he resigned his post before going 'back home after spending eight years in the provinces', rejoining Crystal Palace at the end of the month. The club which, under the Mercer–Allison combo, won the First Division in 1967/68 and the 1969 FA Cup then enjoyed the dual triumph of the League Cup and European Cup Winners' Cup in 1970, was in very real danger of coming apart at the seams. Johnny Hart, an ex-City inside-forward and much-liked member of the backroom staff, was seen by the board as the ideal figure to hold it together.

Although a surprise choice to many, Hart immediately earned brownie points in persuading former hero Denis Law, given a free transfer by Tommy Docherty at the end of the 1972/73 season, to return to the club for whom he'd first played in 1960. Law scored twice in an opening day 3-1 win against Birmingham City. Narrow home wins over Coventry, Norwich and Chelsea, though, were countered by defeats on their travels to Derby, Coventry, Burnley and Newcastle as Hart's reign began in unconvincing fashion. It wasn't until 20 October that City claimed their first away victory, 2-1 at Sheffield United.

However, after a first home league defeat – 1-0 to Leeds – just over three months into the campaign, Hart informed the not-long-installed City chairman Peter Swales he was relinquishing the manager's role. Finding the pressure too much of leaving out players with whom he enjoyed a close relationship, Hart's health had deteriorated to such an extent that he suffered heart trouble. It was a job, he later claimed, he never wanted but feared he would be moved on if he hadn't accepted it.

In Hart's place, Tony Book, City's captain during their recent triumphs, took temporary responsibility for team affairs, the story going that when City's players were consulted on who should be the next manager, their team-mate was a unanimous choice. The side responded well. Walsall and Carlisle were both dumped from the League Cup. Yet City's inconsistent league form continued. A goalless draw at Wolves, a 2-1 defeat at home to Arsenal, then a fortunate 1-0 win over QPR (Marsh's penalty claiming both points against his former club) suggested little significant shift in the gears. After failing to score again in a League Cup fourth-round stalemate at lowly York, Swales decided to act. On assuming control following Eric Alexander's stepping down, Swales' first declaration was his wish to rid the club of its showbiz element. In Swales' eyes there was no better man to fulfil that mandate than Ron Saunders.

Swales, wrote James Lawton in the *Daily Express,* saw 'Saunders' style of harsh discipline and drive as the best available antidote to increasing uncertainty in the Maine Road dressing room'. Feelers had been put out for Brian Clough (now at Brighton) and Ipswich's Bobby Robson, but a recent run-in for Clough with the FA disciplinary commission had given City reservations. Saunders – 'a man of fierce ambition and Shankly-like dedication', Lawton said – was now the number one choice.

Before the fateful Norwich/Everton clash, Saunders, also coveted by Nottingham Forest, was well aware of City's interest. 'At the moment I'm involved in several transfer deals and thinking about getting two points against Everton tomorrow,' he'd said on the eve of the game. 'These are the only things on my mind now.' Whether or not the possibility of the Maine Road job influenced his post-match argument with South is open to question. Now, recognising that Saunders wouldn't be unemployed too long following his Carrow Road resignation, Swales offered him the job at Manchester City. Saunders duly accepted. As at Norwich, he became the club's tenth manager since the war. He'd been out of work for less than a week.

After watching his new charges lose somewhat unluckily 2-1 at Portman Road in a midweek match forced to kick off at 1pm due to recent power cuts afflicting the country, Saunders took control for the first time in the replayed tie with York. A player deputation ensured that Tony Book was officially appointed as his assistant. A 4-1 win, with Marsh notching a hat-trick, made a welcome start, even if the scoreline masked the resilient nature of York's performance. There was a strong feeling among supporters that the club now had the experienced manager required if City were to challenge for honours. But if the fans felt the board had made an error in passing the reins to Hart, it was nothing to the sentiments the players were to feel about Saunders' appointment.

In *Fathers, Sons and Football*, Colin Shindler's account of the lives and careers of three members of the Summerbee family – Mike, his father George, and his son Nick – the author summarises the plight of Mike Summerbee and the other senior pros at Maine Road when Saunders took over, 'City's established stars thought Saunders set out to break their spirits like a sergeant major dealing with conscripts on national service.' Shindler was referring in particular to Summerbee, Lee, Marsh and Law. If Saunders supposed it was a tactic that would work on them, he was grossly mistaken. 'They saw themselves as professional players,' Shindler wrote, 'who didn't need such handling.' Saunders entered an intrigue-riddled dressing room at Maine Road knowing that, in his own words, 'the players there favoured Tony Book for the job.' Talks with Swales and other boardroom members had reassured the incoming boss that 'there were no problems I couldn't handle.' The question was, how would a manager with an authoritarian approach suit a club with a sprinkling of individualists? The answer soon became obvious.

Eager to stamp his authority, Saunders immediately started treading on toes. He didn't care whose. In front of his team-mates, Denis Law was called 'The Old Man'. Francis Lee, although never the slenderest footballer, was cruelly referred to as 'Fatty'. Internationals who had enjoyed long, successful careers were made to feel as though they were finished.

As if to hammer home Saunders' message, training games saw 'the old men' versus the young hopefuls. 'They felt as though he [Saunders] was telling them that the rest of the world might consider them great players,' Shindler wrote, 'but to him they were just superannuated ballboys.' Indeed, Summerbee turned up at the training ground one morning to find Law behind one of the goals acting as ballboy as some of City's youngsters had shooting practice. A deal for Summerbee to go to Leeds United was agreed, only for manager Don Revie to withdraw when Swales began demanding a bigger fee, money he wanted to secure the transfer of Hull City striker Stuart Pearson. When Saunders tried to sell Law to Bradford City, the Scottish international lost all respect for him. The forward had a World Cup to prepare for and told Saunders he wasn't going to do so in England's lowest tier.

'Saunders wasn't the best communicator,' writes Rodney Marsh in his autobiography, *Priceless*. It wasn't just how Saunders communicated but what he communicated that also upset the City hierarchy.

Tactically, too, Saunders left them unimpressed. Reared on the innovative coaching of Allison and encouraged to play with flair, they found that Saunders had very different ideas. 'I don't want my back four to play football,' Mike Doyle was instructed. When City's defenders got the ball they were to 'just lump it forward and we'll go from there.'

Much of Norwich's attacking play had involved the central defensive pair of Forbes and Stringer pumping garryowens up the middle for the forwards to get on the end of. It wasn't pretty but it was effective. To Manchester City's footballers, it was tantamount to blasphemy.

Rumours of unrest soon became rife. Stories even circulated of a wholesale dressing-room revolt, with players threatening a strike. Unsurprisingly, off-the-pitch disharmony was matched by unreliable results on it. Victories, defeats and draws all intermingled as City went on in the same vein as before Saunders' arrival. At the turn of the year, after a 1-1 draw with his former employers at Carrow Road, City were in the table's bottom half.

Their pedestrian progress continued in the first two months of 1974. After a 5-2 FA Cup third-round win at Oxford United, the Blues were dispatched from the competition in the next round, 4-1 at Nottingham Forest, in City's first-ever Sunday game. In the league, although they lost only once before February was out, they also drew three of their eight games.

Travelling by rail to the last of those eight, an away trip to Southampton, the City players were instructed by Saunders they weren't to leave the train car in which they were seated. Summerbee and Law didn't oblige and left Saunders fuming. During the week, the pair, along with Marsh, Lee and even Colin Bell, were all made to train separately from their fellow first-teamers. The following Saturday, City went to Wembley to play in the League Cup Final. It was only in this tournament that they'd displayed any consistency. A 4-2 victory on 19 December over Joe Mercer's Coventry (City's only top-flight opposition on their run in the competition) had meant a semi-final pairing with Third Division strugglers Plymouth Argyle. After a 1-1 first-leg draw at Home Park, a goal apiece by Bell and Lee saw City to a comfortable 2-0 win and a place in their first final since 1970.

Their opponents were Wolverhampton Wanderers. Managed now by Bill McGarry, a man Midlands-based sports reporter Pat Murphy claimed made Saunders seem like 'a pussycat', Wolves at the semi-final stage had ended Norwich's own hopes of a second successive visit to the Twin Towers. Despite their shaky league form, though, City went into the final as favourites.

Saunders fielded an adventurous line-up. Summerbee, Law, Marsh, Lee and Bell all started. But seeing the City teamsheet beforehand only boosted the Wolves players' confidence. Saunders, they thought, had picked a totally unbalanced team. With Law and Lee both struggling with injuries, City, Denis Law relates in *Denis Law: King and Country*, 'were found out very quickly' and he himself 'played as awful a game as I have ever played in that arena'. A minute before half-time a Kenny Hibbitt mis-hit put Wolves ahead.

City came back, however. Just before the hour mark Colin Bell netted a deserved leveller from close range and, now dominating, Saunders' side looked set to get a second. They failed to make it count. Five minutes from time, firing home after Alan Sunderland's cross deflected off Marsh's heel into his path, England international John Richards sealed a dramatic Wolves victory and City's players had nothing to show for their afternoon's toils. After the final whistle, Marsh was so disgusted he headed straight for the dressing room, snubbing the presentation of tankards to the runners-up. If anything, the cup loss only highlighted how troubled the Manchester club had become.

A week later, when a 1-0 defeat at Leeds left them mid-table, Saunders' response was to enter the transfer market for the first time. A double swoop on Sunderland saw Dennis Tueart and Mick Horswill, two of the victorious FA Cup-winning side the season before, move to Manchester, with City midfielder Tony Towers heading to Wearside as part of the package. Just 48 hours later, the expensive new duo were exposed to the heat of a midweek derby at home to Manchester United, now managed by Tommy Docherty. With United desperately fighting relegation, the match proved even feistier than expected. A first-half on-field spat saw City's Doyle and United's Lou Macari both sent off by referee Clive Thomas. When the two players refused to leave the pitch, Thomas ordered the teams from the field, before escorting two policemen into the dressing rooms to ensure Macari and Doyle didn't return to the action. An ill-tempered clash ended 0-0.

The addition of the 24-year-old Tueart failed to spark goals as Saunders hoped. A 1-0 home defeat to Sheffield United was followed by another blank at Highbury as Arsenal ran out 2-0 victors, and City had dropped to 16th. A three-game unbeaten run (all three at Maine Road, including one win, 2-1 over Newcastle United) did little to ease any relegation worries. On the Saturday after a midweek draw with Everton, on home soil again City came unstuck, losing 3-1 to Ipswich. Mike Summerbee's goal that afternoon was to be the last scored by a City player under Ron Saunders.

The following Tuesday, 9 April, 20,461 at Loftus Road saw City lose 3-0 to QPR and surrender so meekly that it appeared, to the watching Colin Shindler, as if the players 'were holding a large banner draped across the width of the pitch proclaiming to the world "We hate our manager"'. On a seemingly irreversible slide and above the relegation places on goal average alone, action had to be taken.

Swales convened a meeting of the entire playing staff and, handed the chance to express their discontent, the anti-Saunders camp delivered their damning verdicts. It wasn't a case of Saunders losing the dressing room; he'd never won it to begin with. The inevitable soon followed. Saunders drove up to Manchester from his Norwich home to meet Swales the following morning. At the resultant get-together, the manager was invited to resign; the premise being City's poor results in the league. 'I flatly refused,' Saunders said. Swales was left with little option. On Good Friday, 12 April, less than six months after his arrival at the club, Saunders was relieved of his duties and, he said, he 'hadn't even got round to signing the contract I had been offered when I took the job'.

Swales had publicly staked his own career on his first appointment. 'I know for sure Ron's the right one,' he'd declared. 'If he goes down, I go with him. It's as blunt as that.' He did nothing of the sort. Instead, beneath the weight of feeling from the very players he'd perhaps encouraged

Saunders to faze out of the club, the City chairman buckled weakly. Only hours after the announcement of Saunders' sacking, with Tony Book once more assuming caretaking responsibilities, City entertained Liverpool, earning a 1-1 draw against Shankly's team. A 4-0 thrashing in a swift reverse fixture at Anfield followed. It was only on 20 April, in City's last home game, a 2-1 win against West Ham, that the shadow of relegation was finally cast off and the fate City's fans so feared was avoided.

On the season's final Saturday, Book took his side to Old Trafford and, on a famous afternoon, former United hero Law back-heeled a goal five minutes from the end that gave the visitors a 1-0 win. Results elsewhere, rather than the derby defeat, meant that, after 36 years in the First Division, six years after winning the European Cup, City's bitter rivals were condemned to the second tier. City, meanwhile, celebrating 50 years at Maine Road, lived to fight another day. Whether this or seeing Norwich City sitting at the very bottom of the First Division pile gave the out-of-work Saunders any satisfaction one can only speculate.

The end of Saunders' Maine Road stay was as abrupt as his behaviour had reportedly been during his tenure. Fired for the first time, the dismissal left Saunders so 'disillusioned about some things in the game', he said, he even considered turning his back on football altogether. That consideration got as far as planning to open a health clinic with a friend in Norwich, where he was still living.

A trip to a dinner in London, however, changed his mind. Following long talks with two friends, Jim Smith, then managing Colchester, and Dick Graham, a former Colchester boss, Saunders determined that football management might be worth another shot 'if I were offered a First Division job or a good job with a club in Division Two'. As it happened, events at Villa Park meant that it wouldn't be long before that good job was forthcoming. Within weeks of 'crashing to the depths', Saunders was back up on his feet again. The health clinic could wait.

Christmas in June

WHOEVER got the Aston Villa job, Vic Crowe said, the new manager would 'think it's Christmas'. On the back of Crowe's sacking, Peter Morris, in *Aston Villa: The First 100 Years*, had written, 'They [the Villa board] must either go for success in the big, bold way or forget about their future.' If anyone represented 'the big, bold way' it was Brian Clough. Clough may have been sincere in his desire to bring the same success to Third Division Brighton that he had at Derby County – the East Sussex club, their chairman Mike Bamber announced, would soon be a force in football under Clough's management – but even a blind man could see that the Seagulls wouldn't be landing anywhere near the top flight anytime soon.

A 4-0 defeat by Walton and Hersham in the FA Cup first round, then an 8-2 home humiliation by Bristol Rovers were losses that Clough later said affected him as deeply as any triumph at the highest level. He was quickly eyeing an escape route. In March, a £400-per-week offer from the Shah of Persia to run the Iranian national team had greatly appealed. Clough was already packing his suitcase but the Brighton board held both him and assistant Peter Taylor to their contracts. 'I'm staying at Brighton to do a job,' Clough said. 'I am not saying I'm happy here.'

The consensus remained that Clough had just taken on a holiday job before he got back to serious, regular employment. So it was little surprise that, when the Villa vacancy arose, the bookies identified Clough as the overwhelming favourite to fill it. Just two days after Crowe's dismissal, branches of Ladbrokes in Birmingham stopped taking further bets on the Brighton boss getting the job. Among the Villa supporters, too, Clough was the unanimous choice as the man they saw bringing the good old days back to Birmingham. In an *Evening Mail* poll, 93 per cent voted for Clough to take over the Villa Park hotseat.

As messy as his departure from Derby was, Clough's credentials were unquestionable. In just over six seasons with the East Midlands outfit, Clough, in tandem with Taylor, had secured the Second Division title, the Watney and Texaco cups, a league championship, as well as a European Cup semi-final place which might well have been a final but for the 'cheating bastards' of Juventus whom Clough claimed had conned their way to a 3-1 aggregate victory on a controversial night in Turin.

That he courted publicity was all the more of a draw; the loud, brash Tommy Docherty had helped put Villa firmly back in the nation's imagination and, while Crowe furthered the club's revival, it was for a more populist figure in the Docherty mould that the Villa fans most craved. Success and publicity was a potent cocktail. In 1967, Villa, just relegated to the Second Division, had actively sought Clough's services. Clough and Taylor's achievements at achievements at Hartlepools United (as they were then known, before they dropped the 's') had registered strongly on the radar of a number of clubs, including Villa. Instead, the pair went to Derby. Now it was Clough, while not exactly touting himself to Villa, who was happy to add his own voice to the chorus of favourable opinion.

In Majorca, where he was enjoying his end-of-season holiday, he informed *Evening Mail* reporter Jim Waters, 'I don't think I could get Aston Villa into the First Division, I know I could.' After confirming his interest in the position and putting Villa alongside Liverpool and Manchester United as one of 'the top three clubs in the country', Clough further championed his own cause by declaring, 'I would not just build a team just for promotion, I would build a team for the top of the First Division.'

If such fighting talk was music to supporters' ears, it failed to strike an enchanting note with Doug Ellis. Ellis had already once before rejected Clough's advances to make himself Aston Villa's boss. According to Ellis's biography, *Deadly!*, in December 1972, during negotiations at the Baseball Ground for the £90,000 transfer of full-back John Robson, both Clough and Taylor had attempted to persuade the Villa chairman to sack Vic Crowe and appoint the pair of them in his stead. Ellis felt now as he had done then: that the presence of Clough at Villa Park would never work; Ellis's reason being that 'there is only one boss at Aston Villa and that's me'. From his Majorcan holiday home, Clough had told the press, 'Doug Ellis has not contacted me and I can tell you that I have not contacted him. Let them come and see me if they want me...but before I become their manager I would want to see that they have the breadth of vision.'

Ellis was not a man who ever felt he had to sell the club to a manager. It was the manager who had to persuade Ellis of *his* worth. Though Ellis didn't say so, the ever-garrulous Clough had talked himself out of a job.

QPR's Gordon Jago was another whose name had been bandied about. Jago, in charge of the side promoted in 1972/73 as Villa finished third, was a progressive, highly thought-of manager responsible for Rangers signing such stellar talents as Stan Bowles, Don Givens and Dave Thomas. But early in May he'd walked out on the Loftus Road club in a fit of temper, fed up with criticism from his chairman Jim Gregory. The break-up was only brief. Gregory apologised to Jago, saying he was happy to reinstate the man who made QPR the top club in London and, with Jago's return on 25 May, one more potential frontrunner for the Villa job was now ruled out. The shortlist was getting ever shorter.

In the same *Evening Mail* poll that had shown Clough's support from the Villa fans, the nearest contender to Clough, registering only four per cent, was Sir Alf Ramsey. Just over two weeks prior to Crowe's departure, the hero of 1966 had been deposed as the national team boss. England's draw against Poland the previous October and their subsequent elimination from the forthcoming World Cup finals in West Germany effectively signalled the end for Ramsey. The man who, in Geoffrey Green's words, 'succeeded in cementing a team spirit, equivalent to that of a successful club side, which has never existed at a national level' paid the inevitable price.

On 19 April, Ramsey was dismissed, the FA, having stuck up two fingers, then giving him a less-than-golden handshake reputed to be £15,000. It was shabby treatment at best. Another job offer wasn't long in coming – coaching Athletic Bilbao in Spain on a huge £40,000-per-annum salary – but it was on a return to day-to-day club management in England, which he'd last tasted over a decade earlier, that Ramsey was apparently keener. Ramsey's claims as a possible Villa boss appeared far more realistic than Clough's and, perhaps because of a lack of other suitable candidates, the bookies now made him the new favourite to replace Crowe.

At a meeting with Ellis and vice-chairman Harry Kartz in a room hired at London's Hilton Hotel, however, Ramsey gave the distinct impression he wasn't overly bothered about the role. The man he actually recommended for the position was a recently sacked manager named Ron Saunders.

Saunders was certainly available and, although he hadn't engaged in any blatant lobbying for the vacancy, it clearly appealed. While not in any particular hurry to start warming a hotseat again, he was adamant that when he did so it would be at one of the country's premier clubs. 'I'd worked so hard to get up there,' he later wrote, 'and having reached the top, there was no way I was going to start all over again from the bottom.'

Villa, despite their present status, could still be included in that category. Nonetheless, it was more in hope than expectation that Saunders expressed his interest. 'Frankly, at the time I posted my application,' he said, 'I wasn't too worried about the response.' The response was positive. Once word emerged that Saunders was in the frame, from being a rank outsider – as he said himself, 'an also-ran' – Saunders was now odds-on for the role. 'I'm not afraid of any challenge,' he responded when asked about the prospect. 'I reckon my record will stand comparison with other people who want the Villa job.'

On 4 June, the news was confirmed: signing a three-year contract with a reported annual salary of £10,000, the 41-year-old Saunders was revealed as the new manager of Aston Villa, their sixth in ten years.

It had been a far from straightforward process, though. The previous night, Saunders had stayed at the house of Doug Ellis. On the morning of the 4th, Villa's commercial manager Eric Woodward picked up Saunders and, in a cloak-and-dagger operation, whisked him through a door on the Witton Lane side of Villa Park to keep his identity secret from the few journalists sniffing around outside for a story.

Having met the Villa board, however, Saunders was then left to wait while Ellis and his fellow directors discussed the merits of the prospective new manager. The deliberations went on much longer than Saunders anticipated. Fed up with the delay, Saunders grew increasingly annoyed until, his patience pushed too far, he informed Woodward, 'I've had enough of this and I'm off!' Only Woodward's persuasive powers got him to stay. The board eventually made up their minds, and the announcement of Saunders' arrival was made public.

The delay, it later transpired, was due to a ponderous debate in which director Sir William Dugdale, along with other board members, spent hours convincing a sceptical Doug Ellis that Saunders was the perfect fit. In his autobiography, *Settling the Bill*, Dugdale wrote, 'Doug was very anti-Saunders and tried to veto his appointment but (director) Harry Cressman said: "Who else is there?" and moved that we appoint him. After much argument and discussion regarding re-advertising, we left Doug to discuss terms with Ron. Whatever happened next we shall never know, but Ron and Doug were not on the same wavelength from day one.'

Journalist Ian Johnson had no doubts that Villa had found the ideal man. On the day that Saunders was handed the reins, after press, radio and TV interviews had taken up all of the morning, Eric Woodward had arranged for Johnson to take Saunders for lunch. 'We arrived so late at the hotel that all they had left was a few curly sandwiches,' recalled Johnson in *The Aston Villa Story*. 'It was a bit of a disaster in that respect, although the staff would willingly have knocked the place down and re-built it if the new manager had requested it.'

The pair talked for a couple of hours. Well, Johnson talked for a couple of hours, because Saunders wanted to know as much as possible about his new club. 'I was so impressed by his personality that I wrote that I would back him with a week's precious wages to make Villa successful,' Johnson wrote. 'Nobody took my bet, but I would have won it eventually.'

With Fleet Street's gaze already firmly fixed on the imminent World Cup finals starting just nine days later, and British football fans – even the odd English one – preparing to sport their Scottish tartan caps, Saunders slipped almost unnoticed through the Villa Park gates. It was, wrote Graham McColl, 'A low-key entrance entirely suited to a man who preferred action to words.' But even those finals were soon to become the backdrop to a sensational chain of events unfolding at England's top clubs. In the summer of 1974, the end-of-season comings and goings – what French football writers termed 'The Waltz of the Managers' – featured the most unlikely dancers.

On 4 July, a day after Holland and the hosts West Germany had sealed their places in the World Cup Final (the latter with a 1-0 defeat of England's qualifying conquerors Poland), Don Revie was installed as the new England team manager in succession to Ramsey. Joe Mercer, while boasting a solid record as caretaker, had expressed his wish not to be considered for the permanent role. Clough, as with the Villa vacancy, had got the popular vote. But the maverick tendencies and fiery outbursts were never going to appeal to the hierarchy at FA headquarters. Although once described by Football League secretary Alan Hardaker as 'totally ruthless, selfish, devious and prepared to cut corners to get his own way', Revie, born only a brisk walk away from Clough in Middlesbrough, was the man they wanted.

Then, on 12 July, five days after West Germany's 2-1 triumph over the Dutch, a dramatic statement emerged from Anfield: Bill Shankly had retired as manager of Liverpool. After nearly 15 years in command, claiming the strain of being involved in top-class football was affecting him adversely, the 60-year-old decided to call it quits. The FA Cup Final victory over Newcastle, two days before Crowe's sacking by Villa, was Shankly's last game in charge. Going to inform his chairman, Shankly said, was 'like walking to the electric chair'. Two weeks later, Bob Paisley, Shankly's 55-year-old assistant, who'd been with the Merseyside club since 1939, was promoted in his place.

The retirement of Shankly would undoubtedly make the managerial landscape much less vibrant. But with Clough still prominent in the picture, it was never short on colour. And it wasn't long before Clough's face and name were being splashed all over the tabloid pages once more.

On 20 July, in perhaps the most unexpected managerial shift of all, Leeds United announced that the new man occupying the chair vacated by Revie was none other than their harshest critic. With Leeds' midfield twosome Billy Bremner and Johnny Giles both vying for the job, the Leeds board, not wanting to upset either player, went instead to the other extreme. While Peter Taylor stayed at Brighton, Clough, lured by the challenge of 'winning better' than Revie, accepted a five-year contract worth a reported £20,000-per-annum. As things panned out, no one could have caused greater upset at Elland Road. Clough, rather than trying to fill Revie's shoes, donned a pair of jackboots and trampled a self-destructive path that led him just 44 days later through the club's exit door.

Warmed by the possibility of the livewire Clough landing in the Midlands, instead, Villa's supporters were left distinctly cool by the prospect of Saunders. With an appetite for much tastier nourishment after two years of solid but ultimately dissatisfying fare under Crowe, they were now, they feared, faced with something all-too-similar. Crowe, a manager who, Geoffrey Green wrote, 'understands the psychology of a player', was at least considered a kind, sympathetic boss. Saunders at Maine Road had displayed an apparent total absence of either understanding or empathy. Dennis Shaw, in the *Evening Mail*, wrote that the new manager 'has to find a short cut to the top of Division One' but warned that Saunders' initial job was to win over the fans.

He made a positive first dint in their minds. 'The potential here is screaming out to be tapped,' Saunders enthused. 'We have the greatest public in football and it is my job and my ambition to tap it for them.' He proved he was no mug at public relations either. 'Villa are a club with a tradition second to none,' he said, 'and I would like to think that we can build a present and a future to match the past.' As at Carrow Road, the ambition, Saunders declared, was to have First Division football within three years. He was confident of achieving it.

That the squad which Crowe bequeathed him had failed to blend successfully was a mystery which Saunders would have to quickly solve. On 15 July, the players met their new boss for the first time. John Deehan, then an apprentice with the club, believes that the 'senior players felt very threatened' by Saunders' arrival. 'It was an unsettling situation,' Deehan says, 'as one manager moves on and another picks up and decides who will go and who will stay.'

There was bound to be some trepidation. Perhaps fearful of a repeat of the Manchester City scenario, Saunders, too, had reason to be wary. Getting to know one another took two or three weeks, including a two-game five-day stay in Germany, by which time the players knew full-well what to expect from Saunders: graft, graft and even more graft. Even before pre-season training began, Ian Ross met with Saunders who confirmed, 'It was going to be nothing but hard slog.' Ross, no stranger to sweat as a graduate of Shankly's Liverpool, was impressed. 'I thought that was good,' he said, 'because I knew we would get nowhere without hard work.'

On the same August day as reserve team coach Bill Shorthouse joined, Roy MacLaren also boosted the coaching staff. A boardroom upheaval at Huddersfield had seen, first, manager Ian Greaves leave, then, a week later, MacLaren. The affable Scot, whose 18-year career as a goalkeeper had taken him from St Johnstone in Scotland to playing in the top three divisions in the Football League with Bury then Sheffield Wednesday, was only out of work for a week. Greaves had put in a good word and, on the strength of that, Saunders rang up MacLaren to ask him to come down to Villa Park for a chat. 'I didn't know Ron – in fact, I had never met him,' MacLaren said, 'and really I didn't know much about Aston Villa and their traditions.' Soon made aware by Saunders of just what a big club Villa was, MacLaren happily signed up as first team coach.

In his book, *Cloughie: Walking on Water*, Clough likens pre-season training to 'taking the first steps on a long military campaign'. It is a vitally important time, to remind the players to do things properly and to remember their common goal: success. 'Make sure you've got your helmet on securely in July,' Clough wrote, 'and it will keep you safe right the way through.'

Saunders took to the task with unstinting thoroughness. It wasn't all gruelling cross-country running. From corner kicks to throw-ins, everything was gone over constantly on the training ground until it almost became like automation. Attacking and defensive moves were practised hundreds of times. By the end of it, everybody knew his job.

'Players like to know what they're supposed to do and what they're not supposed to do,' he'd told Gerry Harrison in his Norwich days. If anyone was going to tell them it was Saunders.

Though a move was mooted for Millwall striker Alf Wood (a frustrated Saunders failing with a £100,000 bid when the Lions wanted £150,000) and an enquiry made about West Brom's midfielder Len Cantello, with Villa still very much living hand-to-mouth – a 'make do and mend' situation, Saunders called it – the new manager contented himself with working with the 'good characters' at his disposal.

Ian Ross was installed as captain. Signed by Liverpool at 17 from junior football in his native Glasgow where he was a school friend of Kenny Dalglish, the 5ft 9.5in Ross was so highly rated as a man-marker, Shankly employed him to perform the role against Bayern Munich's Franz Beckenbauer in the away leg of an Inter-Cities Fairs Cup fourth-round tie in 1971. With Liverpool leading 3-0 from the home leg – thanks to a hat-trick from Alun Evans – they sealed the tie in Germany with a 1-1 draw, securing their progress to a semi-final encounter with Leeds United. Ross not only shackled the West German skipper – earning Ross the nickname 'Der Kaiser's shadow' among Liverpool supporters – he also claimed Liverpool's goal on the night.

But, following a surprise 1-0 FA Cup defeat at struggling Second Division side Watford in February 1970, Shankly had decided it was time for renovation work. 'The wise manager is always looking over the rainbow and planning for the morrow,' Geoffrey Green wrote. Many of that Liverpool team had reached their rainbow's end. Ross's versatility was an asset that Shankly valued but also robbed him of a regular place. In over five years at Anfield, Ross made only 68 appearances in all competitions.

Just two days before Villa were due at York's Bootham Crescent for their opening fixture, Saunders made his first addition. Negotiating his compensation pay-off with Peter Swales, Saunders enquired whether his former employers had any players to sell. He wasn't referring to Messrs Lee, Summerbee, Law et al. Asked whom he wanted, Saunders came out with the name, Frank Carrodus.

At 20 years of age, Carrodus, then playing for Cheshire League side Altrincham, was regarded by Malcolm Allison as 'one of the best non-league prospects ever'. Signed by City, the Manchester-born wideman made his debut in a 1-1 draw with Arsenal in February 1970 but subsequently remained on the first team fringes. It was during 1973/74, under Saunders, that he'd enjoyed his most prolonged spell of action. Despite only handing a disappointed Carrodus a non-playing substitute role for the League Cup Final versus Wolves – opting for the experienced heads of Bell and Summerbee alongside Tony Towers – Saunders was a fan.

Carrodus, not blessed with the greatest ball skills but pacy and renowned for his bottomless reserves of stamina, would add, Saunders believed, 'a few more alternatives in the middle of the field'. Loath to leave Maine Road though playing only 40 matches in five years, once Carrodus saw the Villa Park set-up, his mind was made up. 'I had to be certain that it was the right move,' Carrodus said. 'Ron helped ensure it was.'

The £95,000 deal, however, left Doug Ellis less than impressed. 'Ron had come from Norwich and was staying at Penns Hall Hotel in Sutton Coldfield,' Ellis recalled. 'He called to say he had signed Frank Carrodus from Manchester City. He was a good player but I told him, "The board makes those decisions." I told him to stay at the hotel and I went over. I had to put my trousers over my pyjamas! I told him he could recommend players but the board made the decisions. We did buy Carrodus – but for a lot less than Ron had agreed.' It wouldn't be the last conflict between chairman and manager.

Securing the services of two of Villa's star performers was vital to Saunders' plans. When, in the run-up to the first league match, the 'pay rebels' – Brian Little and Ray Graydon – both re-committed to the club, it was a huge boost. Since his arrival from Bristol Rovers, the 27-year-old Graydon had played a pivotal role in Villa's rise. Little had already cemented a regular first team spot. But as many before and after him found from their own first meeting with Saunders, the young forward discovered just what a hard-nosed figure he could be. With an appointment to see the new boss to discuss an improved contract, Little knocked on the office door and went in. 'Who are you?' was Saunders' greeting. He knew full-well who Little was but, as was his habit, Saunders was making sure the player, Superboy or not, knew he'd be getting no preferential treatment from this manager. 'I think I went away on less money than I was on before,' Little joked years later.

From others, the same curt question produced a different response. When John Gidman was greeted with it, his reply to Saunders was, 'Who the f**k are *you*?' Saunders said, 'Oh, we've got a smart Scouser, have we?' Gidman, a winger in Liverpool's youth side, was asked by Ronnie Moran to play for the 'A' team as an attacking right-back. It became his position from then on. Overcoming the heartache of being let go by his boyhood club – once Tony Waiters was appointed head of youth development, Gidman's 'face didn't fit' – the 16-year-old impressed during a month's trial at Villa (Gidman's father Frank rang Villa to ask them to give his son a trial) and signed professional forms for the Midlands club in August 1971. Aged just 18, Gidman made his full debut the following year against Carlisle United. Named the club's Player of the Year for 1973/74, he'd firmly established himself in the number two shirt, his performances reportedly attracting admirers from several top-flight clubs. That initial exchange with Saunders, however, was symptomatic of the antagonistic relations the two would share in the coming years.

As part of the club's centenary celebrations, Villa had arranged a pre-season friendly at home to Leeds United. The game, on Wednesday 7 August, was Saunders' first in charge. It was also the second match in his Elland Road reign of Brian Clough. Leeds had last visited Villa Park for a League Cup third-round tie in October 1972 when Villa, then top of Division Two, had earned a deserved 1-1 draw, Bruce Rioch equalising spectacularly after Jack Charlton had given the visitors an early lead with a long-distance shot. Crowe's side – beaten 2-0 in the replay – were, in Revie's view, 'The most exciting team I have seen all season.' With 46,815 in attendance, Villa Park, enthused the Leeds boss, was like 'another Anfield'.

Revie's encounters with Saunders, however, had been less amiable. In January 1973, following Leeds' 2-1 win in a league clash at Carrow Road, Norwich boss Saunders was bitterly critical of them. 'Leeds carry professionalism to the extreme. It borders on intimidation,' he claimed. 'Our players have been told not to dispute a referee's decision, but when you play Leeds it seems you have to, otherwise they try to gain an unfair advantage.'

An affronted Revie refuted the accusations, using his weekly column in the *Yorkshire Evening Post* to retort, 'One would have thought Saunders had been in the game long enough to avoid clutching at straws when his team are held or beaten.'

Two weeks earlier the sides had also clashed at Carrow Road in the FA Cup, Saunders arguing after a 1-1 draw that Leeds disrupted the home side's rhythm by repeatedly feigning injury. 'That's nonsense,' wrote Revie. 'Besides, Saunders is the last person who should complain about such tactics when you consider Norwich themselves were accused of this when they won 3-0 at Arsenal in the League Cup.' It was surprising, Revie added, that a coach of Saunders' experience and stature 'should choose to cover up for his team's limitations in this way'.

Predictably, in his programme notes, Saunders gave no name-check to either Revie or Clough, though generously referenced the West Yorkshire club's achievements. 'We could not have asked for better opposition for our

Centenary Match,' he wrote. 'Without doubt, over the last decade, Leeds United have proved themselves the outstanding team in the country, a team whose stars have become household names.'

The game, Saunders felt, would provide Villa 'with an excellent yardstick of how much we have progressed in our preparations for the coming season'. His goals for the club were clear. 'It is the ambition of everyone at Villa Park,' he wrote, 'that ten years hence Aston Villa's players will be held in the same esteem throughout the country. That is the "Everest" that we are all aiming to conquer.'

Climbing that "Everest" meant ascending a Second Division with 'a very strong First Division flavour'. Manchester United, Sunderland, West Brom, Blackpool, Nottingham Forest, Bolton, Southampton, Fulham, Portsmouth, and Sheffield Wednesday were all teams, Saunders mentioned, that 'have made important contributions to the premier division since the war and now find themselves battling to regain their former status'. Saunders acknowledged that 'the competition is going to be so intense', but as manager of Villa, he'd make sure his players shed blood, sweat and tears to reclaim their top-flight place. 'Soccer is not a game for promisers,' Saunders concluded, 'but I can guarantee one thing: everyone who pulls on a Villa shirt, no matter which team (first, reserves or youth) he's playing for, will be giving 110 per cent effort.'

As yardsticks go, the Centenary Match counted for little. On a night of celebration, with nostalgia high on the agenda as former Villa players paraded pre-kick-off before a 29,481 crowd, Leeds won 2-1. Sammy Morgan bagged Villa's consolation. Though had Ray Graydon not spurned two penalties at the Witton End – for which, naturally, he received a hard time from the fans – the home side might have added to the misery of the man in the opposition dugout. As it was, including Frank Carrodus, given clearance to play because it wasn't an official fixture, Saunders got the chance to check out the players that were likely to serve him in the season ahead. Just over a year later, Leeds would visit Villa Park again. The difference was that, then, the two teams would be meeting on a much more even footing.

Jekyll-and-Hyde

IF an instant lift-off was expected, it didn't happen. After York, playing their first-ever Second Division match, had taken a ninth-minute lead from Barry Lyons' free kick, Villa responded well and Ray Graydon, erasing the memory of a penalty miss against the same opponents in a 1-0 League Cup defeat the previous season, deservedly levelled with a header 20 minutes later. Unable to force a winner – 'In the first 20 minutes and for 20 minutes after half-time it was a case of how many goals we were going to score,' Saunders felt – Villa, with Carrodus impressive on his debut, had to settle for a point. Their 'great character in coming back so strongly after conceding an early goal' left their manager relatively content. 'There is plenty here to build on,' Saunders said.

Three days later, they finished level, 1-1 again, at Hull's Boothferry Park then repeated the trick against Norwich in Saunders' first home game (Colin Suggett, one of Saunders' signings for the Norfolk club, cancelling out another Graydon strike). Although a 6-0 pounding of Hull – Sammy Morgan's hat-trick the first at Villa Park by a home player since Bobby Thomson's in an 8-3 win over Leicester in 1962 – suggested a belated launch, the rocket was still struggling to get off the ground.

While convincing on home territory, it took Villa 11 games – a 2-1 win at Oldham Athletic – to register their first triumph on their travels. A 2-0 reverse at Bristol Rovers' Eastville three weeks earlier had prompted Saunders to get out his chequebook again. Cardiff City's Wales international defender Leighton Phillips, an assured footballer and fine reader of the game, who'd made his league debut for the Welsh club in 1967, was attracting interest from a number of clubs, Portsmouth, Sheffield Wednesday, Ipswich and Liverpool among them. Learning that Anfield scout Geoff Twentyman, the man who'd spotted John Gidman playing for Liverpool Schoolboys, had been assigned to watch Phillips in action, Saunders acted promptly. He tabled a bid and, after initially refusing to let Phillips leave for a few weeks, Cardiff's manager Jimmy Andrews finally accepted. On 18 September, Phillips joined Villa, the £100,000 fee equalling the club's record buy.

With Phillips starting life in the Midlands in an unfamiliar role – Saunders feeling his new signing could add some much-needed bite to a toothless midfield – Villa went on an unbeaten run that, by the end of October, saw them in third spot, albeit six points behind leaders Manchester United. Orient, Millwall, Nottingham Forest and Sheffield Wednesday had all been on the receiving end of three-goal blasts. Villa were playing a fast-paced, highly direct game and no one was profiting more than Ray Graydon. By mid-October, the express-quick winger, with 12 in league and cup, was the top scorer in England. Yet Saunders' Manager of the Month award proved the proverbial curse. Beginning with a 3-1 reverse at Fulham, Villa lost all three of their next league fixtures, including their first home setback, 1-0 versus Notts County, followed by an unlucky 2-1 defeat at Old Trafford, Villa bettering Docherty's side for much of a match that turned on a dubious penalty decision for United.

The loss of John Gidman didn't help. On 29 October, already invited by Don Revie to attend a meeting in a Manchester hotel for 84 players the new national team boss saw restoring England's reputation in world football, Gidman was part of the England under-23 team that beat Czechoslovakia 3-1 at Selhurst Park. Less than a week later, the Liverpudlian's entire career almost came to a tragically premature end. At a 5 November party held at Jimmy Cumbes' house, the Villa defender was the victim of a freak fireworks accident: a rocket, rather than flying upwards, rolled on to its side and shot 50 yards across a field, travelling at over 70mph. It hit the player straight in the right eye, propelling him back through a patio window.

Gidman – told later that the accident had a two-million-to-one chance of happening – was hurriedly transported to the nearest hospital, haemorrhaging badly and losing a lot of blood. He woke three days later with his head completely bandaged. The immediate reaction of the medical staff had been to remove the damaged eye, but Gidman's fiancé Clare intervened and wouldn't let them. Nor would the Villa club doctor David Targett who, fortunately, had been on hand at the party. 'He's a footballer, you can't!' Targett told them.

Gidman would remain in hospital for the next six weeks. Because of the bleeding, it was difficult for specialists to determine the extent of the damage. Thankfully, when Gidman was diagnosed, although there was blindness in the right eye, he hadn't lost his peripheral vision. Gidman's season was thought to be over, but the football career of one of Villa's most outstanding talents for years could continue.

At the time of his accident, Gidman had been talking to a QC about the recent IRA troubles. Two days before Villa faced Portsmouth on 23 November, 21 people were killed and 182 others injured by bombs planted in two Birmingham pubs, the Mulberry Bush and the Tavern in the Town. The game with Pompey went ahead – a respectful minute's silence observed by an understandably subdued 16,821 crowd and black armbands sported by both teams – with goals from Hamilton and Little giving Villa a 2-0 win to slightly offset the gloom, but there was a palpable tension mingled with shock and sadness in the atmosphere.

On the pitch, Saunders' chief bugbear remained Villa's away form. A painfully familiar pattern was emerging. Having eased their way past York City 4-0 on home soil, Villa lost their next game 2-0 at West Brom; following a 1-0 Boxing Day victory at Villa Park over Bristol Rovers, they then went to Cardiff on the last Saturday of the year, returning from the Welsh capital on the end of a demoralising 3-1 defeat. This Jekyll-and-Hyde sequence left them seventh in the table.

A whole 11 points ahead, Manchester United had claimed top spot from the off and fully warranted their pre-season tag as the bookies' promotion favourites. As the year drew to its end, Mud were topping the UK music charts with 'Lonely This Christmas' and with United, Sunderland, Norwich, West Brom, Bristol City and Oxford United all above them, Villa were in danger of getting left behind by the promotion-hunting pack.

Successfully unlocking opposition defences was becoming a genuine problem. Various combinations had been tried – Little, Sammy Morgan, Bobby Campbell and Keith Leonard all sharing game time up front – but, aside from Ray Graydon with 18 goals, Villa's forward line had lacked any killer instinct. Morgan's encouraging start had been halted abruptly by a serious groin injury. Youth team graduate Campbell, another burly, Belfast-born, in-your-face forward, had failed to convince.

In October, Saunders had been at Rochdale to watch Reading's Robin Friday, who'd led the attack as the Berkshire side assumed the Fourth Division leadership and though no approach was made – Friday, with a maverick reputation and a heavily tarnished disciplinary record hardly seemed the Saunders type – Saunders was clearly training his antennae farther afield to find a solution to his striking dilemma. As Villa entered the New Year, a two-legged League Cup semi-final was a tantalising prospect. The push for promotion, however, remained the priority. If it wasn't to be derailed, getting back on track needed to happen fast.

Third Time Lucky

SINCE Aston Villa won the inaugural League Cup in 1961, 3-2 on aggregate against Second Division Rotherham United, the tournament, the brainchild of league secretary Alan Hardaker, had steadily gained kudos and, unlike during its formative years, no one complained anymore that the biggest clubs didn't take the competition seriously. The 1974/75 season wasn't a vintage one for the First Division big guns, however. By the time of the semi-finals, the last-four line-up boasted not a single top-flight representative. Holders Wolves had fallen at the first hurdle, losing 3-1 to Second Division Fulham, who would go on in the next round to beat West Ham – the club they'd face later in the season in the FA Cup Final – before eventually going out to Newcastle United. At the quarter-final stage, only the team from St James' Park, Middlesbrough and Ipswich were still fighting the cause.

One of the semi-finalists was Villa.

Their route there had been anything but simple. Drawn at home in the second round to Saunders' first employers, Everton, Villa had controlled much of the game against their loftier opponents, gaining the advantage through a Chris Nicholl header. But a leveller from Brummie-born centre-forward Bob Latchford – a £350,000 capture from St Andrew's – earned the visitors a replay and, expected to show their superior class on home turf, the Goodison Park club were clear favourites to progress.

A confident Toffees boss Billy Bingham spoke of 'a nice League Cup run opening up'. If he thought the tie was in the bag, he was very misguided. Up on Merseyside, Saunders' side completely destroyed the copybook, putting in, as the *Evening Mail* described it, 'An extravagant performance in which they not only beat their First Division opponents, they outplayed them from the first kick to the last.' With Brian Little absent through injury, the twin strike force of Morgan and Campbell completely unsettled the Everton rearguard and, capitalising on their dominance, second-half goals from Morgan, Carrodus – his first for the club – and Graydon silenced the Goodison crowd. So humiliated was home keeper Dave Lawson, he was dropped by Bingham to be replaced by Dai Davies and wouldn't play again for Everton that season.

Their toughest test apparently over, Villa were then drawn away to Fourth Division Crewe Alexandra, the Gresty Road club who'd extinguished Birmingham City hopes in the previous round. The home side's appetite for cup heroics almost proved too strong again; Villa had to fight tooth and nail to earn a 2-2 draw before another close encounter in the following week's replay was settled by a last-minute left-footer from 'Chico' Hamilton. Prior to the move that led to Hamilton's goal, Jimmy Cumbes pulled off a vital stop from Crewe's Hughie Reed that had almost certainly saved Villa from an embarrassing elimination. Another away tie against Fourth Division opposition awaited.

Saunders had, after the Goodison triumph, expressed to his players a feeling that Villa's name was on the trophy this season. If it was, the lettering was still only a faint trace. The match at Hartlepool's Victoria Ground proved another unexpectedly uncomfortable battle; Charlie Aitken, an uncommon sight on a Villa scoresheet, finding the net with an even rarer, right-footed strike to give Villa a 1-1 draw. The replay was far easier. Including a brace of Brian Little goals, the home side made short work of the north-easterners, romping to a 6-1 victory. Little, celebrating his 21st birthday, had even greater cause for celebration: it was the first time at senior level he and his brother Alan had started together in the same team.

Chalk and cheese as footballers – Brian's skilful, attacking game contrasting completely with his brother's take-no-prisoners defensive approach – the two had grown up on the Durham coast where their father found employment as a miner, and had first teamed up for East Durham Boys. Now they were plying their trade as professionals at the same Midlands club, Alan arriving at Villa Park 12 months after his older sibling.

When, in early December, Villa then went to Colchester United's Layer Road in the fifth round, the two were again in the starting line-up. Alan, scoring his first and only senior goal for Villa – 'Brian laid it on, I played a one-two with him on the edge of the box, and I somehow scrambled it home,' he said – and a long-range effort by Graydon helped negotiate an awkward quarter-final against the Third Division outfit managed by Jim Smith, Villa overcoming their hosts 2-1. But the goal that

Alan Little described as 'our greatest moment together' wasn't enough to impress Saunders. Advised by the Villa boss he would never quite make the grade, after just two league starts under Saunders, Little was sold a week and a half later to Southend for £10,000.

With Villa the only team to enter the semi-final hat – the other three quarter-final ties between Middlesbrough and Manchester United, Newcastle and Chester, and local rivals Ipswich Town and Norwich City, were all drawn and required replays – when Fourth Division Chester emerged from the congestion as their opponents, it was seemingly the best possible draw. But Saunders knew they would be no pushovers. Challenging for promotion under ex-Villa outside-right, Ken 'KO' Roberts, Chester had already caused a sizeable shock, comfortably accounting for reigning league champions Leeds United 3-0 at Sealand Road before also securing a famous single-goal replay victory at home to Newcastle to set up the clash with Saunders' side.

On two successive Wednesday nights in January 1975, Chester put up a tremendous scrap. At home in the first leg before a packed 19,000 crowd, scrambled equalisers from Owen and Millington twice pegged Villa back and the 2-2 scoreline left the Midlanders with still plenty to do. 'I expect them to fight even harder tonight,' Saunders wrote in his programme notes for the second encounter, 'but I am equally confident that our lads will be prepared to apply themselves even harder.'

In front of 47,732 at Villa Park, it was another pulsating clash. A Keith Leonard double in the first half-hour looked to have killed off the Chester challenge but the plucky visitors weren't dead yet. First Mason before half-time then John 'Jessie' James after the break, profiting from a Cumbes error, scored to level the tie once more. But with Saunders' team in danger of fluffing its lines, ten minutes from time, Brian Little – turning sharply to fire home after Bobby McDonald nodded down a Graydon cross – ensured the match went according to script and this time there was to be no comeback.

Whatever the semi-final outcomes, a first Wembley final contested by two teams outside the top division was guaranteed. In the other semi, Villa's fellow Second Division pacesetters Norwich and Manchester United faced one another and, though United were fully expected to come out on top, a Suggett goal at Carrow Road edged City to a 3-2 aggregate victory.

The news of their triumph, announced over the Villa Park tannoy at the end of the Chester game, was greeted with almost as much elation as Brian Little's winner. Meeting the Norfolk club in the Wembley showdown was much more appealing than having to face Docherty's high-flyers.

For the neutrals, Villa's clash with the Canaries threw up the intriguing prospect of a face-off between the two managers: Saunders and John Bond. Bond, as Saunders' Carrow Road replacement, had breezed in from Bournemouth along with young coach Ken Brown, having led the south-coast club to promotion as Fourth Division runners-up at the end of his first season and near to promotion again the following season. On taking up the Norwich reins, the loquacious Essex man almost immediately declared, 'I want players to enjoy themselves and to pass on that sense of fun to the supporters.' It was, unmistakably, a direct dig at his predecessor.

Aside from being born within a few weeks of each other in 1932, Bond and Saunders had little in common. Bond, a shameless self-publicist, courted the media spotlight and was always willing to pronounce on any football-related matter. 'I prefer to let performances and results speak for themselves,' was Saunders' mantra. The disparity in their footballing styles was so stark Keith Skipper often wondered 'if this was the same club pursuing the same goals in the same sport'. One Fleet Street veteran once suggested to Skipper, 'If you could melt down those two and mix the steel and organisation of one with the flair and flamboyance of the other, I reckon that'd produce just about the perfect boss.'

Sure enough, with the final approaching, Bond couldn't resist the temptation offered him by the tabloids. Under Saunders in 1973, a stoic, hard-working Norwich side was heavily slated for the negative tactics that spoiled the spectacle of the final against Spurs. Bond pledged that there'd be no repeat; *his* Norwich side's adventurous approach, he bragged, would reap its just rewards. Disparaging remarks were made about the team he inherited from Saunders. He then cranked up the perceived antipathy even further by calling his counterpart a 'short-term manager'.

Once the motor-mouthed 'Bondwagon', as Skipper labelled it, was on a roll, it was hard to put on the brakes. Reporters tried to bait Saunders into a response, but he wasn't biting. What did rile him, however, were comments made by Vic Crowe. In a newspaper interview, Crowe claimed great satisfaction from and no little credit for Villa's season so far. Saunders was clearly offended at what he perceived as a belittling of his own influence on the team's fortunes: 'It would appear from what Mr Crowe has said that I have been wasting my time and would have been better off sunning myself in Majorca.'

Villa went to Wembley in fine form and with confidence high. They'd hauled an impressive 32 points from their previous 18 league games. The

Saturday before Wembley, a 2-0 home win over Manchester United in front of a near-40,000 crowd was another boost. Rather than bigging up their chances, Saunders spoke only about the importance of 'blend and balance' and 'when you pay big money for First Division players you buy that club's problems'.

Maintaining a quiet lead-up to the big day, Saunders kept everything distinctly low-key. The value of victory was stressed to the players. Too many teams, Saunders told them, were happy to go to Wembley simply satisfied to be there. Saunders perhaps didn't quite share Shankly's belief that 'if you are first you are first, if you are second you are nothing', but he was imbued with the same steely determination to succeed. 'There are only winners and losers in this game,' Saunders said. 'There is nothing in between – and losers find themselves out of a job.'

For someone who believed that you make your own fate – 'If you wait for things to happen, invariably they are the wrong things – especially on the football field,' he said – Saunders had more than his share of superstitious quirks. Though there was no Revie-like 'lucky' blue mohair suit in the wardrobe, a rabbit's foot and a bent penny were just two of the various charms Saunders liked to carry on his person, 'to help me along', he once said.

While Revie in his pre-match preparation – including a walk up to a particular set of traffic lights and back – indulged in what he called 'little ceremonies' designed to leave nothing, however illogical, to chance, Saunders' own Saturday routine, he once informed Gerry Harrison, involved essentially no more than harmless rituals that were just something 'you begin with and you stick to'. 'But you hate to be diverted off that course?' Harrison asked. 'Absolutely,' a smiling Saunders replied. Having been in the north dressing room for his previous two losing finals, Saunders applied this time for the south one. He was successful. The omens, at least in Saunders' mind, had just improved considerably.

Once the game kicked off, it was evident that Villa wouldn't need providence on their side, or the subs' bench for that matter. Almost from the first whistle, they looked much the better team. With Carrodus, Hamilton and the impressive McDonald bossing midfield, they quickly established control. At the back, Ross, 'busy as an ant' in the words the following day of the *Mirror*'s Frank McGhee, and Nicholl nullified the twin threat of much-vaunted striking duo MacDougall and Boyer, and the Canaries offered little by way of danger. Aside from a 30th-minute scare when ex-Bournemouth striker MacDougall rounded Cumbes only to see his shot headed off the line by Ross, Villa's backline was barely breached.

While the *Birmingham Mail* would report that Nicholl – 'bold and hard and winning everything in the air' – was 'the best player on the field', if there were a man of the match award, Brian Little would have been deserving of it. Giving a masterclass on close control and trickery to Norwich defenders Stringer and Forbes, Little – with brother Alan a spectator in the 95,946 crowd – was the undoubted star of the show. In the second half Villa upped the tempo. Chances came and went. Graydon, Little, Carrodus and Hamilton all saw efforts kept out by Kevin Keelan. The Calcutta-born custodian of the Canaries' goal had first signed forms as a professional at Villa in 1960 but endured a series of quick-fire moves – from Stockport County to Kidderminster Harriers to Wrexham – before a transfer to Carrow Road in 1963. It was only under Saunders that Keelan really established himself as a Norwich regular and Keelan was happy to acknowledge the debt he owed Saunders for giving him renewed confidence after so many early setbacks in his career.

That confidence was much in evidence now as his virtual one-man salvage operation looked like denying Villa the winner their dominance deserved. In the 79th minute, though, came the one moment of real drama that swung the match. Rising to meet a Hamilton corner, a towering Chris Nicholl headed a powerful goalbound effort that beat Keelan, only for full-back Mel Machin to dive full-length and deflect the ball past the post with his hand. Machin's transgression – labelled in *The Guardian* in 2009 as 'perhaps the most famous iconic – and surprisingly – deliberate piece of cheating in Wembley history' – left referee Gordon Hill with no option.

The question was, who would take the penalty? Ray Graydon, who'd missed the two pre-season kicks against Leeds, had also spurned an opportunity from 12 yards in the home defeat to Notts County. And while both Hamilton and Graydon had converted spot-kicks in the League Cup thrashing of Hartlepool, Hamilton was guilty of a miss as Villa drew at home to Fulham just three weeks previously. It was Graydon who grabbed the ball.

With skipper Ross unable to look, his back turned to the goal as Cumbes gave him a commentary, the Villa wideman stepped up and struck his kick firmly to Keelan's right hand. The diving keeper parried the ball on to the post. Villa's nemesis for so much of the game, Keelan appeared to have kept them out yet again. It wasn't so. Rebounding off the upright, the ball fell kindly straight back to Graydon and, steadying himself, coolly bringing the ball down with his instep, with Keelan struggling in vain to cover the left side of his goal, the forward volleyed a strong shot into the back of the net, giving the Norwich number one no second chance. The Villa fans behind the goal, their hearts momentarily in their mouths, suddenly exploded. As scrappy as it was, it was a fitting reward for the side on top throughout.

Keith Leonard might have added further gloss – his header hitting the inside of Keelan's post – but it didn't matter; Villa closed out the game and Norwich, with ten minutes to do what they hadn't looked like doing all day, never came close to scoring. Ironically, on a day in which the only pre-match entertainment (aside from the Band of the Royal Corps of Transport) was a penalty competition organised by ITV's football preview show, *On the Ball* – teenagers versus West Ham keeper Mervyn Day – the final was settled from 12 yards. Well, about six to be more precise. At the final whistle, Saunders, a League Cup winner at the third time of asking, gave Graydon a joyous bear hug. 'I meant to tell Ray that Kevin always dives to his right, but I completely forgot,' Saunders admitted afterwards. 'I knew he'd play a one-two off the post,' he added, mischievously.

While the Canaries had little to sing about, Saunders couldn't have been chirpier. Wembley, he'd told his players, is 'the worst place in the world to lose'. After the bitterness, he now relished what he later described as 'a very sweet victory'. On whether, after Bond's comments, the win had any added significance, it was fairly clear. 'I've had a lot of good things said about me by managers of proven ability like Bill Shankly, Don Revie and Dave Sexton. I'm not really interested in what lesser managers have to say,' he remarked. 'He did all the talking all week. My players did the talking today.' Bond himself was reasonably gracious in defeat. 'Villa were worthy winners,' he said, who 'never let us settle down.' Feeling that 'we never knocked the ball about as we can', he was disappointed with his own side's performance. His pre-match predictions didn't get a mention.

The following day, the national press lambasted the encounter. 'For most neutrals,' the *Mirror*'s Frank McGhee wrote, 'the feeling when Ray Graydon's goal finally won it for Villa ten minutes from the end was, bluntly, one of relief that we wouldn't have to live through another fortnight of promises and, worse, another replay.' Though one enthusiastic newspaper went with, 'Super Villa Win!' it's doubtful even the most ardent Villa fan would have been enticed by a full-page ad in the official souvenir programme offering highlights on vinyl LP for just £2.30.

Still, it was perhaps a bit harsh of McGhee to suggest that 'at times both sides looked as out of place as provincial repertory players on a West End stage', and that 'a very ordinary Aston Villa team never needed to rise above muddling mediocrity to be distinctly superior to Norwich'.

The statistics told the tale. Villa had 23 goal attempts to Norwich's five. Villa forced 15 corners, Norwich four (two of which went straight into the side netting). 'I was virtually a spectator,' said Jimmy Cumbes. 'I gained a winners' medal without having a serious shot to deal with!'

As the players and fans later enjoyed an evening at the Savoy Hotel, Saunders toasted the team's success. 'I have a problem,' he said. 'Every time I go to Wembley I get the sack – this time it's different. From the oldest to the youngest, from the most experienced to the least, I thank you from the bottom of my heart. I hope we'll work together for a good many years backed by the best supporters in the league.'

After the meal, the players were joined by their families. Doug Ellis bought all the wives a pendant and a bottle of champagne. 'It was a lovely evening,' Ray Graydon recalled, 'and I remember, right at the end of it, walking in the cul-de-sac outside the Savoy with my family and my father turned to me. "Well," he said, "that was a bloody great day." I was amazed. I said, "Dad, I've never heard you swear before," and he said, "Son, if you are ever lucky enough to have a son and he goes on to play for a big club in a Wembley final and scores the winning goal in front of 100,000, then I think you'll swear."'

For some the day had been anything but perfect. Leighton Phillips, cup-tied after an appearance for Cardiff against Bristol City earlier in the competition, hated missing out. 'The knowledge that I wouldn't be playing in the final really got to me,' the Welsh international admitted. 'I felt more sick then than when we actually went to Wembley.' Phillips, along with fellow absentees Sammy Morgan and John Gidman, all travelled, Saunders making them feel part of the squad. But while Morgan found solace in having played there for Northern Ireland, for Gidman, after battling back from his eye injury, being left out of the line-up was, he said, 'the last straw'. Nine days after the final, Gidman demanded a move. His manager turned it down straightaway. As deep as Gidman's disappointment was, his Villa story still had a long way to run.

Not so for two others. Selecting his starting 11 had posed little difficulty for Saunders; the one place really up for grabs was on the bench. Jimmy Brown, another member of the FA Youth Cup-winning side, believed the spot was his when, the day before travelling down to London, Saunders told the Scot to have a haircut. When he did so, to Saunders' eyes it wasn't 'short enough' and Alun Evans got the nod as number 12.

Brown had reached his limit. Still bitter at Saunders omitting him, the midfielder didn't join in with the team celebrations, taking it upon himself to have a party of his own, ordering two crates of champagne and charging it to the club; an act that didn't go unnoticed by Saunders.

Long-term injury victim Pat McMahon, a starter in 1971, was another who wanted little to do with the day's events; he spent the match in a bar near Wembley Stadium before returning shortly before the final whistle. The Villa futures of both Brown and McMahon were effectively over.

What once had looked like being a fairytale story, in Brown's case, was to end very unhappily. Making his debut in a 2-1 midweek defeat at Bolton's Burnden Park on 17 September 1969, aged 15 years and 349 days, the Musselburgh-born Scot became the youngest-ever player to take part in a league game for Villa. Just over a year later, Brown signed professional forms. Then, when Vic Crowe made the 19-year-old captain of the side in the 1972/73 season, Brown earned a second entry in the record books as Villa's youngest-ever skipper.

But a career that had promised sunshine had largely remained in the shade. The blame for the downturn, Brown believed, lay firmly at the feet of Crowe and Saunders. Brown's early introduction into the first team had, he reckoned, burdened the player with both too much expectation and, subsequently, too much experience at too young an age. Exposure to coaches had eliminated much of the ad hoc instincts he'd once possessed. Aged just 21, Brown already felt burnt out.

Kept out of the picture by Saunders, Brown resented the fact that not only was he missing the chance to stake a claim for a regular start but also any opportunity to put himself in the shop window. A mooted transfer to Manchester United, which didn't materialise when Tommy Docherty – the man who'd signed Brown from Midlothian Boys – failed to follow up his initial interest, only added to Brown's disenchantment. Watching from the sidelines, Brown grew ever more resentful, not only towards Saunders but to his team-mates, too. Such was Brown's disillusion, the Scot later admitted that he sat watching the cup success wishing that 'Norwich would stuff them' in the hope that he might feature again in Saunders' plans. He didn't. Saunders saw no place for him. Brown played his last game for Villa in the Cardiff loss and, in October 1975, was sold to Preston North End.

For the Aston Villa fans, 1 March 1975 marked the day when the relationship with their manager moved from a tentative romance to a full-blown love affair. A chorus of 'We want Saunders!' had risen up from the terraces at the end of the 90 minutes. 'Winning at Wembley,' Saunders later emphasised, 'is out of this world,' but winning, full stop, was the best habit to get into. It gave footballers a taste of what the game was essentially all about. 'If a team isn't winning,' Saunders said, 'then they don't know what they're playing for.'

On the day, the manner of victory wasn't really relevant. What was important was that Villa had claimed the silverware and, in doing so, 'There was,' the *Birmingham Mail* reported, 'a sense of something on the move. The rebirth of one of football's most historic clubs.' Rabbit's paw or not, Saunders had had every faith they'd lift the trophy. He'd even predicted it before the season started. But there was belief that it was just a prelude to much grander music. 'This will give us the impetus for our promotion push,' Saunders told the *Daily Mirror*'s Dave Horridge, 'and I'm confident we'll succeed.' Surrounded by Villa fans at the end of the final Saunders had pledged, 'I'll take the Villa into Europe next season as a First Division club.' He wasn't a man given to making idle boasts.

Like Winning the Pools!

THE following Wednesday, a crowd of nearly 40,000 crammed into Villa Park to welcome their homecoming heroes and then watch them fight out a goalless draw with Bolton Wanderers. The flat beer served up after the champagne was perhaps inevitable but the point was still sufficient to lift Villa into third and an all-important promotion berth. That they failed to register on the scoresheet for the first time since the New Year was the real surprise. It had taken some months but, up front, Saunders had finally found the solution he'd been seeking: Keith Leonard and Brian Little.

First paired together at Cardiff, the duo hadn't worked that afternoon. But Saunders persevered. Leonard, a team-mate of Bob Latchford in the South Birmingham schools' side, possessed no great pace. Though 6ft 1in and a natural danger man in the air, he lacked Morgan's brute aggression. Yet Leonard's sure, sharp touch made him ideal for the Villa manager's needs. Ron Greenwood – someone who believed that the game was spoilt by coaches complicating it to make themselves appear clever – stated that football was essentially about the space between two players. Saunders liked his sides to bridge that space as swiftly as possible.

Physically strong, fending off defenders and shielding the ball, Leonard created time for both his fellow forwards and supporting midfielders to bolster the attack. He was no mean finisher in front of goal, too. For Little, he proved the perfect partner. Able to feed off the bigger man, the elusive Little picked his way through defences almost at will.

From January onwards, Villa were easily the most successful club in the country, embarking on a run that saw them lose only one and win 15 of their remaining 18 league games, eight of them away from home. After the Cardiff setback, Doug Ellis told reporters that he had 'for the first time in my chairmanship' gone into the Villa dressing room and 'said things to the players which I never believed I would say'. It's doubtful his intervention came at Saunders' request. 'I was bitterly disappointed and told them so in no uncertain fashion,' Ellis said. 'But I hope all that can be forgotten now, particularly after the way they won today.' The way they won today was a convincing 3-0 win at Oldham's Boundary Park in an FA Cup third-round tie on Saturday 4 January. It heralded a complete transformation.

Whether or not Ellis believed his two pennies' worth was the sprinkling of stardust that sparked it, several other factors undoubtedly helped. Leonard and Little's gelling was just one. The introduction of 19-year-old Scottish left-back Bobby McDonald, filling a vacancy on the left side of midfield (created when the versatile John Robson returned to a familiar full-back role in Gidman's absence), was another. McDonald, playing a significant defensive role, brought a youthful zeal to the team, his probing left-foot passes often finding the runs of Little, Graydon and Leonard to great effect. Phillips and Carrodus, too, became increasingly influential figures, 'dictating the pace of the game' in Saunders' opinion, and 'combining high work-rate with a ration of skilful play'.

Throughout the side, the performance levels lifted several notches. Jimmy Cumbes pulled off vital penalty saves in away wins at Oxford United and Notts County. One of a number of footballers employing their cricketing skills during the summer months, the keeper had taken 18 wickets in six appearances as a fast-medium bowler at Worcestershire before joining up for pre-season training at Villa. On the last day of August, as Villa were going down to a single-goal defeat at Bolton Wanderers – a game Cumbes had to sit out through injury – the Lancashire-born number one learned that he was now the owner of a cricket County Championship winners' medal. All that summer's catching practice was now coming in very handy on the football pitch.

Robson and Aitken were reliable in the full-back berths. In central defence, Ross and Nicholl were a sturdy pairing. The side as a whole clicked into gear and a momentum just grew and grew, propelling Villa upwards.

Their FA Cup progress gained impetus, too. In the fourth round, just three days after booking their trip to the Twin Towers, 35,881 at Villa Park saw them emphatically dispatch First Division Sheffield United 4-1, including three second-half goals and a double-strike from Leonard. A faultless man-marking job by McDonald had nullified the influence of England international Tony Currie, though later the young Scot earned a stinging rebuke from Saunders after McDonald told reporters post-match that Currie 'hadn't impressed me much'. Saunders deemed it a lack of respect and let McDonald know it.

When Villa travelled to Portman Road for their fifth-round tie, they were the only club in the country still involved in all three domestic competitions, albeit 300/1 long shots to complete an unlikely 'treble'. 'It is inevitable that people will talk of the problems of trying to win all three,' Saunders observed, 'but I bet most clubs would swap places with us.' Ipswich, 1-0 conquerors of holders Liverpool in the previous round, were firm favourites. But when goals from, first, Alun Evans (handed a rare start with Little injured) and then McDonald – his first for the club – had the visitors 2-0 up at half-time, another Wembley visit seemed very much on the cards.

Villa, however, managed to grab defeat from the jaws of victory. With the introduction of Bryan Hamilton, the game turned on its head. Ipswich's Northern Ireland international midfielder came off the bench to spark a three-goal salvo in 22 minutes – Johnson scoring one, Hamilton the other two – and Villa's 'treble' dream was shot down. 'I think some of the players thought the game was won at 2-0,' Saunders ventured. They'd 'stopped playing' and paid the price.

Back in the league, the team made quick amends; a 3-2 victory at Portsmouth was followed by the win over Manchester United, Graydon and Aitken getting the goals for a dominant Villa as Docherty returned to Villa Park for the first time since his sacking. The stalemate with Bolton was just another temporary blip.

After Little's goal proved decisive in a 3-2 win at the City Ground, a 3-0 home defeat of Southampton – all three goals arriving in the final 21 minutes – saw them climb into second. As Villa were beating the Saints (the game going ahead thanks to a helicopter used to dry the rain-sodden pitch), Norwich gained a crucial point in a 1-1 draw at Old Trafford, while Sunderland slipped up, held at home by Forest. Villa, Norwich and Sunderland were still tightly bunched but, when an unexpected 1-0 reversal at Orient suggested a nerve-racking run-in, Villa simply sprinted away.

Starting with a 3-1 home win against West Brom, they won all eight remaining games, scoring 26 goals and conceding only three in the process. A crowd of 47,754 watched the Easter Saturday clash with the Albion. Don Howe's Baggies, themselves with a foot still propping open the promotion door, took the lead and might well have been 2-0 up but for an Ian Ross challenge to halt Tony Brown that one fan later described as 'the finest tackle ever seen at Villa Park' and which elicited a deafening roar from the Holte End that almost seemed to spur the home side to a rousing comeback.

An eight-minute three-goal blitzkrieg – Leonard netting another brace – earned Villa a 3-1 win, a bizarre second-half blizzard only adding to the home supporters' sense of wonder. Later that evening, a problem with their cameras meant the *Match of the Day* coverage of the clash started in colour and finished in black and white. Villa's season was enjoying the opposite journey. Three days later, away at Millwall, Villa repeated the scoreline. With a 2-0 success at home to Cardiff the following Wednesday, the side that began so uncertainly was now fully in its stride.

Against the Welsh club, Brian Little's spectacular diving header from a Hamilton cross capped another dynamic display. The 5ft 9in forward wasn't in Saunders' good books during the next home game, however. Already two goals up against Oldham, with Little scoring both, Villa were awarded a 36th-minute penalty. With Graydon absent, 'Chico' Hamilton should have been its taker but Little, despite warnings from his team-mates not to do so, placed the ball on the spot, keen to bag his hat-trick. When his tame kick was hit straight at Chris Ogden, there was only one outcome: at the break Little was 'absolutely slaughtered', Saunders telling the young forward it was the very reason he didn't want Little taking penalties; he *knew* he'd try something audacious. It mattered little. Later in the game, the striker claimed his third and, despite the private rollicking, to the press afterwards Saunders was quick to praise Little for his 'exceptional contribution'.

Villa were almost there. 'Barring the most horrific anti-climax imaginable,' wrote Ray Matts in the following Monday's *Evening Mail*, the club would be back among the elite. Five days later, they went to Blackpool and, with Little illuminating once again, won 3-0. A rumour of a Sunderland defeat spreading like wildfire around Bloomfield Road, meaning Villa were up, proved false though too late to halt either the conga-dancing Villa fans from their premature festivities or the swarms of supporters celebrating on the beach straight after the game.

But the party hats were out in force four days later and this time it was no false revelry. With around 15,000 supporters making the exodus from Birmingham to Hillsborough and the road from the Midlands clogged with claret and blue, it meant slow-moving traffic all the way to South Yorkshire. Once there, they witnessed a poor Sheffield Wednesday side, cast adrift after a sorry season and their passage to the Third Division for the first time in their history already confirmed, that was little more than lambs to Villa's slaughter. Goals from Leonard, and two by Little, one fired in from 25 yards out after he flicked the ball over a hapless defender's head, gave Villa an unassailable lead.

Bay City Rollers' 'Bye Bye Baby' now topped the UK music charts and Villa were bidding farewell to the Second Division. They could even afford to hand winger Steve Hunt his debut (as substitute for Hamilton) and penalty duties to Ian Ross. The skipper, the one outfield player yet to find the net during the season, put away the resulting kick and Villa made certain of their return to the big time. Little didn't risk Saunders' wrath on this occasion.

Saunders had hit the jackpot. He and his players 'needed a few months to get to know each other', he said, 'But throughout the season,' he added, 'they played with skill and immense character.' In his programme notes for Villa's final home game, against Sunderland, the 41-year-old couldn't disguise his joy. 'We're back,' he opened with, 'and it feels like winning the pools!' Whatever he'd achieved in his managerial career thus far, Saunders insisted it 'does not equal the thrill of taking Villa back to the First Division.' With the Wearsiders, in their last fixture, needing a win to hopefully secure the third promotion place, thousands of Rokerites journeyed down, swelling the Villa Park crowd to a season high of 57,266. A packed Holte End was closed about an hour before kick-off, with an estimated 15–20,000 locked outside the ground.

In the scorching April sunshine, the heat and perhaps the occasion was too much for some; various fans fainted and had to be carried down the Holte above the heads of others. On an afternoon of rejoicing, the match seemed almost secondary to the home support. With 11 minutes to go, the game still scoreless, Villa were awarded a penalty which, with Graydon and Hamilton both absent, Ian Ross – 'seemingly phlegmatic as usual' in Saunders' description – duly converted, Sunderland's FA Cup Final hero Jim Montgomery powerless to stop the Villa skipper dispatching it high into the roof of the net.

A story later had it that Jimmy Cumbes was due to take any spot-kick should Villa be awarded one and had practised the day before, hitting 19 out of 20. But on the day, thinking Norwich City would complain if Cumbes squandered the chance, Saunders got cold feet and ordered his keeper back to the other end of the field. Five minutes later, a typically delightful finish from Little, starring once again before the watching England boss Don Revie, wrapped up the match.

The night before, Little later revealed, the forward had actually given two Sunderland fans a lift. 'They were hiking on the A38. I just managed to stop,' he said. 'They were looking at me in the car and saying: "We know you, don't we?" Obviously I dropped them off in Birmingham and they half-wished me good luck.'

To cap the afternoon, John Gidman enjoyed an emotional return to first team action. Made substitute by Saunders, Gidman came on for Steve Hunt to thunderous applause. 'I got the best reception I've ever had,' he recalled. 'It was very emotional. I realised that people cared. I played up front with the instruction to enjoy myself as we'd won promotion. I was like Billy Liddell on the wing.' After months of convalescing, teaching himself to judge the speed of the ball again, with his left eye over-compensating, and even learning to walk once more, the Liverpudlian completed his incredible comeback.

For Sunderland, though, there was no second chance. Norwich had beaten Portsmouth 3-0 at Fratton Park to finish third on 53 points, and the huge contingent from the north-east, cheering all afternoon, were left silently resigned to at least another season in the second tier.

At the final whistle, ignoring the PA announcer's pleas, thousands spilled on to the playing surface. Chants echoed around the ground, 'We're going up' and 'AVFC, Aston Villa are magic' among a repertoire of songs as the on-pitch party which had threatened all afternoon began in earnest. After a long wait, Saunders and his players appeared in the upper part of the Trinity Road stand to receive the fans' acclaim. The Promised Land had been reached and Saunders was the Joshua who'd guided Villa there. 'I have the greatest supporters,' he declared, 'and the greatest bunch of lads in the world.' The promotion, Saunders told the crowd, is 'the greatest moment of my footballing life'.

The following Wednesday night, Villa gave their season's picture one last colourful touch. Missing Little and Graydon, an under-strength side went to Carrow Road but, 'like men addressing their signatures to a masterpiece of craftsmanship' in the *Birmingham Mail*'s description, caned the Canaries 4-1.

John Gidman, latching on to a punt upfield by Jimmy Cumbes, marked his first full appearance since his accident with one of the goals. When, four minutes from time, the game's outstanding player Frank Carrodus headed in to complete the scoring, as one journalist put it, 'Saunders could not have wished for a more satisfying finale.' Even a post-match invitation from Sir Arthur South to share a congratulatory glass of champagne in the Norwich boardroom couldn't sour Saunders' mood. He declined it. 'I was down in the kitchen having a drink with the workers,' Saunders told a *Mail* reporter.

Runners-up, three points behind Manchester United, Villa might well have won the title had the season gone on for a couple more games. 'We were unstoppable towards the end,' said Frank Carrodus. Docherty's side, showing the form of champions, had clinched the title with an emphatic 4-0 home win over Blackpool, meaning both they and Norwich, two of the previous year's relegated sides, were back in the First Division at the first attempt.

In his book, *Manchester United Champions*, Docherty wrote that United's descent into the second tier had 'a cauterising effect'. During their relegation season, in the Scot's view, they'd paid the price for playing negative, defensive football. 'From that point on,' Docherty wrote, 'I decided to manage a United team that attacked.'

Yet it was Villa that outscored every side in both the top two divisions. In all competitions, they netted a phenomenal 110 times. Twenty goals, just one less than Newcastle United's Malcolm Macdonald, saw Brian Little top the Second Division scoring charts along with Southampton's England striker Mick Channon. Hamilton and Leonard were also in double figures. Ray Graydon with 27 to his name, including 19 in the Second Division, finished as the club's top scorer. The blond-haired Graydon who, at Bristol Rovers, had even considered quitting the game for good as 'I didn't seem to be getting anywhere' could also lay claim to have scored the most important goal of all – the winner at Wembley.

Villa's defensive record also demanded huge respect. Only Cardiff and Fulham had put three goals past them in any league match, and just Manchester United let in fewer goals. At Villa Park alone, they conceded a meagre half-dozen times. 'From the turn of the year onwards our all-round form was so good we didn't need a goalkeeper!' said Jimmy Cumbes. The professionalism that underpinned their march was such that giving away any goal made them angry.

Chris Nicholl, told as a youngster by Burnley that he wouldn't make the grade, had proven them wrong in the most resounding manner, deservedly winning the Terrace Trophy as the supporters' club Player of the Year. The long-serving Charlie Aitken was fittingly voted Midlands Footballer of the Year.

Ian Ross, an ever-present along with Aitken, never had any doubts success would follow Saunders' appointment. 'Even before Ron Saunders arrived I felt we might get promoted,' the Scot said. 'What we needed was good leadership and he provided it.' He 'goes quietly about his job but, nevertheless, produces remarkable results', said Jimmy Cumbes at the season's end. 'He trains us hard, keeps us toughened up.' Saunders, the goalkeeper believed, had made them all 'as sharp as tacks'.

At Bodymoor Heath, Saunders paid painstaking attention to how the side was set up. Training drills were repeated ad nauseam until patterns were imprinted upon the players' psyches. Full-scale practice matches took place against the reserves with no forwards involved so that the sole focus was on defending. At other times, players would move upfield without any opposition to familiarise themselves with moving as a coherent unit. Saunders' organisational skills were 'brilliant', according to Charlie Aitken. 'He was the best I had ever known for working the different areas of the team.'

Hours and hours were devoted to these procedures, as Saunders made his players acutely aware of the necessity of working for the collective good. The abiding principle was: good teams make good players, not the other way around. Sir Alf Ramsey's priority, writes World Cup-winning full-back George Cohen in his eponymously titled autobiography, 'was always the assembling of a team of perfectly complementary parts'. Much like the former England boss, Saunders didn't necessarily select the most talented individuals but the footballers best suited to the pattern he wanted to play. A new broom sweeps clean but, instead, Saunders had patiently gauged the strengths of the players he'd inherited. After half a season he found just the ones he wanted.

The long hours pre-season slogging up and down sand-covered hillsides had left the players in peak condition. When the side was struggling or needed that extra thrust in their promotion push, Saunders' remedy was to hammer the players with even more stamina-building sessions. 'After getting to Wembley I stepped up training and became more critical, both with individuals and the team,' Saunders said. His players had 'responded marvellously'. As demanding as it was, the players were quick to note its efficacy. It fostered a sense of invincibility throughout the team. 'We could wear teams down,' said Keith Leonard, 'and no matter how long it took, we simply knew we were going to score.'

Psychologically, too, Villa endured when others wilted. 'Most games are decided in the last 20 minutes,' says Chris Nicholl in Richard Whitehead's *Children of the Revolution*, 'and we had the belief to stick in there.' Convinced the team would win both promotion and a cup, Saunders fortified his squad with the same assurance. 'A manager's job is about motivation,' said Frank Carrodus, 'and he [Saunders] certainly motivated us during the second half of that first season. We knew what we had to do and because we were well-prepared, we hardly had to think about it and simply went out there and won.'

Not all of Saunders' motivational techniques were greeted with enthusiasm, though. Bill Shankly – a staunch believer that players were only injured when they lost concentration – liked to remind any whom he considered were malingering, 'That's not your leg. It belongs to Liverpool

FC.' Visitors to the Anfield treatment room were usually given the cold shoulder, Shankly's thing about injured players almost bordering on a phobia; as if the weak might cast a curse on the healthy.

Saunders was similarly unsympathetic. 'If you take five or six injured players away with you on a coach, they don't want to have what the other players are having, do what the other players are doing,' he told Richard Whitehead. 'They bring in negative things.' Saunders' sole priority, as he saw it, was achieving the best results for Aston Villa with the players he deemed most capable of doing so. 'The only thing that matters is the results of the first team,' Saunders said. 'The youth team, reserves, scouting system and other things are all necessary, but the bottom line is what the first team does.'

Yet some players didn't necessarily have to be injured to get the silent treatment from the Villa boss. Those who weren't into the first team frame were often shunned or, worse, suffered the indignity of having to train with the reserves without proper training tops or balls. The premise was that anyone left out of the inner circle would work all the harder to get back in. The manner of their exclusion was sometimes exceptionally harsh, the training ground a centre of humiliation.

'If you were not in that select first team party you were very much out of the picture,' said Brian Little. 'You even wore a different coloured jersey for training. I remember vividly how sometimes a player would walk out with a blue first team training top on and the kit man would be sent out to take it off him, in front of all his team-mates, because he was not involved in the senior squad that particular day. I know that used to destroy quite a few of the established first team players at the time.'

On one such occasion, as teams were split up, Sammy Morgan was made to stand with the reserves, Saunders telling him, 'You're over there with the shit.' It was a demeaning experience for the forward.

Jock Stein believed that a manager should never be friends with his players. Saunders at times seemed to deliberately set out to make enemies of many. Willie Donachie, then a young full-back with Manchester City, said that what the senior pros at Maine Road particularly objected to from Saunders was being talked down to. Likewise at Villa, Saunders' idea of creating a team effort by habitually making cracks about specific individuals – a tactic Neil Rioch claimed 'he seemed to get a kick from' – jarred with some of the bigger personalities.

Morgan, Pat McMahon and Jimmy Cumbes were common targets. Cumbes came under particular scrutiny in training, Saunders often firing close-range volleys at the goalkeeper – 'it was almost a deliberate session to establish who was the dominating factor' according to Chris Nicholl – though Cumbes never complained, accepting it as par for the course of life under Saunders. 'At the end of it he'd always say, "Well done,"' Cumbes said.

There were, to certain minds, other purposefully provocative acts on the manager's part. One of Don Revie's favourite sayings was, 'Football isn't water – you can't just switch it on and off.' At Leeds, they engaged in full-blooded five-a-sides, replicating the competitiveness of a matchday. Saunders employed a comparable tactic. First team players would take on reserves and both sides were positively commanded by Saunders to be totally committed – or else!

As someone who'd always enjoyed the physical nature of football as a player, Saunders gladly took part in these bruising training encounters, putting himself about and not sparing anyone from a kick or two into the bargain. Yet, while Revie cultivated a club spirit, Saunders' focus was solely on a team mentality. Designed to encourage those out of favour to fight their way back in, according to Jimmy Brown it only 'created this aggressive atmosphere where they would be kicking lumps out of each other'.

As competitive as Saunders wanted them to be, there was still room for individuals to shine. No one was more incandescent than Brian Little. The long-haired youngster, shirt outside his shorts, socks around his ankles, radiated natural talent. 'Don't let them coach this kid,' one-time Villa coach Peter Doherty had instructed director Harry Katz. Finding the net ten times in six successive games in the season's run-in, Little had produced an astounding burst of form.

His goalscoring virtuosity was noted by Don Revie. When England's Home Internationals squad was announced, Little earned a call-up. More surprising was Revie's inclusion of John Gidman. During his recovery, Gidman had drawn strength from the realisation that he had been in hospital at the same time as some of the victims of the Birmingham pub bombings. 'When I realised what had happened to them,' he said, 'I began to think I had nothing to worry about.' Now, his long road back to fitness was rewarded in the best possible fashion.

Close friends whose careers had almost run parallel, Little and Gidman had already represented their country at the 1972 UEFA European under-18 championship, dubbed the Mini World Cup, held in Spain. In a side that also included the likes of Trevor Francis and Kevin Beattie, the pair helped England secure victory in the final against West Germany at the Nou Camp.

It was Little, however, who broke through first on to the full international scene. Coming on for Mick Channon 20 minutes from time in the midweek Wembley clash with Wales, Little became the first Villa player to win a full England cap since Gerry Hitchens turned out against Austria in 1961. With England 2-1 down and in very real danger of defeat for the first time under Revie, a typically jinking run by the forward ended with an early cross from the byline high into the Welsh area and fellow debutant David Johnson rising to head an 84th-minute leveller.

Little's role in rescuing the point earned rave reviews. Revie, too, extolled the Villa player's 'quite magnificent' cameo. With important European Championship qualifiers ahead in 1975/76, it was surely not a matter of if but when further opportunities would come Little's way.

Two days after his forward's dazzling turn, as reward for masterminding Villa's most successful season in over 30 years, Ron Saunders was named Bell's Scotch Whisky Manager of the Year. While there were several strong contenders – Dave Mackay, who'd guided Derby to their second title in four seasons, Jimmy Armfield, called upon to calm the waters at Leeds after the storm caused by Clough and who had steered them to the European Cup Final, and John Lyall, boss at FA Cup-winning West Ham – it was Saunders who, in the voters' opinion, was most deserving. In a mere matter of months he had been elevated from an out-of-work manager to one who was now acknowledged as the best in the country. 'It is a sobering thought,' Saunders said, collecting the trophy, 'to think that the dividing line between success and failure is so thin.'

Tasked, in his own words, 'with the obvious objective of getting the club into the First Division at the earliest possible moment', Saunders had achieved that goal perhaps faster than even he had envisaged. 'We have done three years' work in 12 months,' he admitted. Much of his satisfaction was in knowing 'that the board have proved to others that you do not always have to take the advice of newspapers'.

The decision to employ Saunders, however reluctantly it was taken on Doug Ellis's part, had been more than vindicated. 'I felt right at home from the day of my appointment,' Saunders declared. 'I felt it was right for me – and I felt I was right for the job ahead.' It had been a swift ascent. Villa, Saunders stated in the programme for the Sunderland game, had 'climbed each mountain as it has appeared'.

Now the First Division beckoned and, Saunders had written, 'You can take it from me that never has a club been so eager to follow.' What lay ahead? 'More pressures, more sweat, more dedication as we try to consolidate our new situation.' Whatever peaks were waiting, it was never going to be an easy hike.

A Great New Dawning

WHILE Saunders himself made no such claim, it felt as though the famous Midlands club was now back in its rightful place. Early in August 1975, Kevin Connor's fantasy/adventure film *The Land that Time Forgot* was released in UK cinemas. For Aston Villa fans, that land was the terra firma of England's top flight. Eight years away had seemed an eternity. 'I've spoken to many people since we won promotion,' Jimmy Cumbes told *Shoot* magazine, 'and believe me they're regarding going up as a great new dawning.'

Villa were entering a division with no one team obvious favourites to take the title. The 1974/75 championship – with Liverpool, Ipswich, Everton, Stoke City, Sheffield United and Middlesbrough all having a tilt at the top – had been perhaps the most open yet in the league's long history. Ultimately it was Derby County, despite losing as many as ten games, who topped the pile. Liverpool, in their first season under Paisley, were second, while Ipswich Town, considered by many the division's finest side, eventually paid the price for fixture congestion and a too-thin squad, finishing third.

'We don't have to be afraid of any of them,' was Saunders' assessment. Villa's upward trajectory would continue, he said, 'so long as we show the application and character which played such a great part in our promotion.' While *The Guardian*'s David Lacey was cautiously optimistic, citing Villa as 'possibly the best placed of the promoted clubs', fellow *Guardian* scribe Cyril Chapman was far more positive. 'If Villa can keep out the old enemy, complacency,' he wrote, 'their future could be as bright as their supporters and the football world in general desire.'

Chapman's assertion that 'like a glider carried on thermal currents, a promoted club often spiral to the top' seemed a little over-hopeful, though.

On a sun-draped Saturday afternoon on 16 August, the first test of Villa's credentials was against Leeds United. Now under ex-Bolton boss Armfield, the West Yorkshire club's previous competitive match – a hugely controversial European Cup Final defeat to Bayern Munich – was viewed, to all intents and purposes, as the remaining chance for the side moulded by Don Revie to capture the biggest prize in club football and leave an indelible mark as one of the true greats of the game. Leeds, who despite a decade as one of the dominant forces had failed to claim the glut of trophies that their football perhaps deserved, had fallen short once more. What they needed, though, Armfield decided, was only an oil change, not a total overhaul. Saunders, too, placed faith in what he already had. Having earned the club success, the key now was to maintain it. Inexperienced at the highest level as most of his players were, Saunders felt they deserved the right to prove themselves.

Within eight minutes of the opening game, 46,026 – the country's largest crowd of the day – saw them go a goal ahead. When Graydon's cross was only half-saved by David Harvey, Leighton Phillips, lashing a shot from the edge of the box, sent the ball into the Leeds net and the home support delirious. In dreamland early on, by the end of the 90 minutes they'd had a loud wake-up call. Leeds, with two Peter Lorimer strikes – the first from the penalty spot when John Gidman was harshly judged to have handled; a second when the Scottish international pounced after Cumbes let a soft Aitken back-pass slip from his grasp – ran out 2-1 winners.

After Cumbes' clanger, described by ITV commentator Brian Moore as 'sure to be the goalkeeping mistake of the season', the visitors simply closed ranks and never let Villa back into their own party, wily campaigner Paul Madeley keeping Brian Little under lock and key for almost the whole match.

'I don't think I got a kick,' said Little.

Saunders still took heart from the performance. 'We learned a lot today,' he said afterwards. 'I know we will be all right in the First Division.' Further encouragement came four days later when a Keith Leonard strike earned a 1-1 draw at Loftus Road. But a 5-3 drubbing at Norwich – Ted MacDougall becoming the first player to net a hat-trick against a Saunders Villa team – was another eye-opener. 'Football was the winner,' John Bond chirped. It's doubtful Saunders shared the sentiment. A 1-0 win over Manchester City at Villa Park – the club's first top-flight victory since March 1967 – followed on the Saturday by another single-goal home success against Coventry City (Keith Leonard the match-winner on both occasions) soon had the smile back on Saunders' face but, with the season still in its infancy, events off the pitch now began generating far more headlines.

On 1 September, prior to the club's AGM, Doug Ellis stepped down from his role as chairman, to be replaced by Sir William Dugdale. In vacating the chair he'd occupied since the dark days of 1968, Ellis stated, 'When I took over seven years ago I set myself three goals for Villa.' Those goals – 'to get back in the First Division, then gain entry into Europe and to see the club in a strong financial position' – had, in Ellis's assertion, all been achieved. There was no doubt that Villa, perilously perched upon the edge of extinction just a few years before, was, once again, a thriving, stable club. Yet if Ellis gave the impression he was willingly abdicating his throne, job done, the truth was very different. In *From One Season to the Next* Dave Woodhall writes that Ellis was the victim of 'a palace revolution'.

The revolution was orchestrated by his fellow board members. A diversely talented group, Dugdale, American businessman Harry Cressman, ex-England cricketer Alan Smith, Eric Houghton, Harry Kartz and millionaire accountant Ron Bendall felt that, as they operated as a team, they should be recognised as such. Ellis, who, according to Woodhall, regarded Aston Villa as his 'personal fiefdom', had tended to hoard the glory for all the club's recent achievements. Journalist Ian Johnson was told that Ellis 'was asked at least ten times to stop taking all the credit and styling himself "Mr Aston Villa"'. He didn't desist. Irked by his persistent self-proclamations, the directors acted. One Sunday morning, scarcely six months after his own elevation to the Villa board, Ron Bendall played host at his house to a meeting, convened to put forward a motion to remove Ellis from the Villa chair and install Dugdale in his place.

A lifelong Villa fan, Sir William, or Bill as he was commonly known, had joined the board in 1973. A direct descendant of William the Conqueror, he was the born nobility to Ellis's self-made man. Whereas Ellis dubiously claimed to have been everything from the inventor of the bicycle-kick to the man who popularised package holidays, Dugdale's far more fantastical achievements were based in reality: he had, among his lifetime's achievements, served as a captain during World War Two, winning the Military Cross, taken part in a round-the-world air race, as well as ridden in the Grand National.

While Ellis would blatantly display the trappings of his wealth (recalling his first-ever day at Villa Park, Brian Little remembered how

Ellis showed him – as he did with all the young apprentices – his Rolls-Royce, with the words, 'This is my Rolls-Royce, and I am the chairman of this football club'), Dugdale was more than content to journey about in a far-less-ostentatious Morris Traveller. Despite boasting an impressive CV that also included businessman, politician, colliery owner and High Sheriff of Warwickshire, Dugdale was a modest, very affable man. By further contrast with Ellis, he was a fan of Ron Saunders.

At the get-together, Harry Kartz presented the one dissenting voice, feeling that – as well as being friendly with Ellis – he, as vice-chairman, should be next in line to take over if Ellis was gotten rid of. But Kartz's objections were overlooked. On learning of the plot, Ellis's instinct was to fight back. He thought better of it, deciding, so he said, 'The club is always bigger than the individual.'

Years later, Ellis suggested that he'd actually jumped rather than been pushed. 'I asked Sir William Dugdale if he would take Villa on for a year,' he told the *Birmingham Mail*, 'so I could go back to the office and put things right [with his ailing travel business].' Whatever the political shenanigans, Dugdale took up office and despite Ellis's official line that 'the time is right to let someone else take over at the helm', any real harmony behind the scenes was just a pipedream.

On the field, Saunders had more pressing concerns. After a 3-0 loss at Newcastle to a Tommy Craig goal and two from Macdonald, he was dealt an even bigger blow. Keith Leonard, who'd already proved himself more than capable against many of the country's top defenders, notched another goal as Villa beat Arsenal 2-0 at Villa Park. Leonard's late header – Arsenal getting caught out by a quick throw-in, Graydon whipping in a cross and Leonard, with time and space, nodding it past Jimmy Rimmer – added to an earlier Leighton Phillips strike. In the first half, though, challenging for a high ball in the box with Arsenal defender Terry Mancini, Leonard landed awkwardly and, with the Gunners' keeper Rimmer falling on top of him, Leonard's right knee was badly damaged. By half-time it had started to swell. Although he played the remainder of the match, the day after the knee ballooned. The stiffness was considerable. Following consultation, Leonard was faced with needing a cartilage operation and a long spell on the sidelines, Saunders with a swift search for a replacement.

Amid their struggles, 17 September brought a distraction. A welcome one or not, it didn't last long. Guaranteed by their League Cup triumph automatic entry into the UEFA Cup, Villa made a first foray into European competition. Friendly games against Bayern Munich, Górnik of Poland

and Dutch side Feyenoord – largely the brainchild of Eric Woodward – had given the club a flavour but, now they were in it for real, they wanted to savour it to its fullest.

Arriving in Belgium to face Royal Antwerp, Villa's players and staff were immediately exposed to the psychological tricks employed by foreign clubs to gain advantage over their British counterparts. Just to reach the Bosuilstadion ground, they were forced to walk a quarter of a mile. There, they were greeted with a dressing room that had no heating and the players were left numb from the cold. 'I'd been better treated in juvenile football in Scotland,' Charlie Aitken, the party's most experienced member, told Graham McColl. The discomforts might even have had a casualty in Saunders. When the Villa boss went to light a gas geyser on the dressing room wall, it blew up, caused an explosion and, in Aitken's words, 'Ron nearly got blown away.'

Pre-match, Saunders emphasised the need to keep the tie alive. For 27 minutes they did so, an attacking Villa side, with only Sammy Morgan as a recognised central striker, more than holding their own and unfortunate not to score. But a Heykgen free kick, curled perfectly over the wall and past Cumbes, sparked an astonishing capitulation. In 14 fatal minutes, Antwerp, sitting top of the Belgian league after a blistering start to their own domestic campaign, hit Villa with four goals, including a hat-trick from Austrian forward Karl Kodat. In spite of a second-half strike by Ray Graydon – the winger's long, angled drive registering the club's first European goal – Villa's hopes of progress were effectively over and Saunders' post-match insistence that they could still turn it around sounded flimsy at best.

Two weeks later, in front of 31,513, when Kodat bagged his fourth of the tie, the remainder of the match became a formality. Further sorties on to foreign soils would have to wait. Competing in Europe is 'all about tactics', said Aitken, and 'like a chess game'. Antwerp were hardly grandmasters but nevertheless had completely outwitted a naïve Villa side both mentally and physically unaware of what had been required.

By the time the home leg was played, Saunders had made two highly significant changes to his starting line-up. While Villa Park, though not exactly a fortress, was proving to be a strength, away from home Villa's defences had been penetrated with relative ease. It triggered Saunders to take action. Identifying weak spots in his side's make-up, the manager looked immediately at the goalkeeper. Jimmy Cumbes, after his first-day fumble against Leeds, also bore much of the blame for the hefty defeat in Belgium. Although unlucky with one shot that took a deflection off a Villa defender, Cumbes had looked decidedly at fault for the other three Antwerp goals. 'Villa will do well in Division One,' Cumbes had stated pre-season, 'without setting it alight.' Their chances of turning up the flame, though, Saunders concluded, were being spoiled by costly goalkeeping errors. After five seasons as Villa's regular stopper, the 6ft 2in Cumbes found himself ditched from the side.

Pitched in in his place was 20-year-old Jake Findlay, a Scottish youth international and a member of the FA Youth Cup-winning side who'd long been groomed as Cumbes' replacement. His introduction had little effect. Despite a brave team performance, three goals in the last half-hour from John Toshack, Kevin Keegan and Jimmy Case saw Villa on the end of a 3-0 defeat at Anfield. Saunders told reporters he would have been happy for the game to have ended after 60 minutes. The retired Bill Shankly, being interviewed on *Match of the Day*, said that it did. As Findlay took up residence between the posts for Villa's next game, a 0-0 draw at Wolves, another keeper was watching from the Molineux stands, poised to join the ranks.

John Burridge, nicknamed 'Budgie', had been winning admirers for some time at Second Division side Blackpool. Signed from Workington just before the Seasiders' relegation to the second tier in 1970/71, Burridge was carrying on a tradition of top-class keepers – Tony Waiters, Gordon West, George Wood (the latter two who would go on to enjoy successful careers at Everton) – who'd blossomed at Bloomfield Road. In February, he'd caught the eye before the TV cameras, pulling off a vital penalty save in a game with Sunderland that Blackpool went on to win, Mickey Walsh's decider later voted as *Match of the Day*'s Goal of the Season.

Manchester United had made a £50,000 bid for his services. When Villa trumped it by another £50,000, Blackpool accepted, telling the keeper to travel to Birmingham straightaway. Despite the disappointment of missing out on his dream move to Old Trafford, when a three-year deal was put on the table, Burridge had little hesitation in accepting. Two days later, the 23-year-old was handed his debut. It couldn't have been a more intimidating situation.

A crowd of 53,782 jammed into Villa Park to witness the first Second City derby since 1969/70. In September 1968, in the first Birmingham derby to be televised by ATV, Villa suffered a humiliating 4-0 defeat at City's hands. Now the cameras were there to capture a famous win. Trailing 1-0 at the midway point, Villa turned the game around with Hamilton and Little scoring to earn the local bragging rights. Little's goal – capitalising on an error by Kenny Burns – was seen as justice done by the home supporters; Burns was lucky to be on the pitch after a crude studs-up challenge on John Robson earlier on. At the other end, making some vital, reflex stops, Burridge acquitted himself admirably.

Among the crowd that afternoon, watching in the Witton Lane stand, was a raw 19-year-old Scottish forward. His name: Andy Gray. With Leonard a likely long-term absentee, Saunders was seeking an alternative to lead the line. After working rigorously to regain fitness, Sammy Morgan was under the impression he was the most obvious choice. The man who led him to believe that, Morgan claimed, was the Villa manager. It proved not to be the case. After the home game with Antwerp, the popular Irish striker never donned an Aston Villa jersey again, moving for £10,000 to Brighton & Hove Albion in December, disgruntled he was never given the fighting chance he thought would be his.

Instead, the player Saunders had earmarked for the number nine shirt was Gray. Signed by Dundee United at the age of 17, the Drumchapel-born forward had already netted 46 times in only 62 league games. In only his second season, he'd finished as Scotland's top marksman. Word about the youngster's goalscoring prowess was soon circulating. Liverpool and Everton sent scouts to cast an eye over him. Newcastle, Leeds, and Spurs were, at various times, all rumoured to have the blond-haired striker on their respective radars.

There was speculation that one of the two Glasgow giants – Celtic and Rangers – might make an approach. Only Second Division Nottingham Forest submitted a firm offer, however; a bid of £75,000 rejected by the Tayside club, with manager Jim McLean holding out for a far more substantial sum. Without the Scottish club knowing, Gray had been made a very attractive offer by West German club Schalke 04 but, after some deliberation, he decided that, with a wife and young daughter, moving to the continent was impractical.

Still, despite a recent falling-out with the notoriously short-tempered McLean, Gray wasn't pushing for or expecting a transfer. So when McLean informed Gray the day before a fixture with Celtic that United had accepted a bid from Aston Villa, it was no little shock. McLean, with talk in the air of changes in the law, was worried that Gray might walk away for nothing when his contract ran out at the end of the season. He'd decided to cash in. Though the *Scottish Daily Mail*'s Glenn Gibbons would call it 'like a duellist selling his sword', for United it was economically unavoidable.

However, any deal would only go through if Gray travelled south of the border and put pen to paper that very night. Given McLean's trusted opinion that 'Villa would be a good move', the young Scot duly took the plane from Glasgow to Birmingham, where Saunders and Villa's chief scout Neville Briggs greeted him at Elmdon Airport. It was Briggs whose reports back to Saunders had persuaded the manager to pursue the striker. With Manchester United supposedly readying a bid, Saunders had acted with due haste.

Later that evening the formalities were concluded. Yet, as Sir William Dugdale would recount in *Settling the Bill*, while negotiating Gray's wage demands, the Villa chairman was left baffled when Gray repeatedly went to the window and made tic-tac signals with his fingers to his agent standing below. 'The next time Andy got up,' Dugdale recalled, 'I went to the other window and leant out, which brought the signalling to an end. We reached agreement soon after.'

Gray became a Villa player for a club record £110,000 and was delighted at the move. 'Ron Saunders made up my mind for me,' he told *Shoot* magazine. 'Any doubts I may have had were quickly dispelled as he convinced me Villa were a club going places.' In stark contrast to Gray's joy was the wrath of the local press. Less than 24 hours before the deal was sealed – the fee, a 'gross outlay' in journalist Reg Drury's view – Saunders had flatly denied a transfer was imminent, very likely wary that any leak might alert other prospective buyers to Gray's availability. Saunders, Gray felt, shared an 'honesty' similar to McLean. The local press, as well as Sammy Morgan, begged to differ.

In Scotland, the Tannadice terraces had rung to the sound of 'Who's the boy with golden hair?' Although Gray's debut – Villa drawing 0-0 with Middlesbrough on a bumpy Ayresome Park pitch – was instantly forgettable, the Aston Villa supporters were soon to find out. After a headed consolation goal as Villa relinquished their grip on their League Cup trophy, losing 2-1 at home to Manchester United, three days later, on his home league debut, Gray scored again, nodding home a Graydon cross to give Villa a 52nd-minute lead against Spurs.

Even though the visitors, down to ten men after Terry Naylor's dismissal, equalised late on through a John Pratt header, Gray's performance lit up the scrappy affair. The Villa Park crowds rejoiced in his relentless hunger and commitment. For all Gray's rough edges, it was obvious the club had discovered a gem.

Saunders' hopes of a dynamic front pairing, though, were quickly quashed. While Gray was arriving in the First Division theatre, Brian Little was exiting stage left. As Gary Jones' brace (including a penalty) condemned Villa to a 2-1 defeat at Goodison Park, Little suffered a cartilage injury that would keep the striker out until the following spring. Already seeking to bring a fresh dimension to Villa's attack, Saunders would now have to look even harder.

Another player for whom he saw no future was Alun Evans. Evans might have joined Villa straight from school, having impressed during a trial in 1964, but decided to sign for Wolves instead. But, as on Merseyside following his move from Molineux, the forward for whom great things had been expected at Villa Park had been a disappointment. The League Cup winners' medal (as a non-playing substitute) was as good as it got. After just 17 goals in 71 games, on 14 December Evans was allowed to leave, making the short trip across the West Midlands to join Walsall for £30,000.

One player Saunders surprisingly did want was Rodney Marsh. Following a fall-out with Tony Book – the pair had what Marsh later described as a 'face to face, very physical' ruck – the forward had been transfer-listed by City, accused of 'not giving 100 per cent to the club'. Marsh, who in March 1963, at the age of 18, had scored the winning goal for Fulham on his senior debut against Aston Villa, was a performer whose love of the outrageous meant he wouldn't, in journalist Derek Potter's opinion, 'be happy until he's headed a goal from the penalty spot'. Nonetheless, Saunders was keen on a reunion. Marsh wasn't. When a £50,000 offer was tabled, it was rejected, the player reportedly opting instead to join Belgian club RSC Anderlecht in a £75,000 deal. 'Everything has a habit of turning out for the best in this game,' a philosophical Saunders said.

Ten days later, Home Farm complained that their star midfielder, 17-year-old Martin Murray, had been illegally approached by Villa. According to the Irish club, their English counterparts made waves that were contrary to regulations. Whatever waves they were, a move to the Midlands didn't happen. It was to Everton, linking up with fellow Irishman Billy Bingham, that Murray was lured.

As it was, Little's absence opened the door for 19-year-old local lad John Deehan. Deehan, Solihull-born and a boyhood Villa supporter, had almost joined Arsenal as an apprentice before, at his father's prompting, Villa stepped in and offered the youngster a trial. Deehan scored a first-half hat-trick, convincing Vic Crowe to sign the forward in August 1973. The following April, 'Dixie' as he was affectionately known, put pen to paper on professional forms. Deehan had trained with the Villa senior squad for a few days when Saunders asked, 'You're ready for first team football, aren't you?' It wasn't so much a question as a statement.

The Saturday after a 1-1 home draw with Burnley, Deehan was thrown into battle at Portman Road, making his First Division bow as Villa went down 3-0. Seven days later, his home debut was a completely different story. Heading in from a corner to help Villa to a 5-1 victory over Sheffield United, the youngster earned the adoration of the Holte End, of which he'd only so recently been part. It proved to be Villa's most comprehensive win of the campaign.

As autumn turned into winter, their league form ebbed and flowed. A 2-0 defeat at Old Trafford – with lively winger Gordon Hill making his United debut after moving from Millwall – preceded a 3-1 home win over Everton which, in turn, was followed by a 1-1 with Leicester City at Villa Park, Ray Graydon cancelling out a Frank Worthington strike. The Everton game again evidenced the goal-greedy Gray's insatiable appetite: in a two-goal salvo – both headers – the forward's first came only seconds after he'd returned to the field following lengthy treatment.

Deehan himself scored a brace as Villa beat Norwich 3-2 on a bone-hard Villa Park pitch in mid-December. In Gray and Deehan, Villa boasted the youngest front two in the division but, throughout the side, a lack of top-flight experience was telling. A week later, as Liverpool headed back to the table's top after beating QPR 2-0, Villa went down 1-0 at Leeds, Allan Clarke sniffing out his 100th goal for the Elland Road club. Saunders, knowing his novices needed reinforcing, decided to act again.

Two days before Christmas, Coventry City's stylish playmaker Dennis Mortimer was brought in. Mortimer, Liverpool-born, had been snatched by Coventry from under the noses of Merseyside's big two when he left school, making his Sky Blues debut (against Liverpool) aged only 18. Already capped seven times at England under-23 level and having played over 200 first team matches, Mortimer was unquestionably City's prized asset and one they ideally wanted to keep hold of. But with falling gates (their average home attendance less than half that of Villa's), the Highfield Road club were in desperate need of a cash injection; one Villa were more than willing to administer. Coventry, fearing a struggle for survival, had little choice but to sell, managing director Jimmy Hill stating, 'Our supporters might be disappointed, but this sale ensures Coventry's future for the next five years.'

Saunders met Mortimer at Stonebridge Island and, on the drive to Villa Park, outlined his plans to the player. Convinced that Villa were a club on the up and the move would 'further my ambition to play for England', Mortimer, despite admitting he didn't know any of the Villa players, agreed to the switch. On 23 December, in a festive publicity stunt, Mortimer, standing in a box bundled up in wrapping paper, was unveiled as 'Villa's Christmas present to the fans'. It was a gift that cost a hefty £175,000.

With football suffering the effects of the country-wide recession in the early 1970s, Villa cut their cloth accordingly. Their caution was now being rewarded. That season, only the November £300,000 transfer of Welsh international winger Leighton James, from Burnley to Derby County, exceeded Mortimer's figure. His fee, Mortimer later admitted, did weigh on the midfielder's mind for a while – he felt he had to justify such a sum – but Mortimer would soon show he had ample character to shoulder such a load.

After Villa secretary Steve Stride had driven to the Football League headquarters in Lytham St Anne's on Christmas Eve to get the forms signed in time for him to play, Mortimer's debut couldn't have gone better. On Boxing Day, before the day's biggest crowd – 51,250, with claret and blue balloons ascending from the Holte End into the darkening skies – Villa produced arguably a season's best performance, beating FA Cup holders West Ham 4-1. Two of their goals resulted from passes threaded through by the newest signing. Although, only four games into his Villa career, Mortimer would jar his knee in a reckless challenge by Malcolm Macdonald, suffering ligament damage and sitting out the next six weeks, his influence was evident from the start.

The victory over the Hammers was to be the season's zenith. The following day, with fans and their colourful balloons again out en masse, Saunders' side ventured to the Baseball Ground full of festive cheer, only for their away-day malaise to strike once again. Goals by Steve Powell and Charlie George (a penalty) gave the defending champions a 2-0 win. It was the first in a worrying sequence of 17 league games in which Villa won only once. Within a week of the New Year they were also relieved of any further FA Cup commitments.

On Saturday 3 January, leading 1-0 through Andy Gray at The Dell, Villa looked to be heading into the fourth-round hat when a late Hugh Fisher leveller denied them victory and sent the tie to a replay. Four days later, taken to extra time by Lawrie McMenemy's men, Villa succumbed 2-1 to Jim McCalliog's decisive double and were dumped out of the competition. When the Second Division Saints marched all the way to Wembley and one of the biggest-ever upsets in the cup's history against favourites Manchester United, the fact that they'd come within 30 seconds of exiting to Villa at the first hurdle was no doubt long forgotten.

Further talks were had with Rodney Marsh, still at Maine Road, but it went no further than that. Villa's league form brought little cheer, either. A 0-0 draw at Arsenal was followed by another stalemate, 1-1 at home to Newcastle United. On the last day of January, when second-half goals from John Hollins and Gerry Francis gave title-chasing QPR both points in a 2-0 win at Villa Park, it put the seal on a miserable month.

It also brought to an end the Aston Villa story of Charlie Aitken. For Aitken, survivor of no less than six different managers at the club, that was down to one man: Ron Saunders. Aitken told Richard Whitehead, 'I knew I was finished when Saunders called me in on 19 December 1975 and said to me, "Charlie, I have decided that you can stay here for as long as you want." I thought then that I would be out of the team inside a month. I had seen the way he worked.' The facts bore out Aitken's statement. Following the loss to the Londoners, Aitken, after a club record 660 appearances, never kicked another ball in Villa colours.

The way Saunders worked, according to Aitken, was in a deceitful, underhand manner: kind to your face while sharpening the knives behind your back. Keen to clarify his future, Aitken sought out Saunders, but regular requests for meetings were ignored. On transfer deadline day, Saunders summoned Aitken and informed the veteran full-back the club was giving him a free transfer. It was less than an hour before the deadline. Aitken had next-to-no chance of finding a new club. In Aitken's view, it was an act of calculated cruelty on Saunders' part.

Aitken was furious. Saunders, he believed, 'was such a narcissist', resentful of players getting more attention than him. Aitken, as the most senior professional at the club, enjoyed a special relationship with the fans, his popularity thereby a threat to Saunders. For so long part of the Villa furniture, Aitken was now cast aside like a broken chair. The toxicity between the two intensified to such a degree that Saunders banned Aitken from the dressing room, feeling the full-back was too troublesome to have around. Towards the end of the player's time at the club, Aitken claimed that Saunders actually hated him. Aitken was even forced to train on his own. For such a loyal servant, it was a sorry end to a distinguished career.

While the club's longest-serving player was embroiled in a bitter departure, one of Villa's emerging youngsters was making his entry. On Saturday 7 February, 17-year-old Gordon Cowans made his Aston Vil debut in a game against a Manchester City side three weeks away fr a 2-1 League Cup Final win over Newcastle. Cowans, known to mos 'Sid' after his middle name, had signed apprentice forms with Vil n June 1974, the same month that Saunders signed on as manager. Sau ers regarded the young midfielder highly and had no reservations about pitching him in at the deep end.

Witnessed by 32,331 at Maine Road and the *Match of the Day* cameras, it was a somewhat inauspicious bow. Coming on as an 82nd-minute substitute for Frank Pimblett, Cowans went immediately to cover the far post as Villa defended a City corner. The ball looped into the air as it came into the six-yard box and Asa Hartford, with his back to goal, hooked it past Burridge and over Cowans into the top corner. Villa had conceded before Cowans had even touched the ball.

Hartford's goal capped a late rally by the home side, who snatched a 2-1 victory after Andy Gray's strike on seven minutes – sweeping in from an Ian Hamilton centre – had earlier looked as if it might finally break Villa's away duck.

Seven days later, thousands of Villa supporters made the trip to Bramall Lane fully expecting their team to end the hoodoo. Sheffield United, the First Division's bottom club, had won only once in 28 matches. But even on Valentine's Day the fans' romantic aspirations proved all-too-idealistic. Villa somehow contrived to lose 2-1 to the South Yorkshire side and, while John Burridge might be forgiven for being slightly distracted – the next day, with his team-mates in attendance, the goalkeeper was due to marry fiancée Janet – another defeat on the road only added to Saunders' frustrations.

While a 2-1 home win over Manchester United – Gray, as he'd done on his debut, netting against the Red Devils – was welcome, Villa continually struggled to get the better of opponents. Three successive stalemates – a 1-1 draw at home to Wolves, a 2-2 at Burnley, then a 0-0 against Ipswich (a game so dull a large flock of pigeons settled on the halfway line and were undisturbed by the tedium on the pitch) – meant almost permanent residence in the table's bottom half.

When Spurs racked up a nap hand against Villa in a 5-2 win at White Hart Lane, the threat of relegation was becoming very real. Tottenham's first goal that afternoon came after Chris Nicholl's attempted interception of a Ralph Coates cross-shot diverted the ball past Burridge into his own net. The following Saturday, before 21,370 at Filbert Street, Nicholl not only went one better, he achieved a unique footballing feat: scoring all four goals in a 2-2 draw with Leicester City.

Twice he gifted the home side the lead (his second own goal, an unstoppable header powered past a helpless Burridge, Nicholl would later call the 'best goal I ever scored') and twice he restored parity. There was a goal for each team at each end, all of them from open play.

Perhaps more unusually, the pair he bagged for Villa were with his feet rather than his head. Oddly enough, on the Saturday before, Leicester had beaten Middlesbrough, the game's only goal another own goal, by Middlesbrough's central defender Stuart Boam.

The following day, Nicholl's achievement earned him his fair share of headlines. An Australian paper even printed the story of Nicholl's 'hero and villain' turn with the headline, 'Is This the Irish Joke to End all Irish Jokes?'

Remarkable as it was, Nicholl's accomplishment wasn't unique. On 6 October 1923, playing a Second Division game for Oldham Athletic against Manchester United, left-back Sam Wynne scored four times – from a penalty and a free kick for Oldham, and two own goals for United – though Oldham, unlike Villa, eventually ran out 3-2 winners. Nicholl didn't even get to keep the match ball. The referee, officiating his last fixture, claimed it for himself.

Nicholl's fortunes soon took one more twist. After a 0-0 draw at home with Stoke City and the bitter disappointment of losing 3-2 at St Andrew's, Villa battled to another goalless Villa Park stalemate with Liverpool. Against the champions-elect Saunders handed Nicholl the captain's armband. Ian Ross had been a steadying presence in Villa's rearguard as the team struggled to find their First Division feet. But several heavy defeats had exposed its brittleness. Saunders sought more solidity. When Leighton Phillips, a central defender for the Welsh national side, impressed in his more accustomed role during a reserve team run-out (Phillips had out-marked Francis Lee, now at Derby), Saunders assigned the ex-Cardiff man as the player to partner Nicholl in the future.

For four of Villa's final games, he paired up Phillips alongside Nicholl. The two looked sufficiently at home together for Saunders to decide that Ross was expendable. Although Ross came back for one last appearance, his partnership with Nicholl had run its course. After a summer playing for Santa Barbara in California, Ross would return to England and, following autumn loan spells at Northampton Town and Notts County, in December 1976 he linked up with Peterborough United. 'It wasn't an easy decision to leave and join a club who were then in the Third Division,' the Scot reflected. 'But I have never regretted the move, and I enjoyed being captain of Ron's team. We had a good side, and they were a tremendous bunch of lads on and off the field.' Nicholl, meanwhile, celebrated his promotion to skipper by finding the net yet again, in a 1-1 draw at Highfield Road.

Ironically, it was in Villa's last away fixture of the season, at Upton Park, that the search for success on opposition soil came closest to bearing fruit. Heading into stoppage time, leading 2-1 through Steve Hunt (his only goal in his seven-game career under Saunders) and John Deehan, Villa were denied at the very death when a Trevor Brooking goal 90 seconds from the end snatched away their last chance of maximum points on their travels. When two narrow home wins – over Derby and against Middlesbrough – left them 16th in the table, a comfortable nine points clear of the relegation spots, Saunders summed up the season as one in which 'we have consolidated as well as having played some good matches and some good football'.

The transition from Second to First Division had been anything but smooth yet, but for the Achilles heel of their unproductive away form, Villa would have been much better placed. On their own turf – with only their opening day reverse to Leeds and defeat to QPR blotting their copybook – Villa boasted an impressive record, and the Villa Park turnstiles had clicked; the club's average attendance 38,233 – their highest since 1951/52 – was bettered by only Liverpool and Manchester United. 'It is an accepted fact in football,' Saunders wrote in his final programme notes of the season, 'that a side needs two or three years in the First Division to consolidate and tune to the greater demands this standard of competition makes.' The long campaign had at least allowed Saunders opportunity to assess how his squad would cope with life at the top. 'Some players unfortunately didn't come up to our expectations,' he added, 'but others gave us a pleasant surprise by doing better than we first thought they would.'

The failings were obvious. For Saunders, for whom a parsimonious defence was the cornerstone of all his sides' successes, the Villa backline's charity was totally uncharacteristic. And, though the loss of long-term cartilage victims Leonard and Little certainly hadn't helped, too many teams leaving B6 with a share of the points highlighted a lack of clinical finishing.

In March, Jimmy Cumbes and Pat McMahon had both left for new careers Stateside, reuniting with ex-boss Vic Crowe at Portland Timbers. Neil Rioch would soon join them. Another, perhaps more surprising, departure was Ian 'Chico' Hamilton. One of the club's most popular players, Hamilton had been a regular throughout the season, but Saunders was willing to let him go. The derby defeat was the attacking midfielder's last appearance. After seven years, Hamilton packed his bags for Second Division Sheffield United for £30,000. Hamilton later confessed that leaving to go to Bramall Lane when he did was the worst move of his career.

Further departures followed. Young utility forward John Overton, who'd made his first team debut at Maine Road on the same day as Gordon Cowans, enjoyed only three appearances before a loan to Halifax and a subsequent move to Gillingham. Midfielder Frank Pimblett, an England Schoolboys international and former team-mate of Bolton's Peter Reid at Huyton Boys, was another with a short-lived Villa career, enjoying just nine league starts before a loan spell at Newport County was followed by a transfer to Stockport County. The side arguably moulded mostly in Crowe's image was now being fashioned much more to Saunders' own liking.

Undoubtedly the biggest success story was that of Gray. Although he admitted being 'a bit overawed by the size of the crowds at first', the striker was soon revelling in the Villa Park atmosphere and the terraces immediately took him to their hearts. Despite his relatively short stature – 5ft 10in – Gray's immense leaping power and determination to get to the ball ahead of his marker made even bad crosses look good. His pace on the floor posed a constant menace to defenders.

Saunders, John Burridge said in his autobiography, *Budgie: The Autobiography of Goalkeeping Legend John Burridge*, 'was clever enough to play the long ball game' that perfectly suited Gray's style. That Gray himself believed his season's goal tally – ten in 30 games – was 'a disappointment' demonstrated a measure of the Scotsman's desire to improve.

Their prudent investment in Gray, Burridge and Mortimer emphasised not only the board's ambitions for the club but their backing of Saunders to achieve them. Villa's lowly finish aside, the signs that the nucleus of a new team was forming had its manager chiming an optimistic note. 'I think we will be able to face the start of next season far more confidently and better prepared than we did this season,' Saunders said. 'The lads have learned a lot and are much wiser, and their greater experience will stand the club in good stead.'

As the sizzling summer of 1976 approached, just how much better prepared Villa would be, even Saunders can't possibly have envisaged.

Dreamland

WHEN the 1976/77 Football League season kicked off on Saturday 21 August, the United Kingdom was still in the midst of one of the hottest summers on record. For many of the 39,012 fans – the male ones, at least – crowded into Villa Park that afternoon, it wasn't just shirt-sleeve but bare chest weather. England might have been enduring the worst drought for more than 100 years but at Aston Villa there was a strong undercurrent of belief that the pieces were slowly slipping into place. 'I feel sure that supporters are going to see an improvement this season,' an upbeat Saunders reiterated ahead of the new campaign.

He dipped just once into the transfer market. While Arsenal were splashing out the biggest money – £333,333 on Newcastle's Malcolm Macdonald – Villa's only outlay was a much more modest sum. After a failed £60,000 bid to land Clydebank's 20-year-old winger Davie Cooper, considered one of Scotland's brightest prospects, Saunders did make one successful raid north of the border, in early August signing St Johnstone's Scottish under-23 international defender Gordon Smith for £80,000, a record deal for the Perthshire club.

Informed that an English side were interested, the Partick-born Smith, whose grandfather Willie Salisbury had once played for Liverpool, had jumped at the chance. A naturally right-sided defender, he had expected to be competition for John Gidman's number two shirt. But Gidman, whose buccaneering raids down the flank had won him the fans' Player of the Year award, wasn't going to be dislodged in a hurry. Instead, Saunders had pencilled in Smith for the berth vacated by Aitken.

On the verge of dotting the i's and crossing the t's on a contract, Smith was suddenly sprung with a question – had he ever played at left-back? 'I hadn't in my life,' the Scot revealed to *Villa Times*. 'But I told him I had. I knew how good Gidman was and knew it was either left-back for Villa or stay in Scotland playing in front of 8,000–12,000. A no-brainer really!'

Saunders was pleased with his purchase. 'Some 14 or 15 players have left the club since I came and half-a-dozen new ones have been signed,' he noted. 'We now have a more workable number on the staff and, although we would still like to add two or three new quality players, we're entitled to feel better equipped than we were.' Smith's arrival, however, was greeted with far less bunting by Bobby McDonald.

The Aberdonian had only enjoyed sporadic appearances – ten starts in all – on the First Division stage. With Aitken's days numbered, McDonald assumed that he would revert to his more familiar role as the ready-made replacement. He was wrong. In Aitken's absence, Saunders handed the number three shirt to John Robson. The purchase of Smith now meant even greater rivalry for the jersey. Saunders, though, made it clear to McDonald he didn't rate him as a defender. When, three weeks later, Coventry City boss Gordon Milne made a bid for the player, Saunders let McDonald have talks at Highfield Road and a deal was soon concluded. Despite McDonald's desire to remain at Villa Park, his time with the club was over. Like Aitken, he left on less-than-friendly terms with the Villa manager.

Villa's warm-up fixtures had gone well. They opened a European tour – playing 'some exceptionally good football' according to Saunders – by beating the defeated European Cup finalists and French champions from the previous season, St Etienne, 2-1; the first time the French club had lost on home soil in three years. Most significant, however, after draws in Rheims and against the cosmopolitan talents of Porto, once managed by Tommy Docherty, was a home win over Royal Antwerp. The UEFA Cup games with the Belgians had, in the words of Sir William Dugdale, 'provided a salutary lesson in the somewhat rarefied atmosphere of European football, and we paid heavily for our education'. A 3-1 triumph for Villa in the friendly gave an indication of just how much their players had subsequently learned.

The return to fitness of Brian Little was further cause for optimism. 'I really haven't had time to prove what I can do against the best defences in the country,' the Durham-born striker said ahead of the new season. In the friendly games, he hit three goals – one against Porto and two in the game with Antwerp – and the exhilarating form which had earned him so many plaudits and an England debut was clearly coming back.

One journalist stated confidently, 'Aston Villa, now alive to the ever-changing face of football, are more than equipped to go forward into the

1980s with confidence. Those ghosts of glories past have been laid to rest at last!' Yet, exorcised spectres or no, Villa was not a name on anyone's lips as challengers for the major prizes. Saunders, upon promotion, had claimed that the club was 'near to an explosion' but the bomb was still ticking 12 months later. It was about to go off in devastating fashion.

On that opening day, West Ham United were the first to suffer. Four second-half goals – two apiece for Gray and Graydon (including one penalty) – completed a rout of the London club and while Villa bloomed in the sunshine, by the final whistle, according to the *Birmingham Mail,* West Ham 'the former aristocrats of the First Division were dressed in rags'. Even a Graydon miss from a second spot-kick couldn't spoil the day.

Undeterred by a 2-0 defeat at Maine Road four days later, Villa finally banished their away day blues the following Saturday, the rejuvenated Little adding to a Mick Lyons own goal to give the visitors a 2-0 win at Goodison Park and their first top-flight victory away from Villa Park since February 1967. With five goalless draws in the First Division on the same afternoon, had a league table been produced Villa would have headed it.

A week later, after a 5-2 home trouncing of Ipswich Town, they were officially top. Little netted again, but it was Andy Gray who grabbed the headlines, scoring the season's first hat-trick in the First Division – a second-half 19-minute three-goal burst – and the first by any Villa player in the top flight since Tony Hateley ten years previously. Not since the beginning of the 1962/63 season had the club occupied such a lofty perch.

Reminders of the defensive frailties that had plagued them the season before continued to nag, however. Of their first six fixtures, Villa won three and lost three. One of those reverses, a derby defeat before a 50,084 crowd at Villa Park, was a game that Villa dominated yet, despite taking an early lead through Gray, somehow contrived to lose. After fellow Scottish number nine Kenny Burns equalised for the visitors (his belligerent goal salute in front of the Holte End instantly wiping him off the Christmas card list of a few more Villa fans), a 'beautiful goal', as ITV's Hugh Johns described it, from yet another Scot, John Connolly, sealed a 2-1 City win. Saunders decided that, as reliable as current midfielder John Robson was, what the side required was a more all-round, dominant player who could create and destroy in equal measure.

That player was Arsenal's Alex Cropley. Cropley, a combative but extremely skilful footballer, was a genuine ball-winner but also, as Andy Gray put it in the foreword to Cropley's autobiography, possessed 'a wand of a left foot' that, he wrote in his own book *Gray Matters*, 'could open a can of peas'. Signed from Hibs for £150,000 by Arsenal's Bertie Mee in December 1974, the Aldershot-born Cropley had endured a frustrating time in north London, suffering a hairline fracture to his leg in a match at Middlesbrough shortly after arriving, then breaking it again soon after his comeback at the start of the following season.

At odds with new Arsenal boss Terry Neill and failing to fully settle at Highbury, Cropley, once aware of Villa's interest, was keen to make the move to the Midlands. During protracted negotiations – unusual for Saunders – the Villa manager had sold the club to Cropley. 'Saunders was very affable, putting absolutely no pressure on me,' he wrote in *Crops*, 'simply stating that he had a great bunch of lads and was highly optimistic of doing something with them.'

Cropley himself had witnessed first-hand the Villa team's potential in the previous season's encounter against the Gunners (the game in which Keith Leonard suffered his injury); they were, Cropley wrote, 'a young workman-like side playing with great energy in front of a fantastic crowd' that had impressed him greatly. On 21 September, Cropley, having travelled to Birmingham from Blackpool where he'd been with the Arsenal party for a League Cup tie, was an onlooker at Villa Park as the home side took on Norwich in the same competition. The following day, Cropley completed the formalities, Saunders forking out £125,000 for the 25-year-old.

Thrust straight into action in the number ten shirt against Leicester, Cropley had an immediate impact, winning a penalty (converted by Graydon) and slotting in with ease alongside Dennis Mortimer. An Andy Gray goal sealed a 2-0 victory. There was, wrote Cropley, a 'happy atmosphere' at the club; the Villa players, according to the new signing, had an 'evident desire for success'. Two weeks later, when man of the match Cropley scored an exquisite winner at Roker Park – beating two defenders before executing a perfect chip over debutant keeper Barry Siddall to secure Villa's first win at Sunderland in 14 attempts – Saunders ('not a man to give praise lightly' in Cropley's words) told the midfielder it was 'one of the finest goals he'd ever seen'.

While a ninth successive league game without a victory for the north-east side meant the end for Bob Stokoe – the boss who'd guided Sunderland to possibly the unlikeliest result in FA Cup history, when they beat Leeds United in the 1973 final, resigning the following Monday – Villa's manager couldn't have been more chipper. With Cropley turning in another masterly performance, an almost befuddled Arsenal, in spite of taking the lead through Alan Ball, were blitzed 5-1 at Villa Park, Gray notching another brace, with Graydon, Little and Mortimer also adding their names to the scoresheet.

Bristol City were next on the receiving end. Back in the First Division after a 65-year absence, City started with a surprise win at Highbury. At Villa Park, they went in at half-time 1-0 thanks to Tom Ritchie. But, in front of a happy Holte End, three second-half goals showed what an indomitable force Villa were fast becoming. Even defenders were registering in the scorers' column; Chris Nicholl getting Villa's equaliser, while John Gidman's strike was his first-ever on home soil. Now sitting in second, Villa headed for a top-of-the-table clash at Anfield.

As in the year before, though, they left on the end of a 3-0 defeat. Yet the scoreline masked what had been an impressive display. Villa, with 10,000 fans in support amongst the 51,751 attendance, had more than matched the Merseysiders for 75 minutes, with the home side's goals in the final quarter of an hour – from Keegan, Callaghan and McDermott – a testament to the powers of Liverpool's persistence but giving a somewhat warped reflection of the game. Saunders stated that Villa's performance was '20 times better' than the previous encounter.

When Villa then edged out Manchester United, 3-2 at home, their increasing maturity was in evidence again. United, who'd only recently scored their biggest victory under Docherty's management, Gordon Hill grabbing a hat-trick as they beat Newcastle 7-2 in the League Cup, led for much of the game. But a leveller from Mortimer and two goals by Gray – his second a soaring far-post header – earned Villa another thrilling victory on home turf. Ray Graydon's weak effort from the penalty spot on 68 minutes, easily smothered by Alex Stepney, didn't matter.

Later that evening, Gray enthused about the new spirit at Villa Park, telling *Match of the Day*'s Jimmy Hill, 'We've got the players, we've got the manager, we're all hungry for success. Aston Villa's been in the doldrums for a little bit too long, and we aim to give it success as soon as possible.' But in capturing Gray's winning goal the BBC cameras also landed him in trouble. Suffering a torrent of abuse all afternoon from the United supporters massed at the Witton End, Gray had responded instinctively to his winner with a defiant pose and a double V-sign towards them that was shown over the evening programme's closing credits. The Scot's goal 'celebration' was also snapped by a photographer from *The Sun* and earned the following day headline, 'Andy, You Are a Super Player – Don't Become a Yob'.

Gray had already been the target of the headline-makers for the wrong reasons after his first-half sending-off the month before, along with Czech defender Ondrus, as Scotland lost 2-0 against Czechoslovakia in Prague. Inevitably, he incurred the wrath of the FA. At the subsequent disciplinary hearing Gray was slapped with a £110 fine. Or, as the player later put it, '£27.50 a finger'.

After his penalty woe, Graydon's misfortune got worse. In the following Wednesday's derby match at West Brom, Graydon was 'taken out from behind' by Baggies midfielder Len Cantello, a challenge that left the West Country wing wizard crumpled in a heap and the usually placid Saunders leaping up from the dugout to remonstrate. Having to settle for a point after holding an interval lead was the least of Saunders' worries. Graydon damaged knee ligaments in the tackle. 'It was the worst injury I ever had,' he told *Villa Times*. 'I was out longer than if I'd broken my leg, 12 to 14 weeks.' Graydon's goals and teasing high crosses would be sorely missed. His absence offered John Deehan another opportunity.

Coming in for a central role alongside Gray, Deehan's introduction gave Brian Little licence to roam. It suited the side perfectly. Able to float, Little became a ghost that opposing defenders found almost impossible to track. The new three-pronged forward line struck with even deadlier force. Gray's rich vein continued. His 13th of the campaign – coming to Villa's rescue to earn a 2-2 draw with Coventry after two quick-fire strikes by Mick Ferguson had stunned the home side – was followed by another brace (both soaring headers) at Elland Road, as Villa claimed an impressive 3-1 win. With the football programme decimated by icy conditions, and leaders Ipswich's game with Newcastle abandoned, Liverpool (3-1 winners over QPR) leapfrogged into first. But Villa, fifth just behind Newcastle and Manchester City, were still handily placed.

That weekend, Charlton striker Derek Hales became the costliest player to leave the Second Division, with Colin Murphy, Derby's acting manager following the November sacking of Dave Mackay, paying an estimated £330,000 for his signature. Hales, on his 25th birthday, made his debut for the Rams the following Wednesday in a dour 0-0 draw at home to Arsenal, Murphy afterwards revealing that Derby had also made an offer to Bill Shankly to join them in an advisory capacity. But on that same midweek night the ex-Liverpool manager was elsewhere in the Midlands: watching a game that has since gone down in Villa's modern folklore.

On 15 December 1976, when they arrived at Villa Park, Liverpool were six points ahead of their opponents, though Villa had a game in hand. Just two defeats in their first 16 matches had seen Paisley's team go clear at the top. Following a 5-1 bashing of Leicester in November, the Foxes' boss Jimmy Bloomfield said, 'It is frightening to think what Liverpool are going to do to a team that plays badly against them.' Despite pre-match talk about the absence through injury of John Toshack, Saunders knew it wouldn't make his own side's task any easier. Toshack's replacement, former Everton striker David Johnson, was an England international who'd returned to Merseyside in the summer, signing from Ipswich in a £200,000 deal.

Whoever lined up in the Reds' attack, it promised to be a tough night in the Villa number five shirt for 18-year-old Charlie Young. With Chris Nicholl nursing a broken nose sustained in a clash of heads during training the day before, Young – a 'Scot' born in Nicosia, Cyprus – was drafted in for his debut against Leeds, deputising alongside stand-in skipper Leighton Phillips and giving a good account of himself. Facing the likes of Johnson, Keegan and Heighway presented the youngster with an altogether more daunting challenge. But if Young was anticipating a torrid home baptism, he couldn't have been more mistaken. On a cold, misty night, with blizzards only days away, the reigning champions and UEFA Cup holders were hit by a first-half blast from Villa that left them completely taken aback.

After only nine minutes, following a beautiful link-up between Cropley, full-back Robson and Deehan, Robson's perfect, inviting cross from the left flank was met by Gray, who beat keeper Ray Clemence to the ball to fizz home a trademark header. Barely two minutes later, with the visitors' fans who'd turned up late due to traffic wondering what was going on, Deehan, latching on to an incisive short through-pass by Mortimer and given onside despite the protests of all four Liverpool defenders, perfectly steered the ball through the legs of Clemence to make it two.

In the 21st minute it was three and almost a carbon copy of the second; when Thompson and Gray collided, the loose ball ran into the path of Deehan on the left who clinically slotted home a low shot at the goalkeeper's near post. With their free-flowing, fast-passing style, a rampant Villa were now ripping apart the Reds' defence. In midfield, Cropley, Carrodus and Mortimer – outwitting Callaghan, Kennedy and McDermott – were winning virtually everything. Only two superb saves from Clemence spared the visitors further punishment.

Time and again Little, in imperious form, left a dispirited Emlyn Hughes sprawling on the deck. 'Hughes couldn't even get near enough to foul him,' one supporter later mused. Just past the half-hour, Little got his reward. Receiving the ball on the edge of the box from the advancing

Gidman, Little eyed a packed penalty area in front of him before coolly curling a swerving left-footer into the far, top corner. Clemence could only watch. It was the best goal of the bunch. A packed Villa Park was absolutely buzzing. When Ray Kennedy's low drive pulled one back it was greeted with only ironic cheers from the home supporters. A minute before the break, Gray beat Thompson in the air to meet Mortimer's cross from the right and bullet home a near-post header, and Villa's four-goal cushion was restored.

Shrewsbury referee Ken Ridden sounded the half-time whistle and applause rang out from all four sides of the ground. As the floodlights beaming the legendary 'AV' had sliced through the December dark, Villa had lit up the evening with a 45-minute exhibition of football that would linger long in the memories of all who had witnessed it.

'The 42,851 crowd gave the players a standing ovation – the likes, of which I have never heard before,' recorded the *Birmingham Post*'s Ian Willars in his match report. Holding up their photo-spread of the Villa manager from the match programme, the Holte End burst into a rendition of 'Saunders, Saunders, Saunders'. It was a hairs-on-the-back-of-the-neck moment. The shell-shocked Liverpool players left the pitch arguing among themselves.

After the break, exhibiting typical character, Paisley's side did make a strong fist of it and might have cut the deficit but Villa, too, missed chances to make the margin even bigger. John Deehan spurned an opportunity to grab his hat-trick when set up by Little. Clemence was lucky to see the ball come back off his crossbar when he got a hand to Mortimer's centre. The England keeper also had to pull off fine saves from Deehan and Gidman as well as courageous stops from Cropley and Mortimer near the end.

The following day, the press were overflowing with praise. 'Villa for England!' raved the *Daily Mirror*. 'Aston Villa produced a magical championship-class display to totally humiliate league champions Liverpool,' reported the *Birmingham Post*. The *Daily Mail* called it a 'savaging'.

Pre-match, Saunders had stated, 'I want us to beat them this time and I want us to deserve to do so, but I will happily settle for the result rather than the performance if need be.' He'd been given both. Although Clemence said that the visitors had mistakenly 'let Villa dictate the pace of the game instead of doing our usual away job by setting the pace ourselves', in truth Liverpool had had little choice; as the *Daily Mail*'s Ronald Crowther wrote, 'Villa's swift, stabbing moves and accurate passing bewildered Liverpool from the start.' They'd asked questions the Reds found impossible to answer. 'Everything Villa did went in,' said 'Pool midfielder Ian Callaghan.

But for their goalkeeper, though, who'd last conceded five times in a game 12 years earlier for Scunthorpe A, it could have been far worse. 'Devastation. Pure and Simple,' was the *Liverpool Echo*'s verdict. The 5-1 scoreline represented the Reds' heaviest league defeat since a 7-2 thrashing at Spurs on Easter Monday 1963. It was the first time in ten years that Liverpool had shipped five goals in one match – against Ajax. It would also prove to be Liverpool's biggest defeat in the Anfield Road reign of Bob Paisley. 'Looking at our team, you'd have thought they'd never played together before and that we had no experience,' Paisley said post-match. 'It was just too bad to be true.'

The stats, impressive as they were, were nothing to the brilliance of Villa's football on the night. The best team in England had been destroyed and Villa had done so by playing a Liverpool-style game. The 5-1 scoreline summed up their superiority. Andy Gray later described it as 'one of the greatest team displays I was ever part of' while Alex Cropley would always maintain it was the best game of football that he had played in. For John Gidman, who, just four years prior had been cleaning the boots of Clemence, Keegan and Hughes at Anfield, the victory was almost redemptive.

Gidman, deemed to be lacking both the ability and dedication to succeed, had been let go by Liverpool, with Bill Shankly informing the 16-year-old the club was releasing him because he was 'shite'. It was a word for which Gidman would never forgive the Liverpool manager. 'I always felt like I had a point to prove when Villa played Liverpool,' Gidman told Andy Mitten in *We're The Famous Man United. Old Trafford in the Eighties – The Players' Stories*. 'After the game, Shankly was at the top of the stairs,' Gidman said. 'He shook my hand and said, "How are you son? We made a mistake. Well done." I just looked at him and said, "Thanks."'

Gidman also told of how 'Ron Saunders didn't even know what to say at half-time.' According to the defender, the Villa manager, 'showing a rare flash of humour, said, "Get yourself a cup of tea and have a piss." We were astonished, but he added, "How can I give a talk when I've just seen you play like that?"'

Christmas and New Year had been rolled into one, and B6 transformed into dreamland. The lucky ones who'd seen it were still pinching themselves long after the 90 minutes. Their disbelief was perhaps exceeded only by the incredulity of those hearing the scoreline relayed on their radios. Fans – both Villa's and Liverpool's – as far away as Australia were ringing up Birmingham's BRMB radio station asking for confirmation that it wasn't some cruel hoax. When reassured it *was* real, questions were still forthcoming, 'Did Liverpool have a full side?' and 'Were the conditions poor?' Few could accept it was fact not fiction.

The good fortune of those there that night was only emphasised when it later became apparent there was no TV coverage at all of the game. BBC's *Sportsnight* that December evening had been replaced by *Sports Review of the Year* 1976, with Birmingham-born figure skater John Curry taking the accolade of Sports Personality of the Year. Over on ITV, with Central TV only allowed to cover one game in the region, they'd opted to send cameras to the Baseball Ground for Derek Hales' home debut. The story was that, while his colleagues were watching the dull affair at Derby, ATV's sports bulletin presenter Gary Newbon was at Villa Park sporting a pie, a pint and an ever-increasing look of dismay as the first-half action unfolded.

Hales, who couldn't stop scoring in the Second Division and was seen as the man to bring back the halcyon days they'd enjoyed under Clough, scored a total of four goals in his entire Derby career, one less than Villa managed in those first 45 minutes against Liverpool.

There were subsequent rumours of footage of Villa's famous victory existing – on Super 8mm film – with Andy Gray claiming to have seen it ('the footage is grainy and not good') but, if it's true, it has yet to surface. As the *Birmingham Mail* suggested at the time, 'If only Villa had a ciné film to market this, they would have a best-seller on their hands.'

When, three days later, fifth-placed Newcastle visited Villa Park, there was still no reality check. Two more Deehan goals – with only Alan Gowling replying – put the seal on a perfect week and moved Villa to within two points of the new leaders, Ipswich. The mood at the Midlands club had not been as cheerful for years. Even the disappointment the fans felt about Keith Leonard losing his 15-month battle to overcome his knee injury was diluted somewhat by their delight over the form of Gray and Little.

Now being mentioned in the same breath as Toshack and Keegan, Villa's deadly duo were arguably the best front pairing in the country. 'Teaming up with Brian Little has helped tremendously,' Gray told *Shoot* magazine. 'I think we complement each other and it has been an exciting experience playing alongside him.' The feeling was shared. Little, now revelling in his freer, roving role, enjoyed an almost telepathic understanding with his partner, able to pick him out perfectly wherever Gray found space in the box. 'He has scored some fantastic goals; goals which I don't think I would have got,' said Gray of Little. Now, Little was deriving just as much pleasure from creating chances for his fellow frontman. As a duet, they couldn't have been more on song.

Even in friendly games, Villa had been goal-happy. In late November, Deehan and Little (twice) had earned a 3-1 win against Bundesliga side Eintracht Frankfurt. Though in early October, after Frank Carrodus had put the home side 2-0 up, a not-so-friendly encounter against Glasgow Rangers had to be abandoned on 53 minutes when hundreds of Rangers fans threw bottles and then invaded the Villa Park pitch, leading to a fierce battle with the police. One local paper labelled it as 'Birmingham's day of Tartan terror'.

The headlines weren't exaggerating. More than 100 fans were injured and 50 arrested. An FA inquiry cleared Villa of any blame for the riot but, unless the Midlanders drew Scottish opponents in a European competition, a ban on all Scottish clubs visiting Villa Park was put firmly in place.

Laced with skilful and hard-working players, Villa's balanced team was so capable, Leighton Phillips believed, they 'could have taken anyone out of the crowd and they'd have fitted in'. It wasn't the case, though. What Saunders lacked was the liberty to bring in like-for-like quality replacements, a fact highlighted at the Liverpool game. While the visitors were able to call on Jimmy Case from the bench, 18-year-old Mick Buttress was pressed into service as Villa's substitute.

Two days after Christmas, with Alex Cropley missing (with a pulled hamstring caused by the cold weather during the Newcastle fixture), Saunders was forced to draft in another youngster, David Hughes, for the last match of the year at Middlesbrough. Despite another Gray strike – his tally now 21 goals in 25 games – and a goalscoring debut from Hughes, Villa fell victim to a hat-trick from Boro's transfer-listed David Mills and lost 3-2. 'It is not fair to always pitch so many teenagers into games like this, particularly as we are hoping to continue our championship challenge,' Saunders said. 'There is such a gap between the experienced men and the promising teenagers on the staff. I believe the point was admirably made this afternoon.'

With a League Cup semi-final and a hectic league schedule ahead, Saunders' concern about the lack of genuine strength in depth wasn't without good cause.

From the Blue Half of Manchester to the Red

THREE successive finals meant that Ron Saunders' name had almost become synonymous with English football's third most important domestic competition. After Manchester United the season before had snuffed out hopes of a fourth consecutive Wembley trip, it was Manchester, the city, that linked both the start and end of the story of Saunders' latest League Cup odyssey.

The second-round draw paired Villa with City, winners of the trophy for a second time, on the opening day of September. When the two sides met just seven days prior to the tie, the Maine Road club had eased to a 2-0 league victory, their cup final match-winner Dennis Tueart netting one with centre-back Dave Watson – once a £70,000 target for Vic Crowe in November 1970 when Watson was playing centre-forward for Rotherham – claiming the other. The swift rendezvous on a Wednesday night before 34,585 at Villa Park was an even more one-sided affair.

That was due, almost single-handedly, to Brian Little. Following his cartilage troubles, the forward had trained all summer, he said, 'To make sure I was ready for another challenge.' Against Tony Book's men he bounced back in brilliant fashion. Little's 33rd-minute opener – an overhead volley at the far post after Graydon's corner-kick was only half-headed clear – was followed by a smartly taken second after the break and, when Graydon completed the scoring later on, the cup holders were dumped emphatically from the tournament. Later that evening, Little's two crackers had BBC's Barry Davies nigh on ecstatic in the commentary box.

When Villa were handed a second home tie against another of Saunders' previous employers, Norwich City, it prompted him to remark, 'It seems that the football fates have conspired to throw up such reminders of what has happened over the years.' Not that Saunders needed reminding. He had neither forgotten nor forgiven City chairman Sir Arthur South. On a previous visit to Carrow Road, Saunders had even made the Villa coach driver make a detour to South's house, then park up while the manager stood swearing at it for a few minutes. This time, at Villa Park, Saunders was in a much happier humour. Two Andy Gray goals saw Villa narrowly edging past the Norfolk side 2-1 and into the next round.

The omens that this could again be Saunders' year were good: all of the five previous League Cup winners, including Villa, had beaten Norwich en route to Wembley or in the final itself. With their midfielder-in-waiting Alex Cropley an onlooker from the stands, of equal significance was the presence on the pitch of Gordon Cowans. Still a few weeks shy of his 18th birthday, the whippet-thin youngster stepped up to make his full debut just one month after signing professional terms. Cowans, whose father Walter was Villa's kit man and, for a time, a steward at the club's youth hostel (a job offered to him as an enticement to his son to sign) was first spotted playing for his school in Mansfield as a ten-year-old in 1968. 'You have to be quick off the mark spotting budding talent these days,' said Saunders.

That 41,428 turned up at Villa Park on a chilly Wednesday evening in late October to watch a cup tie versus Third Division opposition was verification of just how attractive a proposition Villa had become. Fourth-round opponents Wrexham, managed by ex-Villa full-back (and member of the successful 1961 side) John Neal, had already twice dispatched top-flight opposition – Leicester and Spurs – and, with young attacking talents such as Mickey Thomas, Bobby Shinton and Billy Ashcroft in their line-up, harboured high hopes of another upset. When Graham Whittle gave the visitors an 11th-minute lead, the headline-writers' pens were poised. They quickly put them away again. With goals by Gray, Carrodus, Little (two), and Nicholl, Villa ruthlessly put the Welsh side to the sword and another hurdle on their journey was safely negotiated.

Playing before their own supporters again, the next round wasn't so smooth. Though, on paper at least, appearing to be the easiest quarter-final opponents Villa could have drawn, Second Division Millwall proved anything but. Despite falling behind to an early Nicholl header, the Lions fought defiantly and, but for two missed opportunities late on – Jake Findlay producing a stunning stop to deny Barrie Fairbrother just moments after the Millwall striker had missed another golden chance – Villa might well have been forced to a replay or even worse. As it was, Brian Little's breakaway goal in injury time gave some gloss to the scoreline and a tangible sense of relief to the home fans.

The two-legged semi-final meant Villa were at long last dusting off their passports, with QPR, who'd emerged from the previous round 2-1 winners over Arsenal, their opponents. 'Like an Everest expedition,' the *Daily Mail*'s Jeff Farmer wrote, 'Villa found the foothills of the League Cup a comfortable trek.' From hereon it was certain to be 'more testing terrain'.

That terrain was worsened by the English weather. An especially severe winter, with heavy snowfalls and temperatures averaging just about freezing, had seen the Pools Panel called into operation on a number of weekends. The first leg at Loftus Road, scheduled for January, was postponed on successive midweeks. On 1 February, when it did go ahead at the third time of asking, despite a thaw and the use of hot air balloons to try to dry out the pitch, conditions were still very poor. The game wasn't much better. Players from both sides struggled to negotiate the difficult playing surface and a largely nondescript affair finished goalless.

The return leg, just over two weeks later, was an altogether more thrilling clash. Ahead on the hour mark when Deehan finished off a fast, four-man move, Villa were pegged back 11 minutes from time with Rangers captain Gerry Francis heading in a Givens cross to send the tie into extra time.

Seconds before that, a game that had seen its share of fearsome tackling threatened to turn ugly. A crude Alex Cropley challenge on another ex-Arsenal man Frank McLintock left the veteran Scottish centre-half with a ripped sock and fuming mad. McLintock took immediate exception, grabbing Cropley and spitting out a barrage of tartan-flavoured expletives that lip-readers would have had little trouble deciphering. Cropley later claimed the tackle was accidental – he may have been hard but he wasn't dirty – the blame being mostly on the heavy Villa Park pitch, the drainage on one side of which was under repair. When Cropley had gone to trap it with the sole of his boot, the ball didn't bounce as anticipated, so it appeared that Cropley had gone over the top. McLintock hadn't seen it any other way but as deliberate.

With order restored, Villa soon held sway again. In extra time, rising to head home a Gidman free kick, Deehan got his second of the night. Rangers, spurning a spot-kick seven minutes from the end – Burridge guessing right to keep out Givens – looked to have missed their opportunity. Not so. Barely a minute later, substitute Peter Eastoe pounced and the tie was forced into a replay.

It was, wrote Jeff Farmer, 'an electric second leg' that 48,439 had paid club record receipts of £73,709 to watch. Rangers' escapes, reported Jeff Powell in the *Mail*, 'would have done the inmates of Colditz proud'. Post-match, however, the drama continued. Cropley, interviewed in the players' lounge by Gary Newbon, found himself confronted by a still-angry McLintock who once more manhandled the midfielder around the neck and was only prevented from inflicting further damage on his fellow Scot by the intervention of some newspaper men. 'Then, in the car park, David Webb shouted over that he would be posting me the stud I'd left in Frank's leg,' Cropley told *The Scotsman* years later. 'Imagine that, coming from one of the game's big hard men! I'm still waiting for my stud, mind.'

Some theatrics were taking place in the Villa boardroom, too. Tossing a coin to decide the neutral venue for the play-off, West Brom chairman Bert Millichip declared 'Heads' the winner, only for Rangers chairman Jim Gregory (grabbing the coin after it had bounced off the low boardroom ceiling) and Sir William Dudgale to both claim victory. A shouting match soon ensued, with Gregory – about whom Tommy Docherty would later say, 'When you shook hands with him, you counted your fingers' – adamant he had three witnesses to testify he'd called correctly. Despite Dugdale's protests, eventually the Old Etonian graciously conceded. 'The great coin-tossing controversy,' as Jeff Farmer termed it, was 'about as fair as a three-card trick' but meant that, instead of Coventry's Highfield Road (Villa's preferred choice), Highbury was set as the stage for the third match. Whether or not Villa had been conned didn't concern an unfazed Saunders. 'It's not so much where you play,' he told a press gathering phlegmatically, 'as how you play.'

The following Tuesday, in front of a 40,000 crowd, the ill-feeling QPR's players still harboured towards Cropley was soon unleashed. From the opening minutes, Villa's number ten was clearly a marked man, scythed down – or 'blatantly done' as Cropley later put it – by Rangers' full-back Dave Clement then clattered by McLintock himself. Combating an initial onslaught on both their limbs and their goalmouth, Villa struggled to get a footing in the game, albeit not for long.

On 22 minutes, Mortimer, capitalising on Masson's poor control, fed Little in the box and Walsall-born keeper Phil Parkes, once approached by Villa when playing in the West Midlands League for Brierley Hill Alliance, was helpless to stop Little lifting it over his advancing body. A second goal soon followed. When Cropley's curled-in corner fell at Little's left foot, the lank-haired number eight fired home to double the lead. 'That's the one I usually use for standing on,' the striker later admitted.

The loss of Cropley, forced to sit out the second period despite a half-time injection, failed to upset the rhythm. Villa rarely looked in trouble, coping competently with the threat of Bowles and Thomas and, in the closing seconds, after the breaking Mortimer turned the ball back to him on the edge of the Rangers area, Little slotted home to seal a resounding triumph over Dave Sexton's beleaguered side. 'Villa didn't simply beat them on a night when nerve, stamina and ability were under the public microscope,' reported the *Birmingham Mail*, 'they outplayed them, outran them and out-thought them, and stated quite decisively that Aston Villa are ready for any challenge.'

Remembering how the cock-a-hoop Hoops had irritated them with their over-the-top celebrations following the 2-2 at Villa Park, after the match the Villa players uncorked the champagne bottles, rejoiced loudly and cared little who heard them doing so. Even Saunders, so Cropley wrote in *Crops*, was 'ecstatic, taking it in turns to congratulate each player individually'. It was the precursor to a very late, drunken evening. As all-round a team effort as it was, one newspaper headline spelled out how Villa had progressed to the final, 'Little by Little by Little'. Rangers, having been left the previous week 'standing on the hangman's trapdoor', wrote Steve Curry of the *Daily Express*, 'saw Little pull the lever that strangled their chances.' Curry suggested that 'Don Revie should blow the dust from the dossier' on the striker and recall Little to the international team's fold.

'Mr Magic' was now at the peak of his footballing prowess. Pat Crerand once declared that George Best gave opponents 'twisted blood'. Little, with a drop of a shoulder and his light-footed, darting movement, had that same ability. 'There was no one to match the natural talent of Brian,' wrote Andy Gray in *Return of the Little Villan*. 'The things he could do with a football were sometimes unbelievable.' Although he had played in the Scottish team with Kenny Dalglish, Gray still felt that Little was the superior all-round player. Gray revelled in the fans' acclaim. Little was almost a reluctant hero. A cavalier footballer but an extremely modest young man. There was never any peacocking on the pitch. Little let his feet do the talking. Their language often left defenders baffled.

He barely even celebrated his goals. 'I used to shrug off goals and say "I've just scored" and walk back to the halfway line,' he reflected to the *Birmingham Mail* years later. 'I liked to take things in my stride and take in the moment rather than go overboard.' At times he even appeared detached from the action going on around him.

'It was his apparent indifference almost,' journalist Graham Clark wrote, 'that ensured he would never become the kind of idol' that Gray became. The fans' love affair with Gray, though, while passionate, would ultimately be brief. For Little, they would have a lasting affection. Little said that he had been coached to caress a football, to keep it to his toe as if it belonged to him. His play had an almost poetic quality. According to John Gidman, Little 'could dance on the pitch'. Pat Murphy said that he was 'beautifully balanced, elusive, intelligent'. To those on the terraces, he possessed even more messianic gifts. 'Brian Little walks on water' was a familiar chant from the masses swaying in rapture on the Holte End.

Villa's Wembley appointment, scheduled for Saturday 12 March, was with Everton. In early January, the Goodison Park club had sacked Billy Bingham, with 18 months of the Northern Irishman's five-year contract still to run. Everton had just beaten Stoke 2-0 in the FA Cup but their early season promise had hit the buffers and despite costly new signings, Rioch and McKenzie, the side had failed to keep pace with their successful neighbours across Stanley Park. A run of eight league games without a win left them in the table's lower reaches and Bingham out of a job. With coach Steve Burtenshaw as caretaker boss, the Merseysiders beat Second Division Bolton Wanderers 2-1 on aggregate – Bob Latchford's goal at Burnden Park proving decisive – to book their date with Villa.

On the lookout for a new permanent manager, Everton had supposedly secured the services of Bobby Robson but, when the press printed that it was a done deal, the Ipswich Town man pulled out, feeling he'd been put in an awkward position. Rumours also circulated that Saunders was on their wanted list. As tempting as a return to his native Merseyside perhaps was, Saunders quashed all speculation. 'I've worked hard to achieve what I have,' he said, 'and I will have to work even harder in the future.'

A 3-0 disposal of West Ham in the FA Cup fourth round on 29 January only prompted a more emphatic declaration. 'We are on the verge of great things at Villa Park,' Saunders said post-match. The following Monday, Everton announced the new man in charge: Gordon Lee. A Villa defender for 11 years, Lee surrendered the reins at Newcastle, deciding that a move nearer to his children who were educated in Lancashire would be more beneficial. His first game in control of the Toffees, ironically enough, was at Villa Park, goals from Gray and Little giving the home side both points.

Through various postponements and cup commitments, Villa were now playing catch-up with the clubs above them in the league. The week before the final, with John Deehan replying to a Jon Sammels penalty, they could only draw 1-1 at Leicester. Staying at a hotel in St Albans, they set up camp in Hertfordshire. There was only light training on an adjacent pitch. The mood in the group was positive. At odds of 11/10 to take the trophy, Villa were fully expected to win. On what ITV commentator Brian Moore described as 'a beautiful, crisp Wembley afternoon made for a cup final', the two teams emerged from the tunnel. Yet if the setting was perfect, the game itself couldn't have been more of a let-down. 100,000 fans witnessed one of the dullest domestic finals ever to be played at the stadium.

In an opening half in which the football seldom rose above the level of the extremely ordinary, Villa spluttered like an engine running on the wrong fuel. Everton, with Martin Dobson bossing the midfield and Duncan McKenzie lively up front, were only slightly better. Neither side mustered an opportunity. After the break, if anything, it only got worse. More passes went astray. Play became untidier. The action, what there was of it, lacked any flow whatsoever.

Everton, determined not to allow Villa's counter-attacking style to flourish, grew increasingly negative, the regular employment of their own goalkeeper Dai Davies inciting a sarcastic chant from the frustrated Villa supporters of 'Pass the ball back' to the tune of 'Clementine'. Fans from both Birmingham and Liverpool could have been forgiven for nodding off in the March sunshine, their interest piqued only briefly when referee Gordon Kew called together all 22 players to scour the pitch for bandsmen's spurs lost during the half-time interval's marching parade. McKenzie might have won it near the end, blazing over a chance that nine times out of ten he'd have put away, but a 0-0 draw – the first League Cup Final without goals – was apt for such a drab encounter.

The watching Princess Anne, sitting alongside Sir William Dugdale in the Royal Box, looked as relieved as anyone when the 90 minutes were up. It was, as Moore commented, 'Not really a dish to set before a princess.' The post-match verdicts of the managers spared no punches. Saunders admitted, 'We never got started. We had a lot of players who probably froze on the day. [It was] very disappointing.' All 'the ballyhoo, the tension, the build-up to the game,' he told Brian Moore, had adversely affected his players. 'Even an old seasoned campaigner like me has a little bit of a bubble in the bottom of my stomach,' he added with a grin. The warm afternoon had also taken its toll, Gordon Lee agreeing with Saunders' assessment that the humid weather had left both teams tired and toiling and they 'seemed to be gasping somewhat'.

'Maybe it was nerves,' said Andy Gray. 'But it wasn't like us at all.' Such was Gray's disappointment with his own contribution, the striker, despite Saunders' urging, even refused to join his team-mates on the post-match lap of honour feeling that it was 'for winners and we hadn't won'. Captain Chris Nicholl could only apologise. 'On behalf of all the players,' said the centre-half, 'I sympathise with the fans.' Like everyone else, Saunders could only hope the replay would be far livelier, but wasn't counting his chickens. 'Unfortunately, this game has a funny way of putting you in your place,' he told Moore. 'Every time you forecast something, it goes the other way. I forecast that some of my lads might freeze, particularly the younger ones,' he joked, 'and for once I was right!'

Aside from the missing spurs and Everton at one point having two number twos on the pitch due to a shirt mix-up, there was virtually nothing of note to write about. The *News of the World*'s Frank Butler deemed it a '£300,000 yawn'. 'Ninety minutes of emptiness,' the *Birmingham Mail* called it. The *Sunday Times*' Brian Glanville, under a despairing headline, 'Heaven Help Us All at Hillsborough', summed it up as 'dull and uneventful as a seaside town in winter'. A competition in the *Birmingham Mail* for the best banner on display at Wembley was won by 'Godsvilla', but the footballing deities had definitely had an afternoon off.

Duncan McKenzie, for one, felt that the huge anti-climax might have been spared if the game had had an additional half-hour to deliver a result. Saunders agreed, calling for penalties to be deployed in future, too, if necessary. McKenzie pessimistically claimed that the Hillsborough replay was now a bit of a 'non-event' and wondered who, outside of the two teams, would be interested in who won the cup on a Wednesday night. Saunders didn't care. 'The trophy and the rewards haven't changed,' he said, 'only the venue.'

The evening after the final, Andy Gray's gloom lifted considerably. At a ceremony at the Fulton Hotel, London, the Professional Footballers' Association sensationally awarded Gray both the Player of the Year and Young Player of the Year awards. It was a unique double, Gray becoming the youngest player to earn the main award, and the first to win more than one of the official three Player of the Year awards in the same season. For good measure, the young striker – along with John Gidman – was also selected for the PFA First Division Team of the Season. Gray wasn't at the ceremony to accept his accolade, however.

Instead, in the rather less glamorous surrounds of his own sitting room, the forward was handed the trophies by his captain Chris Nicholl, the pictures relayed to a screen at the hotel. The reason for that was the

Villa manager. 'Naturally, our boss, Ron Saunders, wasn't on for any of us going to London for the awards,' Gray said at the season's end. 'He wanted the team back in Birmingham for treatment to injuries and to prepare for the replay at Hillsborough the following Wednesday.' Gray accepted his manager's decision, though confessed, 'I did feel a little out of it sitting in my lounge while, 100 miles away, my fellow professionals were toasting me.' It was, Gray said, 'something you have to accept as part and parcel of the job'. Accept it or not, Saunders' refusal to let Gray attend the annual dinner was to have serious implications for their future relationship.

On the Wednesday night, before 54,840, a heavy Hillsborough pitch hosted an encounter only marginally more spirited than the first. With another goalless draw written all over it, in the 79th minute (the same minute that Ray Graydon had scored Villa's last League Cup Final goal two years earlier), John Deehan, an onlooker from the Wembley terraces in 1971, at last broke the stalemate. Fastening on to Mortimer's ball across the area, Deehan turned and hit a soft shot that Everton's bearded centre-half Roger Kenyon, off-balance, could only bundle into the back of his own net. Villa's passport into Europe appeared to be booked. With the claret and blue ribbons attached to the trophy as it was brought down pitch-side, Bob Latchford snatched it away in the dying seconds.

In Everton's very last attack of the game, Jim Pearson launched the ball into the Villa box and, amid the goalmouth scramble, up popped the former Birmingham favourite, virtually on the goal line, to force home the equaliser. When the extra half-hour failed to produce a winner, it meant a second replay – 'but we don't know when or where', the Hillsborough public address system announced – and the dubious honour of the game entering the history books as the longest-ever cup final in British football. While Everton, *The Guardian*'s Patrick Barclay believed, now 'seemed to sense that the cup was within their grasp', for Villa there was only yet more tired legs and walking wounded.

Three days later, having eased through three rounds of the FA Cup without conceding a goal, seeing off Leicester and Port Vale as well as the Hammers, Villa went to Old Trafford for their quarter-final with a Manchester United side unbeaten in 13 matches. Ray Graydon's return after 18 weeks out was heartening but Saunders admitted it would be more a test of Villa's moral fibre than their football skill, especially with Cropley, Nicholl and Gray all missing.

Still, they made the fresher start. After only two minutes, Brian Little picked up the ball just inside the United half, moved forward unchallenged and unleashed a fulminating right-footer that flew straight into the top corner of Alex Stepney's net. 'I was captain that day,' Leighton Phillips recalled to *Villa Times*, 'and Brian Little said, "If we win the toss, take the ball." We won. Brian beat one man then another and shot from 30 yards. Stepney was in goal and it flew in. Stuart Pearson came across and said, "Can we start again?"'

Little's stunning opener was to no avail. On 26 minutes, after Phillips fouled Macari just outside the box, Stewart Houston drove the free kick into the bottom corner of Burridge's net to level. Then, with just less than a quarter of an hour left, Pearson's low cross from the dead-ball line evaded the Villa back four and an unmarked Macari rifled the ball high into the goal for the winner. It had been another highly competitive 90 minutes on an energy-sapping surface. When, a week later, Old Trafford was announced as the venue for the League Cup Final's second replay, any fans who shared Saunders' superstitious nature might have felt slightly cursed: Villa hadn't won at the ground since 1954.

Now eighth in the table, a whole ten points behind leaders Liverpool, even with as many as five games in hand over some of the higher-placed teams, the League Cup was, realistically, Villa's best chance of delivering silverware. They had to wait a whole four weeks after the Hillsborough draw before the next opportunity to do so arrived. During that time, following wins over Sunderland and Middlesbrough and a goalless draw with Bristol City, Villa suffered a slip-up, 2-1 at Derby County. More significantly than its effect on Villa's title aspirations, the defeat, just four days before the second replay, resulted in even more players queuing up at the hospital casualty department.

On a heavily sanded, pitted pitch – 'full of bloody pot-holes' in Frank Carrodus's description – the Villa midfielder tore his knee ligaments, Andy Gray and Chris Nicholl both suffered nasty twists to their ankles, while John Gidman sustained a groin injury that left the full-back facing a fight against time to be fit for the cup game. 'I remember going to the hospital and I was pushing Andy along on a trolley,' Carrodus told *Villa Times*. 'We saw the specialist. He said, "Andy will be out for three weeks. Frank, you'll be out for the rest of the season." I was the one who should have been on the bloody trolley!'

The post-match verdict wasn't positive: Gray was definitely ruled out, Gidman rated extremely doubtful, while Nicholl would be available but only courtesy of a heavy bandage supporting his damaged ankle. 'Injuries had been that bad,' Carrodus said, 'Good Hope hospital phoned up and said, "Can we have our crutches back?" because they were short. We found 11 pairs of them.' To make matters worse on the day, one of the Derby goalscorers was Derek Hales, whose debut had denied the Villa fans any TV coverage of their Liverpool demolition.

'Pressure and the urgency to get results affect me,' Saunders confessed to *Shoot* magazine, 'but I have no fears.' As the second replay approached, the tensions were beginning to show. According to John Burridge, an uptight Villa manager was 'so desperate to get us into Europe', he kept telling his players that, unless they won something, they'd be regarded as failures. In his autobiography, Burridge complained, 'Whereas some managers are good at shouldering the pressure themselves and shielding their players so they don't feel edgy, Saunders never hesitated to share the pressure around.'

Everton, meanwhile, went to Old Trafford on a surge of renewed confidence. Though still only 14th in the league, Gordon Lee's side were FA Cup semi-finalists after a sixth-round triumph over Derby and in resurgent form, having lost just once in eight games, in five of which Latchford had scored. Saunders admitted that, for the first time in the three encounters, the Merseyside club were now favourites to win the trophy.

Saunders' anxieties weren't lessened any in the dressing room pre-match. John Gidman – with the aid of three painkilling injections – was starting, but those injections were only delivered at the 11th hour. David Targett, the Villa club doctor, was caught up in traffic on the way to Old Trafford, leaving 'both Saunders and Gidman going absolutely mental', according to Alex Cropley. When Targett eventually emerged – 'with the biggest needle you've ever seen', Chris Nicholl said – a naked Gidman, his legs held down on the physio table by his team-mates, was finally given his treatment with just ten minutes to spare before kick-off.

Thirty-eight minutes into the game, Everton fully justified the 'favourites' tag. Making the most of McNaught's headed knockdown from a free kick, the predatory Latchford was on the spot again to sidefoot home from close range. Ahead for the first time, the Toffees took their advantage into the break. It looked like being decisive. In the second half, a recharged Villa, though pushing Everton further and further back with a series of well-crafted moves, were repelled time and again by a resolute defence. There were less than ten minutes left when they got the leveller they deserved.

It was a goal that would in due course assume mythical proportions, not least because it arrived in so surprising a manner and from the most unlikely source. Picking up the ball out wide on Villa's right-hand flank, just over the halfway line, Chris Nicholl cut inside, skipped over Jim

Pearson's flailing tackle, then moved forward towards the centre of the pitch before unleashing a 35-yard left-foot pile-driver that swirled and dipped and flew past the despairing dive of keeper David Lawson. The Villa fans massed at the Scoreboard End exploded in both elation and disbelief. Guilty of the foul that led to the Everton goal, Nicholl had made amends in quite jaw-dropping style.

Barely 90 seconds later, Brian Little, showing persistence and strength, robbed Everton right-back Neil Robinson on the edge of the area and, despite being pushed wide, squeezed a low, angled cross-shot under Lawson's body and, after they had their noses in front for so long, Lee's men were rocking on their heels. They soon recovered their composure. A minute later, amid a goalmouth melee following a corner, the ball bounced down off the underside of Burridge's bar, centre-half Mick Lyons pounced to poke home and extra time was called for once again. Choruses of 'We shall not be moved' rang out from both ends.

On 104 minutes, Gidman was forced to admit defeat. Unbeknown to him at the time, the right-back's pelvis had snapped during the game but, so numbing were the injections in his groin, Gidman 'felt nothing'. In his place, on came substitute Gordon Smith. It was the Scot who played a crucial role in the moment that decided the match.

In the 119th minute, with the very last seconds ticking down, the fresh-limbed full-back, galloping down the right to meet a long ball out wide from Dennis Mortimer, sent in a low cross goalwards. Having deflected off the outstretched leg of Everton's Ronnie Goodlass, the ball passed in front of the wrong-footed Terry Darracott who, in an instant of fatal hesitation, let it run, not knowing that the still-sprightly Little was lurking, perfectly positioned, behind him. The Villa number eight danced into the six-yard box and tucked the ball neatly past Lawson. There was barely time for a restart before Gordon Kew blew his whistle. Minutes later, amid flashing camera lights and scenes of wild celebration, Chris Nicholl took the trophy from the Football League president Lord Westwood.

To a reporter before the game who'd asked, 'Who wants to win a League Cup in Manchester on a Wednesday night anyway?' Saunders, as deadpan as ever, had replied, 'Well, we do.' They'd done it with a performance so typical of a Saunders team. Despite their one-goal deficit, Villa, according to BBC commentator John Motson, had remained 'orderly and composed' and, even after Lyons' dispiriting late leveller, they'd stayed mentally and physically strong. 'Villa just prove again that they never, ever give up,' Motson said at the end of his commentary.

Saunders himself acknowledged it had been 'a heart-stopping affair'. The injured Frank Carrodus, watching alongside his manager, later remarked, 'The game was so thrilling, I don't think I could ever sit on the bench again.' But if Villa's boss was in danger of losing it backstage beforehand, he betrayed no emotion throughout the game. 'The only time he jumped up was when Brian Little scored our winner,' Andy Gray told *Shoot*. Flushed with the joys of victory afterwards, though, 'the boss celebrated in traditional style on the coach back to Birmingham,' said Gray, 'and had his share of champagne.'

'The night belonged to Saunders,' one fan later put it. 'He really was our king.' Another supporter simply said that 'the Villa fans' singing of "Saunders, Saunders, Saunders" echoing around Old Trafford, was a religious experience, something I'll never forget.' It had been, in Jeff Farmer's description, 'another 90 minutes of somersaulting fortunes' that 'came belatedly but gloriously to life' before Villa ultimately landed on their feet.

'The final act had to be breathtaking,' Farmer wrote. It was. And fitting, too, that Little, whose opener against Manchester City had uncorked the bottle, provided the closing sparkling moment. Little's dramatic match-winning goal was his tenth in the season's competition. 'It was beyond my dreams that such a thing should happen,' he said. 'As a kid, I used to think about scoring the goal that put my side through to a cup final at Wembley and then hitting the winner.' Albeit at Old Trafford, that childhood dream had been realised. Little may have profited from what John Motson called a 'terrible defensive disaster' but it took a player of his intelligence and guile to capitalise on the calamity. A home-made flag at Wembley had read, 'Little Goals Mean a Lot'. Never had it been more appropriate.

As in 1975 (and 1971, for that matter), it had taken a total of ten games before a titanic tussle was settled. The first triumph had seemed almost like a sprint compared to this marathon. Five hours to decide the semi-final. Five-and-a-half to settle the final.

Some of the Villa players had actually been upset by the prospect of penalties; they had it written into their contracts that a bonus be paid for a 'final' appearance. That included replays. 'We had three lots of bonus in the end,' recalled Chris Nicholl. 'Mr Ellis changed the wording after that season.' Nevertheless, they weren't complaining too much now that it was over. All in all, it had taken 16-and-a-half hours of combat. As Jeff Farmer noted, 'There can hardly have been a more arduous route towards Europe.'

Yet no one at Aston Villa doubted for one moment that it was worth every second.

Just as Villa's League Cup-winning run of two years earlier had begun with a victory over Everton, so their triumph of 1976/77 ended against the same opponents. By a quirk of fate, the victory was just three days short of the 80th anniversary of the game generally regarded as the finest cup final of the Victoria era when Villa, appearing in their fourth FA Cup Final, had beaten Everton at the Crystal Palace. The score? 3-2. By another quirk, the same day on 10 April 1897 also saw Villa crowned league champions and therefore winners of the 'Double'. As Villa celebrated their FA Cup win, 230 miles away at Gigg Lane, Bury were defeating Villa's nearest rivals in the table Derby County, so Villa claimed the league title, too. It is a distinction unlikely ever to be matched.

Their Old Trafford triumph also meant that, as well as entering the record books as the first team to win the League Cup on three occasions, Villa, having beaten Rotherham United 3-0 at Villa Park in the second leg of the inaugural final, now became the first club to win the trophy in three separate cities: Birmingham, London and Manchester. No other final of either the League Cup or FA Cup has been decided by three games and, given that finals are, if need be, concluded with penalties these days, it's a record that almost without doubt will remain unbroken.

The Entertainers

IF titles were given for entertainment alone, Villa might well have run away with it. 'Play with a smile on your face' was never a management trope Saunders was likely to employ, but to all who'd seen them perform it couldn't have been more apparent that the players were enjoying themselves.

Producing what author Simon Goodyear described in *Memories Made in Aston* as 'fast, high-octane, attacking football built on an athleticism that was years ahead of its time', Villa had shown that on their day they were a team capable of not just beating but annihilating the very best. Certainly on home soil, their crowd-pleasing displays had made them an almost irresistible force. At Villa Park alone, they smashed in 55 goals in 21 league games. In a third of those, four or more goals had been scored. A further 20 came in cup competitions. Not one Villa fan was demanding a refund on their season ticket.

Only Birmingham City came away from Villa Park with the full spoils. Disappointingly, Villa's neighbours were the one side to beat them twice, that league double completed in a tempestuous derby at St Andrew's when, first, Leighton Phillips, giving a V-sign to referee Peter Reeves after being penalised for a foul on Trevor Francis on the hour mark, then Blues defender Joe Gallagher, for an ugly stamp on Deehan, received their marching orders.

With a controversial encounter level at 1-1, it was perhaps inevitably settled by another dubious decision: Reeves awarding a hotly disputed penalty when Francis tumbled theatrically over Gray's leg. Francis duly dispatched the spot-kick winner to hoist the home side clear of the relegation area and earn some bitter post-match criticism from Saunders. 'Francis won the [*Evening*] *Mail*'s Player of the Year for *playing*, didn't he?' Saunders said. 'So why didn't he play tonight instead of conning the referee?'

Match official Reeves didn't escape Saunders' vitriol, either. Forgetting the fact that both sides were down to ten men, Saunders added, 'When the penalty was awarded against us, the referee had 22 players laughing at him. If Brian Little got that kind of protection from referees, he would be one of the best players in the world.'

That defeat was just one of a number in which Villa surrendered points against lower-order teams they possibly should have beaten. In the end, it proved decisive.

The New Year opened as the old one had concluded, with a letdown: a 2-0 loss at Old Trafford to a pair of Pearson goals leaving Villa nine points behind leaders Liverpool. Even at that stage, it was a too-big gap to make up. After their League Cup triumph, they were squeezing in games left, right and centre to fulfil their league programme.

April alone saw Villa play nine matches. Buoyed by their cup success, they enjoyed three wins on the bounce – a 3-2 victory at Coventry City, notable for Cowans' delightful winner after Ian Wallace had scored twice for the home side, followed by two narrow wins at Villa Park, over Tottenham and Norwich. But two defeats in five days in north London – relegation-bound Spurs exacting swift revenge with a 3-1 win, before Arsenal, too, gained some retribution for their 5-1 hammering, running out convincing 3-0 winners at Highbury – left Villa sitting in fifth and any lingering title aspirations all but quashed.

In May, a further seven league matches were played in 19 days. Points were dropped in home draws with Manchester City and QPR. Villa also went down 3-2 at Newcastle, Brian Little's brace against his native north-easterners being matched by the home side's Paul Cannell before Graham Oates sealed the victory for the Geordies. Narrow home wins – 2-1 over Leeds and 1-0 versus Stoke (Andy Gray's penalty consigning the visitors to the drop) – exemplified Villa's undoubted resilience, but the early season canter had now slowed to a trot as they approached the season's finishing tape.

When their campaign was finally rounded off on Monday 23 May, nine days after Liverpool were confirmed champions for the second season running following a 0-0 draw with West Ham United, Villa finished fourth in the table on 51 points, six behind Paisley's title-winners. It represented their highest league placing since 1933 yet there was still a nagging feeling that it might have been even better.

'The sign of success in football,' Saunders told *Shoot* magazine, 'is to have too many fixtures.' Nonetheless, their cluttered programme exacted a heavy price. For all Saunders' 'grinding insistence on the merits of physical fitness' (as journalist Alan Dunn put it), the bruising demands of top-flight football on a small pool of players proved too much.

Andy Gray, who'd opened the campaign exactly ten months earlier with a brace against West Ham, ended it by going one better. Gray's hat-trick in a 4-0 win against West Brom left the Scot with 25 league goals and sharing the Golden Boot as top scorer in England with Arsenal's Malcolm Macdonald. Forced to withdraw on the night versus the Baggies, replaced by 17-year-old striker Ivor Linton after suffering a bad ankle injury, Gray left the field to tumultuous applause. It was symptomatic of the striker's second half of the season.

Gray was modest when describing his approach to football, 'I just attack the ball, run at defences and chase everything.' The key, he said, was 'never give a centre-half a minute during a game and, sooner or later, the chances will come'. But the chances did stop coming so often. Gray's disregard for danger in his desire for goals exacted a toll. Niggling injuries and a lean scoring spell meant that only seven of Gray's league goals came from January onwards.

Despite Gray's unprecedented PFA awards, it was Dennis Mortimer who got the vote as the supporters' club Player of the Year, the Terrace Trophy presented to him by Saunders at Penns Hall Hotel. Mortimer's biggest champion was unquestionably his manager, Saunders constantly alerting the football world to take note of the Liverpudlian link-man. Both the anchor that steadied the ship and the engine that drove it forward, Mortimer was an inspirational presence in the centre of the park. It was no secret that Saunders felt strongly that the midfielder deserved an international opportunity.

Instead, it was John Gidman who got the call to the bigger stage, Don Revie rewarding the full-back's form with his England debut in the 5-0 win at Wembley in a World Cup qualifier against Luxembourg on 30 March. In what proved to be Revie's last World Cup match in charge, Gidman gave such a good account of himself – already heavily involved in the first goal, his natural, attacking game was given freer rein the more the game progressed – that Revie described the right-back's performance as 'the best England debut since Duncan Edwards'. However, as with the firework accident in 1974, injury was to halt his international career in its tracks. The groin troubles he suffered at the Baseball Ground ten days later all but ended Gidman's campaign. After the second replay at Old Trafford, he didn't play again for Villa that season.

In 56 games, all told, Villa had netted 104 times. Play to your strengths and don't let anyone exploit your weaknesses was Bob Paisley's modus operandi. With ever-mobile target men in Gray, Deehan and Little, Saunders – 'a very clever, intelligent manager', John Deehan says – simply had his side utilising their assets as best as possible. A former forward himself, Saunders talked Deehan's language and taught the youngster about the runs he needed to make as well as an understanding of what was going on in defenders' and goalkeepers' brains. 'He also explained how individuals on the pitch could be influenced by the movement of players in their immediate vicinity,' Deehan says.

Attacks were strategically worked out, with the Villa frontmen making runs to create space, distract the opposition keeper or block his line of vision, ultimately enhancing a team-mate's chances of scoring if they were timed correctly. 'We all understood the system so well,' Deehan says. 'That is why we scored so many great goals.'

Training was almost wholly geared towards winning the ball and countering. 'Ron's instructions were, on the whole, straightforward,' says Gordon Smith. 'Do not take chances at the back, and get the ball forward early.' It wasn't up-and-under football in any way, but Saunders' desire to hurt the opposition by getting the ball hurriedly into their box resulted, Alex Cropley wrote in *Crops*, in Villa 'often missing out the midfield completely'. Smith agrees. 'As a full-back, I was encouraged to get forward as much as possible and I liked this,' he says. 'However, I always felt we could and should have built the play more, especially with the quality we had in midfield.'

Saunders wasn't a blackboard manager. 'Players take the field and they play by instinct,' he told *Shoot*. 'They can either play or they can't play. It's up to the manager and coaches to make it simpler for them and to encourage them to perform and to improve their technique and ability.' In John Burridge's view, Saunders 'was able to get successful results out of the team mainly by signing skilful players and then training them hard, to the point where they were fitter than any other club in the league.' Training, Burridge wrote in *Budgie*, 'was unbelievably hard', though 'the results on the pitch justified his methods'. John Deehan, too, saw only the positive effects. 'No other side would match us on the field for fitness,' he says. 'Ron was a big believer in weight training which allowed me, Andy and Brian to soar above our opponents when crosses were raining in to our opponents' 18-yard box.'

'Young, keen, and eager to learn,' according to Cropley, the Villa players were also, on occasions, more than willing to educate themselves. In full-scale practice matches against the reserves 'instead of taking things easy as some sides might do, we would try out different things that could be used in games'. This natural desire to improve paid off and, in Cropley's view, 'went some way in helping to mould us into a top-class side'.

As good as they'd been, Saunders wasn't satisfied. 'I still believe we are two or three years away from becoming a top side,' he said. The teams that clicked most smoothly were the ones who'd grown used to success. Like Liverpool. It was a habit he wanted Villa to develop. Despite their Villa Park pummelling, the Anfield club still ended up with the best defensive record in the division on the way to becoming the first to claim ten league championships.

Denied the domestic 'Double' in the FA Cup Final by Manchester United, four days after that Wembley defeat, Liverpool became only the second English club to win the European Cup, beating Borussia Mönchengladbach 3-1 in Rome's Olympic Stadium. 'When you're strong, you make yourself stronger,' was Shankly's adage. Now, combining the aggression and work-rate of British football with the controlled passing game of the continentals, Liverpool, in England and Europe, were peerless.

Saunders began reshaping again. Although he remained at Villa Park for another year before moving to Lincoln City in April 1978, David Hughes' fleeting career in the first team was over. Charlie Young, after only 11 appearances, had played his last Villa game. Mike Buttress was to start only once more for the club. Keith Masefield, with just one start all season in the right-back berth at Spurs, was another who would soon be bidding adieu.

The match at White Hart Lane also proved to be Ray Graydon's swansong. The winger, having returned for four games in the spring, was clearly still suffering and, in Saunders' view, not as effective as he'd once been. After interesting Leicester, Graydon decided Coventry City would be his next destination and one of Villa's most important players of recent years was gone. An even more surprising name was next through the exit door.

Convinced by the performances of Everton's Ken McNaught in the trio of League Cup Final encounters, Saunders decided that the strapping young central defender was the man he wanted to stabilise Villa's backline. While Andy Gray would later claim in his book that, in the Wembley game, McNaught 'had an easier afternoon than he might have expected. If I'd been 100 per cent fit I don't think he'd have been so comfortable,' Saunders was more than impressed by how the number five had handled himself. He asked Gordon Lee about the young Scot's availability.

McNaught, who'd joined the Goodison Park club as a junior in 1971 the season after their championship win, had made his first team debut in the FA Cup against Altrincham on 4 January 1975 and been a regular in the Everton side ever since. The only ever-present in 1976/77, he'd even been handed the captain's armband for Everton's final fixture. But Lee, hoping to buy QPR winger Dave Thomas and Blackpool keeper George Wood, needed to generate funds.

Despite McNaught's desire to stay – he'd only got married in 1975 and just bought a new property – Lee was willing to sacrifice the Kirkcaldy-born youngster.

After initial problems over McNaught's personal demands threatened to scupper a move, an undeterred Saunders doggedly pursued his interest and the defender, realising he'd be going to a club who really wanted him, flew back from Everton's pre-season tour of Germany to complete the deal. On 28 July, the son of Willie McNaught, once a renowned defender for Glasgow Rangers, signed for £200,000.

It was another new transfer record for Villa. It was also a fee that left Saunders with little alternative. Money was tight, so someone would have to be sold. The player the club 'couldn't afford to keep', Saunders wrote in *Ron Saunders' Aston Villa Scrapbook*, was Chris Nicholl. Luckily, Saunders said, Southampton boss Lawrie McMenemy, very keen on the Northern Ireland stopper, 'phoned to ask about his chances of signing Chris, so a joint deal was set up and everyone was happy'.

Whether *everyone* was happy was questionable. The Villa skipper had little inkling that he was about to be jettisoned. Nicholl had enjoyed his first full season as captain, even signing off with the opening goal in the final game 4-0 drubbing of West Brom. Upon his move from Luton, Nicholl had said, 'My dad's team was always Villa so, as soon as I knew I had a chance to sign for them that was it, I was going to sign.' As Villa statistician Frank Holt put it, the already-towering centre-half 'certainly appeared to grow six inches in his Villa kit'. Nicholl was, according to Andy Gray, a 'first-class captain' who 'knew how to wind me up and get the most out of me by geeing me up on the field'.

His transfer came as a total surprise to his team-mates, too. They only became aware of Nicholl's imminent departure when McMenemy appeared one day at the hotel where they were staying during an end-of-season Marbella trip. Nicholl informed his friend Leighton Phillips that McMenemy had made a bid and Saunders had told Nicholl he could leave. The dependable duo of Nicholl and Phillips – 'an ideal back four pairing' in Alex Cropley's view – was no more.

Whether Nicholl was deemed surplus to requirements purely because Saunders had already pencilled in McNaught as a replacement was also open to debate. Nicholl, with his contract up, had been in talks with Saunders about a new one and approached the Villa manager about a possible pay rise. Despite his captain's pleas, Saunders refused. At 22, McNaught had eight years on Nicholl. Saunders might well have valued potential over experience.

Brian Little had a different theory; the Villa side was, what Little called, 'a terrific team to play in, because we had a few characters'. Strong among them was Nicholl. Not only was the modest, much-liked Nicholl a stalwart presence on the field, he was an influential figure in the dressing room. As with Charlie Aitken before him, Little believed that Saunders was perhaps threatened by that growing influence. In Little's opinion, Saunders liked to have players for a couple of years and then 'they were either played out or they had found him out'.

Andy Gray was another who felt that Saunders always preferred younger, more naïve players of whom he could be in charge and dominate. Given that Saunders had stated at the season's end, 'We do not have enough senior or experienced players,' the release of the 30-year-old Nicholl gave more than a little weight to that argument. Nicholl himself later joked that the reason he was sold was: he beat Saunders at golf! 'I used to play golf against Ron and he would beat me every time,' said Nicholl. 'Then I beat him once – and he sold me two weeks later.' Whatever the motive, Nicholl undoubtedly left Aston Villa against his wishes, joining the Second Division Saints for a reported fee of £90,000. Ironically, one of Nicholl's new team-mates on the south coast was Alan Ball, whose father, Alan Ball Snr, then manager of Halifax, had given Nicholl his chance in league football

More changes weren't long in coming. In early August, Villa played in a four-team pre-season tournament hosted by Spanish club Athletic Bilbao. A 2-0 defeat to Bilbao preceded another loss, 4-3 to an RSC Anderlecht side containing Dutch stars Rensenbrink and Haan, though Villa thrilled the home crowd by coming back from 4-1 down and threatening to draw level. The day after the final – Bilbao beating Dynamo Kiev 1-0 – Pat Jennings joined Arsenal in a shock move from their north London neighbours Tottenham, newly relegated to the Second Division. With Spurs boss Keith Burkinshaw eager to give an opportunity to Jennings' long-time understudy Barry Daines, the Northern Irish keeper was surprisingly let go, his one-time international colleague and former manager Terry Neill snapping up the 32-year-old for a bargain £40,000.

Now, with Neill seeing Jennings as 'the man who could give stability to our defence', Jimmy Rimmer, an Arsenal regular for three-and-a-half years after replacing the retired Bob Wilson, was free to leave. The previous summer Rimmer had won his first (and what would be his only) England cap, playing the initial 45 minutes in a 3-2 friendly victory over Italy in New York. Unfortunately for Rimmer, he conceded twice during that time and was substituted at half-time before England recovered to win. But, despite winning Arsenal's Player of the Year award in 1976, Rimmer was unsettled at Highbury. In January, he'd told the club he wanted a transfer. Neill informed him he wouldn't be released until a 'suitable replacement is found'. Jennings was that replacement.

With Rimmer's time with the Gunners up, Saunders acted promptly. Just three hours after Jennings joined, Rimmer was on his way to Villa Park. Only a year previously, Rimmer and Alex Cropley had been living in London, just two doors apart. Saunders had sought Cropley's verdict on his old team-mate; in the Scottish midfielder's view, Rimmer was an excellent keeper. It confirmed what Saunders already thought. 'What do I look for in a good player?' Saunders said in an interview with *Shoot*. 'Basically, someone who will do a job for me better than that person I have playing in that particular position.' Rimmer, Saunders believed, was better than what he already had. He signed the Southport-born number one for £70,000.

As expected, Rimmer's arrival threw into immediate doubt the future of John Burridge. In December 1976, after being replaced by Jake Findlay for seven games, a disgruntled Burridge – 'unhappy at being in the reserves and [who] feels he will have a better chance of first team football at another club', Saunders told the *Daily Mirror*'s Dave Horridge – submitted a transfer request, which was granted by the Villa board. No move was forthcoming. Burridge, fired with a warning shot, responded and subsequently won back his place, the Perthshire-born Findlay relegated to the reserves again. After amassing only 14 appearances in over three-and-a-half years since his debut against Sunderland in April 1974, Findlay would eventually leave for Luton Town in November 1978.

Yet Saunders still wasn't convinced. Essential to the last line of defence, he believed, was a commanding figure, someone who would 'come out and get 'em in the air'. Although a good shot-stopper, Burridge, Saunders later reflected, 'Tended to stay on his line.' It left the Villa back four vulnerable. At Manchester United on New Year's Day, both the home side's goals resulted from their clever preparation, knowing that Burridge struggled with crosses. Rimmer, by contrast, was matchless when it came to bossing the six-yard area. His fine positional sense, agility and distribution made him one of the most proficient keepers in the business.

From an increasingly demanding Saunders, Burridge felt he was expected to perform like a veteran but knew that, still in his early 20s, he was a long way off reaching his peak. He was struggling to cope. On the training ground Saunders liked to join in with the crossing and volleying, often working with Andy Gray as a pair, one on the near post, one on the back. 'Whenever he scored a good goal, maybe one he'd hit on the volley from seven or eight yards,' wrote Burridge in *Budgie*, 'he would be right over me and in my face shouting "You should have saved that!"' It affected the young keeper's confidence. Burridge needed cosseting and praise, not critiquing at every opportunity. Finding Saunders unapproachable and difficult to get on with, Burridge's desire to escape from his harmful attentions only grew.

Burridge's own personality and that of Saunders – 'I had one, he didn't,' Burridge said – were just too dissimilar for the pair ever to get on. The keeper's matchday eccentricities – the handstands and somersaults, the launching himself full-length to tip an imaginary shot over the bar – were lapped up by the Villa Park audience but never going to get applause from Saunders. 'Any showmanship seemed to make Ron bristle,' Burridge said.

What the keeper considered as harmless antics intended to lift his team-mates' spirits, the manager judged simply as juvenile behaviour. As if to rub Burridge's nose in it, Saunders paraded Rimmer at the training ground and introduced him to his new team-mates. The notoriously short-fused Burridge, made to play as a forward during a practice drill, with Rimmer taking his place between the sticks, barged into Rimmer with full force, kneeing him and sending him to the floor. It was nothing personal against the new signing, whom Burridge liked, merely a release of all of his pent-up frustration towards the manager. When Burridge tried it again, Saunders had seen enough, and told Burridge to 'get the f**k off the training ground'.

The goalkeeper would enrage the Villa boss even further during the 1977/78 season. Rather than listen to the team-talk before a European tie, Burridge, with Rimmer starting, wandered off elsewhere. 'Saunders was going loopy in the dressing room, wondering where Burridge was,' Brian Little recalled. 'We found him out on the pitch doing handstands and press-ups and showing off to the crowd.'

An episode on a plane returning from another European game almost certainly sealed the goalkeeper's fate at Villa Park. Andy Gray recalled that, for all the rugged public image that Saunders cultivated, 'he wasn't quite so hard when it came to aeroplanes'. Saunders, in spite of efforts to hide it, had a fear of flying. 'He used to insist on taking the middle seat, with the trainer Roy MacLaren beside,' wrote Burridge.

A practical joker like Burridge couldn't resist the opportunity to make the most of this apparent chink in Saunders' armour. Coming in to land at Birmingham, the keeper sneaked up behind the Villa boss, blew up a sick bag and then, just as the landing gear came down, burst it. 'When he heard the bang Saunders jumped so high he almost smacked his head on the luggage rack,' Gray tells the story in *Gray Matters*. 'He was not amused.' Neither was MacLaren who duly delivered a punch to the keeper's face. 'It was my little way of getting him [Saunders] back,' wrote Burridge of the incident.

Burridge, whom Saunders had already told to 'grow up' after another previous incident, knew his time was up. When the two had it out in Saunders' office one day – Burridge confronting the manager over his treatment of him – Saunders called Burridge 'a pussy'. Relations between them were at breaking point. Burridge submitted another transfer request, which Saunders had no hesitation in accepting. In March 1978, after a short, six-game loan spell at Fourth Division Southend United, while Rimmer established himself at Villa, Burridge became the second 'Budgie' (after ex-England centre-forward Johnny Byrne) to land at Selhurst Park, signing for Terry Venables' exciting young Second Division Crystal Palace side.

A manager's job, Saunders said, is 'to field the best possible team'. He was steadily furthering his options. Another goalkeeper, Nigel Spink, arrived from non-league Chelmsford City for £6,000. In June, John Gregory, able to play in defence or midfield, joined Villa for £40,000 after five years, including two re-election seasons, and 187 league appearances for Northampton Town. Having made his debut for the Cobblers in 1972, Scunthorpe-born Gregory's ability to fill in all over the pitch – he played right-back, centre-back and in central midfield – had put him on the radar of Liverpool scout Geoff Twentyman. Although it was Gregory's team-mate Phil Neal who the Merseysiders plumped for – Neal becoming Bob Paisley's first capture as Liverpool manager – it inspired Gregory to work harder in the hope of securing a similar move.

But, two years later, with little interest apparent from any top club, Gregory contemplated quitting the professional game altogether, thinking instead of playing non-league football and finding employment in a local boot factory. But having been watched several times by director Eric Houghton out on scouting duties, Gregory was spared that alternative fate now that Villa had taken the plunge.

The biggest transfer story that summer also centred on Anfield. On 10 August, Celtic's talismanic striker Kenny Dalglish was signed by Paisley as a direct replacement for the Hamburg-bound Kevin Keegan. Dalglish had been Scotland's highest-paid player but was determined to try his hand south of the border. His £440,000 departure from the Glaswegian giants – thus becoming the most expensive player to be signed by a British club – ignited a good deal of debate, and no little fear, among Scottish football writers who seriously questioned where the game in Scotland was now heading if one of its leading clubs, Celtic, was unable to keep hold of their captain as soon as an English club waved their wallet. It was, according to the *Glasgow Herald*'s Jim Reynolds, 'a dangerous and maybe disastrous turn' from which the game in Scotland might never recover.

The perceived 'brain-drain' – a £3m exodus in the past five years – had seen the likes of Alan Hansen (Partick Thistle to Liverpool), Lou Macari (Celtic to Manchester United) and Arthur Graham (Aberdeen to Leeds United), as well as many others, leave Scottish football for the top English sides, sparking a worry that 'we are little more than a nursery for the wealthy clubs down south'. Villa, in purchasing Gray and Smith, had, of course, themselves contributed. Saunders, as one *Shoot* writer put it, clearly liked 'a streak of tartan' in his line-up.

Most recently, in May, he'd added another Scot to the payroll, signing Dunfermline Athletic's 20-year-old Allan Evans. The 6ft 4in Evans had first appeared for the Scottish club against Glasgow Rangers aged only 16, enjoying an unforgettable baptism when, just prior to the interval, a tackle resulted in Evans breaking his leg. In his career with the part-timers, he'd flitted between defence and attack. But it was up front that Evans was playing when both Villa and Leeds United, there to scout Evans' team-mate, goalkeeper Hugh Whyte, saw the youngster bag a 15-minute hat-trick against Stranraer and were impressed.

Offered trials at, first, Villa and, then, Elland Road the week after – 'I was a big Leeds fan at the time,' Evans said, 'because they had so many Scotsmen in the side – Bremner, Lorimer, the Grays and Jordan' – Evans reported at Villa Park on the Tuesday and by the weekend had become Saunders' latest recruit. Even while he'd found the trial 'physically demanding', Evans had done enough to warrant a contract offer. He joined Villa there and then. 'I made the decision to say "yes" to Villa and forget about Leeds,' Evans said.

Saunders' 11 Bell's Scotch Whisky Manager of the Month awards – seven since he came to Villa – were more than any other manager. What was his secret? 'I'm just lucky,' he joked to *Shoot* magazine. He now had on his hands, the *Daily Mail*'s Jeff Powell wrote, 'a young Villa team who have it in them to become the most exciting in the land'. The average age of the squad was under 24. Saunders wasn't overly concerned with them being exciting. 'If, as well as being successful, you can play attractive, open football, then so much the better,' he said. But winning came first. There'd be four competitions in the new campaign 'and our aim is to win each of them', he said. Unrealistic, yes, 'but the impossible happens now and again, doesn't it?'

Their most cherished ambition remained the league title. That Aston Villa were now considered a force to be reckoned with was emphatically acknowledged by the bookmakers; the odds against the club claiming the championship were slashed to 9/1. The previous season, they'd started as 100/1 rank outsiders. Whether Villa, now one of eight Midlands sides in the top flight, had a cogent case as contenders remained to be seen. The team was capable enough, Saunders was certain, but the squad wasn't. Having 18 to 20 players of equal quality was still his target. The signs all pointed to a golden era for the club. They'd already made huge strides, but crossing the threshold required stronger legs altogether. There was still an extremely long way to go.

The Not-So-Great Pretenders

THE way ahead, Saunders warned, was going to be difficult. Villa, he told all those at the club's AGM, was now the team everyone wanted to beat but, with the same dedication towards success from all the staff together with 'the tremendous support we get from our fans', they could well progress much further. Record season ticket sales reflected huge optimism among supporters. When Villa, even with Gidman and Gray absent, left Loftus Road with a 2-1 opening day victory, it appeared quite justifiable. Saunders remained cautious. It was, he reiterated in the matchday programme for Villa's first home fixture against Manchester City, 'going to be doubly hard' to exceed or even match the achievements of the previous 12 months.

He was right. By the following Saturday, both before their own supporters, Villa had lost their next two games. On the Wednesday night, Dennis Tueart's hat-trick – one of three the England frontman would notch up before January – gave Tony Book's City, the previous season's runners-up, a 4-1 win. Three days later, after Andy Gray's first of the season was trumped by a double from Everton's Duncan McKenzie, Villa suffered a second successive loss at Villa Park. Within the opening week, the fortress had already been sacked more than in the entire 1976/77 campaign.

Heady with hopefulness, the watching Villa faithful were forced to sober up very swiftly. To make matters worse, their mood already grim amid their midweek humbling, some in the Holte End focussed more attention on destroying a fence erected down the centre of the terrace, to segregate home and away fans, than following the action on the field. Their frustrations would only increase as the season progressed.

Bearing the early brunt of them was Ken McNaught. In neither of the two defeats, Saunders admitted, had Villa done themselves justice. While Rimmer and Gregory also took time to settle, it was McNaught who soon became the target for the boo-boys, especially after a particularly difficult baptism against his former club. Bedding in alongside new club captain Leighton Phillips required McNaught to completely readjust his game. Used to a partnership with a similar-style stopper in Mike Lyons, in which they'd each attack the ball only on their own designated side, the 6ft 2in Scot was now charged with fighting all the aerial battles, with Phillips mopping up behind in a sweeper role. An understanding between the two developed slowly.

The form of Villa, in general, was indifferent. Even when they gained their first home points in early September – Alex Cropley scoring late in the game after Gray sent the ex-Gunner through to edge Arsenal 1-0 – Saunders described it as 'our worst performance for two years', with an especially acerbic Villa boss complaining of his 'awful' team 'not even doing the basic things right'. In the next match, Villa travelled to the City Ground. In sharp contrast to their own faltering start, newly promoted Forest had set out on their Division One campaign winning four of their first five with a swagger that mirrored their manager, a certain Brian Clough, who'd replaced Allan Brown in early January 1975.

Pre-match, Peter Taylor, reunited with his partner after a two-year separation, admitted to the *Villa Times* journalist Graham Clark that he and Clough 'watched Villa on a number of occasions last season and each time we did we were impressed and, more importantly, we learned a lot'. Both Clough and he, Taylor said, 'have great admiration for the job Ron Saunders has done and the team he has built. In fact, we use the same principles of teamwork and hard work here at Forest.' As the basis for attacking, attractive football the Clough/Taylor philosophy had already worked wonderfully and, despite a 3-0 setback at Highbury, Taylor was adamant, 'That's the way we'll be playing all the time. To be honest, we don't know of any other way.'

Yet, while happy with their forward line, the Forest management team wasn't so enamoured with the rearguard. In the week prior to the Villa clash, Forest snapped up England goalkeeper Peter Shilton from relegated Stoke City for £250,000. Making his debut against Villa, the 27-year-old Shilton had little to do as goals from John Robertson and Tony Woodcock left the visitors on the end of a 2-0 reversal and Saunders expressing his frustration that his side were 'unable, once more, to produce our true form'.

Further misfortune soon followed. During the game, John Robson had left the field complaining of dizziness. In time, his condition grew steadily worse – Robson, unable to walk, was forced to sleep downstairs at his home – but defied doctors' diagnosis. The following March, a story in the *Evening Mail* would claim that Robson's career was under threat due to acute vertigo. The reality of Robson's illness, however, was far more serious. Two months earlier, in January 1978, he had been diagnosed as suffering from the early stages of multiple sclerosis and, though it would be another eight months before he revealed to the football world the full extent of his illness, the player knew his career was at an end.

It was too early to start ringing any alarm bells. Before a Friday night home game with Wolves, Saunders wrote in the programme of his hope that the long round of derby encounters to come would provide an additional edge to Villa's game and 'produce an extra incentive to bring our performances up to the standards which we expect'. Villa beat Sammy Chung's side 2-0. It was a sign of better things to come. After a 1-0 home defeat to Birmingham City – ex-Ipswich striker Keith Bertschin netting with a free header from a Francis cross – Villa embarked on a six-game unbeaten run that culminated in a memorable afternoon on Merseyside.

After Villa's previous nine visits to Anfield had yielded heavy defeats including 6-1, 5-1, 5-2, 4-0 scorelines and two 3-0s, few Villa supporters among the 50,436 crowd can have expected anything else but the reigning champions meting out more of the same punishment. But on 5 November, with nationwide power cuts forcing most matches to kick off at least 30 minutes early to avoid the risk of a blackout, Andy Gray provided all the fireworks, scoring both in a 2-1 victory as Villa ended Liverpool's proud home record of 38 consecutive unbeaten games.

Gray's opener four minutes before half-time, the striker tucking home the rebound after Clemence pushed Frank Carrodus's shot on to a post, gave Villa a worthy lead and was the first goal Liverpool had conceded at Anfield all season. Even after Carrodus inadvertently turned the ball into his own net to gift the Reds a 64th-minute equaliser, Villa's composure remained unshaken. Eight minutes later, Gray chested down McNaught's long free kick into the box and blasted past Clemence to earn them a famous win.

At the final whistle, the Liverpool crowd gave the visitors a standing ovation and, despite Bob Paisley's somewhat sour post-match claim that Villa had actually played better at Anfield the previous season when they lost 3-0, for Saunders, born on 6 November 1932 in Birkenhead – 'the posh side of Liverpool', he called it – it was a perfect early birthday present. 'Not only did we beat them,' he enthused, 'but we thoroughly deserved to beat them.'

Villa's performance, reported the *Birmingham Mail*, 'established them firmly as a team who are only one or two players away from being championship material'. From Rimmer, in thou-shalt-not-pass mode in goal, to Brian Little, back to his audacious best after an ankle injury had ended a run of 67 consecutive appearances, all 11 players had displayed the hallmarks of a Saunders side at its peak. 'They have skill in all departments plus work-rate, organisation and team spirit,' wrote the *Mail*'s correspondent. Leighton Phillips, who'd marked Kenny Dalglish virtually out of the game, spoke of how they were 'a more professional side now'.

Their shortcomings, however, were much the same. A week after their day to remember, Villa lost at home to Middlesbrough, the visitors' pint-sized 19-year-old striker Stan Cummins – a player Jack Charlton believed would be 'the first million-pound footballer in Britain' – grabbing the only goal of a wholly forgettable encounter. By the time West Brom made the four-mile trip to Villa Park on 10 December, Villa had failed to find the net in three consecutive matches and were looking enviously upwards from 11th spot at a Baggies side sitting in an impressive third just behind Everton and leaders Forest.

Albion, now under the guidance of Ronnie Allen, infamous in the eyes of all Villa followers for scoring the goal in 1959 that consigned the Villans to a bout of Second Division football, had continued building on the foundations laid by previous boss Johnny Giles. Yet, unpredictable as ever, Villa produced a battling performance to emerge 3-0 victors, goals by Cowans, Gray and, direct from a free kick, John Gidman earning a notable win. Any gloss, however, was completely tarnished by an injury to Alex Cropley that left the wiry midfielder with the third fracture of his career and nursing a broken leg that would keep him out of action for at least the remainder of the season.

In a decidedly passionate match in which Ken McNaught had already gone off injured, Albion – Villa's 'oldest and most respected rivals' in historian Peter Morris's description – had shown anything but respect for the opposition. Just before half-time, with both players running at full pelt from opposite directions about ten yards apart, Cropley went into a tackle with Albion's Scottish striker Ally Brown. 'I just managed to nick the ball away from Brown,' Cropley wrote in his autobiography, 'when with all my weight on my left leg he took me, ball, the lot, sending me flying through the air.'

The sound of the break was unmistakable – 'like the gunshot that starts a race', *The Observer*'s Tim Adams later recalled – and, even if Cropley was in so much instant pain he was unaware of it, the reality soon became clear. With his team-mates enraged – Andy Gray taking matters and the Albion player's neck into his own hands – and the home supporters baying for blood on the terraces, Cropley was stretchered off, rushed to Good Hope hospital and operated on immediately. Both the tibia and fibula in his right leg were snapped and the twice-capped midfielder, tipped by many to make the Scottish squad for the following year's World Cup finals, was left facing a lengthy road to recovery.

For Saunders, a dull, grey Birmingham afternoon had grown into an even darker day. Later that evening, the Villa manager went to visit the still-groggy player in his hospital bed but only, according to Cropley, 'to collect my jersey'. Although feeling at the time that Brown had 'done me', the 26-year-old watched the highlights of the win on TV and was willing to believe the forward, whom Cropley had known since his school days in Scotland, had merely mistimed his tackle. *Match of the Day*'s Jimmy Hill attributed much of the blame to referee Jim Bent for not imposing sufficient authority and stamping down earlier on the West Brom players who, from the outset, went out, according to Leon Hickman's *Evening Mail* report, with 'malice as the motive' and clearly seemed more set on stopping Villa playing than winning the match.

Accidental or not, the prognosis was bleak: it would be several months before Cropley returned and Villa Park once more rang to the sound of the fans' tribute song, 'Five foot eight, not much weight, Alex Cropley's f**king great, la la la la la la la la la la la.'

Typically, a week after Cropley's leg break, their burgeoning bogey side Middlesbrough completed the double over Villa, Graeme Hedley popping in the game's only goal just a few minutes after John Gidman was ordered off for a foul after an earlier caution. Heading into the festive period, Villa were a whole 11 points behind Forest, Clough's side widening the gap at the top with a 4-0 hammering of Manchester United at Old Trafford and an irrepressible exhibition that *Match of the Day*'s Barry Davies called 'the best display I have had the privilege of seeing this season'. While Forest looked on course for an extraordinary success – at the end of 1976/77 they'd barely scraped the last promotion spot – Villa continued to be blighted by inconsistency.

A home draw with Coventry followed by a 3-0 win at Derby did nothing to alter that pattern. Plagued by a chain of injuries to first-teamers that had hampered any hopes he had of fielding a settled line-up,

Saunders was forced into one reshuffle after another. Such was the spread of casualties, even Villa's non-playing staff weren't immune; just before Christmas, physio Peter Downs entered hospital to undergo a cartilage operation. When the year ended on another low – Manchester City with a 2-0 win at Maine Road becoming a second side to beat Villa twice – Villa were positioned in mid-table. The lofty pre-season aspirations now appeared outrageously over-ambitious.

The New Year brought no relief to Saunders' headaches. Having surrendered their hold on the League Cup at the end of November in a 4-2 defeat at Forest – the home side going four up in less than half an hour before Carrodus and Little replied – Villa's FA Cup hopes were instantly put to bed in another hefty defeat, this time at Goodison Park. Goals from Everton's Andy King, Trevor Ross (penalty), McKenzie and Latchford saw Villa unceremoniously dumped out of the competition 4-1, their disastrous afternoon completed when Leighton Phillips – already booked for disputing the penalty decision against John Gregory – was dismissed for making a two-fingered gesture at his fellow Welshman, referee Clive Thomas. Andy Gray netted Villa's lone reply against the Merseyside club but a week later, as a single King strike saw Villa go down again at Goodison Park in the league, the Scottish striker suffered knee ligament damage, limped out of the ground on crutches and an already stretched squad was strained even thinner.

After failed advances for Luton Town's full-back Steve Buckley, brother of Walsall striker Alan – the defender opting for a £163,000 move to Derby instead – Saunders' endeavours to secure new players were at last rewarded towards the end of January. Gary Shelton, an attacking midfielder with Walsall, the club he'd joined straight from school, was first to arrive. Despite having played only a handful of first team games for the Saddlers, the 19-year-old had already been recommended to Saunders by his scouts as 'the most promising youngster in the country'. It persuaded the Villa boss to snap up the Nottingham-born player as quickly as possible. A week later, Newcastle United's Tommy Craig joined him.

With the whiff of relegation hanging heavily in the air over St James' Park – in mid-October, bottom-of-the-table United lost a club record tenth consecutive league match – Craig had been hankering for a move away from the struggling Geordie outfit. Just after Christmas, Bill McGarry, appointed as Newcastle manager after Gordon Lee's replacement Richard Dinnis's brief, unsuccessful reign, had invested £250,000 in strikers Mark McGhee from Morton and Clydebank's Mike Larnach. Needing to balance the books, McGarry was willing to let Craig go.

The red-haired midfielder had actually twice spurned opportunities to wear the claret and blue of Villa. Nine years earlier, Tommy Docherty had tried to sign him from Aberdeen, Craig's hometown club, while Saunders himself had made a previous bid for his services when Villa were still in the Second Division. On both occasions Craig had chosen to join clubs in higher divisions: Sheffield Wednesday first tempting him (when still a teen) in a £100,000 deal, before Craig departed Hillsborough to join the North Tyneside club. Craig had been in the Wednesday side that entertained Santos shortly after the Brazilians played at Villa Park and, as he told the *Daily Record* a few years later, had spent the last ten minutes of that game following Pelé just to get his shirt at the final whistle.

That Saunders went after a player of Craig's calibre was perhaps surprising given what Eamon Dunphy had written in his 1976 book, *Only a Game?* Player and manager, Dunphy felt, were cut from far too differing cloths. Craig was a strong player with great skill but, in Dunphy's opinion, his insufficient graft made him superfluous to the 'counterproductive, bad for the game' kind of football that Dunphy felt Saunders encouraged. 'If he wanted to play, if he had the desire and application and courage to go out there and play for 90 minutes, he would be a hell of a player,' Dunphy wrote. 'But he doesn't.' Saunders clearly saw qualities Dunphy didn't.

But if it was a case of third time lucky for Villa, that luck didn't last very long. Having made his debut in a 1-0 home win versus Bristol City – the midfielder's impressive start even sparking whispers that here, perhaps, was a club captain of the future – Craig would play only three more games before an injury left him requiring a scrape to cure a roughening of the bone under the knee and languishing on the sidelines for the season's remainder. It was yet another harsh blow for Saunders. Quoting an old idiom, he rued the club's plight. 'It never rains, but it pours' summed up the situation succinctly.

It was true of the English weather, too. Hazardous conditions – heavy downpours in the autumn months, hard frosts in the New Year – took their toll on the Villa Park turf (tons of sand – some of it in the centre circle dyed green – was often required just to make a home game playable) and, tellingly, on the fixture list. In February, Villa managed only two league games, both away from home. On the 4th, on a swamp of a Highbury pitch, Villa beat Arsenal 1-0 for a second time in the season, the outcome decided when, following a 23rd-minute corner, Pat Jennings punched the ball against the shoulder of Malcolm Macdonald and it rebounded back into the Arsenal net.

Afterwards, Saunders joked that he'd wanted referee Lester Shapter (the first match official to send off Manchester United legend George Best, no less) to inspect the ground half an hour before kick-off 'just to see if it was there'.

Three weeks later, Villa suffered an unwanted league double of their own, again falling to a single-goal defeat to Birmingham City. The 90 minutes very much encapsulated the story of Villa's season thus far: numerous chances created but none converted – the dominant visitors hit the woodwork on four occasions and Brian Little somehow missed with the goal at his mercy – while Birmingham barely had a kick of the ball yet sneaked a victory. 'We deserved to win and lost,' Saunders reflected ruefully. 'They deserved nothing and got two points.' It was as simple as that. And while Saunders reasoned that 'this sort of result is possibly one of the things which makes soccer what it is', it was no comfort after one more fruitless afternoon's work.

The victory for City was actually the last they enjoyed under the temporary command of Saunders' opposite number, Sir Alf Ramsey. The man put in place as Willie Bell's successor would soon announce his final retirement from football management in England after an unhappy six months at St Andrew's during which he'd been involved in a conflict with the Birmingham board, mostly over the issue of the sale of Trevor Francis. City appointed Blackburn Rovers manager Jim Smith as Ramsey's replacement shortly after.

Throughout the spring, almost on a week-by-week basis, Villa kept tearing up their own form guide. Two wins were followed by two draws, which were followed by two losses. The brace of victories, beginning with an easy 4-1 win at home to West Ham (Villa putting four past the hapless Hammers at Villa Park for a third year running), yielded seven goals in all, but Villa's lack of potency continued to leave them vulnerable to sucker punches. On 1 April, making fools of the Villa back four, a devastating Liverpool attack exacted clinical retribution for their November defeat, chalking up three goals after only 21 minutes, with Kenny Dalglish slotting home the first two.

Dalglish, in his first season in red, had fitted seamlessly into the number seven shirt vacated by Keegan. 'From the off,' his manager Paisley later said, 'Dalglish read my team better than *they* understood *him*. That's the hallmark of a great player.' Together with the acquisitions of fellow Scots, central defender Hansen and Middlesbrough's midfielder Graeme Souness, the signing of Dalglish was yet another example of Liverpool's ability to integrate new players and improve their side with barely a blink. How Saunders must have wished for such smooth transitions.

The following Wednesday night, the Villa boss watched his side dominate for much of the match against Nottingham Forest, outplaying the champions-elect for long spells and, but for an impeccable display from Peter Shilton, they would have earned a deserved victory. Yet it was a familiar tale. A goal didn't materialise and, with five minutes to go, Tony Woodcock – the England forward who'd made his Forest debut in a Second Division clash at Villa Park in 1974 – headed in to gift the visitors a win they barely merited. With closest rivals Everton losing the Merseyside derby at home to a single David Johnson goal, Forest were now four points clear with three games in hand, their victory at Villa Park virtually ensuring the East Midlands club the league title. Clough's side had already furnished their club cabinet with silverware, a John Robertson penalty in the League Cup Final replay at Old Trafford against Liverpool ending Forest's 19-year wait for a major trophy. For Villa, UEFA Cup football was as much as they could hope for.

They gave it a good shot. After a 1-1 draw at Newcastle, Villa embarked on a sequence of five victories in a row including a 2-0 win in a swift reverse fixture with the north-east club nine days later that confirmed Newcastle's relegation to the Second Division. Villa's first, a sublime strike from Cowans who bent it into the top corner after Mortimer touched a free kick to him, signalled the growing maturity of the raw midfielder. Frustrated earlier in the season after being in and out of the side – Saunders 'resting' the youngster, feeling he wasn't quite ready for regular action – Cowans had come to realise 'the boss was right'.

Now, fully acclimatised to the demands of Division One football, the guileful playmaker had made the number ten shirt his own, imposing himself on matches with a self-assurance that belied his tender years. When Cowans netted for a third game running in a 3-0 win at West Brom and Villa defeated Leeds 3-1 at Villa Park, it meant European football was still a mathematical possibility. But the fact it was only a remote chance showed just how frustrating a campaign it had been.

Before the last home game against Ipswich Town, Saunders reflected upon 'a season in which all the players and myself have been somewhat disappointed'. Writing in the matchday programme, Saunders bemoaned the 'absolutely staggering' injuries that had 'affected the balance and rhythm of the team' so badly. At the season's start, Saunders had stated how everyone at the club was 'more determined than ever to carry on where we left off last May', but that determination had been continually undermined as player after player faced spells on the sidelines. And while, overall, Saunders remained optimistic that Villa 'can only approach the future with anticipation and hope', possessing a first team squad 'now stronger than ever before', where Villa had fallen short in 1976/77, they'd done so again.

Against the Suffolk side, Villa enjoyed their most impressive result of the entire campaign. Goals by Cowans, Deehan (two), Gray, Carrodus and Little gave them a 6-1 win, though it's safe to assume that the minds of Bobby Robson's players were already thinking ahead to their following Saturday fixture: a date with Arsenal in the FA Cup Final. Par for the course for Villa's season, however, they failed to finish it on a high note. The following Tuesday, 2 May, Wolverhampton Wanderers beat Saunders' men 3-1 at Molineux, Carrodus having the honour of being the first and last Villa player to score in the season (their actual opener was an own goal by QPR defender David Webb) and what would be his final goal in claret and blue.

It was a result that ensured Sammy Chung's side lived to fight another day in the top flight, remaining there at the expense of John Lyall's West Ham United who, despite a late revival and winning six of their last nine games, had lost their final match 2-0 at home to Liverpool, and left Villa eighth in the First Division standings and missing out on a UEFA Cup spot.

Big numbers had still squeezed through the Villa Park turnstiles – Villa regularly played before crowds of over 35,000 – but the paying customers had been short-changed by many of the displays. After raining goals the previous year, Villa had endured several dry spells and, of the top ten teams in the table, their total of 57 was the lowest. In only eight of their league games did they manage to score more than twice in any one match. Even Manchester United who'd finished a disappointing tenth under the stewardship of the more studious Dave Sexton – Sexton replacing Tommy Docherty, sacked shortly after the 1977 FA Cup Final triumph for an extramarital affair with the wife of club physio Lawrie Brown – managed to find the net ten more times than Villa.

Andy Gray, the division's leading scorer earlier in the campaign, eventually finished way down the scoring charts behind a whole host of other marksmen including Trevor Francis, Malcolm Macdonald, West Brom's Tony Brown, and Kenny Dalglish. Ultimately, it was Bob Latchford who topped the list, the striker notching the two goals necessary to reach the 30-mark in third-placed Everton's last match of the season, a 6-0 destruction of Chelsea at Goodison Park. It was a tally that no other First Division player had achieved since Manchester City's Francis Lee in 1971/72, and was more than relegated Leicester City, with just 27, managed in all three major domestic competitions.

Greater disappointment was to come for Gray; when Scotland manager Ally MacLeod announced his final 22 to go to Argentina, Villa's number nine was a controversial omission. With Dalglish, Joe Jordan (now at Manchester United following a cross-Pennines move from Leeds) and Rangers' one-time Villa trialist Derek Johnstone virtual certainties to go, the last striking place up for grabs appeared to be between Gray, Coventry City's Ian Wallace and 30-year-old Joe Harper of Aberdeen, the club MacLeod managed before his promotion to the international stage. Much to Gray's despair, it was Harper who got the nod.

Saunders declared himself 'amazed' that Gray was not selected for a squad that had, of late, lacked any sort of scoring punch and only recently finished a winless third behind England and Wales in the Home Internationals. 'He has not been 100 per cent fit for most of the season and needed his last half-dozen games or so to get to his match peak,' Saunders said. 'Yet, despite all this, he has scored 20 goals in 40 games in the most difficult club competition in the world.'

MacLeod claimed to have watched Gray on five occasions towards the season's end but, *The Observer*'s Hugh McIlvanney wrote, 'The forward never once showed evidence of the killing touch that has convinced so many of us that he is one of the deadliest and most exciting front players in the game.' In light of his country's subsequent showing at the finals – Britain's sole representatives exiting on goal difference for the second World Cup tournament in a row – excluding Gray (what McIlvanney termed 'masochistic eccentricity' on MacLeod's part) was the wrong decision. It was hardly compensation for the Villa man that he later entered Panini folklore as one of the few players to make a World Cup sticker album but not the tournament itself.

In the end, defying expectation and even logic, Forest virtually romped to the title and became only the third club in history to claim the league's 'Blue Riband' a year after winning promotion. When they finished the campaign with a goalless draw at runners-up Liverpool, it was the culmination of a 26-game unbeaten league run that stretched back to the previous November and left them a whole seven points clear of the Anfield Road club. The addition of Peter Shilton, voted PFA Player of the Year, was a masterstroke; it had made them better organised and almost unbeatable. What the Clough and Taylor double act had achieved with one unfashionable side in Derby County six years earlier – taking them from the Second Division to become league champions – they'd now repeated at the Trent club. Leeds' and England's loss had conclusively been Forest's enormous gain.

A second successive European Cup was Liverpool's somewhat significant consolation prize, Dalglish capping his campaign with the only goal of the final at Wembley with Belgian champions Bruges. It meant the Merseysiders were the first English club to retain a continental trophy. In December, Paisley's side had also completed a 7-1 aggregate annihilation of Keegan's Hamburg to win the European Super Cup. Saunders had no such glories to reflect upon.

While their frontmen were firing blanks, Villa's defensive solidarity was a plus. Rimmer, an ever-present in his first season, had fitted in perfectly, fully deserving the supporters' Player of the Year award. John Gidman, after recovering from a torn tendon and broken pelvic bone, had flourished once again in the right-back role, forging a fine marauding partnership with fellow full-back Gordon Smith, a regular on the opposite flank. For the second year running, Gidman's impressive form earned him a place in the First Division Team of the Season at the PFA awards (a team that surprisingly excluded any member of the Liverpool side, prompting an enraged Tommy Smith to write in the *Liverpool Echo*, 'It has ruined my faith in the awards and when I say that, I believe I speak for many Liverpool players,' and vow to never vote again). It also brought another international call-up.

Gidman and his fellow John, Deehan, were included in the England squad for the friendly at Wembley with Brazil on 19 April. Deehan acknowledged the thanks he owed to Saunders, a manager who would 'encourage your team-mates to give you the best service in the penalty area'. The young striker had been asked by Eire boss Johnny Giles (then player-boss at West Brom) whether he'd turn out for the Republic – Deehan qualified through his father – but said, 'Ron Saunders told me he thought I would play for England one day,' so he chose England.

Although neither John was called into action from the substitutes' bench – a Keegan goal giving the home side a 1-1 draw with a Brazilian team 'thuggish in their approach' according to Ron Greenwood – it was heartening that both players remained in the national manager's plans, in spite of their club's stop-start domestic form. Sadly, encouragement didn't manifest into caps. Unable to oust the preferred choices, Liverpool's Phil Neal and Forest's Viv Anderson, Gidman would remain on the periphery. Arguably the best full-back in the country, Gidman was restricted to just one full England cap. Deehan was never called up again to a full international squad.

Taking further positives, after his initial difficulties, Ken McNaught had found his feet, forming a concrete pairing with Leighton Phillips. Yet the partnership wasn't to last. Saunders remained unsure about the best central defensive line-up and, so he later said, 'could not erase the conviction that what was really needed was two big men together who could not only man-mark, but who could cover each other'. It was, however, a helpful word of advice from McNaught that prompted any change.

With six games to go, when Phillips was struck down with a virus, McNaught suggested to his manager that he bring Allan Evans to the back. 'Ron would listen to his players,' the big defender told Paul Brown, editor of the official Villa website, in 2013. 'He listened to my thoughts about Allan as a centre-half. But that was Ron. He would take things on board. Others would have dismissed the notion.' Ironically, only the week after the ex-Dunfermline man had claimed his first goal playing as an out-and-out centre-forward in the draw at Newcastle, Evans made his first appearance in the number four shirt in a 2-0 victory at home to Chelsea. The two Scots gelled instantly. 'The thing about Allan was, he was quick,' McNaught said, 'he could always recover well. I just felt he was more suited to being a defender.' After only a handful of games together, it already looked as though, in their compatriot, both Evans and McNaught had found an ideal partner.

Villa chairman Sir William Dugdale, for his part, regarded the 1977/78 season as one of 'solid progress and endeavour towards making Aston Villa what it should be', with over £1m invested in the new North Stand, as well as £810,000 spent on players and basic ground improvements. Considering the club's dire financial plight just nine years previously, these were quite incredible figures. In addition, a large sum of the budget was earmarked for a much-needed resurfacing of the Villa Park pitch.

Yet it was hardly a satisfying scenario. Where giant strides were expected, only baby steps had been taken. Predicted by pundits to be pretenders to Liverpool's throne, instead it was Forest who'd unexpectedly stolen the Reds' crown.

Uncertainty concerning Saunders' future continued, with further rumblings of discontent within the boardroom. The row, inevitably, was between Ellis and Saunders. In March, the simmering tension between the two was rumoured to be on the brink of boiling over. Realising he didn't have the full support of a board – and Ellis, in particular – reluctant to grant him the contract he felt he deserved, Saunders was believed to be considering quitting.

Such was the weight of press speculation, Dugdale felt obliged to issue a strong statement of denial. 'The board wish to assure the supporters of Aston Villa,' he said, 'that all members of the board support the ongoing policies of the club towards providing Aston Villa fans with a team and club worthy of support.'

Few were fooled by the paper-thin portrait of harmony the chairman felt obliged to paint. For all the positive sentiments, there was no denying that Villa remained a divided club. In the coming months, the cracks – and not just at boardroom level – would only get wider and wider.

A Passport into Europe

COOKING on a low flame for most of their First Division campaign, it was only in the UEFA Cup that Villa's kettle really came to the boil. After the high drama of their League Cup win over Everton, Saunders had promised, 'We shall be better prepared for Europe this time than two years ago.' The team, he insisted, was 'almost completely different' and, he said, 'The players we have signed since then have enabled us to improve with almost every match.' There was a quiet optimism that Villa could travel much further than on their previous foreign venture. 'If we can be reasonably lucky in the draw and survive an early round or two,' Saunders said, 'who knows what we might achieve?'

Villa approached their automatic re-entry into European competition needing, in Jeff Farmer's words, 'to prove their quality in the wider arena after their false start' in the league. First-round opponents Fenerbahçe, boasting a strong record in games with English sides, meant a tough opening challenge. Pre-match, Saunders told his players he wanted a 2-0 lead at Villa Park to take into the second leg. As it was, he got far more. Two goals to the good at half-time, through Gray and Deehan, a dominant home side doubled their advantage after the break, with, first, Deehan grabbing his second on the night (both headers), then, ten minutes from time, Brian Little adding a fourth. It could have been even better. Villa, in a display of pace and power, also hit the bar three times.

Two weeks on, confident but not complacent, they travelled to Istanbul and, despite the febrile atmosphere inside the Municipal Sports Stadium, Villa showed a new maturity on the European stage, coping admirably with the hosts' desperate attempts to reduce the deficit. When an early strike from John Deehan, capitalising after the Fenerbahçe keeper failed to hold a Cowans shot, put Villa a goal ahead, whatever wisps of hope the home team had of getting back in the tie were dissipated.

After Leighton Phillips was headbutted by the big striker he'd shadowed throughout, leaving the Welshman with a gashed face, mayhem ensued as players from both sides jostled one another. But once calm was restored, that was about as hostile as it got. Little's beautifully hit left-footed chip from the angle of the box, completely deceiving the Turkish number one, wrapped up an emphatic 6-0 aggregate victory. Ultimately, on the night, negotiating a rain-sodden pitch and a shower of rotten fruit pelted at half-time by the Fenerbahçe supporters proved far more difficult for Saunders' men than dealing with their opponents.

A fortnight later, it was revealed that Saunders had been approached by Saudi Arabia to become the national coach – its 'soccer leader' – on an 18-month contract. Far out-scaling Saunders' current annual wage of £36,000, a salary of $175,000 (almost £100,000) was on the table.

His star in the ascendancy, Saunders was the latest in a line of British managers who'd received a lucrative offer to work in the Middle East. According to Andy Gray's autobiography, Saunders informed his squad of the proposal and asked them to tell him what they thought. 'Given the season we'd just had,' Gray wrote, 'it was natural that none of the boys wanted the manager to leave.' Gray, along with three other first team members, went to his office and told him so. Saunders, Gray suspected, was probably using his players' backing as leverage against the board. Though, despite Gray's assertion that 'whatever he [Saunders] asked the directors for, they obviously gave him', the opposite was true.

Sir William Dugdale, telling Saunders that Villa could never match the money the Saudis were proposing, effectively gave the manager the go-ahead to leave if he so desired. He was really calling the Villa manager's bluff. Saunders had little intention of accepting the offer, and Dugdale knew it. It wasn't a pay rise Saunders wanted, but a long-term contract he felt he warranted, the knowledge that he could get on with his job without the constant distraction of further negotiations. Though no new deal was forthcoming from the Villa boardroom, after pondering the Saudi opportunity for several days, Saunders opted to remain at Villa Park, declaring, 'There are some things that money just can't buy.' The matter, if not totally forgotten, was put to bed. At least for the time being.

In the programme notes for Villa's match with Norwich City, Saunders wrote, 'The traumas of the past few days are now behind us and it is essential that we all get our minds on the job in hand.' That job was a UEFA Cup second-round tie with Górnik Zabrze. In December

1971, keen to keep the club name in the public imagination and generate some income into the bargain, Villa had entertained the Polish club in a friendly at Villa Park. A decent turn-out – 14,662 – had braved a cold winter evening in Birmingham to see Vic Crowe's Third Division team hold the Polish champions to a 1-1 draw.

The most successful Polish team of the post-war period, Górnik had also been the first from their country to reach a European final, losing 2-1 to Manchester City in the 1970 Cup Winners' Cup in Vienna. Ever since 1974 when the national side had deservedly finished third overall at the World Cup finals in West Germany, Polish football had been afforded far more respect. As Villa were dispatching Fenerbahçe in the previous round, another Polish club, Widzew Łódź – then bottom of their domestic top flight – were surprising Manchester City, earning a win on the away goals rule after a 2-2 draw at Maine Road.

Górnik, like Villa, were a disciplined, supremely fit unit. However, still in something of a transitional stage, they'd failed to win any domestic trophy for the past five years. Of the four Górnik players that had helped the Poland team in 1974, only centre-half colossus Jerzy Gorgon remained, star strikers Lubanski and Szarmach having left soon after the finals. So imposing was Gorgon's appearance in a red shirt, he'd earned the nickname 'The Telephone Booth'.

On 19 October, however, it was another tall, blond central defender who stood out. Two headers from Ken McNaught – one in either half and both resulting from Dennis Mortimer corners – gave Saunders' side a merited 2-0 win and, just as importantly, would signal a sea-change in fortunes for the young Scot. The target of the terrace critics after taking time to settle, McNaught acknowledged that they perhaps had a right to get on his back but was determined to prove his worth.

Following McNaught's two-goal strike, a tide of goodwill would begin flowing his way. Saunders' faith in the defender to come good played a huge part. 'Ron helped me through it,' McNaught would say. 'He might have left me out of the team but he stuck with me. I developed a good rapport with him because he helped me get through the bad times. I wanted to repay him on the park.'

Heading to the second instalment, there were still, Jeff Farmer wrote, 'questions to be answered on a damp, grey afternoon in industrial Poland'. Eager to claw their way back into the tie, Górnik forced Villa into a heavy rearguard action for much of the first half. A 40th-minute strike from Janusz Marcinkowski put the outcome very much in the balance. Expecting the Poles to crank up the pressure even further, Saunders provided the perfect response; he adjusted the formation to 4-4-2 and it paid almost instant dividends.

Shortly after the restart, following a swift counter-attack, Frank Carrodus found a clear path on the right-hand side before crossing for Gray to head a precious away goal past keeper Fischer. The pressure now relaxed, Villa played out the game in a proficient, professional fashion, easing to an aggregate victory and not even the fog at Kraków which led to an overnight delay of their return to England could dampen Saunders' joy at their progress. Earning their European wings, gaining experience and confidence with each new adventure, Villa were showing they were more than capable of matching the competition's best teams.

Athletic Bilbao, the oldest club side in Spain, were their next obstacle. Beaten UEFA Cup finalists the year before (only losing a two-legged final on away goals to Italy's Juventus), Bilbao were a team the noted writer about foreign football Leslie Vernon rated 'a better cup side than Barcelona'. En route to the third round, the Spaniards had seen off Swiss club Servette and Hungary's Újpest and, on home soil in particular, they were formidable adversaries, having lost just once in two years in the Spanish league and suffered only a solitary defeat in 29 European ties at their Sam Mames stadium. Saunders, having witnessed first-hand in the teams' pre-season friendly clash what 'a very accomplished side' Bilbao were 'with some outstanding individuals', knew they'd provide Villa with a stern exam. 'We are under no illusions whatsoever,' he said, 'that, without doubt, this is the hardest game we have had in the UEFA Cup.'

The first leg at Villa Park would mark a return to the ground where Bilbao's 34-year-old goalkeeper and captain José Ángel Iribar, the most-capped Spanish international of all time, first performed 11 years previously, representing his country at the 1966 World Cup finals. It proved an unhappy one. On a late November night of torrential rain, on a pitch slowed by the downpours, Villa produced what Jeff Farmer termed 'their finest performance in Europe'. They were helped in no small way by Iribar. In the 34th minute, the keeper, nursing a shoulder injury and under pressure from McNaught, inexplicably pushed Alex Cropley's lofted corner straight into his own net to leave the hosts 1-0 ahead. With 12 minutes remaining, Deehan, getting on the end of Gidman's free kick, headed past Iribar and Villa, wearing an all-white away strip as they had at home to Górnik, clinched another vital first-leg victory.

Going into the second leg in northern Spain on 7 December equidistant in the league from table-toppers Forest and bottom club Newcastle United and on the back of a 2-0 defeat at Ipswich, Villa once more put their erratic domestic form to one side, turning on an even better performance. In Bilbao's intimidating stadium, with its steep terracing chock-full with a fervent home following, the visitors gave a first-half exhibition of swift, offensive football that at times left their hosts looking bamboozled.

Two minutes before half-time, Dennis Mortimer, dipping to power in a rare header from a Gidman cross, gave them the lead they deserved. The silence among Bilbao's notoriously vociferous fans was striking. Bilbao didn't go down easily. But, constantly rebuffed by a craggy defence of Gidman, Smith, Phillips and McNaught, and with Jimmy Rimmer answering when called upon, all the Spaniards' efforts at a fightback floundered. Had it not been for an 86th-minute equaliser – Dani finally breaching the defences – Villa would have left the San Mames stadium as only the second English club to win there in 11 seasons.

It mattered not. Villa, to a man, had turned in an elegant, classy showing and done more than enough to earn their aggregate victory. At the final whistle, the visitors gravitated to the centre circle and were greeted by a standing ovation, an outbreak of spontaneous applause from the Bilbao fans prompting Leighton Phillips to reflect afterwards, 'I have played all over Europe and never had a reception like *that*.'

The Spanish press were in full agreement about Villa's dominance, the Bilbao morning newspaper *La Gaceta Del Norte* producing a full-page headline the following day announcing that the Spaniards had been given an 'English Lesson' by their visitors from Villa Park. According to Saunders, a magnificent Villa, 'superior in every department', had given 'the best performance I have seen from any Villa side since I took over three years ago'. Given that it was just short of a year since the annihilation of Liverpool, that was quite some statement from the usually diffident boss. Saunders' opposite number, Bilbao boss Koldo Aguirre, didn't disagree, feeling 'it was justice that the English team reached the quarter-finals'.

The UEFA Cup was highly regarded and hugely competitive, its standing probably best gauged from the fact that the previous five winners all won their national championship in the same season. When the quarter-final draw was made in Zurich on Friday 20 January 1978, Villa were keeping company with some experienced European campaigners, in the hat alongside PSV Eindhoven of Holland, Bastia from France, the Swiss side Grasshoppers, Eintracht Frankfurt of West Germany, the East German duo of Magdeburg and Carl Zeiss Jena and the Spanish giants, Barcelona, victors over Ipswich Town in the previous round.

For the fourth time in succession, they were handed a first-leg home tie. And it was Barcelona with whom they were paired. Having already played host to Pelé and Franz Beckenbauer (on 23 January 1973, while Villa were re-establishing themselves in the Second Division, Bayern Munich, the 'Europameisters' as the match programme labelled them, played out a 1-1 friendly draw before 22,699), Villa Park would now welcome another of the greatest players ever to grace a football pitch, Hendrik Johannes Cruijff, commonly known as Johan Cruyff.

If Barcelona were the aristocrats of Spanish football, Cruyff was the lord of their manor. Dutch captain at the 1974 World Cup, Cruyff had declared himself unavailable for the forthcoming finals in Argentina and, at the end of the season, though still only 30, was to retire from Spanish football to pursue pastures new in the United States. The first leg at Villa Park – so Cruyff assured the audience at a lunch held in his honour by the Midlands Soccer Writers' Association – would be his swansong on English soil. The three-time European Footballer of the Year, who'd joined Barcelona from Ajax in 1973 for a world record fee of £922,000, promised something special.

In February 1977, a Cruyff-inspired Holland side had triumphed 2-0 over England in a friendly at Wembley, the scoreline barely reflecting the dominance the Dutch had exerted. Able to skim past opponents with devastating speed, often from a standing start, and switching play with both short and 40-yard passes, Cruyff gave an imperious 90-minute display. By the final whistle, Revie's men looked out on their feet. For many observers, including Revie, it was the most emphatic showing by an away team against England since the magnificent Magyars of 1953. But the post-match extolling of the dynamic Dutch didn't deflect the football writers from their criticism of the England team and, in particular, its boss.

The scalpels with which they began dissecting the home team's performance were, in effect, doubling as daggers digging deeper into Revie's back. Sensing his cards were already marked by the public and an FA keen that Ipswich's Bobby Robson would make a better job of it, Revie elected to jump before he was pushed. On 11 July 1977, a day after his 50th birthday, Revie resigned as England manager following three unsatisfactory years at the helm. With a hotseat now vacant at Old Trafford following Docherty's dismissal, there was some immediate and quite strong speculation that Revie had been lined up for a return to club management. The conjecture couldn't have been wider of the mark.

Barely 24 hours later, Revie revealed in an exclusive to the *Daily Mail* that he'd accepted a four-year contract worth £340,000, tax-free, to take charge of the United Arab Emirates national team, making him the highest-paid football manager in the world. The lucrative deal gave rise to allegations of financial misdealing. Charged with bringing the game into disrepute, Revie was suspended from football for ten years, a decision he later contested and had overturned by the court. But the damage was done. While his former Leeds players remained faithful, as Michael Henderson wrote in *50 People Who Fouled Up Football*, 'The rest of the world saw only an unhappy, disloyal man who, when he could have done so much for the game, opted to befoul and then betray it.'

The day following news of Revie's defection, the *Daily Mirror*, in tandem with Ladbrokes, gave its readers the opportunity to vote, via a poll, for his successor. A list of ten prospective replacements was drawn up. The names – with one surprising omission in Bob Paisley – included the two favourites for the role, Brian Clough and Jack Charlton, who'd resigned as Middlesbrough's boss at the end of the previous season, as well as Jimmy Armfield, Jimmy Bloomfield, Les Cocker, Ron Greenwood, Bobby Robson, Dave Sexton and Terry Venables. Also on the list was Ron Saunders.

Predictably, it was Clough who came out on top, notching up a comprehensive 84 per cent of the votes. Charlton was his nearest challenger, albeit with a paltry six per cent. The percentage of votes for Saunders wasn't declared but it's unlikely – as they say in cricket parlance – to have troubled the scorers. Most amusingly, the football-watching public nominated a few candidates of their own, with Sir Alf Ramsey still producing a twinkle in the eyes of some and, perhaps even more humorously, Bill Shankly, a Scot as Scottish as bagpipes, winning a few votes. In the event, the public clamour for Clough went unheeded. The FA, unsurprisingly, plumped for a far safer option: Ron Greenwood, general manager at West Ham United.

With missing out on Argentina now almost inevitable following a 2-0 qualifying tie defeat to Italy in Rome the previous autumn, the country's game was perceived to have reached a new low. On taking up his role, Revie had said, 'My own concern is to marry the best of our domestic game with a realisation that what we produce at home every Saturday is not ideal for international competition. At home we give the fans what they want – football played at 100mph. We have been bred on that kind of all-action game and in its own way it typifies the English game. But at international level I doubt if this is where we can achieve progress. We need to slow down and work more at the skilful aspects of our game.' The marriage, thus far, had failed.

Saunders saw little wrong with football in the country. 'The British game should remain true to its strengths, instead of trying to play an alien continental style,' he said. 'Why should we abandon the natural assets of our game – our speed, stamina, determination, and fitness? These are the strengths which scare the continentals.' How many of the top continental clubs would be good teams in the English First Division, he argued, if they had to play 42 high-pressure league games, contend with commitments in two domestic cup competitions and, possibly, a European tournament as well? All the technique and flair in the world and possessing a good soccer brain were nothing if a footballer couldn't play with the same intensity for 90 minutes. 'When players can't run,' Saunders said, 'it's time for them to retire.'

Nevertheless, the frustrations remained over a national side increasingly out-thought in one-off matches against teams able to slow down then quicken the pace again at the appropriate moments. 'Speed is something very particular,' argued the West German director of coaching, Karl-Heinz Heddergott. 'It isn't just a matter of run and run. It's how to run and where to run.' A Cruyff-led side had caught out England time and again. 'What total football really meant,' wrote Michael Henderson, 'was a dissolution of hard distinctions between defending and attacking.' To Sir Alf Ramsey, 'a meat-and-two-veg Englishman' who 'preferred limited football', the concept was something quite beyond him. Revie, too, had been found wanting.

On 1 March 1978, another 'meat-and-two-veg Englishman' was preparing for his own encounter with the Dutchman. Cruyff once said of himself, 'I have an instinct to do the wrong things. That's probably my secret.' At Villa Park he did many 'wrong things'. From the very start, his continuous movement leaving midfielders and defenders chasing shadows beneath the floodlights, Cruyff gave a slick football exhibition. One of Saunders' regular psychological ploys was to, pre-match, survey the opposing teamsheet in the dressing room and then dismiss their best player with a disparaging remark or deliberately get his name wrong before screwing up the piece of paper and hurling it away.

'Gruff – he can't play!' he'd told his team. But Gruff could play and, nearing his 31st birthday, with Saunders failing to assign a man-marker to track him, the Dutch master was totally running the show. According to Dennis Shaw in *A Game of Three Halves*, Villa paid the price for Saunders' 'stubborn insistence on all things being done his way'. In their La Liga fixture immediately prior to the UEFA Cup clash, Barcelona had been held to a goalless draw by Bilbao. Saunders' assistant manager Tony Barton, accompanied by Shaw, had been sent on a spying mission and reported back to Saunders that Bilbao's success was based on a close-marking stifling of Cruyff. But Saunders – a man who 'didn't like being given tactical advice' – took exception to Barton's 'stop Cruyff' suggestion (especially when it featured in Shaw's newspaper preview of the Villa game), and gave his assistant 'a rollicking'. Now, Cruyff was showing just how sage Barton's advice was.

In the 20th minute, picking up possession from a stray pass close to the halfway line, the flying Dutchman ran unchallenged at the heart of the Villa defence, his long, loping stride moving him gracefully to the fringes of the penalty area. There, with the backing-off Phillips vainly attempting to jockey him wide, Cruyff cleanly clipped a low, accurate shot from 20 yards out that spun over the turf and swooped past Rimmer into the corner of the net. Promising something special, Cruyff was keeping to his word.

In the Spanish title race, the Catalonian club, while not yet surrendering all hope of catching Real Madrid, hadn't been performing particularly well, but even without Cruyff's Dutch compatriot Johan Neeskens their vast European know-how was simply stopping Villa in their tracks. Not necessarily legally.

Brian Little, in particular, was on the receiving end of some rough treatment and the lenience of Portuguese referee Cesar Correia only encouraged the tough-tackling Spaniards to continue in the same rugged vein. When the entire Barcelona team – not just Cruyff – did play by the rules, however, they were a clear class apart. In the 78th minute, they were two ahead, a header from a left-wing cross by Zuviria looping over the hapless Rimmer to leave Villa looking dead and buried. His job seemingly done, Cruyff, protecting an ankle injury, was substituted eight minutes from time, the standing ovation he received from all four sides of the ground an indication of the respect the watching crowd held for the departing Barça captain. Even certain Villa players joined in with the voluble applause. Cruyff 'was that good,' Gordon Smith later said, 'it was frightening.'

But just as the presence of Barça's destroyer-in-chief had inspired his own side, his departure stirred Villa to a rousing finale. Within minutes, Ken McNaught, meeting a Smith free kick, powered in a diving header to narrow the margin. In the 64th minute, Saunders had replaced one Evans for another, striker Allan coming on for fellow debutant 19-year-old right-back David to lend some muscle to the Villa forward line. Allan Evans had been impressing in the Central League, claiming a double hat-trick in a 10-1 thrashing of Sheffield United just days before. Pitched into battle, with his team-mates firing a barrage of balls into the box, the big

Scot battered the Barça back four. With two minutes left, if not exactly handsomely, Saunders' gamble paid off.

Chasing after Mortimer's lobbed ball into the box, a charging Evans collided with Artola and, with the keeper helpless on the ground, John Deehan, standing on the six-yard line, stretched out to jab the bouncing ball into an empty net. Right at the very death, Villa had grabbed a lifeline to hold on to. It was, Saunders claimed afterwards, 'a moral victory'. His Villa players, he felt, had been 'bullied' by their opponents and thrown off their normal game. 'In the first 20 minutes of the match,' he said, 'the flow of our game was utterly destroyed by the ruthlessness of some of the Barcelona players. Had it been an English league match, I feel certain that the referee would have clamped down on the trouble-makers during the first ten minutes – and then, perhaps, we would have seen a different result.'

Regardless, 49,619 – the biggest-ever crowd for a European tie at Villa Park – had witnessed a classic. Asked years later whether the match was the most exciting of his time at Villa, Saunders told the *Heroes and Villains* fanzine, 'They were all good nights. I can't pick out the best games. After all, if you play the likes of Hartlepool in a cup-tie they are there by right. Whoever they are, the opposition have to be beaten.' The battle with the Catalan giants, however, was, without question, a thrilling spectacle for all who were there.

Perhaps feeling the effect of their emotionally draining evening, when Villa returned to domestic duties they could only manage a goalless draw three days later at home to Leicester City, following it with a 2-1 defeat at Carrow Road, substitute John Gregory grabbing Villa's goal. Andy Gray was still sidelined. All the same, when the second leg arrived, Saunders was more than hopeful of going through. 'I honestly believe we can win,' he said.

After only 24 minutes that belief took a monumental blow. John Gidman, already nursing a bleeding nose (later revealed to be broken) after a bruising opening to the game, was elbowed in the left eye by Barcelona striker Jesus de la Cruz – a sly foul missed by the officials – and when the Villa number two, playing in an unorthodox midfield role, lashed out at de la Cruz, Turkish referee Dogon Babacan instantly banished Gidman from the field. De la Cruz, meanwhile, recovering quickly from a dramatic fall to the floor, went unpunished. A man light against opponents for whom Cruyff again was the star man, Villa's mountain had grown even steeper.

Only Rimmer's saves from Cruyff, Rexach and Zuviria got them to half-time still level. Yet they dug in deep. Twelve minutes into the second

Doug Ellis and his wife Heidi (right) celebrating with Saunders and his wife Breda following the 1975 League Cup triumph.

Villa's players are applauded on to the Villa Park pitch against Sunderland after sealing promotion in 1975.

A celebration cake in the dressing room after the 2-0 victory over the Roker Park club.

Andy Gray rejoices after scoring a goal against Manchester United in 1976.

Saunders in joyous mood after the 1977 League Cup triumph.

10 July 1977, Villa's players are put through their pre-season paces at Bodymoor Heath.

September 1977, Saunders and his players board the flight for a UEFA Cup clash in Istanbul.

Leighton Phillips shakes hands with Barcelona's Johan Cruyff before the UEFA Cup encounter at Villa Park.

John Gidman is dismissed at the Nou Camp as Villa's UEFA Cup dream ends.

Man of the Match Gordon Cowans shadows Ricardo Villa. The home debut of Spurs' Argentinian duo, Villa and Ardiles, ended in a 4-1 win for the visitors.

22 May 1980, Saunders welcomes Peter Withe and his wife to Villa Park.

Dennis Mortimer ecstatic after netting a vital goal versus his boyhood heroes Liverpool.

28 February 1981, Wolves' Andy Gray confronts Tony Morley as referee Joe Worrall steps in to intervene.

2 May 1981, a concerned Saunders watches on from the dugout at Highbury.

Gary Shaw celebrates another crucial strike (against Manchester City) on Villa's road to league title success.

It's party time in the Highbury dressing room for the newly acclaimed champions of England.

February 1982, Saunders talks to the press after his resignation.

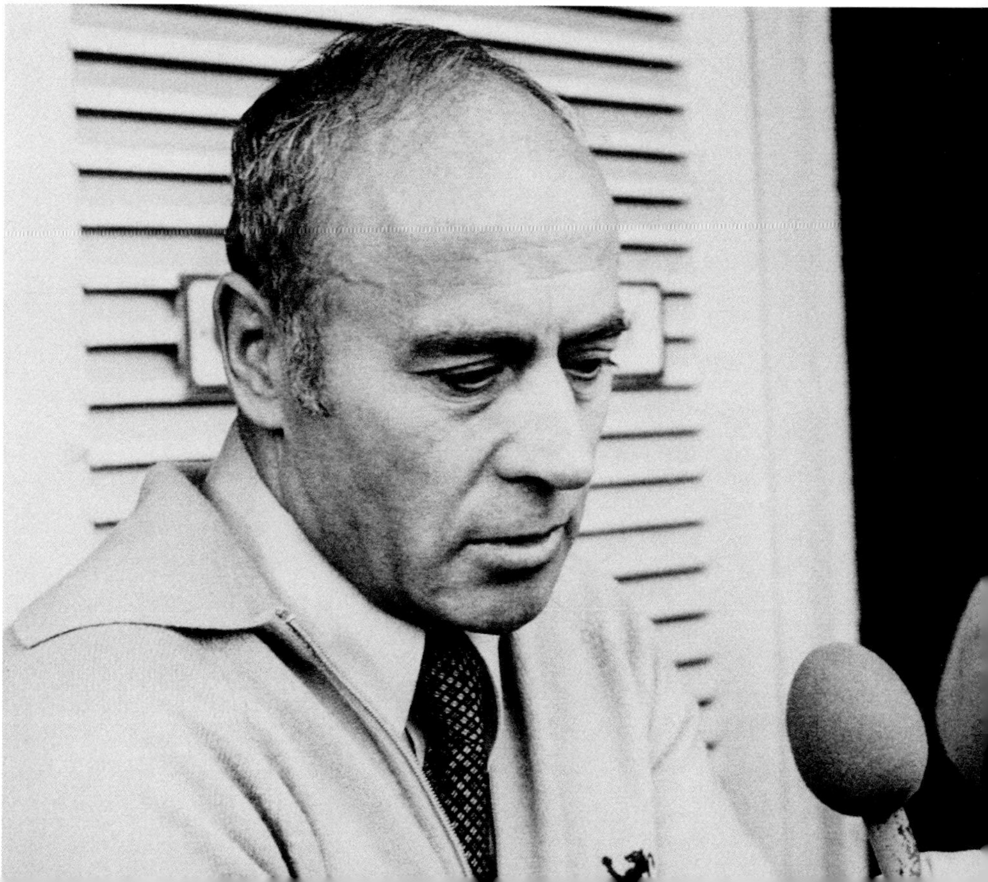

Ex-Villan Chris Nicholl clears for Southampton, the night following Saunders' resignation.

26 May 1982, Gary Shaw, Tony Morley and Peter Withe with the European Cup trophy.

period, when the Spaniards' defence failed to effectively clear a Smith free kick, Brian Little reacted, whisking the ball into the net and 90,000 Catalonians glowering down from the Nou Camp's towering stands were stunned into silence. They weren't quiet for long. After a hashed opportunity by Little to double the lead, Barcelona, firstly through defender Migueli on 67 minutes and then Asensi ten minutes later, stirred from their slumber and, although McNaught's late header rattled the bar, Villa couldn't claw their way back.

'We deserved at least a draw,' was Saunders' post-match feeling. Declaring himself 'proud of how my ten players conducted themselves on the night', the Villa manager left little doubt what he thought had been the deciding factor. After his dismissal, John Gidman's evening only got worse; he'd even received a good dig off police in the tunnel as he left the pitch.

His frustration aside, Saunders took great heart from the club's sterling efforts. Pitting their wits against continental styles in environments vastly different to the norm in England had, in Saunders' words, given his players 'invaluable knowledge'. And while, as Jeff Farmer wrote, 'The torch that had been lit at Old Trafford a year earlier in that epic League Cup Final second replay was finally extinguished in Spain,' against unfamiliar opposition, they'd repeatedly proved how adaptable they were. 'We can look to the future with confidence,' Saunders stated.

When next the club had a chance to show itself in such elite company, Aston Villa's torch was to burn brightest of all.

An Air of Uncertainty

THAT Ron Saunders' contract at Aston Villa was in its final year was well known in football circles. Saunders, already among the highest-paid managers in the country, had long made it plain that he felt his efforts should be rewarded with a new, improved deal to secure his future. Sir William Dugdale had been in favour of giving Saunders what he sought. Other directors erred on the side of caution. One, in particular, opposed it altogether. For Doug Ellis, it wasn't a case of whether Saunders warranted better terms, but whether he should even be retained as boss.

With discussions still taking place – Ellis considering it less than a pressing matter – the birds were circling in the hope that Saunders might be tempted away. Leeds United, in the market for a replacement for Jimmy Armfield, were the first to express an interest. As reported in the *Glasgow Herald*, United, 'frustrated in their attempt to persuade Lawrie McMenemy to take over as their manager, may now be looking to a man of a quite different ilk to assume the Elland Road command'. That man was Saunders.

Ahead of a line of candidates that included the Arsenal coach Don Howe, Jack Charlton, now manager of Sheffield Wednesday, and another of Big Jack's former colleagues in the Leeds glory days, Johnny Giles, in charge of Shamrock Rovers as well as the Republic of Ireland team, Saunders 'with the reputation of being the sergeant major of the managerial ranks' according to the *Herald*, 'could be the next man called up for inspection by the Leeds board'. When a request was made from their Elland Road counterparts for formal permission to approach Saunders, though, Dugdale quickly dismissed it outright.

So cheesed off was Saunders with the constant internal wrangling and disunity over his position, however, that the prospect of a move up north became quite beguiling. 'The blunt-spoken Saunders, who would certainly make no claims to match the McMenemy charisma,' wrote the *Herald*, 'has been in some hard talking with the Villa board and it is no secret that he does not see eye to eye with some of them.' A contract from Leeds was all but on the table and, according to Ian Johnson in *The Aston Villa Story*, 'All he [Saunders] had to do was fill in the figures himself and add his name.'

Saunders considered it very seriously and, wrote Johnson, 'He almost weakened.' But ultimately, Leeds' courting wasn't sufficient to entice him. Their advances rejected, the West Yorkshire club instead wooed recently resigned Celtic boss Jock Stein. Though, in an ironic spin of the managerial merry-go-round, after only 44 days (the same tenure at United as Clough), Stein would vacate the hotseat to take over from Ally MacLeod who had just quit as Scotland manager, Sunderland's Jimmy Adamson becoming the next man to take hold of the Elland Road reins.

Dugdale's rebuttal of Leeds had been, the *Evening Mail*'s Ray Matts wrote, 'the highest compliment' Saunders could have been paid, yet still Villa delayed tying down the manager to the club. Ellis, inevitably, was leading the argument against it. Saunders, so Ellis believed, had created a bad atmosphere at Villa with his manipulation of directors and the rule of fear he imposed upon his staff.

But the too-long delay in offering Saunders a contract wasn't the only issue causing divisions. The announcement by Ron Bendall, now the club's biggest shareholder and vice-chairman, that at the forthcoming AGM his 26-year-old son Donald would stand for election to the board against director Alan Smith (now the Warwickshire County Cricket Club secretary), gave rise to suspicions of nepotism. Bendall, his fellow board members believed, was now using his majority shareholding to wield increasing power, contrary to Ellis's demand that Aston Villa 'remain a democracy and never be under the control of one man'.

On 9 August, two weeks after Leeds' approach and just ten days before Villa's opening fixture, the political in-fighting at Villa Park made the back-page headlines again. Chiefly in frustration over the dilly-dallying with Saunders, Dugdale, along with Smith and fellow director Harry Cressman, quit the club. 'Maybe our departure will force the issue,' the resigning chairman said, 'and Mr Saunders will be given the security he desires and deserves.' It did.

Twenty-four hours later, the four remaining board members – Bendall, Ellis, Kartz and Houghton – finally made up their minds and, despite the predictable querying from Ellis of the proposed deal's length, Saunders was tended a six-year contract to continue as boss. 'I think Ron Bendall did that,' Dugdale later said, 'to show that he was now in charge.' Saunders couldn't hide his delight. 'This gives me the security I was looking for,' he told reporters. 'As a manager, I believe a club like Villa must have an atmosphere of permanency. My contract, together with the long-term contracts negotiated last year for the players, provide that situation.'

With Dugdale gone, the next obvious step appeared to be for Ron Bendall to become the new chairman, but his position as a tax exile living on the Isle of Man prohibited him from spending sufficient time at the club. Harry Kartz was unanimously selected instead, with Bendall remaining vice-chairman. The following week, at the AGM, Bendall Snr got his wish; Donald Bendall was duly appointed to the board. Harry Cressman had resigned, he said, 'because I felt like daddy had bought a football club for his son.'

Kartz, a keen Villa supporter since boyhood, said all the right things: his chief desire was for a 'harmonious board'. A lack of cohesiveness continually threatened to destabilise the club and the board's job, Kartz said, was 'to provide the stability which gives everyone the chance to go about their work' and 'to make sure Ron Saunders and his players are happy'. After persistent unrest that would have unsettled even the most cocksure of managers, striking such tuneful notes must have been music to Saunders' ears.

Unity both off and on the pitch was key. 'We'll be there at the finish if we can steer clear of the kind of injuries that crippled us last season,' said Andy Gray. Villa, in Gray's view, were 'a superb young side' who'd 'grown up and matured together' and were definitely 'on the brink of becoming one of the really top sides'.

Following his slap in the face from Ally MacLeod – a 'numbing experience', Gray called it – the striker remained philosophical. 'I'm still young and there's plenty of time for all sorts of things to happen,' he said. The Scot, forced to miss both Barcelona ties, spoke of how he was 'dying to play in the European Cup', but, he added, 'There's the small matter of winning the championship first!'

Opening the new campaign as they'd closed the last – with a fixture against Wolves – Villa, in a tightly fought clash played out in sweltering heat before a home crowd of 43,922, won 1-0 with Gray's 60th-minute strike all that separated the two sides. Displaying his characteristic razor-sharp reflexes, Gray latched on to a low centre by Gordon Smith, nipping in between Wolves central defender Bob Hazell and keeper Paul Bradshaw to get Villa off on the right foot. Yet, late in the game, the Scottish number nine received a thigh strain, was replaced by John Gregory, and would miss the next two matches. An injured Gray was to be a common theme throughout the coming months.

Having started with a straightforward 4-4-2 formation – Gray up front alongside Little – Saunders was immediately obliged to have a re-think. But as Villa went into their next game – at White Hart Lane – it was the home side's line-up that captured the press's attention.

The World Cup in Argentina had focussed English managers on the possibility of cheap foreign purchases to be had. For some time, there'd been strong lobbying from factions within the game for British football to get in line with the rest of Europe where international barriers to the movement of players were removed long ago. Now the door was ajar and Spurs were the first to prise it open wider.

On 10 July, just over two weeks after the hosts' 3-1 final victory against the Netherlands, the newly promoted north London club caused something of a sensation with the signing of two of the Argentines' cup-winning squad, a small, supremely skilful playmaker named Osvaldo Ardiles and the tall, bearded Ricardo Villa. Ardiles and Villa weren't the first Latin duo to add a cosmopolitan touch to the top flight – the Newcastle United FA Cup-winning side of 1951 contained two Chileans, the brothers George and Ted Robledo – but they were the first to make front-page headlines.

With Tottenham's odds of winning the title now cut from 66/1 to 25/1, the two fresh imports both made their bows on the opening day – Villa scoring the equaliser and Ardiles impressive in a 1-1 draw at champions Nottingham Forest – but it was their first outing at White Hart Lane that was most eagerly awaited. Taking to the field on a balmy August evening in the capital, streamers cascaded and ticker-tape was showered down, Buenos Aires-style, from the stands; the home fans' reception mimicking scenes so familiar to Argentina's players during the summer finals. 'All it needed,' reported the *Birmingham Mail*, 'was the Argentinean national anthem.' Any expectations of the big night belonging to the home side's new heroes, however, were hastily deflated.

Villa, minus Gray, Deehan (victim of damaged tendons in his right foot pre-season), Craig, Phillips and Cropley, and with Brian Little the only recognised forward, completely rewrote the script to suit their own requirements. On 36 minutes, Allan Evans fired them ahead. While his decision to leave out Leighton Phillips was a shock to many – the stylish sweeper, whom Emlyn Hughes called 'one of the most underrated players in the league', was still a regular choice for Wales – Saunders was now convinced that centre-half was Evans' position. Honest enough to admit he didn't think he'd make the grade as a First Division striker, Evans was happy to revert. His goalscoring instincts were already proving useful.

Shortly after the interval, John Gregory, deputising for Gray and looking 'perfectly at home' according to the *Mail*, added a second. The fever pitch atmosphere inside White Hart Lane was now decidedly flat. Ardiles and Villa were virtually invisible. As David Lacey of *The Guardian* reported, 'Villa did not so much stop playing [the Argentineans] as ignore their presence; the pair simply did not see a lot of the ball...at times they almost became lost in the crowd.'

Although rallying briefly when Hoddle replied from the penalty spot following a foul on Ardiles, Spurs' response was inconsequential; Brian Little, with a wonder strike, extinguished any chance of a comeback. When Shelton, making only his second start and sparkling on the right, scored a fourth, volleying home from Gidman's cross, a memorable night was rounded off. Villa, in journalist Norman de Mosquita's words, had 'proved selfish guests as they took all the spoils from what was to have been Tottenham's party'. Burkinshaw's men were 'eclipsed and embarrassed', enthused the *Birmingham Mail*, by 'a performance of power and class'.

Not renowned for his tactical acumen, Saunders had, on the night, got it just right. With Gordon Cowans pulling the strings in midfield – 'the best I've seen him play', said Saunders before, true to form, adding, 'but he can do better' – and Gregory and Shelton as nominal frontmen, Villa employed a fluid, flowing system – with midfielders and forwards rotating – that left the hosts baffled and the Argentine duo taught a tough lesson about life in English football.

'If we had played that way for the rest of the season,' Dennis Mortimer would later reflect, 'God knows what we would have done.' They didn't even manage it in their very next game. Unable to counter in the same swift fashion at Ashton Gate, Villa 'never really got started' according to Saunders and lost 1-0 to Bristol City. The one bright spot on a disappointing afternoon was the first appearance of Gary Shaw, the 17-year-old goalscoring prodigy coming on as sub for Shelton, having joined from schoolboy football only the summer before. The defeat was indicative of a failing that bedevilled Villa so often under Saunders: the flashes of brilliance that outshone the very best teams were all too quickly succeeded by a dimming of the lights. It was also the first of an 11-game run that yielded only two more league wins and a meagre ten goals.

New sick-notes were being handed in practically week-by-week, as players headed for the treatment room on an almost rotational basis.

Frank Carrodus was troubled by cartilage problems in a 1-1 home draw with Southampton – Chris Nicholl, for the visitors, replying to a Gray goal – and would play only two more games before his season (and, subsequently, his Villa career) was brought to a halt. The following Saturday at Portman Road, as Gray's penalty – Villa's first for 18 months – helped his side to a 2-0 win, John Gidman received what he later described as 'one of my daftest injuries on the football field'. Running upfield to bolster an attack, with the ball over 50 yards away, Gidman put his foot in a pot-hole, slipped and, having left the pitch writhing in agony, discovered that he'd torn his ankle ligaments and tendons.

In the same game, Gordon Smith suffered cartilage damage. Youngsters were pitched in. England youth international midfielder Lee Jenkins, a recruit in June 1977, made his debut against Ipswich. In a 1-1 home draw with Everton, 18-year-old Gary Williams, another product of the youth system, also made his first team bow, substituting Shelton. On the same afternoon, David Evans was brought in for the injured Gidman, though Saunders clearly didn't see the West Bromwich-born defender as a long-term replacement; after another start in the following Saturday's 1-0 defeat at QPR, Evans made his final appearance before moving to Halifax Town in June 1979.

On a rainy last day of September, heading into the home fixture with Nottingham Forest, Saunders bemoaned the 'absolutely ridiculous' injury situation in which the club found itself. 'Trying to sort out a team early in the week is a waste of time,' he said. Forest, fresh from knocking out holders Liverpool in the European Cup first round, a goalless draw at Anfield completing a 2-0 aggregate success for the East Midlanders, were the very models of consistency. Avoid defeat and Clough's side would equal Leeds' all-time record of 34 league games unbeaten.

Despite holding a deserved half-time lead – Tommy Craig putting home a 19th-minute penalty after a foul by centre-half Larry Lloyd – Villa succumbed after the break as Forest, first through Woodcock in the 49th minute and then Robertson's contentious 79th-minute penalty (Dennis Mortimer had clearly tripped Ian Bowyer outside of the box but, despite vehement Villa protests, the referee refused to change his mind), marched victoriously into the history books. Just to add to Villa's crippling injury crisis, Gordon Cowans, after accidentally kicking the bottom of Archie Gemmill's boot, broke a bone in the instep of his right foot. Now down to the bare bones, Saunders wasn't able to select a side, only pick the players who were available; even then, one or two took to the field with knocks.

The predicament elicited little sympathy. A plea to the Football League to postpone Villa's following game, away at Highbury, fell on deaf ears. Attempts to add to their numbers came to nothing. In October, Villa were said to be keeping a watchful eye on Gerry Armstrong's situation at Tottenham, the Northern Ireland international forward expressing growing dissatisfaction at being played out of position. Armstrong remained at White Hart Lane. As Villa limped on, Liverpool, by complete contrast, were cantering. After only four league matches, including a 7-0 flattening of Spurs (Ardiles, Villa et al) at Anfield, their goal tally stood at 16. By September's end, a Jimmy Case hat-trick in a 3-0 win over Bolton had Paisley's team two points clear at the top ahead of near-neighbours Everton.

There were moments when Saunders could afford a rare smile. A 2-2 home draw with Manchester United – John Gregory giving Villa a seemingly commanding two-goal lead before a strike apiece from McIlroy and Macari saw United fight back – was, in Saunders' view, 'A wonderful advert for British football.' Then, after five defeats on the trot against their Second City rivals, a lone Andy Gray strike from a sweeping end-to-end move brought Villa a 1-0 victory at St Andrew's. But the joys were short-lived. The team soon returned to type.

A Friday night fixture at home to Middlesbrough – brought forward because of the weekend's motor show – culminated in a 2-0 defeat. The following weekend, Saunders saw his side only manage a 1-1 draw at Villa Park with struggling Manchester City. It was a game that brought down the curtain on the career of another Villa player: Leighton Phillips. Having witnessed the departures of Ian Ross and Chris Nicholl before him, Phillips recognised that being Villa captain bought no immunity from Saunders' cut-throat approach.

'The season before I left, Ron Saunders had asked me to be captain,' explained Phillips in an interview with author Colin Abbott. 'Even though it was a great honour, I had to think about this because Ian Ross hadn't been captain long before he was on his way and then exactly the same thing happened to big Chris Nicholl. Ron told me not to worry as I'd just signed a three-year contract.'

But, with the Evans/McNaught combo increasingly ticking Saunders' boxes and reserve team centre-half Brendan Ormsby, captain of the England youth side, emerging as another challenger for a defensive spot, Phillips had become an ever more peripheral figure. 'I was coming up to 30 and I needed to be playing first team football,' he said, 'but there were some promising youngsters coming through and there was no guarantee.'

John Toshack, who'd left Liverpool at the conclusion of the 1977/78 season to take up the player-manager position at resurgent Swansea, had introduced at the Vetch Field what Shankly termed the 'Liverpool recipe': a family atmosphere in which everyone at the club from the ground staff boy upwards was made to feel part of the same big adventure. Once Toshack, with whom Phillips had grown up and knew from his Cardiff days, came in for him, Phillips was happy to become one of the clan, swapping bench-warming in the Midlands for a return to his homeland and the Third Division.

The door to the Villa treatment room continued revolving. On 8 November the club's fortunes took an even bigger downturn. In the League Cup, having squeezed past Third Division Sheffield Wednesday then taken a three-game path to negotiate Crystal Palace – Villa eventually disposing of the Second Division side 3-0 in a second replay at neutral Highfield Road – Saunders' side were paired with more second tier opposition in Luton Town. The Hatters hadn't progressed beyond the fourth round in their history, yet Villa suffered a shock 2-0 home loss to the Kenilworth Road club and were out of the tournament.

It was a disastrous night all round for Saunders. Andy Gray took a hefty knock to the knee, was carried off – replaced by Cowans – and had his leg put in plaster as he awaited the doctor's verdict on the extent of the injury. He'd damaged both ankle and knee ligaments and would be sidelined for a couple of months at least. Then, after the game, Saunders, fuming at the exit, gave John Gidman a verbal rocket, accusing the right-back of not trying until after the visitors had scored. Gidman immediately submitted a transfer request and, although it was just as quickly withdrawn – Gidman took his place in the starting line-up for the next game, away at Wolves – a match had been put to a bonfire that would burn for months.

The gloom lifted slightly. A spell of game-time for Alex Cropley did its bit to help. Coming on as a substitute 20 minutes from the end of John Robson's testimonial as Villa played out a hugely entertaining 6-6 draw against an International XI (Ricky Villa turning out in a Villa away strip), Cropley was greeted with rapturous applause as the crowd welcomed back to the fold one of their favourites. While John Deehan grabbed the goalscoring honours, netting four times, it was Cropley who received the loudest cheer when, with only his second touch, he volleyed a cracking shot past Ray Clemence.

Three months after breaking his leg, when further surgery was required, the dejected midfielder had declared, 'I can see no point in going on.' But though the battle back to fitness had been even tougher than first imagined, he'd done it.

John Robson hadn't been so fortunate. 'The specialists have finally decided that he has no chance of playing again,' Saunders had told the press in September. Although it was Vic Crowe who signed Robson, Saunders had actually made a £100,000 bid for the player when in charge at Carrow Road. Derby's regular left-back when they won the Second Division title in 1968/69 and a member of their championship-winning side three seasons later before joining Villa, Robson was someone of whom both Clough and Saunders thought highly.

Their admiration was reciprocated. Robson believed it was the duty of a footballer to perform for his manager, regardless of any particular character traits that manager might possess. 'Personally, I don't think it matters what temperament the manager has,' Robson said. 'What does matter is their record of success.'

In the case of Clough and Saunders, those records were impossible to dispute. Robson was grateful to Saunders for the speed with which the testimonial was organised. 'When I learned the extent of my illness in January,' said the 28-year-old, 'I saw the best of Ron Saunders. It was a hard time for me, but he told me to wait until my health was better and that I shouldn't worry because the club would look after me.'

To Villa's credit, even as players dropped relentlessly out of the picture – Brian Little, with a stomach muscle injury, becoming another long-term casualty – results picked up. A 4-0 victory at Molineux – where Saunders felt 'we were a little bit more like our true selves' – preceded a 2-0 home win over Bristol City, including a stunning volleyed goal from John Deehan he later called 'the best of my career'. Saunders continued to give youth its head. Colin Gibson, a Bridport-born defender who'd only signed professionally in April, made his debut, albeit a very brief one, coming on as a late sub for Evans against Alan Dicks' side. Then, following a 2-0 Tuesday night defeat at The Dell, where Alan Ball's missed penalty spared an even bigger margin, Gary Shaw was pitched in for his first taste of a Midlands derby, making his full league debut as Villa drew 1-1.

On 9 December, as the string finally snapped for Forest – Liverpool's Terry McDermott hitting two goals, the first a penalty, to end Clough's side's 42-match unbeaten league record – Villa hammered another nail into bottom side Chelsea's coffin at Stamford Bridge. Allan Evans, on hand in the 15th minute to knock in after Chelsea keeper Bob Iles failed to hold a Gidman shot, got the only goal of the game. When Cropley came on for Shaw with eight minutes left, it was almost a year to the day since the West Brom game in which he had been injured.

For all the endless incarnations of their starting line-up, Villa were now tenth in the table, but only three points behind fourth-placed Arsenal. A push for a UEFA Cup spot was very possible. As Cropley made his welcome return against the Londoners, another Scot was saying goodbye. Gordon Smith had fallen out with Saunders. Following a disagreement at Bodymoor Heath, Smith stated that he 'could no longer work with the manager' and duly demanded a move. 'I was young and headstrong and opinionated,' explains Smith. 'Ron didn't like it unless you agreed with his opinion and complied with his methods.'

Smith, on arriving from Scotland, had accepted that he'd be on a lesser wage than some of the players. In his second season, having heard the dressing room talk about who was on what money, Smith went to see Saunders and, feeling he warranted 'a fair balance', requested a rise. He found himself dropped from the team 'as I had the audacity to ask for more'. In the dispute, there was only ever going to be one winner. 'Things were to be done his way or the highway,' Smith says, 'and regretfully I was out.' Smith felt it was a shame – 'I was happy at the club and treated very well,' he says – though did accept some culpability for the quarrel. 'When I look back, he handled me wrongly,' Smith says, 'but I handled the situation badly, too.'

The following February, Villa agreed a £150,000 deal with Spurs – Keith Burkinshaw had been impressed by Smith's performance in the number three shirt at White Hart Lane – and Smith left for London for almost double the fee Villa had paid St Johnstone.

There were further moves made into the transfer market. With Gray undergoing surgery on his knee and Little sidelined, Saunders turned to a striker he'd noticed not in league football but in a recent *Daily Express* Five-a-Side Tournament. Chelsea's Kenny Swain, who'd arrived at Stamford Bridge via Wycombe Wanderers in August 1973 relatively late at 21, was disillusioned with the direction that the London club was taking under manager Ken Shellito and, increasingly on the fringes of the first team, was keen to leave. Having seen him in the five-a-side competition at the old Earl's Court, Saunders sent Tony Barton to watch Swain play for Chelsea reserves. Meeting Saunders at Bodymoor Heath, Swain, another son of Birkenhead, was immediately taken with both the manager and the Villa set-up. He sensed, he wrote in his book *A Game of Three Halves*, he'd be joining 'a real football club' with a winning mentality. Despite his impression of Saunders being 'a fearsome character' who was 'so straight-laced', Swain saw something extremely appealing in his fellow Scouser and the thoroughly professional way he was running the Midlands outfit.

When the finer details of the transfer were ironed out – Saunders 'just sat there with daggers coming out of his eyes and I felt like I was pinned to the wall by his stare', Swain wrote – the Chelsea forward was offered a 'take it or leave it' deal. He had little hesitation in accepting. Despite a delay – Chelsea chairman Brian Mears informing Swain that he would soon be sacking Shellito, so the player might be staying after all – a move was eventually sealed; ex-Villa youth team boss Frank Upton took temporary charge of the Londoners and his first job was to sanction the transfer. Swain joined Villa for a £100,000 fee.

For Saunders, it was the end of a three-month quest. The Villa manager had long identified the need for more width within the side, a vital ingredient missing since Ray Graydon's departure. Willie Young, signed from Scottish junior side Arthurlie in July had made an impressive debut versus Manchester United but, after a brief, three-game flirtation with the number 11 shirt, the 22-year-old never played for Villa again, though remained at the club before moving to Torquay United in October 1981. Another purchase from Arthurlie, 20-year-old Tommy Graham, hadn't worked out either. Graham – younger brother of Leeds' Arthur – didn't even reach the first team fringes before ending his relatively short stay at Villa Park and joining Barnsley in their Fourth Division promotion bid.

In early November, Saunders had added another Scottish wideman to the staff; Dave Cunningham, a 25-year-old left-winger noted for his dribbling ability, signing for a nominal fee from Swindon Town. Cunningham, however, was one more who would fail to provide the answers Saunders was seeking, and was sold the following season to Hereford United in a £25,000 deal without making a single start.

More of a supporting striker than a winger, Swain announced that he was looking forward to playing up front 'as long as people don't expect me to be scoring like Andy Gray at his best'. Wearing the number nine shirt, he made his debut – and broke a finger! – in a 1-1 draw at home to Norwich City on 16 December, an own goal from the Canaries' Mick Maguire levelling the scores. Swain was the 25th player to pull on a shirt for the first team since the season's start. He wouldn't be the last.

That honour would go to Joe Ward. A week after Swain's signing, Saunders brought in the Glasgow-born Clyde centre-forward, one of the most sought-after strikers in Scotland, with the Scottish side's manager Craig Brown collecting a club record £80,000 for their goalscoring ace. It would be a whole month, though, before Ward made his first appearance. The reason for that was the inclement English weather. In one of the worst winters in league history, over 100 matches were lost to the elements. Heavy snow and frozen pitches forced postponements throughout the four divisions.

The Villa Park turf, in particular, suffered. Following their 2-2 Boxing Day draw with Leeds United – Gregory claiming another double-strike – Villa didn't play on home soil again for over two months, a period which, Saunders said, 'prompted intensive research into a new method of protecting the pitch' (Villa later acquiring a new cover that could be placed in position in a matter of minutes).

During that time, they only mustered three away games. In the FA Cup, the dream was over before it had even begun, an Allan Evans own goal contributing to a 2-0 defeat at the City Ground. Andy Gray had been expected to return for the tie but, when his knee swelled up after training, he was immediately taken to hospital where cartilage trouble was diagnosed. The injury jinx that had dogged Gray throughout the season had struck once more. A rueful Saunders could only conclude it was 'unbelievable bad luck'.

Villa were unfortunate, too, to only get a 1-1 draw at Everton in the league, a Dave Thomas equaliser 27 seconds from the end denying the visitors a win they perhaps deserved. Ironically, the referee for the Goodison game was the same one who'd officiated the previous season when Kenny Swain was in the Chelsea side thrashed 6-0 at Everton, Swain – a boyhood Toffees fan – getting booked for contesting the penalty decision that allowed Latchford to reach his 30-goal target.

Twenty-four days later, Swain netted his first goal as Villa earned another 1-1 away draw, this time with Manchester United. Joe Ward, once a team-mate of Andy Gray in the Glasgow Schoolboys side that played against Manchester at Old Trafford, now found himself deputising for Gray at the same ground. By the time Villa Park was fit for duty again for the derby clash with Birmingham City on 3 March, 67 days had elapsed since the second of John Gregory's goals against Leeds. Against their local rivals, thanks to a Gordon Cowans strike, Villa emerged 1-0 victors, the twin return of Little and Gray providing another welcome boost.

When, four days later, at home again, they put three past Bolton Wanderers without reply, it left Villa eighth in the table and a serious late challenge for a European place remained feasible. For all the lack of momentum, Saunders stressed, 'I have always made it a point not to complain about misfortune or make excuses.' He and the players were, he said, 'now more determined than ever to roll up our sleeves and get on with it'.

Yet, always playing catch-up with the sides above them, Villa were left trailing by their failure to get into any steady stride. Middlesbrough beat them yet again, 2-0 at Ayresome Park. Three days later, a Gidman penalty, Evans and Mortimer gave Villa a 3-1 home win over QPR. Then, the following Saturday, Gidman repeated the trick, his first-half spot-kick together with a Gray goal putting Villa two up against Spurs. But, with just 11 minutes left on the clock, three quick goals – two from Hoddle and a dramatic late winner from Chris Jones – were conceded, leaving many in the 35,486 crowd shaking their heads in disbelief and Saunders confessing that the result 'took a lot of digesting by everyone'. Villa's triumph at White Hart Lane in August now seemed just a distant joyful memory.

The Villa boss remained philosophical – 'One swallow never, ever made a summer and, equally so, the good or bad result never, ever achieved much,' he said – but his mood would soon grow far darker. The filling in the sandwich of two 1-1 draws with Coventry City (Allan Evans, having scored in the home game with the Sky Blues, was then sent off at Highfield Road for headbutting Tommy Hutchison, walking off the pitch without waiting for the ref to produce the red card), was a midweek match on 4 April at Nottingham Forest's City Ground.

Clough's men, still fighting to retain their title, were building up a head of steam. The previous week, Irish midfielder Martin O'Neill had bagged a hat-trick in a 6-0 drubbing of Chelsea. With England's first £1m player Trevor Francis now added to their ranks, the 24-year-old having made the move to the East Midlands after eight seasons at St Andrew's, Forest possessed an impressive attacking armoury.

And, on a chilly Wednesday evening, as Manchester United were edging past Liverpool courtesy of an 80th-minute Jimmy Greenhoff header to take them to their third FA Cup Final in four years, Forest's strike force proved far too strong for Villa. After a 13th-minute own goal by Evans – the Scot unfortunate to deflect Woodcock's low cross-shot past Rimmer – had handed the home side a half-time lead, Villa surrendered to a three-goal second-half blast from Woodcock, Francis and O'Neill that left them on the end of a demoralising 4-0 rout with only the heroics of Jimmy Rimmer preventing further embarrassment. It was the first time in Saunders' reign that his side had lost by such a margin.

Yet it was the manner of the defeat that was most surprising. Villa didn't so much lose as completely collapse. 'There appeared to be no pride in their performance,' reported the *Birmingham Mail*. 'Players who would once have walked through brick walls in the name of Aston Villa were guilty of the most slipshod soccer imaginable.' The effort and application that were prerequisites of any Saunders side appeared to have gone AWOL. 'The defence had a nightmare,' wrote the *Mail* reporter. 'The midfield were unable to do much constructive as they were so busy helping out at the back, and the attack was virtually non-existent, carrying the knockout power of a bantamweight against Muhammad Ali.' A harsh assessment, but doubtless mild compared with the one dished out by Saunders at the final whistle. Half an hour later, the *Mail* recorded, Saunders boarded the team coach 'grim-faced and tight-lipped'. A tipping point with certain individuals had definitely been reached.

A 3-3 home draw with Derby County – Colin Gibson unfortunate to concede an own goal on his first full appearance – and a 1-0 defeat to a Paul Hart header at Leeds meant that, as Villa prepared to face leaders Liverpool on Easter Monday, they hadn't won for six matches and were now in the table's bottom half.

Saunders acknowledged that, through circumstances, the younger players had been pitched in more often than he'd have liked. Saunders believed that if Villa had one player come through each season and established in the first team, the youth team had done its job. Maturing under the guidance of Keith Leonard (the retired striker taking over after Frank Upton left for Chelsea), the side had lost narrowly, 1-0, in a one-off FA Youth Cup Final at Highbury to a richly promising Crystal Palace team at the tail end of the previous season. Now, Gibson, Williams, Ormsby and Shaw from that team had all sampled top-level football and, while they'd undoubtedly benefited from the experience, Saunders knew they still required 'a certain amount of nursing in their early days' if they weren't to be 'killed by too much pressure too soon'.

Liverpool, naturally, were the perfect example of how it was best done. 'We want to bring our youngsters along in the same careful way,' Saunders said. Villa were staring at a 21-point gap between themselves and the team from Anfield, whose nearest challengers, West Brom, trailed them by six points. But, before Villa Park's biggest league turn-out of the season – 44,029 – Saunders' side pulled off their best result when it was least expected. Ignoring the absence of Little and Gray – Evans and Deehan forming the front twosome – and with John Gregory filling in at centre-half alongside McNaught, Villa harried and hassled the visitors from the start. Mortimer, Cowans and Cropley, closing down the opposition and snuffing out any threat, completely dominated the midfield.

With the champions-elect out of their stride, Villa took advantage. In the 33rd minute, Clemence could only parry a Cowans shot from long distance into the path of Allan Evans, who fired the ball into the empty net. Nine minutes later, the big Scot, on the end of a Swain cross, powered a firm header goalwards and Phil Thompson, now captain in Emlyn Hughes' absence, deflected an attempted clearance past his helpless keeper. In the 55th minute, Deehan, nutmegging Clemence, gave Villa a third to make the game all but safe. Deehan's goal completed a whirlwind weekend for the Villa striker; the day before, his wife Linda had given birth to their first child, daughter Emma Jane. Although David Johnson reduced the arrears ten minutes later, Villa remained resolute and were full value for their 3-1 victory.

The result, putting an end to Liverpool's 13-game unbeaten run, was all the more outstanding because in no other match in the season would the Merseysiders let in more than one goal. In the entire campaign Liverpool would only concede 16 times. Despite Bob Paisley's assertion that his team were 'absolute rubbish' on the afternoon, it didn't detract from Villa's performance – 'a triumph for teamwork', Saunders believed – that saw a return of 'the old fire and passion' in the manager's eyes. Why they couldn't produce it on a frequent basis remained a mystery.

The win against the Reds was the first of a four-game winning streak, a 5-1 home thrashing of Arsenal, with a Gary Shelton hat-trick earning Villa a season's best victory after they went in trailing at the break, easily the most notable. But following a narrow 2-1 success at Villa Park over relegation-doomed Chelsea – Kenny Swain enjoying a 'Roy of the Rovers' moment against his former employers with the decisive goal – the team lost their footing yet again. By the time they went to Anfield on the back of two stalemates against Ipswich and Bolton, Villa's hopes of a UEFA Cup spot had nigh on dwindled to nothing. On the night of Tuesday 8 May, Villa faced Liverpool with the home side requiring a win to clinch the title – their 11th – with two games still to go.

The momentous evening was weighted with even greater significance; it was the 40th anniversary of Bob Paisley's arrival at Anfield as a then-young, unknown footballer. Paisley's charges were determined to give their County Durham-born boss the perfect anniversary present and any chance that Villa might gatecrash the party vanished after only 47 seconds when full-back Alan Kennedy opened the scoring. After that, witnessed by 50,576, it was largely a game of containment for the away side. Further goals from Dalglish and McDermott saw the Reds romp to victory and the road to their third title in four years, signposted for so long, had been reached. After giving their opponents a one-year break, normal service had been resumed. They'd accumulated 68 points, a comfortable eight ahead of their nearest rivals, and a record under the two-points-for-a-win system.

The former second-in-command Paisley, voted Manager of the Year for a third time, had proved he was second to none. Liverpool's football, as a rule, was fairly functional – Paisley, not the most imaginative of tacticians, was very much an advocate of the traditional 4-4-2 – and won few fans outside of Merseyside. Journalist Martin Swain is quoted in Paul Rees's book, *The Three Degrees: The Men Who Changed British Football Forever*, an unsentimental and often moving account of West Brom's Cyrille Regis, Laurie Cunningham and Brendon Batson, as saying that watching Liverpool was 'a fairly joyless experience' akin to witnessing the West Indies cricket side of the time: both teams, for all their admirable qualities, possessed a 'brutish efficiency'. Nevertheless, it was an effectiveness every other club was striving to emulate.

Runners-up Forest were making a pretty good fist of it. Their footballing fairytale yielded yet more happy endings. A Trevor Francis header against Sweden's Malmo brought the European Cup to the East Midlands, where it joined the League Cup in the City Ground silverware cabinet, a 3-2 win over Southampton having earned a second successive triumph in the competition in March.

Ron Atkinson's third-placed West Brom, enjoying the club's highest league finish since 1953/54 when they were runners-up, were very much deemed the free spirits of the division. Their football had an undeniable feel-good factor about it and an exhilarating televised 5-3 win at Old Trafford on 30 December left an indelible impression on the millions who witnessed the TV highlights. And it was the Baggies, a whole 13 points better off than Villa and with every right to claim their place as the West Midlands' 'Top Dogs', who inflicted their neighbours' last defeat of the season, 1-0 at Villa Park.

Saunders' side ended the campaign on a high note with a 3-2 success at Manchester City, but the tune had been all too familiar. Eighth-placed for the second year running with an identical 46 points, European qualification was missed out on again and their fans might be forgiven for experiencing a frustrating feeling of déjà vu. For all the mitigating circumstances, there was a sense that, after the heady heights of 1976/77, the potential was being frittered away.

The club, in many respects, had plateaued and, while Saunders remained focussed on the ascent, it seemed that climbing boots had been swapped for carpet slippers. His side had virtually hobbled over the finishing line. The spate of injuries – 'the worst in living memory at the club', Saunders termed it – meant Jimmy Rimmer, an ever-present again, seeing the personnel before him change with alarming rapidity. 'Most teams would have been relegated if they'd had the injuries to key players which we had,' Saunders reasoned. Even if he knew his best first XI, the manager had seldom had the chance to select it.

There were, perhaps, certain consolations. Villa's vibrant youth policy was still rich soil. With a huge supporting cast being called upon, the blooding of so many young talents had given them vital experience and Villa's supporters a tantalising glimpse of players who might well fill future starring roles. Returning from his injury against Forest, Gordon Cowans' worth grew by the game. Tigerish in the tackle, deft in possession, with an eye for a telling pass, Cowans was now a regular name on the teamsheet, his displays earning him admirers at both Villa Park and beyond.

Dennis Mortimer, too, had played some of the most inspired football of his career, anchoring the midfield with almost metronomic consistency. Promoted to captain with the shortest notice from his manager – 'Okay, you lead them out,' Saunders had told him – Mortimer dismissed the suggestion that there was a jinx on wearing the armband (after the departures of the three previous incumbents). 'It's just a coincidence and something we have a laugh about,' Mortimer said.

While Alex Cropley's valiant late-season return was a blessing, Tommy Craig had proved a huge disappointment. After finally kick-starting a Villa career disrupted by injury, the midfielder only rarely offered glimpses of the form that led Saunders to make him the club's record signing. Gary Shelton, even while Saunders felt the player 'found it difficult to add strength and consistency to his game', proved a far more fruitful acquisition; his eye for goal yielding a season's tally of eight in league and cup. Shelton's goal return was matched by John Gregory but not one player reached double figures; John Deehan, filling in mostly as a straight swap for Gray, finishing top scorer with a paltry nine.

As in 1975/76, Brian Little's injury-riddled campaign brought only a single goal. In the latter half of the campaign, Saunders felt Little's 'mental attitude was not up to it', and the once-prolific marksman missed much of Villa's run-in. Both Little and Gray, perhaps unfairly given their lack of match fitness, were also subjected to some harsh remarks by certain sections of the local press.

For Andy Gray, the season, he said, had been 'a complete and utter disaster'. All in all, the Scottish striker managed only 19 league and cup games and the various, mostly injury-induced, troughs Gray experienced had dumped him in the depths. 'If there's anything at all good about it,' he told journalist Mike Beddow, 'then it is that I have the whole summer to get completely fit before my next match.'

But Gray's next match wouldn't be in Aston Villa's claret and blue. Despite his declaration that 'Villa come first with me' and a pledge to work hard to make up for lost time – 'I owe a lot to the club after this season,' he said – Gray had played his last game for the club under the management of Ron Saunders. He wasn't the only one. An air of uncertainty at Villa Park had developed into one of disillusionment. In the dressing room, Saunders' stock was definitely decreasing. Some of the players were now questioning the manager's tactical ability. Others, strong characters such as Gidman, Little and Gray, were increasingly fed up with how Saunders treated them.

For some time, Little claimed, Saunders' abrasive management style had rubbed up certain individuals the wrong way and 'the friction he created to keep the team winning' was having quite the opposite effect. Now, with ever-louder murmurings of mutiny emerging, the press began to speculate about exactly what the truth was behind the rumours of player dissatisfaction. That summer, their questions were perfectly encapsulated in one headline in the *Sports Argus*, 'What Is Going On at Aston Villa?' In the months to come, it was a question that would be asked over and over again.

The Boy With the Golden Hair

IN June 1979, as terrorism returned to mainland UK in the shape of letter bombs – 13 such devices being either exploded or defused at post offices in the Birmingham area – matters at Aston Villa were threatening to be explosive in their own way. The uneasy peace existing between Ron Saunders and various members of his playing staff and the board was in danger of breaking out into open hostilities. Just over ten years after the takeover that had transformed the fortunes of the football club, the whiff of revolution, if not exactly bloody, was undeniably in the air once more.

It all started off tranquilly enough. In the same week that month, two new faces arrived. In Tony Morley, the Villa fans who, since Ray Graydon's leaving, had been chanting 'We want a winger' finally got their wish. A promising wideman noted for his bursts of speed and excellent control, Morley, in February 1976, had signed for Burnley from Preston for a club record £100,000, essentially as Leighton James' replacement. But, plagued by inconsistency at Turf Moor, his career had stalled.

All the while convinced that what Morley really needed was 'someone to give him the confidence to turn on the style on a more regular basis', Saunders approached Burnley boss Harry Potts with a £200,000 offer. Morley, having once rejected an opportunity to move to Arsenal believing he wasn't then ready for the big time, now felt the moment was right. Despite only recently moving into a new house in Lancashire, he had little hesitation in quitting for life in the Midlands.

Also joining was Terry Donovan. During three seasons with his hometown club Grimsby Town, the 21-year-old Eire striker had established himself as a prolific scorer, netting 28 times in 63 league and cup outings with the Blundell Park outfit. Saunders had been in Everton's youth team around the time that Donovan's father, Don, was full-back and captain at Goodison. Remembering the Villa manager as 'a determined young man with a high work ethic, something you could see in the Villa teams Saunders had gone on to produce', Donovan Snr was delighted with his son's £70,000 move. 'I know he [Saunders] is an honest man who is good for young players,' he said.

But as Saunders' rebuilding programme got under way, other pieces started to come loose. John Gregory was the first. On signing for Villa, Gregory had stated, 'To be honest, I'm not fussy where I play.' A good job. In his two seasons since, Gregory had done what he termed 'a lot of shifting around', his versatility a godsend for Saunders in the midst of the club's chronic injury crisis. Having donned the number 8 shirt against Liverpool on Easter Monday – just before kick-off, Gregory plucked up enough courage to ask Saunders if he could wear it and, to the player's surprise, Saunders ratified it – the multitasking player boasted a proud record: after only 57 games since joining he'd worn shirts 2 to 12 and played in all ten outfield positions for the Midlanders.

But with the last-day win at Maine Road, Gregory sported Villa colours for the final time. Despite playing two divisions higher than he'd ever done before – 'I had to catch up with the quality that was in the squad,' Gregory said – he adapted well to First Division football and, after several standout performances, he felt he should be offered improved terms on his contract. 'They were paying me £225 and I wanted the top line, which was £250,' Gregory told *The Independent*. As with others before him, Saunders refused to grant him his wish.

When Brighton, just promoted to the First Division for the first time, came in for him, the lure of what Gregory later called 'a few pennies' was too strong. 'All my life I'd lived on the breadline,' said Gregory, 'and suddenly there was a chance of making more money.' Gregory headed for the south coast in a £250,000 deal, Villa making a tidy profit on the £40,000 fee they'd forked out to Northampton. But there were mutual recriminations between himself and Saunders. Gregory certainly had a legitimate argument for warranting a £25 hike in his weekly wage. Saunders, after all, had fought time and again to better the terms of his own contract. In Saunders, however, Gregory found himself up against a rock that wouldn't be budged.

Only 14 months after his arrival at Villa Park, Tommy Craig was also on his way out. 'When you are buying players,' Saunders said, 'not only do you look for ability; you look for a certain type of player to do a particular job in your team. Craig, while not an exact fit for Cropley, was cast from a similar mould. He was a clever footballer and skilful ballplayer but, standing dictating the action from the centre of the pitch, Craig was far too immobile to suit Villa's style. He lacked Cropley's aggression, too, and, unlucky with injuries, when Craig did start, Saunders felt he was subtracting from rather than adding to the team – the side was playing to suit Craig, not the other way around.

It fast became evident that no matter how many round holes Saunders tried to fit Craig in, the Scot would always be a square peg. Ex-Liverpool star Ian St John had once opined, 'A manager must not only have the wisdom of Solomon, he must have the patience of Job.' Saunders had clearly run out of patience and few could question the wisdom behind the midfielder's sale. As with Leighton Phillips, Swansea City, now a Second Division side, was Craig's destination.

If Craig's departure wasn't entirely unexpected, the name of the next player who looked to be leaving was. Brian Little, who'd arrived at Villa Park as a 14-year-old schoolboy after considering apprenticeship offers from no fewer than 14 league clubs, among them Leeds, Manchester City and Arsenal, was still only 25, his best years seemingly still ahead of him. But the player who 'fell in love with Villa' because 'there was something magical about it' was now no longer enchanted by life at the club. After two frustrating seasons struggling to find form and fitness, Little had reached a stage where his career, he said, 'perhaps needed a boost'. Citing a desire to prove himself once more, he asked for a transfer.

Little's status on the terraces was unparalleled. In claret and blue eyes, no one had been more instrumental in Aston Villa's renaissance. The Peterlee lad who grew up supporting Newcastle United was, to the supporters, a dyed-in-the-wool Villan. Discovering that Little was seeking to move was shattering enough. When it emerged where his next destination was to be, it left them quite incredulous. Having pocketed £1m from the February sale of Trevor Francis, Birmingham City, despite relegation to the Second Division after a disastrous first full season for Jim Smith, were flush. Little was the player they'd earmarked as the ideal replacement for their departed former wonder kid.

Despite believing that, when Little was on song, he was among the very best front players in English football, Saunders still had questions about his forward's overall involvement in any one game. With the rapid rise of Gary Shaw and Saunders' preference for at least one bigger central striker, it looked increasingly difficult to accommodate both the youngster and Little in the same side. More crucially, Shaw was eager and willing to learn – something that Little, to Saunders' mind at least, was not. Agreeing that the time was right for Little to move, Saunders gave it the green light. 'I think he'd had enough of me by then,' Little said later. Little, while never questioning Saunders' qualities as a manager had had 'quite a few arguments' with the Villa boss. There were, Little recalled, 'hundreds of occasions where Ron wanted to kick me and shake me before a game'.

Little liked the set-up at St Andrew's. He got on well with Smith and, he said, 'It didn't bother me too much that I would be playing in the Second Division.' But with Little's bag already packed, the move was dramatically called off. A displaced vertebra in Little's back was picked up by the Birmingham doctor during the routine medical examination. The hitherto undiagnosed problem had caused Little occasional trouble over the years but was one he hadn't considered too serious. When a second specialist confirmed it, feeling that it had most likely gone undetected since birth, City, with £615,000 at stake, decided they couldn't take a risk on the player. Soon after, they took much less of a gamble, spending £175,000 on Walsall's Alan Buckley.

To the immense relief of Villa fans, their hero – by divine intervention, some believed – would be remaining at Villa Park. For the forward, the aborted transfer, as Saunders later put it, was a 'traumatic experience', though Little 'tried to remain philosophical'. Offered two options – leave things be and carry on playing, or undergo a complex operation that would mean a long period out of the game – the striker opted to continue playing. His hopes of a fresh start over, Little rejoined his Villa team-mates ready for the 1979/80 season. Whatever joy Saunders felt about retaining the services of one of his top players, however, was quickly tempered by the news that another couldn't wait to get away.

Andy Gray had spent part of the summer in a Bel Air mansion, property of Brummie heavy metal band Black Sabbath, whose bassist and lead lyricist Geezer Butler was a diehard Villa supporter. Gray may have been subjected to Butler's fanaticism, but it had little effect. When the players reported back for pre-season, the Scot demanded a transfer. The forward who had, in his words, 'jumped at the chance' to join the club was now positively itching to leave. The reason? He could no longer tolerate working under Saunders.

Such was Gray's desperation, he not only informed Saunders of his desire, but told the Villa board and the national press, too. The long-standing differences between manager and player had now, in effect, become public knowledge. When Saunders turned down the request, informing Gray that he wouldn't let him go, the Scot reiterated his determination in no uncertain terms. 'I said, "I want to leave and I won't be happy until I do,"' Gray wrote in *Gray Matters*. '"That's the situation. You know it and I know it. I'm telling you now so I don't have to come banging on your door every day asking for a move."'

When, the following day, Saunders was quoted in the newspapers as saying, 'Andy Gray has now withdrawn his transfer request,' Gray was left dumbfounded. It was all starting to get very murky.

'Beyond everything I've ever dreamt of' and 'a season full of magic' were how Gray described 1976/77 at the time. But two years on, his explosive impact diminished by prolonged absences, the blissful picture had taken on a nightmarish hue. The omission from MacLeod's Scotland squad capped what was mostly a miserable few months. At the end of 1978/79, beset with injuries, Gray was almost at rock bottom. But the root cause of his unhappiness was Saunders. Given their respective personalities, the relationship was never going to be anything less than turbulent. Gray, 'a massive character, bristling with aggression, bubbling with good humour and overflowing with opinion' in the view of journalist David Harrison, a man who knew Gray well and ghosted his weekly column in the *Sports Argus*, was virtually the antithesis of his manager.

The initial cracks began to show in that successful first full campaign in Villa colours. Gray, perhaps the victim of his own youthful naivety, wanted to play at every opportunity whether he was fully fit or not. But he also felt that Saunders was forcing him to perform when the striker would have benefited more from a spell on the sidelines. Still occasionally suffering from the remnants of an injury that had once threatened his career while at Dundee United, Gray believed an unsympathetic Saunders was blinkered to any pain the player might be enduring.

Saunders was convinced, according to Gray, that 'even when I was 60 per cent fit my presence unsettled the opposition and created opportunities for others.' He was right, of course. But Gray's unflinching approach – he not only put his head in where it hurt, but threw his whole body in for good measure – would inevitably make him a magnet for niggles and much worse. His dismay with the manager was already growing.

The rift was widened the day after the Wembley stalemate with Everton. Refused permission to attend the evening's PFA awards ceremony, Gray missed out on what should have been one of his proudest moments. Despite the entreaties of PFA chairman Derek Dougan – the ex-Villa forward, equally renowned for his forceful character, making various suggestions to Saunders, including offering a flight for Gray back to the Second City after the ceremony – Saunders was adamant that travel would aggravate Gray's ankle problem which had flared up again during the final. Gray would remain in Birmingham and that was that!

Saunders had form. After the 1975 League Cup Final, Jimmy Cumbes – Villa's PFA representative – along with a number of other players weren't allowed to attend the dinner. Saunders told the goalkeeper that returning to Birmingham for the following day's victory parade before the Villa fans was far more important. Despite Cumbes' request that he and his team-mates be allowed to travel back down to London after the parade and be given the Monday morning off training, Saunders refused. 'I thought it was a bit petty,' Cumbes said.

In denying Gray, the striker believed that Saunders was being deliberately vindictive and trying to teach the Scot a lesson. Eventually, a compromise was reached between Saunders and Gray but it wasn't a happy one. 'The whole thing was really downbeat and awkward,' Gray wrote in his autobiography, 'certainly not the way a player should remember one of the real highlights of his career.' The seeds of resentment towards Saunders would only grow into outright hostility. They were given further nourishment on the weekend before the return match with Barcelona.

Gray, having missed the home leg with a muscle strain, was still struggling to regain fitness. On the Saturday, he'd had a run-out – his first in eight weeks – for the Villa third team, but then had to withdraw from a reserve fixture. On the Sunday afternoon, the day before the Villa squad were due to fly out to Spain, Saunders paid Gray a visit to enquire if he'd be fit enough to play in the Nou Camp. The young forward, unable to make any promise, could only say that he hoped so.

According to Gray, Saunders wasn't satisfied with such a non-committal response. 'He said, "That's not good enough. I need to know now,"' Gray recounted in *Gray Matters*. When Gray repeated his vague answer, Saunders informed Gray that he would be staying behind in the UK. On the Monday, Saunders told the press, 'He came out of Saturday's game with a thigh strain and there was no point in playing him again so soon. There is no chance of him being fit for Wednesday.' The statement masked a whole other story.

To add insult to an ever-worsening injury, Gray was later told that, on the plane back from Barcelona, Peter White, a journalist with whom he was friendly, asked Saunders if Gray's presence might have made any difference to the result. Saunders' reply to the question, White told Gray, was, 'Let me tell you something about Andy Gray – he not only cheated this club, he has cheated its fans and he's also cheated himself.' Whether Saunders believed he had good reason or not, to a player who prided himself on his blunt honesty both on and off the pitch, it was the ultimate slur.

There were numerous examples, Gray cited in his book, of times when he'd defied injury, eschewed a further spell on the treatment table or simply ignored common sense/medical advice to pull on a shirt, albeit with the aid of painkilling injections. 'I spent more time on ice than Torvill and Dean,' Gray wrote. 'Was that the action of somebody out to defraud the club and the fans? I don't think so.'

While, on the surface at least, it was still all smiles, privately Saunders' words had left Gray seething. The Villa boss had told *Shoot* magazine in 1977 that 'managing football clubs is 99 per cent man-management. It's getting players to respect you and for you to respect them, and to build up a rapport between the two.' Any lingering respect Gray had had for Saunders was lost.

Gray's World Cup heartache did little to soothe his bitterness. On 17 December 1975, two months after signing for Villa, Gray, the boyhood Rangers supporter, had collected his first full cap as Scotland drew 1-1 with Romania in their last European Championship qualifying match, ex-Villa skipper Rioch scoring their goal from a free kick. But his career on the international stage hadn't prospered in the manner many, himself included, had imagined. Aside from his Argentina omission, injuries and the three-match international ban he'd received for his sending-off in Prague, Gray didn't win nearly as many caps as he felt he deserved. The main reason, he believed, was Saunders. Concerned about the risk of his forward aggravating injuries, the Villa manager, Gray claimed, put pressure on him to withdraw from the Scottish squad time and again until, reluctantly, Gray gave in. 'That should have been my time,' Gray insisted, 'but it slipped away.'

Understandably, Saunders was a manager for whom the club's best interests came first. For some time, in Saunders' view, those interests weren't being best served by Gray's lifestyle. Gray, 'a mercurial figure' in journalist David Harrison's description, 'lived life to the full' and 'could usually be found around the city, holding court in a pub or wine bar with his circle of friends'. His off-field antics were fast becoming as newsworthy as his all-action exploits on the pitch and made the Scottish striker what Dave Woodhall termed 'the first true celebrity to emerge from Midlands football'. It was an achievement on Gray's CV with which Saunders was bound to be unimpressed.

One of a generation of players who'd plied their trade in the pre-mass media age, Saunders had no truck whatsoever with the showbiz or the pop culture that 1970s football had increasingly embraced. Another Ron – Greenwood – was, apparently, so wary of players having their heads turned by the outside attractions of fame and fortune, he advised his players to get married, as it encouraged responsibility and, more to the point, kept them out of bars. Saunders took a different tack. If, post-match, reporters expected him to speak in glowing terms about Gray, they were greeted instead with a comment about a more unsung hero like Frank Carrodus.

Saunders, 'the unbending Liverpudlian' according to Dennis Shaw in *A Game of Three Halves*, 'had an almost pathological dislike of anyone else in the club getting any sort of "star" treatment'. Should any player receive too much exposure or demand an improved contract, Shaw said that the Villa manager 'would dismiss them as effing idiots'. Too much limelight for any individual, Saunders made out, disrupted the team or created resentment among other players. To Gray, that was nonsense. 'What Saunders really resented,' he claimed, 'was not that star players took the focus off the team, but that they took the spotlight off him.'

Although his professionalism meant that he never went out after Wednesday if he was playing a Saturday game, Gray certainly liked the Birmingham nightlife. Further front-page publicity followed when Gray became part-owner of a nightclub, The Holy City Zoo at Hockley, managed by Gray's younger brother Duncan and a popular haunt with local 'celebrities'. It's doubtful that Saunders was a regular.

Saunders would later maintain that Gray's meteoric rise had come 'too swiftly for the player to handle'. In his book, Gray denied it vehemently. But Gray's growing profile undoubtedly lent weight to his manager's belief that the forward was getting distracted from performing the job he was paid so handsomely to do. When a photograph appeared of Gray walking barefooted across Corporation Street, Saunders went ballistic. 'I always felt that was one of the moments when he decided the striker would have to be moved on,' said David Harrison.

After the 19-year-old Gray arrived at Villa Park in October 1975, he soon found himself sharing a house with John Gidman, Saunders ringing up the right-back – then single and living alone – to inform him that the club had just signed a young lad from Dundee United and 'he's going to be good'. Also, Saunders told Gidman, 'He's moving in with you.' Over the course of a year, the pair lived together and forged a strong friendship. 'He didn't drink when he arrived at Villa,' Gidman relayed to Andy Mitten in *We're The Famous Man United. Old Trafford in the Eighties – The Players' Stories*. 'He did after I'd introduced him to the country pub in his first week.' In August 1979, shortly after his 'great mate' Gray, John Gidman submitted his own transfer request to the Aston Villa board.

Despite two years remaining on his existing contract, Gidman wanted improved terms. Having struck a deal with the club secretary – 'She left me the players' contracts on the desk and I walked in the office and saw them' – Gidman was 'gutted' to discover how his wages compared with many of his team-mates 'because I was one of the better players'. Dennis Mortimer, for one, was on a lot more money than Gidman's £300-a-week. Both Gray and he, Gidman told Mitten, 'got bladdered and agreed to put transfer requests in the following day'.

Yet, while supposedly about a salary increase, Gidman's chief dissatisfaction, like Gray's, stemmed from his strained relationship with Ron Saunders. Gidman, writes Gray in *Gray Matters*, was 'a big, flamboyant character, popular in the dressing room and on the terraces', and, in Gray's opinion, 'just the sort of player the manager hated'. The feeling was mutual. Saunders and Gidman had, in Gray's words, 'fallen out in a big way' and the Villa defender was eyeing the exit signs, desperate to escape the manager's clutches.

The right-back's surging runs down the flank often had the Villa fans in a ferment. Gidman's crossing at speed was an art form in itself. But a player whose poise appeared occasionally to border on the arrogant, Gidman was, in reality, suffering. His confidence already dented by the series of unfortunate injuries that had disrupted his career, what Gidman took as Saunders' belittling tactics made an even deeper impression. Even if he'd had a good game, Saunders 'knocked me all the time', Gidman said.

The defender 'just couldn't get on' with his fellow Liverpudlian, the 'personality thing' between the two only becoming more pronounced. After missing out on the 1975 League Cup Final and their fall-out following the Luton defeat, getting blamed for Villa's exit in Barcelona was, Gidman felt, 'the turning point'. The situation had seemingly escalated to the point of no return.

Training at Bodymoor Heath soon after, Gray and Gidman received a message to get changed and go to Villa Park. They'd been summoned to a secret boardroom meeting. Told that they weren't to discuss with anybody what was about to unfold, the pair were quizzed by the directors on why they wanted to leave. They gave a list of grievances about the manager. 'If we sack Ron Saunders, will you stay?' one of the directors asked. Gidman said he would. It was either Saunders or him, he'd decided.

Gray, however, declined. 'No matter how much I disliked Saunders,' Gray wrote in *Gray Matters*, 'I wasn't keen to start plotting behind his back.' Gray was adamant he wanted a change of scenery regardless of Saunders' position. It made no difference. According to Gidman, 'The board said that nobody was bigger than the club and that they would sell us.'

The Gray/Gidman situation aggravated an already-existing division within the Villa squad. The unsettled duo had a mutual adversary in Dennis Mortimer. Gidman didn't see eye to eye with the midfielder while Gray, although crediting Mortimer in his book with being 'a good player and a terrific captain' said that the two of them had never got on. They'd even clashed a few times in training. Mortimer, in both Gidman's and Gray's view, was not so much Saunders' strong right arm on the pitch as his eyes and ears off it. Things they felt should have remained in the dressing room – players going out drinking or about to submit a transfer request – were getting back to the manager. Gidman even went so far as to call his team-mate 'a snitch'.

A definite anti- and pro-Saunders divide among the players grew wider. Three members of the latter camp – Mortimer, McNaught and Rimmer – met with chairman Harry Kartz to air their take on the situation. For Mortimer, the reason behind the two players wanting away was they 'thought they could get more money somewhere else'.

Saunders, according to Kenny Swain, ran 'a tight ship' with nearly all the players getting very similar money. The wage structure was kept to a level the club could sustain. Yet Villa's players were always incentivised under Saunders. Success, he believed, should be rewarded, so a bonus system was put in place. Frank Carrodus, interviewed by the *Birmingham Mail* in 2008, recalled an incident in which himself, Brian Little, Chris Nicholl and Ray Graydon were sitting in the bath after the 1975 League Cup Final and suddenly realised that, with £750 for appearing and £1,000 for winning, 'Bloody hell, we've just earned nearly two grand today!'

Gray maintained that he was seeking a move 'to learn more about the game and, more importantly, win honours'. Nevertheless, the rumour mill around Birmingham couldn't resist churning out gossip about the 'real' reason Gray wanted away. With the failure of his nightclub, one story had it, Gray had run up massive debts and was looking for ten per cent of any transfer fee to bail him out. Without credence or not, it didn't suppress the speculation. Almost on a daily basis, the futures of both Gray and Gidman were played out on the tabloids' back pages. The plot had more twists than the average soap opera but the central storyline remained the same: the players' inability to work for their manager.

When negotiations with the two came to nothing, Saunders finally decided that neither wanted any longer to play for Aston Villa. That they no longer wanted to play for *him* was, seemingly, inconsequential. He recommended to the board that the club be open to offers. The price of holding on to disaffected players (even if he himself had caused the disaffection) was too high. In the programme notes of Villa's opening home fixture against Brighton – written to 'keep the record straight' regarding the transfer requests – Saunders stated, 'This does not mean that they will go to the first bidder or to the first club that is interested. What it does mean is that they will leave Aston Villa when the right players in part-exchange or the right cash for their services is available to Aston Villa; in other words, they will go at our convenience.'

It had been, Saunders wrote, 'a few upsetting weeks in the club'. The mood wasn't about to become any more agreeable. While he would later stress that he wasn't 'completely daft' and, at the time, 'I knew exactly what I was doing', Saunders' judgement came into serious question. He may have retained 'the backing of the majority of the directors' (Ellis is unlikely to have been one of them) and believed that the 'genuine supporters' were behind him, but the selling of two of Villa's most outstanding talents seemed, to many, like a colossal act of folly. Was Saunders not only losing his best players, they wondered, but also losing the plot?

Villa, pre-season, enjoyed mixed fortunes, the team spending a few useful days in Scotland in the build-up to the new campaign. At Hearts' Tynecastle, they impressed in a 3-1 win (Deehan getting on the scoresheet after only 30 seconds), but a Paul Sturrock hat-trick saw a strong Dundee United run out 3-0 winners at Tannadice Park. In a slightly surreal moment, Andy Gray, back at his old lair but out of the side with injury, received a tremendous welcome from the home fans, loud applause breaking out when he spoke briefly over the tannoy before the game.

In just under four years since heading south of the border, the boy with the golden hair had stamped himself indelibly on the pages of Villa's history. His was a story punctuated with glorious highs and depressing lows. Yet when the Midlands club, minus their effervescent striker, made their poorest start yet to a league season under Saunders, there were very few neutrals questioning any more why Gray was so keen to bring to a close this particular chapter of his football career.

Broken Records

ON Saturday 8 September 1979, Andy Gray cut his ties once and for all with Ron Saunders. Putting pen to paper on the Molineux pitch before the home side's 1-1 draw against Crystal Palace, the Scottish international forward signed a contract with Wolves that saw him move across the Midlands for a colossal £1.469m. It followed a convoluted tale in which the British transfer record – which, only ten years earlier, was still the £165,000 Leeds had handed Leicester City for Allan Clarke – was smashed twice in the space of a whirlwind three days.

Its two main protagonists were Gray and Wolves midfielder Steve Daley. In June, Manchester City's Malcolm Allison, now back at his old club, had made it clear that Daley was a player he wanted at Maine Road. When John Barnwell, brought in at Wolves after Sammy Chung's dismissal, demanded £400,000 plus Asa Hartford in exchange, it was rebuffed. Another Barnwell request for cash plus Dave Watson was also refused. Allison preferred a straight cash deal and to keep hold of his players (though ironically Hartford and Watson were sold not too long after). An unsettled Daley – rumoured to be having marital troubles – still wanted a move sorted out. With Barnwell now targeting Gray (of which even the Wolves chairman was unaware) and needing to raise over £1m, he upped Daley's fee, though feared the price might deter the Manchester club. It didn't.

Fortunately for Barnwell, City came back in with another bid and, after various negotiations, paid £1,437,500 for Daley. Allison later claimed that he'd agreed a much lower fee with Barnwell but Peter Swales had intervened on a chairman-to-chairman basis and secured the transfer instantly but at a greatly inflated price. As it was, the transfer record lasted a mere 72 hours. Able to pursue the 23-year-old Gray, Barnwell struck a compromise with Saunders – Villa's boss reducing his initial demand for £2m – and a deal was finally agreed.

There had been some talk of Liverpool being interested in Villa's want-away forward, but not at such a price. Told another story, that Spurs might consider an exchange deal involving Gray and Osvaldo Ardiles, Saunders had reacted playfully by saying that it didn't seem such a bad idea. But Saunders had never expressed any desire to enter the foreign market.

When once asked why he preferred not to sign foreign players, he jokingly replied, 'Because they wouldn't understand when I abused them!' John Gregory, in *Geoff Twentyman: Secret Diary of a Liverpool Scout* by Simon Hughes, says of Saunders, 'He could never pronounce foreign names. I remember when Ossie Ardiles signed for Tottenham, he [Saunders] had real problems with his name. "Ardeeleees", he'd call him.' Saunders' counterpart Gordon Lee was another renowned for never getting to grips with more exotic monikers. Informed one time that his Everton secretary had gone to London to see *Evita*, the Brummie-born boss replied, 'Don't tell me he's down to speak to that little Argentine player from Spurs!'

When it became evident that the Black Country club would be Gray's next destination, the scepticism surrounding his stated desire to 'win things' resurfaced. Wolves, the striker insisted, were 'a club with ambitions'. It was a barely disguised dig at his former employers. Or, rather, at Saunders. The long-running saga had come to its end, yet still the enmity lingered.

On the same afternoon that Gray added his signature to his contract, Villa were well beaten 3-0 at home by Manchester United. With his mood no doubt already soured by defeat, Saunders took umbrage when a *Match of the Day* interviewer intimated that Gray's departure was due to his differences with the manager. Saunders stated that Gray had denied to him that this was the reason. In effect, he called Gray a liar.

As ambitious as Gray was for honours, the truth was, as he later wrote, 'Saunders was my sole reason for leaving Villa Park.' Gray's last game for Villa under Saunders – the 4-0 defeat at Nottingham Forest that also proved to be the swansong for Tommy Craig – was, Gray wrote, 'a fitting way' to end the relationship with the Villa boss.

Villa had begun the season in solid enough fashion. On a cool, damp day in Lancashire, Gordon Cowans earned them a fairly undistinguished opening day draw, sidestepping Bolton keeper Jim McDonagh before planting the ball in the net to level Neil Whatmore's opener for the home side. Four days later, newly promoted Brighton & Hove Albion, vanquished 4-0 at Highbury in their first fixture, were the visitors to Villa Park and 28,803 turned up to see Villa register both points, an

Allan Evans penalty and Morley's first for the club bringing a 2-1 win. But the crowd were also witness to one more demoralising injury blow to Alex Cropley.

With Mortimer suffering from a groin strain, Cropley came into the midfield but, early in the game, he went down following a challenge with Albion skipper Brian Horton. Unable to continue and helped from the pitch by trainer Roy MacLaren, Cropley paid an enforced visit to Birmingham's Good Hope hospital where X-rays revealed a fractured ankle bone. When the Scot had returned for John Robson's testimonial the Holte End had chanted, 'Cropley is back, Cropley is back.' Now they were faced with yet another prolonged spell with the hero they dubbed 'Braveheart' on the sidelines.

It didn't help Saunders that Cropley's replacement, Lee Jenkins, was carrying a knee injury for virtually the entire time he was on the pitch in what would prove, as with Cropley, to be his final game for Villa. Jenkins had never achieved the bright future that many predicted and, although he would remain at the club until November 1980 before moving to Port Vale, the young midfielder didn't figure again in Saunders' plans.

The side's soft underbelly was soon revealed once more. When Brian Little's substitute, Ivor Linton, also got injured along with Gary Williams, Villa finished with ten men and were beaten 2-0 at home to Bristol City. 'Battle-Scarred Villa Are Shown the Way' ran the *Sunday Mercury* headline. A six-game run then followed in which Villa would only score one goal – Tony Morley's against his boyhood favourites Everton in a 1-1 draw at Goodison Park. They only narrowly avoided an embarrassing League Cup exit, too.

Heading into the second leg of their second-round tie at home to Colchester United, with a 2-0 advantage secured by Gary Shaw's brace at Layer Road, the outcome looked a formality. But Saunders' cautionary pre-match words – 'The object of tonight's exercise is not to let Colchester get back at us early on. I am sure the players realise what is necessary' – fell on deaf ears. Villa were humbled 2-0 by Bobby Roberts' Third Division side and, with the aggregate level at 2-2 after extra time, had to take part in their very first penalty shoot-out. So successful were the takers that, with the scores at 8-8, it took a miss from U's stalwart goalkeeper Mike Walker and Morley's decisive spot-kick to save Villa's face.

The unconvincing cup passage only added fuel to the growing fire that Villa were, if not a club in crisis, then certainly one in ever-deepening trouble. The 3-0 home loss to Dave Sexton's Manchester United ended a hugely unsatisfactory week.

His pockets newly bulging after Gray's sale, Saunders invested some of the money almost immediately. On 12 September, Mike Pejic, the ex-England international left-back, signed from Everton for £200,000, the 29-year-old becoming Villa's oldest outfield player to highlight just what a young squad Saunders had under his charge. As Gray made a scoring debut for Wolves in their 3-2 win at Everton, Pejic's Villa bow was less successful, two Jerry Murphy goals without reply at Selhurst Park keeping intact Terry Venables' young Eagles' unbeaten record. The defeat left Villa three places off the bottom of the table. It also heralded the goodbyes of both of Villa's starting front two, John Deehan and Joe Ward.

If Gray's departure was the inevitable conclusion to the player's all-too-public fall-out with Saunders, the sale of Deehan was simply baffling. Already an England under-21 cap and tipped by many, including Saunders, to make the grade at full international level, Deehan looked likely to have a vital role in the new-look Villa side as Gray's successor. The half-century of goals to his name was only marginally bettered by Gray's 69 in his 140 games. But, having the close-season before already resisted one West Brom attempt to lure the forward away, once Baggies boss Ron Atkinson, flush with the proceeds from the summer sale of winger Laurie Cunningham to Real Madrid, made a renewed offer of £500,000, Saunders decided this time it was too good to turn down.

The Villa manager called the player one evening to inform him of the bid. 'I asked Ron what I should do,' Deehan told Colin Abbott, 'and he replied, "If I was you I'd go over and talk to them." That basically told me that I was no longer part of his plans.' Saunders convinced the Villa board to accept Atkinson's bid and, on 21 September, just short of two weeks after Gray, Deehan was also on his way, joining two other recent recruits at the Hawthorns, the Manchester City pair Gary Owen and Peter Barnes, in a re-jigged Albion line-up. The Solihull-born forward was the first Villa player to be transferred to the Baggies since 1909.

Ward, signed from Clyde only nine months previously and with only three Villa games under his belt, was now heading back north of the border, Hibernian-bound. The Glaswegian was the makeweight in a deal that saw defensive midfielder Des Bremner travelling in the opposite direction. Bremner, like his namesake and fellow Scot Billy, was a tenacious player but without the malice that so often led the ex-Leeds skipper into confrontation, with opponents and match officials alike.

At Easter Road since turning professional in November 1972, after playing over 200 times in that seven-year spell, Bremner felt he needed a new challenge. A move for his services from Newcastle was mooted two years earlier but failed to materialise when Gordon Lee left for Everton. Saunders, though, had been keeping tabs on Bremner for some time. Capped once for his country – coming on as sub for Kenny Dalglish in Scotland's 1-0 victory over Switzerland at Hampden in April 1976 – Bremner was a consistent performer renowned for his driving runs down the right flank and tireless tracking back. His work ethic on behalf of the team made him ideal for the Villa manager's needs.

With Hibs boss Eddie Turnbull insisting that his midfielder wouldn't be going to either Rangers or Celtic, but would be allowed to leave for an English club, once Villa expressed their interest, Turnbull had little choice but to let him go. The Sunday following Bremner's appearance in a 3-0 defeat against Celtic, Turnbull phoned to tell him to board a plane the next morning from Edinburgh. 'We're going to Birmingham,' Bremner was informed. 'It's Aston Villa we're going to see.' Bremner, accompanied by Turnbull and Hibs chairman Tom Hart, travelled south and, after meeting Saunders and Harry Kartz, the clubs reached agreement following a lengthy board meeting. Later that evening, the 25-year-old became a Villa player in a £275,000 deal, ironically succeeding Alex Cropley as the most expensive player sold by the Edinburgh club. The move to Villa, he said, was 'a dream come true'.

Saunders' purse strings were soon loosened again and David Geddis was the next recruit. A member of Ipswich's FA Youth Cup-winning side of 1974/75, Geddis had failed to hold down a regular first team spot at Portman Road, his star burning brightest when impressing in the Suffolk club's unexpected FA Cup Final triumph. It was Geddis's cut-out cross that led to the trophy-winning strike by Roger Osbourne. With the blond-haired striker on the margins – restricted to 15 appearances the previous season after Alan Brazil burst on to the scene – when Saunders put in a club record offer of £300,000, Bobby Robson accepted and it concluded a whirlwind ten-day spending spree for the Villa boss.

Along with Bremner, Geddis made his debut as Villa fought out a goalless draw at home to Arsenal. Though after being, in Saunders' view, 'rather fortunate not to be three or four goals down by half-time', Villa were unlucky themselves not to claim both points, Ken McNaught having a perfectly good header disallowed for apparently climbing on an Arsenal defender's shoulders. Villa couldn't score for love or money. Two further 0-0s followed, at Villa Park in the League Cup versus Everton then at Ayresome Park the Saturday after, McNaught's misfortune continuing with a sending-off against Middlesbrough that forced Saunders into yet more reorganisation. As Palace, still unbeaten after eight games, topped the division on goal difference from Manchester United and Forest, Villa were much too near for comfort to fellow strugglers Derby, Stoke and Spurs.

Saunders admitted that, so far, Villa had been unable to find any rhythm or blend to their play, conceding, 'When managers bring in two or three players they always point out the fact that it takes time for players to get to know each other and to understand each other's strengths and weaknesses. I am no exception.' He had, he added, 'every confidence that we can overcome that problem quickly'.

The alarming lack of firepower, though, brought into ever sharper focus his decision to sell two of his best strikers. With Tony Morley also sidelined by a nasty ankle injury, the side's cutting edge was blunted even further. The impotency of the forward line gave rise to some black humour on the terraces – 'Villa score, Villa score, once you get one, you'll get more' a chant from the Holte End – but the fans' patience was clearly in short supply. 'Saunders is a w**ker' was another song now getting an airing on matchdays. For the first time in five years, the near-adoration Saunders had enjoyed was in danger of being swept away by a rising tide of criticism. The choristers might still only have been in a minority, but the implicit trust the Villa faithful had in their leader to get the club back on track was definitely eroding.

'I personally feel that one of our biggest problems has been that we have become over-anxious and consequently have played with a certain amount of impatience,' Saunders reckoned. If anything, Villa's players were trying too hard to put things right. Their efforts were soon rewarded. A 3-0 home dispatching of Southampton – Des Bremner cracking in his first for the club – ended the goal drought and despite, three days later, returning from Goodison Park on the receiving end of a 4-1 defeat at Everton in the League Cup third-round replay (that man Latchford again scoring against Villa – this time, twice – in the competition), Villa's steady revival continued. A 0-0 draw at home to West Brom preceded a 3-1 victory at the Baseball Ground, with Gary Shaw, now part of a trio alongside Little and Geddis, bagging his first league goal of the campaign.

Two days before the Derby game, the bitter divorce of Saunders and Gidman was at last confirmed. Gidman had returned for the League Cup tie at Layer Road, then played in all but one of the next seven games (none of which Villa won), but, he admitted, he 'had pushed things too far' and his problems with Saunders were clearly not going to be resolved. The Liverpool-born right-back who admitted 'it seemed like the end of the world' when Bill Shankly rejected him as a youngster, was now returning to his native Merseyside to sport the blue of Everton. Gidman had few qualms about the move and, in a defiant parting shot, stated, 'I've got absolutely no regrets about leaving Villa.'

It was only years later that Gidman revealed his sorrow at his departure, reiterating that he never wanted to go but was 'forced out by the manager' and that 'matters were out of my control'. Gidman signed for the Toffees in a deal worth around £750,000.

Part of the transfer package was 19-year-old ex-England youth international Pat Heard. The Hull-born youngster had played only a dozen games for Everton, although his debut, a 1-1 New Year's Day draw against Bolton abandoned at half-time because of snow, never went into the record books. Although unsure about the move, the player – driven by Everton chief scout Harry Cooke down the M6 to meet Saunders (Heard didn't have a car) – was persuaded by Saunders 'in a matter of minutes' that coming to Villa Park would be good for him. It was all dependent on the Gidman deal going through, however.

'The phone kept ringing in Ron's office,' Heard later told *Bluekipper.com*, 'as it appeared Giddy was holding Gordon [Lee] to ransom saying that I was getting this and getting that.' Eventually, both moves were concluded and Heard, valued at £100,000 and able to fill in at both full-back and in midfield, became another useful addition to Saunders' growing pool.

It was Gidman's replacement, however, that gave Saunders the greatest source of satisfaction. Prior to a pre-season 2-0 home victory over Dutch side FC Twente (the side from whom Ipswich had purchased midfielders Frans Thijssen and Arnold Mühren), the Villa manager dropped a bombshell on Kenny Swain, asking him if he'd play at full-back. It wasn't so much a question as a request. Swain confessed he'd gone through a 'settling-in period' the season before, partly due, Saunders later said, to the player 'clocking up more than 1,000 miles a week, by car and train as he commuted between Villa Park and his home in London'. Still, Swain felt he'd done fairly well and was very excited about the coming campaign. The prospect of becoming a defender never entered his head.

Initially dreading the thought, Swain reassured himself he'd only be a stopgap 'until "Giddy" sorted out his problems'. Saunders, though, emphasised how he felt Swain could do a job for him. 'He showed so much faith and confidence in me,' Swain said, 'I just had to give it a try.'

Aside from a few games when he reverted to his original winger's role as Gidman returned to the side, Swain filled the number two shirt with such authority he might have played there all his life. When Saunders, after the Derby game, asked Swain if he was comfortable in his new position – if not, he'd sign a right-back and Swain would, Saunders told him, 'be in the swim with all the other forwards' – the ex-Chelsea man declined the get-out clause. It wasn't just the prospect of competing with the likes of Shaw, Little and Geddis that made up Swain's mind; he actually found playing in defence relatively easy.

For Saunders, Swain was like a new signing without having to spend a penny. The gap left by Gidman was barely noticeable. The protracted nature of Gidman's departure detracted significantly from the devotion the Villa faithful had always had for him. Whatever machinations may have been taking place, on the surface it appeared as though Gidman had been angling to leave for financial reasons and, according to Swain, the full-back 'couldn't quite accept it when he asked for a move and the fans turned against him'. If the dividing line between success and failure for a manager was a thin one, the line between love and hate from fans towards players could be even thinner.

By the time of Villa's next game, at Molineux, much of the affection the Villa fans had for Andy Gray was also a thing of the past. Britain's most expensive footballer, after swapping claret and blue for gold and black, had flourished, his four goals in his first seven matches helping Wolves, now captained by their other high-profile signing Emlyn Hughes, into fourth in the table.

Inevitably, the pre-match talk centred on the reunion with his former employers and a crowd of 36,267 turned up at Molineux to see it. The banter between the two sets of supporters was predictable – Wolves fans singing, 'Thank you very much for Andy Gray' and Villa's replying with 'Thank you very much for 1.5 million' – but when Gray, as ITV commentator Hugh Johns put it, did 'the one thing that Aston Villa must have feared', volleying the home side ahead, it was Barnwell's team who definitely looked to have got the better deal. Gray's less-than-understated goal celebration left little doubt as to where his loyalties now lay.

Later in the first half, though, Gary Shaw levelled, his fine left-footed strike flying past goalkeeper Paul Bradshaw and 1-1 it finished, ironically a repeat of the scoreline from Villa's very first game in the newly formed Football League on 8 September 1888 – away at Wolves.

The game wasn't without further incident, however. In the second half, a highly charged derby-day atmosphere was ramped up another notch by Brendan Ormsby and Wolves striker John Richards. Going up for a header, Richards' elbow caught Ormsby flush in the face and the fiery-haired centre-half reacted instantaneously with a punch that sent the Wolves player collapsing rather theatrically to the floor. The pair were sent off immediately.

For Ormsby, it was unfortunate. Not only did the 18-year-old defender leave the pitch with a bloodied and what was later revealed to be a broken nose, having claimed a starting place over the suspended McNaught, he now had to relinquish the number five jersey to the Scotsman once more. McNaught was not an easy man to displace. But while the double dismissal grabbed the headlines, it was in the boardroom, as so often with Aston Villa during the 1970s, that the real drama was about to come to pass.

The Egos Have Landed!

THE Midlands club had always had its share of gloom and doom merchants – 'the peripheral people', Saunders called them – only too eager to pounce at the slightest slip-up. 'These are the people who think they are the experts,' he said. 'They think they know more than the professionals.' Saunders, after speaking to the press following a game, would go to see his family via the directors' tea room and often, he said, 'had reason to take it up with those individuals' for knocking his players. They were a minority 'who shouldn't be allowed around Aston Villa because they do no one any good'.

Now, busy predicting a period of struggle and possible relegation, they were having their say again. Doug Ellis, an increasingly marginalised and frustrated figure backstage, was their leading spokesperson.

Shortly after Villa's defeat at Crystal Palace, Ellis seized the opportunity to launch an offensive. Requisitioning an EGM to take place at 6pm on Thursday 1 November at Villa Park, the self-styled 'Mr Aston Villa' was ready to fight to regain the position of power he so desperately craved and from which he'd been forced four years earlier because, he claimed, 'My colleagues complained of the personal publicity I attracted.'

Earlier in the year, in May, a new era was dawning at Downing Street as Margaret Thatcher swept to office at Number 10. Now Ellis, the son of a widowed mother from a poor family in Cheshire, who made his fortune from selling package holidays – the epitome of the Thatcherite ideal – was also seeking to bring a new era to B6. His aim? Ostensibly the removal of Harry Kartz and the two Bendalls from the Aston Villa board. However, his principal target was unquestionably Saunders.

Detecting a growing anti-Saunders sentiment among the playing staff and supporters, Ellis smelled blood. Instead of steering the Midlands club to glory, Saunders, Ellis was convinced, was taking it down a fast path to ruination. Even though promising that 'the only certainty is that I would not be a party to the sacking of a successful manager', no one was fooled. Saunders wasn't 'successful' in Ellis's eyes. A victory for the Hooton-born businessman, over eight years Saunders' senior, and the chair in the manager's office would soon be vacated.

Despite Ellis's later claim that the strain 'was not immediate by any means, but it would have been within the first 12 months', from the moment Saunders crossed the Villa Park threshold – to be kept waiting as Ellis queried whether he should be given the manager's job – the pair were butting heads. The disagreement over the Frank Carrodus fee was an ominous portent of things to come. 'Talk about The Egos Have Landed!' exclaimed Dennis Shaw in *A Game of Three Halves*. Ellis, in rejecting Brian Clough's claims, had correctly envisaged a battle between two domineering characters. But Saunders, the antithesis of Clough in many respects, was equally as individual and single-minded. Conflict between them was inevitable. Club secretary Steve Stride put it down simply to 'a clash of personalities'. It was one unlikely ever to be resolved amicably.

'He was an impossible man to deal with,' said Ellis of Saunders later. 'He had management ability, no doubt about that, but he was so selfish and he could not see the other person's point of view.' It was a description that his detractors felt could easily be applied to Ellis. Ellis would declare his biggest weakness as being 'a devil for seeing the other fellow's point of view'. He may well have seen it, but he very rarely entertained it. Least of all Saunders'. Both on and off the pitch, Saunders' managerial style met with opposition. 'Some managers operate on loving players and putting their arm around them. Others operate on fear,' Ellis told the *Birmingham Mail* in 2006, 'and I think Ron operated on fear.'

By the end of the 1974/75 season the animosity was evident for all – well, the Villa staff at least – to see. On a Caribbean cruise that followed promotion, Saunders and his wife shared a table with the Ellises one night. The next evening, the Ellises were there first. Saunders wasn't amused. 'You're sitting in my seat,' he told his chairman. Ellis's attempt to make a joke only met with Saunders' best Queen Victoria impression. Breaking up the trip to return to England to collect his Manager of the Year award, Saunders warned his players not to talk to Ellis while he was away.

A near-paranoia soon took root. Dennis Mortimer, upon signing, had been told by his new manager to 'be aware' of Ellis's presence. A bridge of mistrust was only going to grow longer. Even when it appeared that the waters were calm, the undercurrents of disharmony were still strong. Ellis believed they were of Saunders' stirring. Saunders saw

Ellis as instrumental. That the differences between the two men were 'irretrievably wide' was, for Dennis Shaw, 'one of the great misfortunes of Aston Villa's history'.

Matt Busby had set a precedent for demanding autonomy over playing matters when, after a director questioned the then-35-year-old manager's judgement at Old Trafford, Busby was given assurance from the Manchester United chairman that he alone would have say over who was picked and who was not. Saunders sought a similar sovereignty, but Shaw believed it was Saunders' desire to have control over other aspects of the club that left him so at loggerheads with not just Ellis but all the chairmen he'd served under at Villa.

'He wanted more power, more security, and less interference,' Shaw wrote in his book. 'Rightly, in my view he was never going to get all of that at Villa Park.' Shaw felt that, in service terms, Saunders was 'a superb non-commissioned officer'. But 'what he wanted to be, however, was a brigadier.' It was a role for which Shaw believed Saunders was ill-equipped. Had Saunders stuck to the footballing side and Ellis to dealing with finances, Aston Villa would have been much better served.

Alfred Hitchcock, when first moving to Hollywood, found himself up against an old-style Hollywood producer in David O. Selznick, a man who wanted the movie made his own way and to take all the acclaim for it. To many, the relationship between Saunders and Ellis was comparable. Just who was 'Hitchcock' and who was 'Selznick', though, no one could quite decide.

The presence of Ellis on the Villa board had long been an emotive issue. It wasn't uncommon for full-blown arguments and even fisticuffs to develop between supporters over the matter. His defenders argued that it was Ellis who'd revived a club on its dying legs and, had it not been for his forward-thinking, all the subsequent successes and modernisation would not have come to fruition. For others, he was a manipulative, selfish figure who, even if rightly, claimed the role of chief orchestrator in the '1968 Revolution' (though many still felt that Pat Matthews was the real instigator behind putting together the rescue package) and sought the sole credit for it. No other club in English football experienced as much backstage bickering through the 1970s as Aston Villa.

Ellis often made all the right noises. 'The success of any team in football or business is the happiness of its members and we have had this at Villa Park,' he'd said in late 1977. 'Together we have built a family called Aston Villa.' But togetherness, his doubters felt, was never top of Ellis's agenda. Although he stressed, 'At all times, I am ready to serve them

[Aston Villa] in whatever capacity helps the club,' the sceptics refused to accept that Ellis desired anything other than to be master of all he surveyed.

No manager was immune to fall-outs with chairmen and directors. Shankly's relations with the Anfield board had frequently been acrimonious. 'At a football club, there's a holy trinity – the players, the manager and the supporters,' he once said. 'Directors don't come into it. They are only there to sign the cheques.' Don Revie, too, had had many a run-in at Elland Road. During his last season with Leeds, Revie praised the United directors for allowing him 'the freedom to manage', but it wasn't always a bed of Yorkshire roses. Revie and the board were regularly in dispute and Revie had often considered leaving the West Yorkshire club. Saunders, too, felt that directors – particularly those who'd never played the game – should keep their noses out of things about which they knew next-to-nothing. 'Football hooligans – well, there are 92 club *chairmen* for a start,' became another famous Brian Clough quote. Saunders believed there was one 'hooligan' in the Villa boardroom who, in his resolve to be hands-on, was prepared to put the boot in at every opportunity.

For the most part it had been, as Alan Hardaker had once described the relationship between the Football League and the FA, 'a cold war' in which 'no triggers are squeezed, no blood is ever drawn'. Although neither aired it publicly, that each wanted shot of the other was football's worst-kept secret. Now, sensing it was an ideal hour to strike, Ellis was ready to bear arms.

Through the *Sports Argus*, Ellis made a public statement. In a 'letter' to the club's shareholders, presenting the mounting evidence in his case against the current regime, Ellis outlined his reasons for taking such 'drastic action'. Villa, he wrote, were no nearer the 'magic targets' of the title and FA Cup triumphs than they were a decade ago, 'despite spending literally millions of £'s'. The club was a boat in danger of capsizing 'with the loss of all hands' and only Ellis, doubtful of 'the leadership and ability of my colleagues on the board to put things right', was able to halt 'its current slide into mediocrity'.

Ellis went at it full tilt. 'Genuine and recognisable improvement has been turned into a slump of alarming proportions,' he continued. The sale of 'almost all of our most valuable players', not to mention Brian Little's proposed move to Birmingham City – all of which Ellis had opposed – had seen 'a wonderful team, believing in themselves, working for each other and feared by every other team in the First Division, as recently confirmed by Emlyn Hughes on television' become one that 'lacks flair, imagination and leadership – an unhappy state of affairs which has clearly fermented unrest among the players'.

Ellis didn't mention Saunders' name directly but the allusion was obvious. Money was being lost, season tickets weren't being renewed, assets were being eroded, and there was only one culprit. 'I know, without false modesty,' Ellis concluded, 'that I am better qualified to revive Aston Villa's potential for real success than any other serving member of the board. Unless we have happiness at the top, generating the right spirit and high morale, we shall not succeed.' With Ellis's battle plan effectively laid out, in the following weeks what amounted to open warfare was fought out on the pages of the local and national press and in radio phone-ins.

Bitter arguments gave an indication of the depth of feeling within the Villa ranks. Supporters were conflicted over their loyalties. A 'Stop Ellis' campaign group was formed. The Villa Shareholders' Association – only 340 strong but big in influence – also came out against him, their half-page advertisement in the *Birmingham Post* urging fans to back the board.

When the EGM and AGM took place over two nights at the start of November, things got even uglier. In the charisma stakes, Ellis clearly had the lead over the dour Ron Bendall. With the majority of the 7,000 small shareholders even now haunted by the spectre of Villa's mid-to-late-1960s decline, a show of hands resulted in a convincing victory for the man they still regarded as the club's saviour. Bendall hardly helped himself by expressing obvious disdain for the evening's proceedings. Yet Ellis, with his 16 per cent shareholding, simply lacked sufficient muscle to regain power. Bendall, with 28 per cent, had too big an advantage. A card vote, with over 84,000 votes cast, was taken. With the exception of Eric Houghton, every man who had ever served (and fallen out) with Ellis voted against him.

Whether or not it was a deliberate act of revenge on their part, it appeared that the ghosts of Ellis's own past had caught up with him. Ellis further shot himself in the foot by putting forward David Rhead as a potential director. Rhead claimed to be a fan of both Villa and West Brom but was willing to plant his colours solely in the Villa camp should it be required. In Ellis, the former Birmingham City director, his critics believed that Villa had already experienced one chameleon condescending to give his loyalties to the club. The last thing the board needed was another.

Unsurprisingly, Harry Kartz sided with the Bendalls but, more significantly, Sir William Dugdale also threw his weight behind the Bendall/Kartz axis. Dugdale – whom Ellis assumed was abstaining –

decided to give them his vote largely because they offered him nothing in return. Ellis, on the other hand, had dangled all manner of carrots: the vice-chairmanship and the presidency. He'd even asked if he could buy Sir William's holding. Dugdale wasn't remotely tempted by such inducements. His 4,000 shares proved a decisive shift in the balance of power.

With his attempted coup having failed, Ellis had no option but to lick his wounds and surrender his seat. In December, he resigned as director, selling the majority of his considerable shareholding to his opponent, Ron Bendall, claiming, 'I bowed my head for the sake of the club to try and bring back harmony.'

Eric Houghton, too, the victim of aligning himself with Ellis, also resigned. The departure of the widely respected Houghton was the source of some sorrow; such was the high regard in which he was held for the 50-plus years of outstanding service he'd given to his beloved club as player, manager and director.

Ellis's leaving, on the other hand, left few reaching for their hankies. 'Without Ellis around,' Harry Kartz had said at the AGM, 'we might get around to talking about players and the manager.'

Bendall's victory was conclusively as much a vote in favour of Saunders as it was a rejection of Ellis. Saunders, like Shankly, a passionate boxing fan and one often to be spotted watching bouts at the Villa Leisure Centre, had proved himself a skilled and stealthy fighter, one not without persuasive powers. Taking Ellis's criticisms as a personal affront and a slur on his abilities, Saunders made the point at the AGM. It swung a significant amount of shareholders in his favour.

'I never asked whether my position was in danger...I carried on being the manager of Aston Villa and let the rest of them get on with it,' Saunders would say shortly after. But there's little doubt that he was aware of how vital a Bendall victory was for his own future. As he underlined at the AGM, 'until such time as everyone connected with the club wanted what was best for Aston Villa – and was prepared to sweat blood to that end – the club would never achieve the greatness which so many people wanted for it.' Maybe now, at last, that time was near.

The Musketeers

THE day after the AGM, walking to the dugout prior to kick-off in the home match with Bolton Wanderers – won 3-1 with a highly polished, mature performance – Saunders received a resounding standing ovation, the like of which he'd not enjoyed before. Contrary to Ellis's contention, the rank-and-file Villa fans were still solidly behind the Villa manager. Returning to the role after his reluctant politician's cameo, Saunders was overseeing a new-look outfit that was, in Dennis Mortimer's view, 'shaping very nicely'.

Terry Bullivant, a young midfield anchor man who'd been impressing in a Second Division Fulham side that included other much-admired assets such as Richard Money, Tony Gale and Gordon Davies, became the latest signing, the 23-year-old snapped up from the Craven Cottage club in a £220,000 deal. Draws at home to Leeds and away at Ipswich Town and Norwich, plus a home win over Stoke saw Villa edge their way up the table. Saunders praised the 'all for one and one for all' attitude of his players. The Musketeer spirit, he said, was 'becoming quite pronounced'. Not only were they displaying 'tremendous character' but 'an abundance of natural skill and enthusiasm'.

It was all still very much a work in progress, though. On 8 December, in the aftermath of a 3-1 home defeat by Liverpool – Little's goal a sole consolation as second-half strikes from Ray Kennedy, Hansen and McDermott sealed the visitors' victory – Saunders reflected that the Merseysiders 'show us what standards we have got to set ourselves before we can think of achieving the success that they have achieved over the past decade'. The Anfield club's ability to live and cope under pressure when every game played was like a cup final was, Saunders believed, the difference between them and everyone else.

By their own relentlessly high criterion, Paisley's side, partly due to injuries, had made a strangely lacklustre start to their title defence. After a 3-1 win over Arsenal in the Charity Shield, the runaway 11/6 title favourites won just two of their first seven league games and a 1-0 defeat at Forest left them ninth at the end of September. A week later, they also exited the European Cup, knocked out in round one 4-2 on aggregate by Dynamo Tbilisi. But any hopes their rivals harboured that the reigning champions were in decline were forlorn. The Liverpool machine quickly kicked into geared again and, after embarking on a long unbeaten sequence, the victory at Villa Park saw them topping the table once again.

For Villa, defeat brought a double blow. As Bullivant figured for the first time, the unfortunate Mike Pejic, after featuring in just ten games, suffered a groin injury that not only ended his season, it put a full stop to the left-back's career. Undiagnosed at the time, it was only some years later after Pejic aggravated the injury in a charity game that a specialist identified it as a double hernia. Pejic, fit and injury-free for most of his playing days, never recovered. When the battle became insurmountable, recognising that he couldn't reach the levels he'd always set himself, the player called it quits, his retirement confirmed the following June.

While Saunders' eye for talent was still roving among the transfer market, earlier in the year one player had actually sold *himself* to Villa. Eamonn Deacy, a full-back with his hometown team, League of Ireland's Galway Rovers (who'd only formed in 1977), had taken the audacious step of writing to every First Division club asking for a week's trial, even offering to pay for his own travel expenses. Villa were the only one willing to take a punt.

In February 1979, handed the chance to show his capabilities, Deacy duly impressed. Yet, despite assurances from the coaching staff that Saunders liked him, the young Irishman felt he'd failed, so he was taken aback when the Villa manager offered him a contract. Deacy later recalled how Saunders broke the news to him. Summoned to the boss's office after training, Deacy was asked by Saunders if he was 'from near Tipperary', the town from where Saunders' wife Breda hailed. 'If you are,' Saunders joked, 'my wife says I have to sign you.'

A deal was promptly agreed, Deacy, an ex-midfielder, joining Gibson (ex-winger), Williams (ex-centre-half) and Swain on a growing list of full-backs at the club who'd shifted from another role. Deacy would say that the day he made his debut for Aston Villa he realised his entire life's ambition and, after just one game in the English top flight, he knew he'd achieved inner peace. That debut came at White Hart Lane as Villa made a swift return to winning ways with a 2-1 victory. Against a Spurs side fielding Gordon Smith, Deacy came on 12 minutes from the end in place of David Geddis. It concluded an afternoon of mixed fortunes for Geddis.

Having scored his first Villa goal – 'a huge relief', he said afterwards – firing into the roof of the net on 21 minutes to put the away side ahead, Geddis was carried off late in the game with an ankle injury that would keep him out until the following February. Saunders' remodelling of Aston Villa would require yet more tinkering. Four days later, his decision to promote Terry Donovan to the frontline reaped immediate results, the Liverpool-born striker netting on his debut in a 3-0 triumph at home to Coventry City and, approaching Christmas, Villa had climbed to fifth position. It was no small achievement.

When Villa went to the City Ground on Boxing Day, Brian Clough acknowledged the strides Forest's opponents were making. Villa's recent form, Clough wrote in the match programme, was 'champion stuff' and, he felt, 'There is no doubt that they are the team of the moment.' Saunders in particular came in for praise, his 'steadfast and resolute attitude', Clough wrote, had seen the Midlands club through 'a traumatic time'.

Clough himself had had to navigate an often-bumpy course through the season thus far. Forest had raced to the top of the table, winning their first four games but, as at Villa, there'd been friction in the background. Clough had fallen out with his paymasters, in October even daring them to sack him. Tony Woodcock's shock £650,000 move to Cologne in November only accentuated the uneasiness. Clough's transfer dealings weren't exactly successful. As well as an erroneous signing of Asa Hartford, £250,000 was spent on QPR's 30-year-old Stan Bowles. By the following July after, predictably enough, failing to get on with Clough, the player would be gone from the club.

When Forest faced Villa, they'd won just once in eight games, a run that had all but scuppered any title chances. However, when Bowles, scoring his first goal since joining, gave them the lead and a John Robertson penalty doubled the advantage, despite a Gary Shaw reply, the Christmas cheer was all Clough's.

Villa were somewhat unlucky; Robertson's spot-kick had nearly been kept out – not by Jimmy Rimmer, but Nigel Spink. The indomitable Rimmer – a player of whom Spink would later say 'was always one who played with a bandage somewhere' – hadn't missed a league game for two seasons. Even after stepping on some broken glass in the dressing room and suffering a nasty cut that required eight stitches on a pre-season trip to Yugoslavia in 1978, Rimmer had recovered in time to take his place between the sticks for Villa's opening game. Now, with Rimmer nursing a septic toe, Spink was drafted in for his debut, the 21-year-old only finding out an hour before the kick-off.

In January 1977, Spink, rejected by West Ham after conceding seven goals in a reserve game, had been spotted by Tony Barton playing for Chelmsford City in the Conference League (in the same side as ex-England scoring legend Jimmy Greaves). One of two young keepers Villa's chief scout had been watching – the first, wanting to concentrate on his studies, declined the chance of a trial – Spink grabbed his opportunity with both hands. In a reserve team try-out – a 1-0 defeat at St James' Park – the Essex youngster made a very favourable impression and, on the Monday, Saunders offered him a one-year contract. Spink had played only 19 first team games for his hometown club. It would be another two-and-a-half years before he made another appearance in Aston Villa's goal.

Three days after finding the net at Forest, Shaw further emphasised his potential, the teenager cracking the first hat-trick of his professional career against Bristol City in a 3-1 win at Ashton Gate, the ground where he'd made his league debut. Labelled by Saunders 'a goalscoring machine' after averaging more than a goal a game in the Central League, Shaw was now fast forging a name for himself in the First Division.

A Villa fan from the age of six, the youngster had been spotted playing for his local amateur side, Coleshill Town. Offers of trials at other clubs were plentiful, but it was only his boyhood club to whom he was going to commit. Disappointed he'd never had the opportunity to partner one of his heroes, Andy Gray, except with the reserves, Shaw was now ensuring the memory of Villa's previous blond-haired striker became ever dimmer.

Something in the south-west air obviously suited him. Shaw bagged another goal – this time at Bristol Rovers' Eastville – as Villa negotiated the FA Cup third round with a 2-1 win. It was Villa's run in the competition that provided the central story of the season's second half. Cambridge United proved stiffer opposition than expected in round four – after a 1-1 draw at the Abbey Stadium, Villa won convincingly 4-1 in the replay – and it took another two games to overcome Third Division Blackburn Rovers. A freak own goal in the dying seconds at Ewood Park by Allan Evans – the 'worst moment' of his career, he said at the time – had earned Blackburn a late reprieve. Four days after, though, the Scottish centre-back was redeemed, heading home an 81st-minute winner to finally kill off the Lancashire club's challenge.

Unlike with the League Cup, Saunders' record in the world's most famous cup competition was poor. A quarter-final tie at West Ham – the seventh successive time Villa had been drawn away in the competition – offered the very real prospect of changing that. Although West Ham, relegated in 1978, sat fifth in the Second Division, unbeaten in their last 12 games, Saunders' side, themselves having lost just one of their previous 13 matches in all competitions, could hardly have been hotter favourites. But badly weakened in defence – Evans missing following a sending-off in the 1-1 draw at Brighton five days before and Kenny Swain ruled out with a knee injury suffered in the same game – Saunders was forced to draft in Ormsby at centre-half and Ivor Linton at right-back.

Predictably, the usually steady backline looked shakier on its feet. With Lyall's hungry side on top, playing with a 'flow, intelligence and fire' according to *The Observer*'s Julie Welch, Villa found themselves up against it for much of the match and were fortunate to escape after several near-misses. However, nearing the 90-minute mark with the game still goalless and the visiting fans, Welch wrote, 'hooting anxiously for the final whistle', Villa's luck ran out. When Ken McNaught rose with West Ham number nine David Cross and defender Alvin Martin to head clear a Trevor Brooking corner, his right hand appeared to hit the ball before his head made contact. To the Villa players' amazement, referee David Richardson immediately pointed to the muddy penalty spot. Rimmer, whose inspired form had held the Hammers at bay, grabbed his goal net in disgust. His aggrieved team-mates' arguments with the official were to no avail.

'John Lyall just wants to see the ball put in the back of the net, and the man who has got to put it there is Ray Stewart,' commentated ITV's Brian Moore. The 20-year-old Scottish right-back, whose unerring nerve and accuracy from the spot had already helped to account for Leyton Orient in the fourth round, duly stepped up to slam a shot low to Rimmer's right and into the net. When one last Villa effort – a low drive from a 25-yard free kick by Cowans – went straight into the safe grasp of Hammers keeper Phil Parkes, that was it: the long afternoon's defensive battle had been lost and a chorus of 'Bubbles' echoed around Upton Park. For Villa, beaten by West Ham for the first time in the FA Cup, the semi-final dream had been burst.

Speaking afterwards about the handball decision, McNaught claimed his hand had been 'pushed on to the ball' by Martin's shoulder, while Saunders also disputed the penalty's award. Having watched it back several times, Saunders described the incident as 'an absolute freak', feeling certain that it was Martin who, in jumping up, had caused the perceived offence. Nevertheless, Saunders' magnanimity immediately following the end of the match earned a tribute from his opposite number. 'Directly the whistle sounded, Ron congratulated me and wished us luck in the semi-finals,' Lyall said. 'I appreciated that more than I can possibly say, for he must have felt sick – I know I would in the circumstances.'

Years later, in his autobiography *My Life in Football*, England international Trevor Brooking would write of the vital spot-kick, 'Had I been a Villa player, I would not have been happy with the decision,' though he still believed that West Ham 'thoroughly deserved our victory despite the dispute at the time'.

Nevertheless, the blow, Dennis Mortimer admitted, had left the players 'devastated'. If they thought the club's name was on the cup, it had been cruelly scratched off at the last. The disappointment was only compounded further by the fact that both semi-finals – a West Ham/Everton clash that finished 1-1 (with Stewart sent off in the first half for fighting with Brian Kidd) and two of the replayed matches between Arsenal and Liverpool – took place at Villa Park. Saunders and his players could do little but watch, 'and all the time we were thinking, "If only..."' he later said.

It was little consolation, too, that, for the third time in five seasons – after Southampton in 1976 and Manchester United in 1977 – Villa had been put out en route by the eventual winners of the trophy. In May, the Hammers, with a Brooking header, went on to clinch the FA Cup in a 1-0 win over London rivals Arsenal, the second time in five years that Lyall had guided them to the trophy.

The cup loss took its toll. After only one defeat – 3-1 at Highbury – since the turn of the year, Villa's form took a sudden slump. On the following Monday night, just two days after their gruelling Upton Park clash, Villa entertained Wolves in a rearranged league match that would bring totally contrasting fortunes for the two players who had only recently formed the most lethal partnership in Aston Villa's history: Andy Gray and Brian Little.

In a disjointed, tepid performance from Villa, while Shaw scored for the second time in the season against John Barnwell's side, the team from the Black Country ran out 3-1 winners. Worse still, in the second half, Little, collapsing under a challenge, suffered a recurrence of an injury to the same knee that had sidelined the striker for much of the 1975/76 campaign. Though continuing to play on, Little knew there was serious ligament damage. Although he would later return to the starting XI – for a goalless draw at Leeds United and a 2-1 defeat at Manchester United – without the surgery available to help the problem, the battle to salvage his career would be lost. 'As time went by during the recovery period,' he said, 'it became obvious to us that my knee was never going to recover.'

The following February, doctors confirmed the news: at the tender age of 26, Little's playing days were done. A goal in a 2-1 win at West Brom on 23 February was his last in an Aston Villa shirt. Somewhat poignantly, on 23 April, when Little donned the claret and blue for the final time, it was five years to the day since he'd helped clinch promotion with two goals at Sheffield Wednesday. English football had been cruelly robbed of a supremely gifted footballer.

In his time at Villa, no one had suited Little's style more than Andy Gray. As fate would have it, Gray could not have been more grateful that his old side succumbed to their late cup defeat. Facing a one-match suspension and the prospect of missing out on the following Saturday's League Cup Final against Nottingham Forest, a replay between Villa and the Hammers would have resulted in the Wolves fixture being cancelled and Gray forgoing what turned out to be a memorable date with destiny. As it was, Gray sat out the game with Villa, served his ban and, as Villa were losing 2-0 at Southampton, the Scottish striker – capitalising on a mix-up between Peter Shilton and defender David Needham – notched a 67th-minute winner in the big clash with Clough's men to bring Wolves their first silverware since their League Cup win six years earlier, captain Hughes collecting the only major honour to have eluded him during his highly successful Liverpool career. Ironically, it was a final refereed by David Richardson.

After such a tumultuous opening to Villa's season, its denouement was relatively serene. The loss at The Dell, followed by further 2-0 defeats at home to Middlesbrough (before only 15,319) and away at Stoke, effectively ruined any European aspirations. The side still had its moments. A 2-0 home win over Norwich City saw a remarkable bow into First Division football by Villa youth team skipper Robert Hopkins. With Villa leading from a Gordon Cowans penalty, Hopkins, a last-minute substitute for Ivor Linton, entered the fray, told by Saunders to 'just go on and play the clock down'. The youngster, whose team-mates knew he was a Birmingham City supporter ('I used to go into training always wearing something blue,' Hopkins said) had been on the pitch for only 20 seconds when Tony Morley whipped in a cross from the left and the 17-year-old slipped home a shot from a tight angle to put Villa 2-0 up. It was Hopkins' only touch of the match. A 3-2 triumph over Forest (an own goal from Larry Lloyd two minutes after the break proving decisive) was another notable home win.

Yet when Villa finished seventh again, for the third season running a UEFA Cup spot eluded them. Above them in the table, a creditable sixth only a year after finishing 18th, were Gray's Wolves. Further up, fifth-placed Forest were again the Midlands' top club, the loss of their League Cup more than compensated for with a second successive European Cup triumph when a first-half Robertson goal gave them victory over Kevin Keegan's SV Hamburg in Madrid in May. In doing so, Forest became the first club to have won more European Cups than league championships.

It meant a disappointing end to Keegan's German career. In February, the England captain made the shock announcement that, after three seasons in the Bundesliga in which he was twice named European Footballer of the Year, he'd be returning to English football with Southampton in the 1980/81 season, joining Lawrie McMenemy's Saints for £400,000.

Arsenal, in fourth, endured a heartbreaking season's finale. Terry Neill's team, just four days after their FA Cup Final loss to West Ham, also came off second-best in the European Cup Winners' Cup Final versus Valencia. Goalless after extra time, a penalty shoot-out saw misses from Liam Brady and Graham Rix and the Gunners losing 5-4 to the Spaniards.

Going from third-bottom in December to third-top and a UEFA Cup berth by the season's end, Ipswich Town enjoyed a remarkable renaissance; while, in the runners-up spot, Dave Sexton came very close to ending Manchester United's long wait for a league title. Despite eight wins from their last ten games, it wasn't enough. A disastrous 6-0 thrashing at Portman Road at the start of March (it would have been worse had goalkeeper Gary Bailey not saved first-half Thijssen and Beattie penalties) dealt a decisive blow to the Red Devils' hopes. At the top, unsurprisingly, it was the Liverpool dynasty that continued to conquer.

Near the campaign's conclusion, Saunders had summed up what he'd been endeavouring to do with his players in the past few months, 'For long periods each season, so-called experts criticise expressions like "work-rate, effort, running and team effort" and drool over phrases such as "natural ability, balance, skill, class", etc. And it is only when cup football comes along that they seem to start realising that without the effort and running ability, and will to win, players will never be able as individuals or as a team to show their "class, ability" etc. Sides that win things unite these two different aspects of the game into the team.'

No side followed that template more closely than Liverpool. Although United ran them close, the Anfield club's inexorable progress towards their fourth title in five years was never seriously in doubt. As Sexton's side slipped up, 2-0 at Leeds United in their last league game, a win for Liverpool in what was their penultimate fixture and the title would be clinched. Their opponents? Aston Villa.

As with the previous season, Liverpool wrapped up another championship triumph with a convincing home victory over Saunders' men. Shrugging aside the setback of defeat just 48 hours earlier in a marathon FA Cup semi-final with Arsenal (Liverpool finally surrendering 1-0 in a third replay at Highfield Road), the Reds ran a hapless Villa defence ragged, slamming four goals past Jimmy Rimmer, with only an Avi Cohen own goal to show for Villa's efforts. The Israeli Cohen scored for the home side, too, his 50th-minute strike putting Liverpool 2-1 ahead before a Noel Blake own goal topped off two David Johnson goals, and the title went to Paisley's men once more.

The 1970s had undeniably belonged to the team from Merseyside, 'the new masters of the game' as journalist Colin Benson termed them. Shankly may have set the wheels in motion, but Paisley had steered them to even greater distances. Another journalist had once written of Herbert Chapman's all-conquering Arsenal side of the 1930s, 'They are as near to the precision of a machine as any football team had come.' The same description could now quite easily be applied to Liverpool.

Ominously, Bob Paisley said that he had never seen a Liverpool side play better than in the run of results they'd produced in mid-season. If, in the 1980s, any club were to break this near-monopoly over the English game, it would take a mammoth effort on another side's part, and a monumental dip in form on Liverpool's. The form book suggested it was unlikely. Even when Derby, Leeds and Forest had enjoyed their moments in the sun, Liverpool had returned to put them back in the shade.

The latest title had been won in familiar fashion. An unyielding defence, a tough and tireless midfield, together with a goalscoring front pairing had again proved the correct formula for success. Paisley put it in simpler terms. 'When you're in a fog, you must stick together. Then you don't get lost,' he said. 'If there's a secret about Liverpool, that's it.'

The fog that had enveloped the first half of Aston Villa's 1979/80 season had all but been lifted. The board (in spite of or maybe because of going back on an agreement with the Shareholders' Association to replace Ellis and Houghton with new directors) were now, seemingly, as united as they had been during Saunders' reign. The feeling that, through a series of wrong steps, Villa had lost their way had been traded for a belief that, with the shadow of Doug Ellis no longer stalking his every footstep, Ron Saunders could now perhaps enjoy a clear path in front of him.

'If – some people would say when – Villa go on to achieve top honours in the years ahead, they will look back on the current season as the vital turning point,' wrote the *Birmingham Mail*'s David Harrison. 'It has provoked a multitude of emotions, ranging from hope to despair, but looks bound to end in a note of optimism, even if there are no trophies in the boardroom cabinet.'

The way the youngsters Saunders had blooded had, in Harrison's view, 'responded with unwavering enthusiasm' meant that that optimism was well-founded. None of them had looked out of place. And while not all the signings were successful, Des Bremner, whose arrival coincided with the season's most difficult phase, had slotted in almost like a dream and, according to Harrison, 'epitomised the new fighting spirit which brought the revival'. Heard and Bullivant, too, though playing only bit parts, had each proved themselves capable of more prominent roles.

'I cannot praise too highly the overall character and commitment of our playing staff,' Saunders said, 'especially our more senior players.' No one typified that commitment more than Kenny Swain, whose unselfish switch to defence was so complete that, writing in the *Sports Argus*, BBC reporter and former Villa favourite Larry Canning nominated Swain as the best right-back in the Midlands – ahead of Forest's England international Viv Anderson. 'I can now honestly say I have never had any real urge to play up front again,' Swain declared.

The *Evening Mail*'s Ray Matts wrote, 'In my younger days of soccer journalism I used to believe that it was immaterial whether players liked or disliked a manager, so long as they respected him. Wrong. If they do not like their boss there is no way they will perform to their peak.' Injuries 'rather than any feeling of disillusionment with the man at the top', Matts believed, had had an unsettling effect on the side's form.

With none of Villa's regulars immune to a visit to new physio Jim Williams' treatment room, an astonishing 29 players had been called upon. But despite the constant reshuffling, Saunders was convinced it was all valuable experience and felt, 'The full benefits gained from this season will be reaped in the next couple of years.'

Waiting further in the wings was yet another budding crop of youngsters. Villa's youth team had won both the FA Youth Cup – overcoming a strong Manchester City team 3-2 on aggregate – and Southern Junior Floodlit Cup. Of the side, captain Hopkins and 6ft

2in teenage central defender Noel Blake – 'built like a tank' in Allan Evans' view – had already been handed their debuts. Paul Birch and Mark Walters were first-teamers in the making.

At the season's end, Saunders was awarded a testimonial match – billed as 'The Second City Cup Final' – against Birmingham City who, under Jim Smith, had recently regained their First Division status. It seemed somewhat ironic that a manager who, had certain factions had their way, would not even have been at Villa Park was now being rewarded by the club.

Even more ironically, Saunders, a man who 'has worked tirelessly for the good of the game', Smith said, was now Villa's longest-serving manager. Chairman Harry Kartz expressed his certainty that the outlook for the Midlanders with Saunders at the helm was a bright one. 'When I think of the future for Aston Villa, which I do frequently, especially when watching the youngsters playing at Villa Park,' he wrote in the testimonial programme, 'I realise that this side of the club is in the best of hands.'

Just what those hands were about to pull out of the bag, though, not even Nostradamus could surely have foreseen.

The Last Piece of the Jigsaw

RON Saunders was, as one scribe put it, 'piloting a revival of fortunes with one of the best crop of youngsters in the country'. After the tremendous transition of the previous 12 months, the club, in general, Saunders believed, was in 'a very healthy state'. Local talents and shop-bought goods had coalesced into an effective mix and the large pool of players Saunders had been trying to build up, he'd more or less achieved. Strong competition existed for each position.

'We have a lot of international-class players here at the moment,' Saunders stated, 'so my problem is to pick the best ones who will blend together and give us the best end-product.'

With Villa's goal-shy forwards mostly misfiring, however, Saunders' search for additional firepower had become even more of a priority. During the season's finale the number nine shirt was worn by no fewer than five different players at various times, all with limited success. When Shaw and Little were injured, both Swain and Allan Evans temporarily revisited their attacking roles, while the home fixture with Forest even saw Ivor Linton forming an unlikely alliance alongside Terry Donovan.

David Geddis had said upon signing that Saunders 'wanted someone young who could offer my style of play', maintaining that fans shouldn't see him as a direct replacement for Gray and 'have to accept players in their own right'. Geddis had pace to burn but his style had brought its troubles. For so long used to an authentic target man, players now had to familiarise themselves with hitting long balls over the top for the striker to run on to.

It was a difficult adaptation – for both Geddis and his new team-mates. Geddis's 19 league games yielded just two goals and, even more frustratingly, after netting in a 1-1 draw at Manchester City, the club's record buy then got sent off in the last minute, leading to a suspension. Despite Geddis believing, 'Brian Little and I built up an understanding fairly quickly. We complement each other. He has the close control and flair, I provide the hustle and bustle,' Little's injury had put paid to that partnership. A vacancy clearly still existed for a proven marksman. The phenomenally talented Shaw, heading the scoring charts with 12 in league and cup, was already being earmarked by neutrals for big things in the game, but spearheading the team on his own was too much to expect of the youngster.

Saunders' antenna had been up for some time. The previous November, shortly after securing Geddis, Saunders turned his attention towards Manchester United's 19-year-old Andy Ritchie. Ritchie was fast earning a reputation as one to watch in the Red Devils' ranks, but largely found himself playing second fiddle to the far more experienced and battle-hardened Joe Jordan. Tommy Docherty, who'd first signed Ritchie for United, had wanted to take him to Queens Park Rangers, the latest stop on the Doc's managerial journey. Chelsea had also expressed an interest. But it was Saunders, offering £350,000, who made a concrete bid.

With Dave Sexton willing to let the youngster go, Ritchie went for talks at Villa Park. 'I had a look round and, although I liked Ron Saunders and the club, I was still convinced I had something to offer United,' Ritchie told *Shoot* magazine. Feeling that 'a transfer would mean adjusting to a side playing a different style of football', Ritchie turned down the move (and 'a large amount of money'), opting to remain at Old Trafford and prove he was 'worthy of a place' at his hometown team.

Early in 1980, Villa invited another striker, Dumbarton's Graeme Sharp, to come for a week-long trial. In 1976, a 15-year-old Sharp – then playing amateur football in Glasgow with Eastercraigs – had been asked down to Birmingham for a similar try-out. But, despite Villa being Sharp's favourite English club, it had proved a miserable experience and the young Scot was happy to return home (his chief recollection from the week being of Brian Little bringing his dog into training).

Two years later, Sharp, having matured into an exciting prospect, signed his first professional contract for Scottish First Division side Dumbarton. His goalscoring prowess was monitored by a number of top English clubs, as well as Rangers and Celtic. But none had made any approach. Now, with Villa reportedly eyeing up the young Scot as a potential replacement for his fellow countryman, Andy Gray (and Wolves, ironically, also rumoured to be interested in Sharp – as an understudy to Gray!), Sharp returned to Villa Park for a 'secret trial', the Boghead board happy to allow their prize asset to go and possibly secure some much-needed finance for the cash-strapped Scottish club.

Unlike the difficult trial he'd first endured, this time Sharp flourished. Convinced of Sharp's finishing ability, Saunders told the striker he was keen to sign him and the young Scot was interested in coming to the Midlands. But, having returned to Dumbarton, believing the two clubs would sort out the move, Sharp heard no more about it. 'I don't know whether the two clubs got together and couldn't agree on a deal,' Sharp wrote in his autobiography, *Sharpy*, 'or if Ron Saunders changed his mind.'

Saunders hadn't changed his mind. He claimed that on Tuesday 25 March he'd agreed a deal for the 19-year-old goal-grabber, only for Dumbarton to ring him the following night to say they'd accepted a bid from Everton, one which the Scottish club and the player found too good to turn down. Dumbarton general manager Alex Wright insisted that, prior to Everton's bid, he hadn't spoken to Saunders for weeks and that when Goodison boss Gordon Lee put in the offer for Sharp, he'd 'tried to phone Saunders but couldn't get hold of him. We regret the way we had to do the deal.'

But Saunders was furious, feeling they'd simply sold Sharp to the highest bidder. 'As far as I was concerned, a deal had been done,' Saunders griped, 'and then they told me it's off because they had a higher bid.' It was, the angry Villa manager said, 'a disgraceful way to do business' and 'the sort of thing that brings the game into disrepute'. Alex Wright defended his decision. 'Graeme had a full week's trial at Villa Park,' he said. 'They had every chance to sign him then.' Whether Saunders had, albeit briefly, had second thoughts about Sharp after that second trial, the delay had proved fatal, Sharp signing for Everton for £120,000. The search for Gray's heir would continue.

Everton's Bob Latchford was another name bandied about. A story even circulated in February 1980 that Villa were interested in Austrian international Hans Krankl, though the Barcelona forward went instead on loan to First Vienna, viewed largely as a stepping stone to a permanent return to his homeland and former club Rapid Vienna. Rumour or not, Saunders was still clearly scouting around for an answer to his quandary. Within days of the 1979/80 season ending, he hoped he'd finally found it.

With his two-year contract at Second Division Newcastle up, Peter Withe was attracting several potential suitors. Leeds, Sunderland and Everton were each fluttering their eyelashes. To Withe, a Scouser who used to sell matchday programmes outside Goodison Park, a move to his boyhood idols must have been very appealing. Fighting off their attentions, though, it was Saunders who sealed a £500,000 deal for the 28-year-old. 'Choosing Villa was not a spur-of-the-moment decision,' Withe said. 'I gave it much thought and I am pleased to be back in the Midlands and in the First Division with a club that will win things.'

Impressed by Saunders' 'positive attitude', Withe opted for Villa because he believed in all that his new boss was aiming for. Withe, Saunders told him, could be the 'last piece of the jigsaw' he was building. In paying half a million pounds for a striker supposedly in the twilight of his career, Saunders had displayed a huge act of faith.

It was a career that had seen Withe's suitcase rarely gather dust. After taking in the sights of Southport and Barrow, Withe enjoyed a stint in South Africa with Arcadia Shepherds before Wolves boss Bill McGarry brought him to Molineux in 1973. At the end of the 1974/75 season, Withe then took his scoring boots abroad again, turning out for Portland Timbers in the NASL, before returning for a second spell in the Midlands, joining Birmingham for £50,000 in August 1975. When City boss Willie Bell – 'who did not think I was good enough' – wanted rid, Brian Clough, a long-time admirer, snapped Withe up. It was at Forest that the Liverpudlian had his most successful period.

An unselfish leader of the line alongside the speedier Tony Woodcock, Withe was a major feature of Forest's rise from the Second Division to the league championship. He'd scored the very first goal in the title-winning season against his childhood favourites at Goodison. But after 'a difference of opinion between me and Brian Clough over money' – Withe felt he was entitled to more; Clough didn't agree and Withe 'wouldn't back down from my principle' – in the summer of 1978, the centre-forward was transferred to Newcastle, Bill McGarry bagging him for a second time. Clough, rarely one to admit self-failure, later claimed that the sale of Withe was 'my biggest mistake'. His second biggest? 'Not buying him back.'

Withe himself had no regrets about missing out on Forest's European Cup successes. 'I've never been one to think about what might have been. That's a quick way to the graveyard,' he said. Shortly after swapping the Trent for the Tyne, Withe had told reporters, 'Naturally, my main job is scoring, but it's also important to create chances for others.' Withe regarded himself 'more as a team player…a rover who will work in all areas of the field.' They were just the attributes Saunders was looking for. 'I have always admired his ability,' Saunders said of his new signing. 'He is enthusiastic, puts himself about, and he will complement our other players. I am sure he will be a tremendous asset.'

The previous season had seen a number of moves involving strikers and large sums of money. Steve Archibald moved south from Aberdeen to Tottenham for £1m, while the same fee took Kevin Reeves from Norwich to Manchester City. Big-spending City had also forked out three-quarters of a million for Preston teenager Mick Robinson. In light of those transfers, the fee for Withe was a relative snip.

Yet his acquisition still raised eyebrows. With Andy Gray's success in his first few months at Molineux, supporters were sceptical about the wisdom of investing a club record fee for a journeyman forward whose restless travels were perhaps indicative of a lack of true quality. Withe's goal-getting record was hardly outstanding. Commenting on the possible reason for Withe's nomadic footballing life, Saunders told James Mossop, 'People are often critical of strikers if they are not constantly scoring, and that may be why he has had so many moves. But I know one thing: I am glad he is on our side.'

Saunders wasn't just seeking a goalscorer. After the aborted attempts to sign younger forwards like Ritchie and Sharp, what Saunders recognised he most needed was an older, wiser head that would bring invaluable experience to the frontline, a seasoned campaigner with established quality. Whereas Geddis, according to himself, was 'not the finished article', Withe, Saunders felt, was 'the ready-made product'. A genuine, hard-working professional who, said James Mossop, trained 'like a demon', Withe was determined to make the most of every opportunity given him.

'Anyone can play off him,' Saunders enthused. 'He makes it easy for the other players. He's always there wanting the ball. Ask any of the players at his previous clubs and they will tell you how sorry they were to see him go.' Withe, Saunders hoped, would be the perfect foil for all his new team-mates. 'It's not just the forward line,' he underlined. 'You have to have 11 players who will knit in as a unit and work for each other. Obviously the more players you can get to score goals, then that takes the pressure off, but you never score as many goals as you would like.'

Withe was a player the Villa manager had first tried to sign prior to the eventual deal. However, he hadn't necessarily been Saunders' first choice. It transpired that Saunders had also made overtures about Mick Ferguson of Coventry. Ferguson, a tall, bearded number nine like Withe but three years younger, had enjoyed a fruitful partnership at Highfield Road with Ian Wallace. In January 1979, though, Coventry and Forest agreed an exchange deal that would send Ferguson to the City Ground with Martin O'Neill plus £500,000 coming Coventry's way. The deal fell through, however, and both players remained at their clubs. As it turned out, it was Wallace who, in July 1980, would join Clough's European champions.

Saunders, alerted to Ferguson's possible availability, told chairman Harry Kartz he was keen on a move for the player. 'He [Saunders] wanted to take Ferguson,' said Kartz, 'but I'd seen him play and wasn't impressed.' Kartz believed that Withe would be ideal for the youthful Villa side and, in his opinion, 'was a far better player than Ferguson would ever be'.

A disagreement ensued, leading ultimately to Kartz's resignation from the Villa chair. 'You daren't say to any manager, "Sign this player,"' Kartz recalled in an interview with the *Birmingham Mail* years later, 'but I feel that a club must have a chairman who is able to get on with his manager, so I asked Ron Bendall to take over.' The proposed move for Ferguson came to nothing, with Saunders eventually persuaded to plump for Withe. But the falling-out had come at a cost: Kartz had, for the most part, been a close ally to Saunders. Now the Villa boss would have yet another new supremo on the club's board with which to deal.

As a new decade of English football began, a cloud of gloom loomed over the game. Under Margaret Thatcher's nascent government, as unemployment topped two million and a worsening recession hit harder, most football clubs were feeling an ever-tighter pinch. The dramatic drop in attendances was a major talking point. The national team had fared miserably at the summer's European championships in Italy, Ron Greenwood's side entering the competition tipped as favourites to win but making an early journey home, while their rioting fans grabbed the headlines off the pitch. The scourge of hooliganism was prompting ever more desperate measures on how to combat it.

Given the acute economic situation, it was something of a surprise when the *Evening Mail* revealed that Villa's players would benefit from a new 'win bonus' scheme to the tune of £1,000 a man if the side was in the top four. After the club's form in the previous three years, the Villa directors perhaps expected not to have to pay out that often. The press made something of an issue of the money but Saunders dismissed the reported figures as 'a lot of nonsense'.

Despite confirming that it was potentially a 'substantial amount', Saunders felt a suitable financial reward was in every way justified. 'To me, it's as simple as this: you're telling people you're ready to pay for success, and challenge them to show they can achieve it,' he said. 'So, to earn it, they've got to be successful, and if they are successful, then they've earned their money.' The scheme also meant that the players wouldn't receive a penny if the team was in the bottom six. Players and supporters alike had every faith that that was never going to be the case.

'The thing about Villa is that we have never gone daft on spending money,' Jimmy Rimmer said. 'We work on what we've got.' It was a policy, the goalkeeper believed, that 'makes for a better team spirit and encourages the youngsters'. The fight the side had shown in the face of adversity couldn't have sent out a clearer message.

Still, not even the most sanguine Villa supporter could question the 25/1 odds against a serious title chase being mounted. Forest, Arsenal, Ipswich, West Brom and Manchester United remained the bookies' best bets to stop runaway favourites Liverpool. Local football writers weren't exactly quick to champion Villa's chances either, the *Evening Mail*'s Ray Matts warning, 'The patience of supporters is beginning to wear thin and unless a major honour comes Villa's way this season, there will be a demand for change at the top.'

Certain areas of the Midlands press had written off the club as still 'lacking ambition'. However, Matts did consider that Villa was definitely a club where the most prestigious silverware would find a worthy home. 'Put yourself in the centre circle of Villa Park,' Matts wrote. 'Survey the towering stands and terraces...and I defy any football devotee not to sense that this would be the perfect setting for the championship trophy.'

A journalist in the 1981 *Shoot* annual had written, 'No club is more tired than Aston Villa of the title "Yesterday's Team".' But shaking off that tag still seemed unlikely. 'We hope and expect to improve on last season,' Saunders would only say. 'With a little bit of luck – and everybody needs luck – we might win something. Anything is possible.' Told that some of those notorious peripheral people were beginning to suggest that Villa were capable of achieving success, Saunders replied, 'But they don't know, do they? They only *think*.'

Yet, as Allan Evans said, 'an air of expectancy around Villa Park' was very evident as the next campaign approached. With the precocious Cowans, if not quite yet the midfield general, rising ever upwards through the ranks, Morley itching to kick-start his career after enduring a tough first season and Shaw's ability for finding space and the back of the net, there would be a definite emphasis on attacking football as Villa set about recapturing former glories.

As Kevin Keegan was leaving West Germany, Villa headed there for a short three-game trip. Withe couldn't have enjoyed a better start for his new club, making a goalscoring, match-winning debut in a 1-0 victory over FC Bocholt. On the scoresheet in both the 2-1 defeat to Nuremberg FC and a 1-1 draw with VfL Bochum, then netting the first as Villa won 2-1 when Bochum visited Villa Park four days later, a newly invigorated Tony Morley also shone in the warm-up games. With Gary Shaw already looking to have formed a strong understanding with Withe, the signs were encouraging.

Withe had told journalist James Mossop that 'years ago I had a dream about playing for Villa' when Vic Crowe was in charge. When Withe went to Portland Timbers, where Crowe was then the manager, the striker thought that 'he had broken my dream'. He was wrong. Now he had Withe on board, the jigsaw Ron Saunders had been working towards since his arrival in 1974 was coming together. Putting all the pieces into the right places would still require great skill, but it would take a very brave man to predict that Saunders couldn't do it.

Do You Want to Bet Against Us?

ONE HUNDRED and seventy-seven seconds into the 1980/81 Football League season, Aston Villa found themselves 1-0 down to the fastest goal scored anywhere in the country that afternoon. When Eamonn Deacy – replacing the injured Colin Gibson – upended Leeds' diminutive midfielder Brian Flynn in the box, Flynn's fellow Welshman Byron Stevenson calmly dispatched the kick from 12 yards to put the home side ahead before Villa had barely drawn breath.

Two minutes later, a header from Leeds' Scottish winger Arthur Graham was saved by the legs of Rimmer. In the eighth minute another of Leeds' Welsh contingent, Carl Harris, saw a snap-shot from the edge of the box palmed away by the Villa keeper. If Saunders had written a script for the campaign ahead, it was ripped up almost immediately.

However, Villa, so muted early on, soon turned up the volume. Prompted by the inspirational Mortimer and Cowans, they began to press. Shaw and Withe saw chances go just wide or blocked. After their whirlwind start, Leeds, mid-table finishers the previous season, were hit by a blizzard from the visitors. A minute before half-time Villa were level. Cowans floated a perfect pass to Morley who, in a blur of movement, controlled the ball, moved it on, before firing a snap-shot from 25 yards that took everyone by surprise, especially keeper John Lukic.

In the second half, first to the ball, quick to break, and always positive in possession, Villa totally outran their West Yorkshire opponents. 'They were,' reported the *Sunday People* the day after, 'yards faster in thought and action', and Leeds, said the *News of the World,* 'neither had the speed nor the know-how to keep them at bay'.

On the hour Villa got their reward. Mortimer, picking up a pass from Morley, put in a low cross which, after Withe perhaps fortunately missed it, arrived at the far post for Gary Shaw to slot home. For the remaining half-hour, they never looked in serious trouble of conceding. A solid back four, with Gary Williams in for the suspended Evans alongside McNaught, nipped any Leeds fightback in the bud, and in the August sunshine, Villa eased to a deserved win. 'Gentle as lambs in the face of early aggression,' according to the *Sunday Mirror*, they'd transformed into lions from then on. 'For 75 minutes,' Leeds boss Jimmy Adamson went so far as to say, 'Villa tore us to pieces.'

'The only two games that matter are the last and the next,' was a stock Saunders phrase. He wasn't going to make any rash forecasts on the back of one victory. 'But if, after 12 games, we are in the top six,' he said, 'I feel that we will be there or thereabouts at the end of the season.' With a dozen games gone, Villa, on goal difference only, were second to Ipswich Town.

If Saunders was seeking any omens from the Leeds result, he might have been encouraged by the fact that, for the first time in Villa's history in three opening day fixtures against the West Yorkshire side, Villa had finished on top. Funnily, all three games (four if you threw in the Centenary fixture, too) had ended 2-1.

Their winning start continued. At Villa Park, a 1-0 defeat of Norwich with a dominant home side playing some crisp, inventive football had Saunders enthusing afterwards, 'At times we were brilliant.' Three days later, despite letting slip a two-goal lead in the last seven minutes to only draw 2-2 at Manchester City – Saunders grumbling that Villa hadn't been ruthless enough – the Villa manager took the plusses from a game in which, again, they'd outplayed their opponents with a display of swift, one-touch football. 'If we can learn from that result and it helps to make us a better side,' he said, 'we may yet look back to that game as one of our stepping stones to the future.'

Three victories on the bounce soon followed. A 1-0 home win over Coventry – Shaw's fine, glancing header from a 65th-minute Mortimer corner proving decisive as strike partner Withe celebrated his 29th birthday – was the meat in the sandwich of two successful legs of a League Cup tie with Leeds. Now even Saunders was prepared to forgo his usual caution. 'I regard this team as the best of any I have managed,' he told reporters. After flattering to deceive for so long, 'everything is coming right', he enthused.

That the disappointment of the dropped point at Maine Road was felt so bitterly by the players was, Saunders felt, a 'reflection of the attitude within the team'. Winning was everything, he always pushed upon his players, but great things were only achieved if individual ability was allied to work and graft. Just how much everyone was now pulling their weight and wanted to succeed was highlighted by the example of Tony Morley.

Arriving as an old-fashioned winger from Burnley, Morley, naturally enough, assumed that the job he'd performed at Turf Moor – 'to stay out wide and provide crosses' – was one he'd be replicating in his new claret and blue colours. Saunders had other ideas. Rather than merely parading up and down the flanks, Morley was expected to play a far more active role, dropping back when Villa were forced on the defensive and breaking out to provide width when they attacked.

According to Gordon Cowans, being the flair player Morley was, it took him longer than other players to 'come to terms with Ron Saunders and the way he wanted him to play'. Morley, by his own admission, had to adjust completely 'to fit into Villa's style'. It didn't come easily, but he was determined to fulfil his potential. Following a pre-season operation to clear a troublesome knee injury, Morley had trained so hard that, *The Observer*'s Tim Adams wrote, when a session was over 'you could see the furrow left by his studs all along the left-hand side of the field'. Now, feeling fitter and stronger, Morley was slotting in perfectly to the 4-4-2 formation that Saunders employed.

'I am sure the Liverpools of this world will not be able to keep us out of the limelight much longer,' said Allan Evans. There was, of course, only one Liverpool, but it was actually high-flying Ipswich who were attracting the glare of publicity. With Dutch midfield duo Arnold Mühren and Franz Thijssen marshalling operations, the Suffolk side were, in the view from the press box, the continental flair to Villa's British aggression and deservedly topping the table.

On 6 September, when Villa came away from Portman Road on the end of a first loss, it only confirmed the general opinion that Bobby Robson's side were the most likely challengers for the Reds' crown. Even while a fluid, interactive Villa – producing some 'absolutely fantastic stuff', said Dennis Mortimer – outplayed their hosts for much of the contest, a number of chances went begging and when Thijssen's innocuous first-time shot squirmed over the line, despite the best efforts of Evans, Ipswich – with 'a silly goal', Mortimer called it – gained a 56th-minute lead that they wouldn't relinquish. '*We* had all the chances,' Saunders said, a statement with which his counterpart Robson graciously agreed.

The following week at home to Everton, however, Villa played as if they were suffering a heavy hangover from the loss. Two goals in the space of four minutes just after the half-hour mark by Mick Lyons and Peter Eastoe put the visitors in command and, despite Saunders' surprisingly blinkered post-match analysis that Villa had 'had 35 minutes of the first half and 45 of the second', in truth it was a mostly inept performance that lacked any creative spark. The Toffees – without a single win on their travels in 24 previous fixtures – were barely troubled for the entire 90 minutes. The back-to-back defeats knocked Villa hard. 'Maybe we thought we were a better team than we actually were,' said Allan Evans shortly after. But rather than denting belief, the deficit set them right.

On a greasy playing surface at Villa Park, Wolves were beaten 2-1 with the aid of a fortunate rebound off Emlyn Hughes and a late close-range header from David Geddis, making his first start and replacing the ear-infected Gary Shaw. The returning Shaw then netted the only goal of the game at struggling Crystal Palace, his right-footed volley into the roof of Paul Barron's net coming with just five minutes left. When sixth-placed Sunderland, who'd thumped Leeds 4-1 the weekend before, were on the end of a four-goal blast themselves, the 4-0 romp was Villa's most resounding win so far. The team were playing well again.

After an incident-laced 3-3 midweek thriller, with George Courtney awarding a controversial penalty to each side in torrential rain at Old Trafford, two more dubious spot-kicks were given as Villa emerged 2-1 winners in the Second City derby at St Andrew's. Benefiting from a baffling 'handball' decision by referee Neil Ashley that gave Cowans the chance to put the visitors 1-0 up, Villa were pegged back by Worthington's reply from 12 yards before the encounter was settled four minutes from time. Allan Evans' left-foot volley – smashed past Jeff Wealands after McNaught's long free kick reached the Villa number four in the box via Peter Withe – was a goal the centre-half would come to consider the best he ever scored in Villa colours.

Quickly closing down space and not giving opponents a moment to settle, Villa were 'probably the worst type of team that you can play against', said ATV co-commentator Jimmy Greaves. 'As far as the ball is concerned, they're like flies round the honey pot.' With Liverpool and Ipswich drawing 1-1 at Anfield, Villa were now third, level on points with Paisley's side. Asked if he was optimistic about Villa's title challenge, Saunders grinned. 'All managers are optimistic,' he said. 'Anyone that gets over confident becomes "all our yesterdays".'

That 12th game, before 30,940 at Villa Park, a season's biggest crowd so far, saw two Tony Morley goals either side of half-time killing off Spurs and the 3-0 victory putting Villa joint top. 'Now we must wait and see how we are placed after the next 12 games,' Saunders said. By the end of the next 90 minutes, they were sitting at the summit. While Ipswich were busy beating Bohemians Prague in a UEFA Cup second-round tie, Villa produced another fine home showing to see off 18th-placed Brighton & Hove Albion. Despite taking a 27th-minute lead through ex-Villan John Gregory, the south-coast strugglers, with new signing Andy Ritchie having decided to fly the Old Trafford nest after all, were hit by four goals in 16 scintillating minutes of football either side of half-time, and Villa now headed the table. Had ATV not shelved plans to show highlights of the game – a refusal by Brighton boss Alan Mullery to change his team's logo-bearing shirts meaning it couldn't be covered – far more than the relatively small 26,367 crowd would have witnessed the moment.

Laid low with flu earlier in the week, Saunders only just recovered sufficiently to witness it himself. About being in pole position, he remained typically downbeat. 'It doesn't mean anything to me,' he reasoned. 'We've got a hard match on Saturday; that's what we've got to think about.'

That home gates only hovered just above break-even point had far more to do with the recession than the fare Villa were serving up. Their fluent, attacking game definitely compelled the onlooker to come back for more. 'You can only play to the players' strengths and that's what we're doing,' Saunders maintained. 'Fortunately, we're geared to play attractive football.'

They had netted 16 times in their previous five games. Morale was 'excellent both on the pitch and during training', Allan Evans told *Shoot*, and, he continued, 'I think it's fair to say that we are now a team without a weakness.'

The press remained uncertain. Following a 2-1 win at Southampton that completed a third of Villa's league games and a near-perfect record in October, Saunders rightly received the Manager of the Month award, but the compliments were still perfunctory at best. Instead, their top-spot placing meant that Villa were easy targets for the snipers' pot shots. With several players suffering the effects of a stomach bug prior to the win at Crystal Palace, the national papers had made headlines of the fact that Saunders' remedy for his players' ailments was to give them a glass or two of brandy before the game.

Social get-togethers were nothing unusual at most clubs, not surprisingly many managers believing they fostered a healthy bond between team-mates. The night before Forest's League Cup Final against Southampton in 1979, Brian Clough had not so much offered his team a drink as demanded they get drunk. On champagne! They went out on to the Wembley pitch bleary-eyed and 'blotto' according to one team member, and won 3-2. Brandy was no stranger to the Villa dressing room. A flask of the stuff was regularly placed on a table before the players went out. Objecting to football's booze culture didn't stop Saunders from encouraging his players to take a nip if it gave them an extra little shot of confidence. While not all of them embraced the ritual – some of the younger players spat out the drink as soon as they were on the pitch – it was clearly having the desired effect.

If Villa were to stay on top, Saunders wrote in the programme notes for the game with Leicester, they would 'have to compete with an extra edge in every game, for the simple reason that you are an extra challenge on the day to whoever the opposition may be'. The clash with Jock Wallace's side was a case in point. A lowly 19th, Leicester fielded a five-man backline and it took two goals in four second-half minutes (Shaw 65, Cowans 69) for Villa's perseverance to eventually pay off. 'No matter how good a side is,' Saunders accepted, 'some games turn out to be sheer hard work.'

Four days later at Carrow Road, as Ipswich were suffering a season's first defeat against Brighton, Villa were indebted to a second-half transformation that saw them seal a 3-1 win after Norwich's veteran midfielder Graham Paddon, the one player still with the Canaries since Saunders' days at the club, had given the home side a half-time lead. Graft as much as craft had again been required. There was now five points' daylight between Villa and their nearest challengers. 'We are rather like a boxer after six rounds of a 15-rounder,' Saunders said. 'We are ahead on points at the moment and feeling good, but there is still a hell of a long way to go.'

A boxing fan who'd often attend bouts in and around Birmingham and even gone a few rounds as a Birkenhead teenager, Saunders was fond of a pugilistic analogy. 'And, we mustn't forget the other bloke who can hit a bit as well,' he added.

After the hardships of 12 months previously, Saunders must have felt he was in clover. Speaking to journalist Brian Scovell, Joe Mercer – now a director of Coventry City and 'still chuckling after 51 years in the madhouse of football' – said that Saunders had excelled on a shoestring. 'He works at it,' the 66-year-old said. 'He buys cheap and sells dear.' Saunders, whom Scovell called 'a determined, almost zealous disciplinarian' and 'a private person' appeared to tick most of the Mercer boxes of what made a good manager: bravery, motivational skills, an eye for talent, a sound business sense, a certain animal cunning and a scrupulous honesty. An innate gift for self-promotion, however – 'You're selling your club so it's no use hiding,' Mercer said – wasn't one generally associated with the Villa manager. There was any amount of extroverts happy to play to the gallery. Their number didn't include Saunders.

With a dislike for the London-based national press bordering on contempt, Saunders brooked as little intrusion as possible into his inner sanctum or his innermost thoughts. For the most part, resentful members of the newspaper corps faced a manager with a fixed stare whose monosyllabic comments revealed little except for the interviewee's attitude towards their questioning. By contrast, Bobby Robson was far more approachable. The jovial Geordie took his football seriously but possessed an endearing harmlessness.

'Always good for a quote,' according to Pat Murphy, Robson's seemingly innocent remarks such as, 'We didn't underestimate them; they were just a lot better than we thought' only increased his allure in the press's eyes. And while Saunders' own pre- and post-match comments were sprinkled with amusing non sequiturs – 'If you're going to commit suicide, you don't do it yourself' and 'allegations are all very well but I would like to know who these alligators are' were just two – Saunders' dourness 'did nothing to make them [the press] warm to Villa', Murphy said. 'Not that Saunders or his players cared a toss about that.'

Saunders, 'when he chose to be', Dennis Shaw wrote in *A Game of Three Halves,* 'could be charming and friendly company.' But with the press that desire clearly didn't strike him very often. This disregard stemmed, Jimmy Cumbes claimed, from Saunders' desire 'to control everything'. The more he acquiesced to the press's demands, the less in charge he was.

'Often the art is saying a lot but revealing only what you want to reveal,' Joe Mercer had commented. That was a knack that Saunders certainly had. 'One of his favourite tricks,' Ray Matts told Dave Woodhall in *Champions Revisited*, 'was to say, "I don't want to say..." then he'd give me the most incredible story, finishing off with, "but you could say..." and he'd tell me what he wanted written.' Perfectly aware he was being manipulated, as long as Saunders was feeding him stories, Matts didn't mind. Matts spoke of how obliging Saunders was, always keeping the journalist informed. While, nationally, Saunders maintained a cold distance, locally, he was far more welcoming. 'Once you won his trust as a reporter,' said Pat Murphy, 'he wouldn't let you down.'

Saunders knew the people he could talk to and entrust to tell things as they were – or rather, as he told them they were. Cross a line, though, and you soon knew about it. Most managers were the same. Even Shankly, who basked in the limelight, would take issue with any journalist who'd written or broadcast anything about him or his team with which he didn't agree, often letting them know in very colourful language. Shankly regularly had a cross to bear over the way football was reported.

'It should be an easy task for an educated man to sit down after a match and write about the goals, thrills and spills,' he once said. 'Yet, after every match, the reporters cluster round dressing room doors waiting for managers like myself, Don Revie, Tommy Docherty and Brian Clough to emerge. They want a quote on which they can hang their story, want an opinion which will give them a guide all the way through. I find this wrong.' Saunders was very much of the same mind.

It was still Ipswich about whom the football writers were waxing lyrical. A poor run of only one win in six games had the scribes once again pooh-poohing Villa's title credentials. Two frustrating 1-1 home draws with Leeds and Arsenal bookended a heartbreaking late defeat at Anfield. A 3-0 win at home to Birmingham – David Geddis, in for the suspended Withe, finally coming good with a brace before setting up a third for Gary Shaw – was flanked by a couple of shock losses at Middlesbrough and Brighton. The defeat to Liverpool was particularly tough.

With Paisley's side unbeaten at Anfield since losing to Birmingham City on 21 January 1978 and chasing an English league record of 60 games without defeat on home soil (the previous record of 59, held by Millwall, had stood for 13 years), the match promised to be, as the Liverpool boss commented beforehand, 'a very special occasion'.

It was one that Saunders was forced to watch wearing a surgical brace; an attempt to cure the trapped nerve in his spine that had meant him missing the previous five weeks' training. His health would have improved when Evans' curling 78th-minute left-footer following a McNaught free kick looked to have earned Villa a deserved point after Dalglish's 66th-minute opener. With just 35 seconds left on the clock, though, Dalglish, the poacher-in-chief, somehow squeezed a scuttling shot through a packed penalty box to have the final word.

It was little consolation that Paisley afterwards praised the visitors who 'again showed that they are not afraid to play adventurous football'. Nevertheless, Saunders repeated his mantra. 'We've learned from every setback,' he said, 'and we'll learn from this.' When, in blizzard conditions at Ayresome Park, Villa were dealt another late body blow, a first-time drive from the left by striker Duncan Shearer capping a sensational spell of three goals in the last six minutes in which Gary Shaw levelled 60 seconds after Boro's Aussie forward Craig Johnston had put the home side ahead, Saunders again remained philosophical. 'If you challenge for the title you have to expect upsets every so often,' he said. 'It's how you come back from them that is the point.'

Even Saunders couldn't mask his disappointment after the 1-0 defeat at the Goldstone Ground, however. Trailing to an early Michael Robinson strike after a rare Kenny Swain mistake and second-best for virtually the entire 90 minutes to a Brighton side 20th in the table, an off-colour Villa were 'awful' in their manager's assessment. 'It's the worst we have played for two or three years,' Saunders said. If Villa's stuttering run wasn't to turn into a fatal stumble, they needed to get back on their feet fast.

Prior to the Boxing Day visit of mid-table Stoke, before any of the crowd were admitted to Villa Park, the ashes of Villa's legendary centre-forward Thomas 'Pongo' Waring, a son of Birkenhead like Saunders, were scattered in the goalmouth at the Holte End. So it was perhaps fitting that Peter Withe, the latest inheritor of Waring's number nine, should claim the only goal of the game, making no mistake from a 34th-minute rebound after Peter Fox had palmed out Shaw's looping header.

Aside from his goals, Withe's work-rate was phenomenal. The meaning of lost cause simply just wasn't in his vocabulary. Having strained every sinew in the 90 minutes, at the end of each home game Withe would fling his wrist bands (made popular by Ray Graydon) into the Holte End. Sweets would be given to a lady season ticket holder seated in the Witton Lane stand. Withe had quickly become an adopted son of Villa Park. The Liverpudlian had, Dennis Mortimer believed, 'graduated from an average player to an excellent frontrunner'.

His influence was being strongly felt. Alongside his more experienced, muscular partner, Gary Shaw was revelling. Like Andy Gray before him, Withe's physically robust approach often led the striker into confrontation with officials. As Dave Woodhall put it in *From One Season to the Next*, Withe 'tended to regard the referee's whistle as an opening of negotiations rather than a final decision'.

It was a leg injury, not suspension though, that forced his absence the following day at his old employers, Forest. It was a game that Saunders was adamant Villa 'should have won' – Shaw had what looked like a perfectly legitimate goal chalked off early in the second half by referee Pat Partridge, while strong penalty claims when Lloyd clearly handled in the area were ignored – but ultimately had to settle for a draw. Despite Shaw putting the visitors 2-1 ahead, scoring in the 68th minute what, at the end of the campaign, he considered his most outstanding goal – half-volleying past Shilton from Kenny Swain's low, driven cross into the Forest box – with only four minutes remaining, Martin O'Neill, seizing upon

Williams' attempted clearance, drilled home from just inside the area to level. Even Peter Taylor, without actually admitting that his side were lucky, paid Villa a great compliment in saying that they 'played the way we did two years ago when we were at our best'.

It was another valuable point and as the year drew to a close, the title race was, in effect, between three teams. Liverpool were the one the neutrals thought would win it, Ipswich the one they wanted to win it. Villa, meanwhile, remained mere interlopers who were bound to fall away sooner or later.

On the first weekend of 1981, the FA Cup third-round draw contrived to pair Villa and Ipswich at Portman Road. As in their league encounter, Villa gave a fine account of themselves and 'monopolised the second half' in Saunders' post-match assertion. But, similar to that first fixture, a solitary goal – England striker Paul Mariner swooping to slam the ball past the helpless Rimmer on 12 minutes – proved decisive, and on a cold January afternoon in Suffolk, everybody's second-favourite team prevailed again.

Robson's players were not only garnering the press's plaudits but international recognition. Young central defenders Butcher and Osman were called up into the England squad alongside the experienced Mick Mills. Mariner was now the number one choice for his country. Praises for his prolific partnership with Eric Gates and Alan Brazil, supplemented by prolific midfielder John Wark, were sung loud and clear. Outside of the local press, few gave a shout-out for the talent on show at Villa Park. Saunders cared little for such starry-eyed notions about the respective merits of the two teams. Nor did he give credence to the criticism that Villa had still failed to beat any of the top-six sides. The week following the cup exit, the perceptions about the Midlanders were to alter dramatically.

On 10 January, when Liverpool came to Villa Park, they'd lost only once in 31 games in all competitions and were level with Villa on 34 points after 25 games, heading the division on goal difference. Although the Anfield club were enduring a relatively pedestrian campaign compared with previous years, the feeling was that, soon enough, Paisley's side would swap their daywear for evening suits and stroll towards another feast at the table come the season's end.

On this afternoon, however, with Morley a threat from the touchline and the enterprising Shaw linking neatly with Withe, it was Villa who looked the more positive from the off. On 19 minutes, Withe, the boyhood Evertonian, fired a low drive past Clemence at the Witton End for a merited 1-0 lead. At the other end, Evans and McNaught – 'steady defenders who do not give much away' in the view of the Scotland manager Jock Stein (watching, with a game in Tel Aviv against Israel imminent) – largely snuffed out the danger of fellow countryman Dalglish. But it was in midfield that the game was really being won. The inexhaustible Bremner – 'the engineer with the untiring heart' as one journalist put it – stifled every Mersey tide; Cowans and Mortimer triumphed in the duel with Souness and McDermott. Villa, throughout, gave as good as they got, and more often better. Even when Liverpool upped their game, Villa stood firm, held fast and occasionally rode their luck (a Dalglish shot leaving Rimmer stranded but clipping the crossbar).

On 82 minutes, they scored again. It was a goal that typified the teamwork so vital a factor in Villa's success. Bremner, selflessly chasing back into his own half, halted an Alan Kennedy surge in its tracks with a ball-winning tackle. The ball fell to Kenny Swain, who raced forward before cleverly back-heeling it to Gary Shaw. With the Liverpool backline pressing up almost on halfway, Shaw spotted an unmarked Mortimer barnstorming through the middle of the park – 'his speciality' as *Match of the Day* commentator David Coleman said – and dinked a through-pass with the outside of his boot into the path of his on-running captain who, with the whole ground seemingly to himself, hit a low sidefoot shot to the left of the advancing Clemence.

A cue for total pandemonium on the terraces and one of the iconic images in Aston Villa history: Mortimer, the bearded skipper for whom netting against his boyhood heroes had 'always been a dream', turning, arm raised in triumph in a euphoric moment which all those Villa fans fortunate enough to be in the 47,960 crowd that day would never forget.

The goal was given even more gravitas by the commentary of Coleman, his voice now seldom heard on TV, the game one of the last he would ever cover for the BBC. He even threw in one of his memorable 'Colemanballs' for good measure, 'Both of the Villa scorers – Withe and Mortimer – were born in Liverpool, as was the Villa manager Ron Saunders who was born in Birkenhead.' The 2-0 scoreline flashed up on the new electronic scoreboard at Villa Park. There in black and white – or, rather, bright yellow.

But more than just the two points that elevated Villa to the top again, the victory was a huge mental lift as well. 'If we've beaten Liverpool, we've done something special,' Saunders said. They hadn't simply beaten Liverpool, they'd won a decisive psychological battle. 'We know that a lot of people have been waiting for us to fail and that we have been regarded in some quarters as super-fit robots,' said Mortimer. 'Perhaps now we will get some wider recognition.'

It came. In the *Daily Mail*, Jeff Farmer stated that the win 'must remove any question about the validity of Villa's championship challenge'. According to *The Telegraph*'s James Mossop, the victory – secured by 'two goals straight from the treasure book of scoring feats' – 'provided emphatic evidence' that the Midlands club had the talent to win the title. Their aspirations, at last, were being taken seriously. Saunders' men, Farmer suggested, were more than 'suitably equipped for this series of showdowns that could decide the title contest'. In 90 minutes that the *Sunday Mercury* labelled 'a credit to English football', Villa, Jeff Powell wrote in the *Mail*, had beaten Liverpool 'at their own game – with concentrated teamwork, imaginative goals, and the ability to keep their nerve in crucial situations'.

Having successfully squared up to the Merseysiders, Villa, their manager asserted, were now 'ready to look them straight in the eye'. Hardly a man renowned for his vocal flourishes, Saunders still wasn't about to go shouting any odds. When he'd taken his table-topping team to Anfield in November, Saunders stressed to the press that it was just another game. 'At the end of the day,' he'd said, 'no matter who you are playing, you get two points for a win, one for a draw, and if you lose they laugh at you.' Now, after the return match, nothing had changed. Villa's victory, Saunders told them, had simply put their destiny in their own hands. The *Sunday Mercury*'s claim that 'the title is surely heading for the Midlands' was plainly more than a little hasty.

The following Tuesday, Ipswich trounced Birmingham City 5-1 at Portman Road to head the table for the first time since 24 October. But the booster shot of confidence Villa gained from the Liverpool triumph arrived at the perfect time. They edged a close encounter at Highfield Road 2-1. Then, following a well-earned break and some much welcome mid-winter sunshine in Marbella (as the FA Cup fourth-round ties were played), on the last day of January, they overcame a resurgent Manchester City – now managed by Saunders' old adversary John Bond – at Villa Park, Gary Shaw after just two minutes latching on to an Evans knockdown to lash the ball past Joe Corrigan from six yards out for the game's only goal. 'The last 25 minutes were the survival of the fittest,' said Saunders afterwards.

The ability to 'win ugly' had characterised Liverpool's performances for so many years. Their predatory instinct to exploit any slip-ups by rivals, however, now seemed to have gone. That same afternoon, at Anfield, despite being handed a 15th-minute lead through an Alan Young own goal, Liverpool suffered a humbling 2-1 defeat at the hands of bottom-placed Leicester. It was the most unlikely of results and finally put a seal on Liverpool's phenomenal unbeaten home streak. By the start of April, they'd win just two more league games and, unable to claw back into genuine contention, the title race became all but a two-horse affair between Villa and Ipswich.

To every marker the Suffolk club laid down, Saunders' team responded in kind. On 7 February, at Goodison Park, Villa produced their best away display of the campaign. One man in particular sparkled. Tony Morley, from a line of Evertonians and desperate to play against his childhood idols, had been led to believe by Saunders that his place in the side would be taken by Pat Heard, Saunders informing the winger that he thought he'd be showboating before his family and friends. It was simply mind games on Saunders' part.

On the day of the match, Saunders told Morley that he'd had a change of heart; Morley would be playing after all. Saunders had no intention of dropping the winger but, as Morley later realised, 'had done his homework'. Saunders' 'great management' worked a treat. After only three minutes, Morley, 'like a bottle of pop', burst into life. Collecting the ball from a neat lay-off by Gary Shaw near the halfway line, he sped directly towards the Everton goal, cutting inside from the left before unleashing a rasping drive from the edge of the area that beat Martin Hodge all ends up. Clearly still rattled by Saunders' psychological tactic, Morley gave a two-fingered gesture towards the bench, one that later earned him a fine from the Villa boss. But it was worth every penny.

In May, Morley's strike would win him the BBC's Goal of the Season award. More immediately, it set his side on course for a 3-1 win in which Villa stamped their authority and planted another firm footprint on the title map.

The nip and tuck with Ipswich continued. Week in, week out, Villa refused to yield ground to their rivals. There were never going to be any soft touches. Crystal Palace, propping up the table, put up stubborn resistance in a 2-1 defeat at Villa Park. Withe, scorer of both versus the Londoners, then claimed the winner against 18th-placed Wolves in a particularly tetchy encounter at Molineux. Tony Morley's poor two-footed tackle after 18 minutes on Peter Daniel lit the touchpaper. Generously described later by John Barnwell as simply 'one of those unfortunate incidents', Morley left the Wolves defender with an injury later revealed to be a broken leg. Thereafter, tackles flew in and tempers were quick to flare. When, early in the second half, Gray, clearly seeking retribution, sent Morley sprawling, the Scottish striker and Dennis Mortimer had a set-to that threatened to get out of hand but for referee Joe Worrall's intervention.

But it was the Villa skipper who enjoyed the last laugh. On 82 minutes, an error by Allan Evans presented Gray with a clear shot on goal but the ex-Villa number nine fluffed his lines, sending his effort sailing over Rimmer's bar. Moments later, at the other end, after Evans had flicked on Morley's corner, Withe rose highest to plant his header into the back of the Wolves net. Ipswich, 4-0 victors at Coventry, still held the edge, but only by two points.

The following Saturday, while Robson's side were fighting out a 3-3 draw at Forest in the FA Cup quarter-final, Villa capitalised. With a flu-ridden Saunders not making the long journey to Sunderland, Tony Barton and Roy MacLaren assumed the managerial reins. But it mattered little. On a blustery north-east day, Villa had the wind in their sails, were 2-0 up after 19 minutes and eventually won 2-1 to draw level at the top. 'When people talk about what we have to do or have not to do between now and the end of the season, that sometimes is quite amusing,' Saunders wrote in the programme for Villa's next fixture, at home to ninth-placed Manchester United. 'The answer is simple; we have just got to keep on winning.'

Doing so wasn't that straightforward. Mirroring the match at Old Trafford in October, an enthralling clash finished 3-3. But Villa, 2-0 then 3-2 up, were denied a post-war club record eighth league win in a row by a last-minute McIlroy spot-kick after Williams upended Steve Coppell, and Saunders, post-match, couldn't disguise his annoyance at the spurned opportunity. 'We should not have allowed the two-goal lead to escape us,' he said. 'After playing magnificently in the first half, we threw it away.' His disappointment ran even deeper when he learned that Ipswich had beaten Spurs 3-0.

Villa, Coppell told the press, 'lacked the killer instinct' which would ultimately prove their undoing in the title quest. Stung by the England winger's criticism, the players stuck the comments on a notice board at Bodymoor Heath as a daily reminder. A similar dismissal of their title credentials by Birmingham's Archie Gemmill provided another enormous spur.

Two more dropped points, though, in a disappointing 2-0 defeat in strong, swirling winds at White Hart Lane – reportedly blowing at 70mph and perhaps to blame for the usually reliable Gordon Cowans skying a 63rd-minute penalty over Milija Alexis's bar – had Saunders unsparing in his assessment, 'We had five players out there who went missing.' Thankfully, with Ipswich also going down, 2-1 at Old Trafford to Coppell et al, the slip-up in the capital wasn't as costly as it might have been.

The Suffolk club, having seen off Forest in their replayed FA Cup tie and completed a 7-2 aggregate victory in the quarter-finals of the UEFA Cup over a Saint-Etienne side containing Michel Platini and Johnny Rep, were still chasing an unprecedented 'treble'. 'An extraordinary mélange of Dutch, English and Scottish talents,' was how *The Guardian*'s Robert Armstrong had depicted Robson's side after a league win at Forest. Villa's blend of English and Scottish plus the one Irishman, Deacy, were still being furnished with far less poetic portrayals. To those who slammed them as an effective but dull side, however, Saunders gave an unexpected retort. 'Remember the fact that the knocker's art requires no brains at all,' he put in his programme notes for the home game with Southampton. It was a line from the Chinese philosopher Confucius.

Back to winning ways with a 2-1 success against the third-placed Saints, Villa were still in second after Ipswich smacked Sunderland 4-1. But when, three days later, Robson's side went down 3-0 at Elland Road, both clubs had played the same number of games, with only one point separating them.

April was to prove a defining month. The next Saturday, on the same afternoon that Bob Champion on Aldaniti was romping home in the Grand National, while Ipswich were on the end of a 3-1 reverse at West Brom, Villa's stylish 4-2 win at 20th-placed Leicester saw them surge to the summit once more.

In Dublin later that evening, Buck's Fizz won the Eurovision Song Contest for the United Kingdom. 'And soon you will find that there comes a time...for making your mind up,' they sang. The bookies – perhaps sensing widening cracks at Portman Road – had changed theirs and Villa were installed as 8/11 favourites. But only a fool would have put good money on the outcome. 'As long as we can stay at the top,' Saunders had said, 'the extra competitiveness in all these games can only help towards making us a better side.' The theory was about to be tested.

A crowd of 47,998 – the highest at home of the season – thronged into Villa Park for the Wednesday night derby against third-placed West Brom. But for a ground capacity reduced due to safety reasons, with hundreds more locked outside, it would have been even bigger. It was, Saunders later reflected, 'no place for the faint-hearted'.

With the more physical Geddis brought in for Shaw to help combat the central defensive duo of Robertson and Wile (the Baggies captain making his 500th appearance for the club), it set the tone for the evening.

Saunders acknowledged afterwards, 'The commitment was always going to stifle attractive football.' The game, according to the *Daily Mail*'s James Mossop, was 'a contest of constant action but little end product', the tension on the terraces echoed on the pitch. Defences dominated. Errors were plentiful, chances few. Villa were lucky to escape when Cowans' misplaced pass presented Cyrille Regis with a one-on-one with Rimmer. Ten minutes from time, when referee Lester Shapter had to be substituted by the senior linesman who, in turn, was replaced by a member of the crowd, it looked like being the most significant drama. It wasn't.

The home side began to rediscover a little more coherence. Mortimer's rasping drive was held by Godden, and Morley started to get the better of the visitors' backline. With less than two minutes remaining, when Jimmy Rimmer's drop-kick landed deep in the West Brom half, full-back Brendon Batson, attempting a needless back-pass to his keeper, under-hit the ball and the ever-alert Peter Withe, holding off Robertson's full-bodied attentions, was gifted a simple opportunity which, in Mossop's words, he 'gleefully converted'. Withe's first-time lob over Godden, moving almost in painfully slow motion before bouncing into the net, sent a roar rising from the claret and blue contingent that could have been heard up the M6. At the full-time whistle the mix of ecstasy and relief was palpable and Villa were three points clear.

Yet, while his players, suffering the following day a reaction to anti-typhoid injections given for the end-of-season tour to South America, might well have been swept up by championship fever, Saunders refused to get carried away. 'The only time I will be prepared to go overboard is when we have a lead that means we cannot be caught,' he said. 'When you start talking about gaps between you and your rivals is when you might start to take it easy. That, we simply cannot afford to do.'

Saunders insisted on playing things down. To arrive as a team, he constantly reminded the players, they had to be successful. 'He'll be the first to pour the champagne if we have anything to celebrate,' said Dennis Mortimer, 'but it won't even go on ice until we have achieved something.' No matter how hot it became, 'You won't notice any difference in Ron Saunders,' Mortimer said, 'and that's an important asset at a time like this.' The title was never a topic of conversation. Winning the next game was always the focus, and 'see what happens after that', Saunders would say. The next game was at home to Ipswich.

If Lady Luck had smiled down on Villa Park against the Baggies, she was positively beaming over the ground three days later. Ipswich, already flagging after a narrow midweek UEFA Cup semi-final win versus Cologne, were taken to extra time in their FA Cup semi-final – the first semi in the competition's history to go to an additional half an hour – against Manchester City. It was goalless after 90 minutes, then, in the 100th minute, City skipper Paul Power curled in a left-footed free kick and, hot favourites before the match, the Portman Road club experienced a demoralising blow. Defender Kevin Beattie had also been taken off with a broken arm.

Among the 46,537 crowd that afternoon was Ron Saunders. Although a neutral spectator, even the stone-faced Villa boss must have struggled to suppress his delight that Robson's players had had to endure an extra energy-sapping half-hour before their return to Villa Park the following Tuesday. Inevitably, ignoring the 7.30pm kick-off, the game with Villa was billed as a winner-takes-all High Noon face-off. Long queues formed outside the ground an hour before kick-off. The Holte End was so heaving, regulars were forced to stand at the opposite end to their usual spot. For the visitors, it was, as the BBC's Barry Davies put it, 'a bit like asking the body to return to the scene of the crime'.

Defeat, according to Robson, was 'unthinkable' and 'a word we can't consider'. They were gifted a tonic after only four minutes. Caught ball-watching near his own penalty area, Ken McNaught allowed Mariner to nip in, feed Alan Brazil, and the Scottish striker had little trouble stroking it past Rimmer. Saunders, with his fondness for a pugilist's parlance, described it post-match as 'like a boxer walking from his stool straight into a right-hander'.

The early blow left Villa visibly shaken and, for much of the first 45, Ipswich looked the more assured side. After the break, Villa recovered. More direct in possession, they began to get the upper hand. Morley went close with a drive. Withe and Shaw both wasted opportunities they would normally have snapped up. Shaw, scythed down in the box by Osman, had a penalty appeal completely ignored by referee Brian Hill. Then, just as they were threatening to level, in the 79th minute Villa fell victim to another calamitous self-inflicted error.

When a suicidal back-pass by Des Bremner presented Mariner with the chance to go forward, he fed the ball to Eric Gates, and when the diminutive striker's long, right-footed drive hit the roof of Rimmer's net, an audible gasp could be heard around Villa Park.

The home side rallied. Withe chested down Swain's throw-in, and Gary Shaw flashed a left-footed volley past Cooper. But it was all to no avail. Referee Hill blew up and, in the away stand, the Ipswich supporters broke out into loud song as if the title was theirs. In the dressing room their players did likewise. Villa's two defensive lapses had left them with 'one helluva hill to climb', said a rueful Saunders. They'd 'created enough chances to win by a street', he said, but paid the price for being 'able to put only one of them away'. There were no excuses. 'It's our own fault,' he said, 'but it makes it interesting, doesn't it?'

If the writing was on the wall, Saunders refused to read it. Entering the crowded interview room (situated just beyond where a home dressing room housed a squad of sickened Villa players), Saunders, rather than waiting for a reporter to throw a question his way at the press conference, posed the first one himself. 'Would anyone like to back against us winning the title?' he asked. There was silence in the room. 'Thank you for your confidence, gentlemen,' he announced. The mischievous twinkle in his eye said everything.

Trailing by only a point with a game in hand and a better goal difference, the odds appeared to be back in Ipswich's favour. Saunders, inevitably, wore a different pair of spectacles. Interviewed shortly after by Barry Davies, when the BBC man asked, 'So it's all to play for still?' Saunders responded, 'I think so. Do *you* want to bet against us?' There wasn't a hint of doubt in his voice.

Despite Ipswich skipper Mick Mills's confident assertion that 'if we don't win it now, we need shooting', his manager Bobby Robson wasn't counting any chickens. 'This result has opened it up again,' he said. 'But there is still too much football to be played for it to be over.'

Villa, in the view of the *Evening Mail*'s Ray Matts the following day, had been 'unable to pluck the apple which hung so invitingly before them', and 'looked the artisans compared with the artists'. Ipswich, in Matts' opinion, had been 'individually superior and collectively more composed' and 'demonstrated cultured, menacing football throughout'. Yet, while believing that Robson's side 'showed on the night what observers have been saying all season, that they are the classiest combination in the league with their Dutch midfield maestros and skilfully swift attackers', Matts also conceded, 'It would take a naïve man to discount the still-valid claims of the Second City side despite the dejection and disappointment they must have experienced.'

Both teams were 'like two leg-weary marathon men' who 'stagger towards the tape in dramatically erratic fashion – defying anyone to predict, categorically, who will get there first'. The end-of-season contest, Matts wrote, promised to be 'the most thrilling finale to the championship race for many years'.

Saunders might well have paraphrased Mark Twain's famous quote. The reports of Villa's death had been greatly exaggerated. On Easter Saturday, 'an exceptional performance', in Saunders' estimation, during which 'each and every one of the Aston Villa players showed tremendous character, coupled with undoubted ability', saw Villa beat Nottingham Forest 2-0 before a vociferous 34,707 at Villa Park. The decibel level was raised even higher when the scoreboard flashed up the result from Portman Road – Arsenal, through Nicholas and Sansom, had claimed a 2-0 win of their own to end Ipswich's run of 46 home games without defeat.

Peter Withe, who'd delivered a pointed reminder to Brian Clough by sealing the win on the stroke of half-time, netted again two days later. Withe's relatively tame header from a Mortimer free kick, fumbled by Peter Fox, gave Villa a lead at the Victoria Ground, but it lasted barely three minutes before Stoke's Brendan O'Callaghan glanced in a heavily deflected equaliser from a Paul Maguire corner. It was a nervy, largely uninspiring performance in a match 'which had all the atmosphere of a cup final' to Saunders. 'Once again the traditional virtues of the English game had ground out the result for Villa,' wrote the *Daily Mail*'s Jeff Powell. It was one more backhanded compliment about their style.

Saunders, as always, fought their corner. 'We did not play particularly well,' he admitted, 'but at the moment it's about 11 players grasping like hell for a result.' Ipswich's 1-0 defeat at Norwich in the East Anglian derby only emphasised how precious the point at Stoke was. It left Villa four points clear and Bobby Robson claiming that Ipswich's defeat 'has probably cost us the title'. Despite still having a game in hand, Robson insisted, 'The only way we can win the title now is if Aston Villa do what we have done – that is, to give it away.'

The implication that Ipswich were surrendering the title rather than Villa winning it wasn't lost on Saunders. 'If we should win it,' the Villa boss stressed, 'we will have done so because of our strength and stamina.' They were qualities that were continually knocked, 'but that's what English football is about', Saunders said. Villa were a side, Ray Matts had written after the Ipswich defeat, which 'managed to combine entertainment with the industry that gets denigrated on occasions when it fails against a team of Ipswich's undeniable quality'. They may not be 'the best collection of individual talent' but if they were to finish top, Matts stated, 'It is because they are the best TEAM in the First Division.'

The draw in the Potteries meant that, remarkably, Villa had not lost all season against a fellow Midlands club, only West Brom claiming a solitary point from the various derby matches. For Saunders' money, it was another factor that had been blatantly overlooked by the press. With so much regional pride at stake, every point was twice as difficult to earn. Ipswich, with only Norwich as a close rival, arguably had a much easier league fixture list. The draw also guaranteed that, with a win at home to mid-table Middlesbrough and an Ipswich failure to overcome their FA Cup conquerors Manchester City, Saunders' side would secure the crown.

'I don't want to think about the league title at the moment,' he told the media on the eve of the Boro game. 'And I certainly don't want to talk about it.' Villa, he wrote in the programme notes, had 'got to produce all the things we are capable of.' On a rain-soaked April afternoon, they did, and more. Dominant from the start, 'Villa laid on a banquet of creativity, power and skilful football befitting a champion team,' reported the *Birmingham Mail,* and the patches of standing water on the Villa Park pitch proved no hindrance to their sleek, streamlined play.

After Gary Shaw, sweeping home from Withe's set-up on 23 minutes, had settled any nerves, it was all one-way traffic. On 51 minutes, Withe's header from a Morley cross made it two. Ten minutes from time, Evans drilled home from Mortimer's half-cleared corner to complete the scoring but it might have been double figures. 'We played tremendously well,' Saunders said, 'particularly when you bear in mind the pressure on the players.'

If it was a relatively run-of-the-mill win on the park, though, on the terraces it was 90 minutes of conflicting emotions. After news of Ipswich taking a 51st-minute lead had dampened the mood, a rumour that Manchester City had levelled late on sent a burst of sunlight spreading through the crowd. Believing that Villa were champions, loud celebrations erupted around the ground. The last few minutes were played out in almost surreal fashion, with ears pressed hard to transistors for confirmation from Suffolk.

At the final whistle, the Villa Park pitch was swallowed up by a claret and blue tide. Some Villa players started to celebrate, too. But it was all too hasty. It transpired that a steward had told Jimmy Rimmer that Ipswich were only drawing, information that the Villa goalkeeper passed to his team-mates and which quickly filtered through to the supporters. The reports had been false. Ipswich – through Terry Butcher, whose midweek goal against Cologne had helped secure a UEFA Cup Final place – had held out for a win. Their thinning title hopes were still alive, albeit gasping for breath.

Once the score came through from Portman Road, there was a vivid sense of anti-climax. Years later, Saunders was asked if he was aware of the rumours on the day. 'I remember people shouting at the bench,' he said, 'but I always tried not to pay any attention.' Afterwards, Middlesbrough boss John Neal, Jack Charlton's successor, declared it 'a shame they [Villa] didn't win the title today. They deserved to, because they are a tremendous side'.

Saunders once again paid tribute to his underrated charges. 'If we win the title, perhaps people might start accepting what we have done,' he said. 'They might look at the management and how the players have conducted themselves as ultra-professionals.' Not the ultra-professionalism of which Clough accused Revie's Leeds, but a desire and determination to battle for each other that had seen them amass a 60-point haul, surpassing a club record that had stood since 1961.

At the end of that last home fixture, Villa's players trotted around the pitch to the acclaim of the 38,000 crowd, bearing scarves and bobble hats thrown to them by their fans. It was fitting recognition of their efforts during an outstanding season. With one game to go, Villa had a foot over the threshold. For so long snapping at their heels, Ipswich were reliant on their Midlands rivals stumbling fatally at the very last.

The Transistor Champions

BIRMINGHAM City Council's plans for a lunchtime celebration and tour of the city centre the following day were all in place. The lord mayor suggested that they go ahead regardless of whether Villa won or not. It was a proposal given short shrift by Ron Saunders. The Aston Villa manager – remaining 'cooler than a bottle of champagne' according to journalist John Wragg – refused to even think about. 'We don't want the accolades until they have been earned,' he said. Seventy-one years of dust had perhaps been swept from the spot in the club's cabinet reserved for the championship trophy, but the silverware still wasn't close enough to smell the polish.

Villa's visit to Highbury, wrote journalist Norton Jones, was 'tantamount to a trip through a minefield when one mistake could wreck everything'. A single point from the final game of a long season and the Midlands club were guaranteed the title. Slip up and Ipswich, should they win at Ayresome Park, would host Southampton after the FA Cup Final in a last-match decider. The consequences of a Villa defeat were too catastrophic for anyone of a claret and blue persuasion to contemplate.

In Arsenal, Villa would be up against an in-form team on a run of eight unbeaten league games. A 3-1 win at Molineux on the penultimate Saturday had seen Terry Neill's side climb into third and they were perfectly poised to secure a place in the following season's UEFA Cup. Victory over Villa was still required to seal qualification. Avoid defeat and Arsenal would also establish the record of going through a whole season without losing a league game at Highbury. Saunders had few fears that his side would be caught up in the emotion of the occasion. 'My problem,' he joked, 'is to find out what I did to get the players as relaxed as they were against Middlesbrough.' That relaxed approach, it emerged, was partly due to a moment of clever man-management by none other than Peter Withe.

The striker, aware that Boro, having won at Villa Park on their previous three visits, were considered by many Villa players as a bit of a bogey side, had duped his team-mates into a false sense of security. Announcing in the dressing room before the game that he had never been on the losing side against the Teesside club, Withe warned them that he wasn't about to start now. 'It was rubbish,' Withe later admitted. 'I had just made it up to get them in the mood.' Bobby Robson, meanwhile, was indulging in his own brand of psychology. 'Villa won't sleep too well next Friday,' he'd told reporters after Ipswich's win over Manchester City, 'and may just have a nagging doubt.'

If there was any uncertainty it was over Ipswich's opponents. The ease with which Villa saw off Middlesbrough gave little hint that the north-easterners might cause Robson's side any trouble. Despite the London bookmakers quoting Villa at 9/4 on to take the title, both Saunders and Robson were loath to concede that Villa were home and dry. Far more certain that Villa would hold their nerve, however, was Bill Shankly. 'I can already see in my mind the streets of Birmingham bedecked in claret and blue,' the former Liverpool boss had written in the *Birmingham Mail* earlier in the week, 'and celebrations lasting well into the summer.'

Terry Neill was playing a diplomatic game. 'I've known Ron Saunders and Bobby Robson as pals for a very long time,' said the Arsenal boss, 'they are both marvellous people and I don't mind which of them wins the championship.'

Throughout the campaign the English press had blatantly nailed their colours to the Ipswich mast. Even the foreign papers loved them. Ipswich, one Malaysian newspaper put it, had 'made entertainment a fashionable word in English soccer again'. The beauty in the eye of the beholders all belonged to the Suffolk club, though not all their international colleagues believed they were the rightful heirs to the throne. The *Montreal Gazette* claimed that, as Villa prepared to face their test against 'the Gunners' dour, robot-like build-up', that 'it can only be good for football if Villa succeeds and lifts the title with its more entertaining, free-flowing style'. A cynic reading that might have assumed that the Canadian pressman had clearly been watching a whole different ball game.

Even the Highbury staff failed to acknowledge the likelihood of Villa's coronation; they'd only made the game all-ticket on the Monday, allocating 16,000 tickets for the Midlands club. The importance of the match was perhaps lost on the north Londoners, but not to the Villa followers. Reared on stories of feats from a past so distant they might have come from a book of fairytales, they were desperate not to miss out. The tickets sold out within hours. Double the allocation could easily have been sold.

Saturday 2 May 1981 was a bright, sun-soaked day in the capital. Estimates of how many made the pilgrimage from Birmingham range from 12,000 to 20,000. In any event, they headed to London in their droves. A convoy of coaches – a record 71 organised by the Villa travellers' club – snaked along the motorway. Cars full of fans ventured south in full expectation that Villa were about to reach the glorious end of a journey stretching back over seven decades. Half an hour before kick-off an agonising gridlock on the North Circular Road was still holding up some supporters, a police escort required to come to their aid.

Those already there mixed with the Arsenal fans in the overflowing pubs and streets near the ground. There was a heady excitement in the air. Ticketless fans queued outside. Inside, Highbury had a carnival atmosphere. Some 57,472 fans, the largest attendance in England all season, were there, the Villa contingent massed mostly at the famous Clock End. When scores of Arsenal supporters charged down the stand on the left, skirmishes broke out, spreading on to the pitch before police quickly quelled them. The kick-off was delayed by several minutes.

Another surreal ingredient to the pre-match pot was added with the presence of Pelé. The Brazilian legend, on a promotional tour and a guest of the Gunners, was introduced to the crowd to loud applause, a chorus echoing from the North Bank of 'Sign him up, sign him up, sign him up' only for boos to greet him from the Clock End when, walking off, he failed to wave to the Villa fans. As the two sides emerged from the tunnel, balloons, released from the centre circle to herald the players, sailed up high into the north London sky.

'My team won't freeze in the white-hot atmosphere of Anfield,' Saunders had once memorably promised before a game at Liverpool. Now – to paraphrase the Villa manager's verbal faux pas – in the afternoon heat of Highbury, his players did freeze. Weighted with expectation, they looked leaden from the start. Arsenal, spring-heeled and purposeful, took only 12 minutes to go a goal up. When Des Bremner conceded a free kick just outside the penalty area, Kenny Sansom swung a high ball in for Alan Sunderland to flick on to Brian McDermott. His back-header found Willie Young and the red-headed Scot volleyed in a low, hard drive past a static defence and into Rimmer's goal. After 35 minutes, the already bleak mood among the Villa fans darkened further: news came through that Paul Mariner had put Ipswich ahead.

At Highbury, just before half-time, it was two. When Jennings' punched clearance from a Mortimer corner was hoofed to the halfway line, with the Villa defence out of position, McDermott headed downfield, outmanoeuvred both Gibson and Swain and, despite Swain's best efforts to bring him down, the young Arsenal forward toe-poked the ball goalwards past Rimmer.

It was agonising for those on the terraces. Watching their team give its least effective display in the last game of the season, it appeared as if their worst fears might be realised. In the Villa dressing room at half-time, there was a deathly silence. 'I lay there feeling I had cost Aston Villa the league,' Kenny Swain wrote in his autobiography. A disconsolate Jimmy Rimmer felt he himself was at fault for both goals. Saunders, positive and calm, urged his dejected troops to 'just keep doing all the good things you've been doing all season', but a feeling that glory could be snatched away engulfed the whole side.

In the second half, for all their huffing and puffing, they made little headway. Mortimer was unable to influence matters. Up front, Withe and Shaw were easily stifled by Young and David O'Leary. Withe, David Lacey wrote in his match report, 'looked as much like England's next centre-forward as Basil Fawlty'. A superior home side remained in control. Tense Villa supporters, their nerves on edge, craved good news from Teesside. Around the 55th minute they got it. Gary Shaw, set up by Withe, fired hopelessly wide. Suddenly, small pockets of Villa supporters began jumping up and down. Roars erupted. Ripples of joy quickly became a sea of jubilation. Boro's Yugoslavian forward Bosco Jankovic, they'd learned, had levelled matters at Ayresome Park. The dream that had seemed vanquished was back on again.

Clutching radios ever closer and clinging to hopes, the fans were almost fully focussed on the drama taking place nearly 250 miles away. In front of them, Gordon Cowans had a powerful 70th-minute 25-yarder tipped over the bar by Jennings. Five minutes later, Shaw saw a shot comfortably held by the Irish keeper. But minds were elsewhere, fearful that a late comeback from Ipswich could still ruin the party.

The game at Highbury was winding down, the hands ticking around on the ground's imposing timepiece. Then came another eruption. With about five minutes remaining at Highbury, those listening to their transistors heard BBC Radio 2 commentator Bryon Butler utter the start of a line, 'Let me be the first to congratulate Aston Villa...' the last part of which was lost in a deafening uproar. It meant only one thing: Aston Villa were Football League champions. Two minutes from the end at

Middlesbrough, Jankovic, the forward so anonymous the week before at Villa Park, had netted a second to seal his name into Villa legend and decide the destination of the First Division title.

Peter Withe jogged to the Clock End, cupped his ear to hear the score then ran back to tell the rest of the team. Kenny Swain took a throw-in. Arsenal fans were giving him the thumbs-up. Middlesbrough were 2-1 up, they said. In 'a quite extraordinary' moment, commented *Match of the Day*'s John Motson, the Villa fans were 'celebrating, even though their own team here have done nothing to help themselves'. At Harrogate referee David Hutchinson's final whistle, as the two teams darted from the pitch, supporters from both ends flooded it in their thousands, police forming long lines to segregate them. Some fighting broke out between them. Others danced together on the halfway line. Nail-bitten fingers grabbed tufts of Highbury turf for keepsakes. 'We're going to win the league' shifted tense to 'We've won the league.' Never has a set of football fans been so ecstatic in defeat. In the players' tunnel, the news was relayed to Saunders. His staff and players heard it confirmed. Aston Villa had won the title. A morgue at 3.45pm, the away team dressing room was now alive with celebration.

But it was a bittersweet sensation. Unable to return to the pitch to acknowledge the fans due to the disturbances, the players remained put. The professional pride that Saunders had instilled in them made it tough to simply gloss over the poor performance. Saunders had, of course, hoped Villa would win 'in style' but, he acknowledged, 'one or two players were trying to do too much' and 'this was not one of our better days'.

Nerves had played a part. Even Saunders had felt them. The last 20 minutes, after he'd heard that Ipswich were being held, were 'inexplicable', he said. Jimmy Rimmer felt he'd had a 'nightmare' against his former club. Gordon Cowans would describe the day as anti-climactic. Gary Shaw spoke of how difficult it was playing out the game as he was watching what was going on on the terraces. Many players admitted later that it took a while before the realisation of their achievement really sank in. The champagne was uncorked but the full intoxication of Villa's success didn't hit for some time.

For *The Guardian*'s David Lacey, the settling of the season by a Yugoslav at Middlesbrough was 'as unlikely a turn of events as anyone could have predicted last August when it seemed that Liverpool simply had to keep their noses clean to take the title for the third successive season'. After nine months of see-sawing fortunes, fate had taken a most unlikely late hand. The script of the headline writers busy penning their obituaries of

Villa's title dream hadn't accounted for the hitherto unknown Jankovic. Boro's first overseas player when he'd signed from Zeljezniicar FC in February 1979, Jankovic had tripped as he ran on to the pitch for his first team debut as a substitute. Now he'd planted his feet and name firmly into Aston Villa folklore.

There was a rumour years later that Jankovic had returned to his native Yugoslavia and died during fighting in the Balkans War. Other reports claimed that he left football to begin a law practice back in Sarajevo, Bosnia. Or that he had he passed away in 1993 of a cancer-related illness. Whatever the truth, Villa fans would forever hold the balding forward in their debt.

Yet the title wasn't decided by one man or one fixture. Mick Mills ungraciously stated, 'The result at Highbury proved that Villa are not worthy champions' (Mills conveniently forgetting that Ipswich had lost by the same score to Arsenal just days before), but the defeat, as disappointing as it was, was one of only eight in a 42-game campaign. Forty-two games in which Villa had won 26, more than any other side, and drawn eight others. Forty-two games that, by the end of them, Villa's players, in journalist Ian Johnson's words, were 'converted from a group of keen and ambitious young men into an oil-smooth outfit who knew they were better than all of the rest'.

'I suppose the knockers will come out,' Saunders told reporters, 'and say we didn't deserve to win the title.' After inadvertently straying into 'Carry On' territory, the Villa manager felt duty-bound to remind them, 'We've played some tremendous football up and down the country. I've not only got tremendous players with tremendous ability but they're also very good people. They've sweated blood and put up with me. Give the lads what they deserve. They're a little bit special.' If anyone questioned Villa's right to be champions, 'Then they don't know what they're talking about,' he said.

For Scottish sports writer Hugh McIlvanney, Villa's triumph was a prize 'earned by a long season of spirited endeavour', while David Lacey described it as 'a tribute to the collective determination of the players and the management, which has inspired such a strong cadre spirit'.

Faced with a typically unimaginative line of questioning in the aftermath of Highbury, Saunders was asked how happy he was. 'I'm probably a little bit more delighted than some of you people are,' he ventured. But, McIlvanney wrote, Saunders 'should not see it as a conspiracy of injustice if many neutral observers have difficulty in acclaiming Villa as a great side'. Lacey, too, remarked that '(it is true to say) there would have been more heartfelt rejoicing among the non-committed had Ipswich, with their Dutch skills and forward thinking, taken the title'.

Lacey conceded, though, 'Those who forever search for ideals in soccer are bound to be disappointed. There is no ultimate way to play the game and while the English league is criticised for its insular outlook, its treadmill fixture system and the resistance to the sort of changes which might produce better players, managers like Saunders and teams like Villa can hardly be blamed if they succeed with a style best suited for the circumstances.'

In all three duels with Ipswich, the Suffolk club came out on top by a single goal but, Saunders emphasised, 'It's not the individual battles that matter…winning the war is all that counts.' The 1-0 league defeat at Portman Road had, strangely enough, given Villa's players even greater belief in their own abilities. In Dennis Mortimer's opinion, Villa had 'battered them' that afternoon. It was a big mental step forward for him and his team-mates. Ipswich's victory at Villa Park also brought a paradoxical effect; it kept the title race open until the final Saturday when a Villa win on the night might have seen the home side pull too far ahead; it also served to galvanise Saunders' players who could otherwise have let the defeat be a crushing blow.

Kenny Swain wrote, 'From the gloom that was almost tangible in our dressing room, we could hear the noise and euphoria coming from the Ipswich dressing room. The walls were reverberating with their celebrations.' The silence in the Villa quarters only magnified their despair and the visitors' joy. But, having showered and changed and witnessed 'the spring the Ipswich players had in their step as they were leaving', something surreal happened. 'The Villa players started to look around at each other and, as one, the thought spread among us, "They think it's all over,"' Swain wrote. 'No one actually said it but we were thinking it and rather than licking our wounds the next day we were licking our lips.'

'Whenever you have a setback you emerge a little stronger,' was Saunders' credo. Facing a stern test of character having failed a Cambridge exam – a lacklustre Villa had exited the League Cup with a shock 2-1 third-round loss at Second Division United – his side responded immediately to carry on their winning streak. It was a familiar tale throughout the campaign.

In *Only a Game?* Eamon Dunphy writes, 'At some stage in the season, failure is going to stare you in the face. Even with a team like Arsenal when they did the 'Double'. At some stage that year they lost 5-0 away from home. It is the way you react to defeat, or to the signs of failure when they come, that determines everything.' What Arsenal did, Dunphy wrote, 'was to come to grips with that defeat'. They 'reasserted their desire to succeed' and 'did not succumb to the temptation of opting out'.

Yet, even in 1971 when Bertie Mee's superbly organised side claimed that historic twin success, Arsenal were knocked for their dour football and a lack of flair. Their league triumph, Bryon Butler wrote in *The Official Illustrated History of the FA Cup*, 'owed more to character, resourcefulness, organisation and steely consistency' than creative individualism. However, Butler felt these were admirable traits. Marshalled by the stately Mee, who began life as a physiotherapist, the Arsenal team were 'a prime example of collective efficiency, the whole greater than its parts'. It was almost a precise description of Villa's team.

Early exits from both cup competitions enabled them to focus on their principle target. Additionally, while Bobby Robson's players' international participation only increased their fatigue, Saunders' group suffered none of the distractions of extra midweek duties. But if Ipswich, wearied from long European journeys and involvement in 66 games in all plus the pressure of maintaining consistent form, were the victims of their own success, that was scarcely Villa's fault.

It was David Lacey's view that, although the combined skills of Thijssen and Mühren had helped 'raise the standards of an English team far above the normal level', Robson himself was perhaps culpable in Ipswich's failure and 'surely risked self-fulfilling prophecy when he began to talk so early about injuries and fixture congestion'. Liverpool's strength, Lacey maintained, 'has been their insistence on never looking beyond the next game and also their ability to put defeats firmly behind them'. Burdened with expectation and the weight of matches, Ipswich hadn't proved durable enough; they 'were inclined to brood on their misfortunes', wrote Lacey, and that weakness at some of the most critical moments was their ultimate undoing.

Inevitably, as the season drew to its close and the outcome of each game became ever more important, the Villa players played out the matches in their minds beforehand, working out where points might be won or lost. But Saunders made sure they retained their focus. Whether you were given a bouquet or a beating, Saunders believed you had to meet it with the same response. While the Portman Road side buckled with the strain, Villa, moulded in the image of their manager – whom Bryon

Butler termed 'bluff and uncompromising' – refused to bend. In the final run-in, Villa's taste for the fight had been far keener.

Bobby Robson was hardly the most modest in defeat. While acknowledging, 'They [Villa] never let us go. They got their noses in front at the right time and they won the title on merit,' Robson contended, 'If we don't win the [UEFA Cup] trophy, people will forget that we were the best team in England in 1981.' Ipswich did win the trophy, managing to pick themselves up and see off Dutch side AZ Alkmaar 5-4 on aggregate. In between the two legs they lost their final league match 3-2 at home to Southampton to trail Villa by four points. The European triumph – plus the small satisfaction of having Norwich City accompany Palace and Leicester down to the Second Division – were consolations, but the feeling remained from all those connected to the Portman Road club that Villa had snatched the main prize from its more deserving owners.

Saunders was having none of it. 'There are other people in the game,' he told the press, 'who believe that we are a credit to English football.' Bill Shankly, a long-time champion of the Villa cause, had already said that, after Villa had won at Everton, it was the best football he had seen played by any team, including his Liverpool giants, in his lifetime.

In his *Sports Argus* column, Shankly stressed that no team ever wins the league through luck. After successive seasons, though, when Villa's medical staff had seen more of his players than Saunders had, the Villa boss recognised that the one piece of luck they did need was freedom from injuries. Any football season was a feat of endurance over an unforgiving course. 'In the league, you're fighting for survival,' said the then-Welsh team manager Mike Smith. 'It's not like training a racehorse for one race; you've got 60 races in the year.'

The good fortune Saunders hoped for, he'd benefited from. Throughout the campaign, only 14 players saw first team duty, a figure ironically only matched by Shankly's Liverpool in their title-winning 1965/66 season. Seven were ever-presents: Rimmer, Swain, McNaught, Mortimer, Bremner, Cowans and Morley. Gary Shaw missed just two fixtures, Allan Evans three and Peter Withe six. Each were practically nailed-on fixtures in their respective positions. It was only the left-back berth that was open to contest, with Gary Williams and Colin Gibson sharing the number three shirt most frequently and Eamonn Deacy drafted in when required.

Not all of those 14 players were 100 per cent fit all the time – McNaught limped off at Villa Park after a tackle by Manchester City's Steve Mackenzie that later required ten stitches; Dennis Mortimer left the Abbey Stadium pitch with his arm in a sling following a collision with Cambridge striker Tom Finney – but the pain barrier was beaten time and again. Away at Southampton, Jimmy Rimmer had insisted on carrying on despite a stomach upset that almost led to the keeper collapsing at half-time.

It was typical of what Tony Morley termed 'the incredible spirit' within the camp. 'We all played carrying a knock of some sort,' Kenny Swain wrote in his book. 'It wasn't macho; you just wanted to play.' The fear of not getting back into the side was a factor. 'A big part of it was that we just didn't want to lose our places in the team,' Shaw said. 'From about the second month of the season there was a real feeling in the camp that we could achieve something.' No one wanted to miss out on the journey. The bonuses, while another incentive, were only ever a secondary consideration. 'We had mortgages to pay,' Ken McNaught said, 'but we also played for the love of it.'

The players' physical staying power had seen them survive many a rain-heavy, frost-hard and often unplayable surface. But, contrary to his stereotype, Saunders didn't push them beyond their own limits. 'The gaffer was happy to leave it to us, fitness-wise,' said Ken McNaught. 'He would just look at things and decide if he thought one of the youngsters needed putting in, but it didn't happen very often.' Villa conserved their energy for when it really mattered. 'We didn't train an awful lot as the season deepened,' said Shaw, 'because we were playing a lot of Saturday, Wednesday, Saturday, Wednesday, so were fit enough.'

The wily Saunders, of course, 'encouraged' them not to drop out and, Gordon Cowans said, 'would make it clear that there was always someone ready to step in' if they did. Able to virtually rubber-stamp the teamsheet each week, Saunders enjoyed a priceless commodity – continuity – denied to him in the previous three seasons. It was a huge asset and one Saunders was determined to preserve. Even if it sometimes meant putting in players who weren't perhaps fully fit or playing in their natural positions, Saunders very rarely deviated from the path.

So when, say, Allan Evans was injured, Gary Williams was shifted across from the flank rather than Saunders opting for a more natural replacement, an orthodox centre-half like Brendan Ormsby. Villa's quick-interchanging football demanded that the players were in tune with one another. 'It's great being in a side where you know that when you go out on the field of play every player is going to be working hard for you,' Dennis Mortimer said, 'where you know each other's play so well and you read one another so easily.'

A week and a half after the season's end, the headline writers used far more ink eulogising another Villa than they did in penning praise for Saunders' team when the Argentine Ricardo's winning goal against Manchester City caught the eye in a memorable FA Cup Final replay. A moment of individual brilliance in any one match was clearly more newsworthy than the honest endeavour of a team over 42 games.

'Villa's much-vaunted teamwork hides a lack of class,' had been one naysayer's view. Workmanlike and relentless, they outlasted rather than outplayed the opposition. Another cruelly labelled the new champions 'the battery hens of the British game, programmed to keep plugging away whatever the conditions'. The same scribe went on, 'Despite the captaincy of Mortimer, the aggression of Withe and the ability with which Shaw, Cowans and Mortimer sprinkle the team, Saunders has worked miracles in driving this team to Villa's first championship in 71 years.' It was yet more grudging acclaim. Saunders had worked miracles. To the writer, however, it was because Villa were such a mediocre outfit.

Kenny Swain, for one, was willing to concede that Ipswich contained 'some fantastic players', but believed that the press were blind to the balance in the Villa ranks. 'We had technical qualities, aggression, pace and sound defending,' he wrote in *A Game of Three Halves*. Shankly was quoted as saying, 'A football team is like a piano. You need eight men to carry it and three who can play the damn thing.' Lawrie McMenemy once proposed, 'The perfect balance for a team is seven road-sweepers and four violinists.' Villa, in Cowans, Shaw and Morley down the left side, perhaps possessed three virtuosos but all of the road-sweepers were just as capable of harmonising. In midfield, for example, as a Wolves programme writer put it, Mortimer, recognised as the *Birmingham Mail*'s Footballer of the Year, 'orchestrated and Bremner and Cowans ensured the music flowed sweetly'.

Every player made a valuable contribution. Jimmy Rimmer kept 15 clean sheets behind an obdurate back four that only conceded 40 goals all season. The defensive authority of Evans and McNaught – a 'formidable tartan barrier' said David Harrison – was a vital foundation of the success. Kenny Swain's performances earned him the recognition of his fellow professionals – he was selected for the PFA First Division Team of the Season, along with Evans and Shaw – plus he received a call into Ron Greenwood's squad for England's friendly at home to Brazil and the Home Internationals.

In truth, deserving as many Villa players were of international call-ups, Saunders' resolve to bring silverware to the club meant that he had scant regard for the requirements of the Home International sides when their respective bosses were on the phone. Tony Morley relayed a story of how, towards the campaign's end, he was 'told' by Saunders that he and Gary Shaw were 'injured' and therefore unable to compete in a forthcoming England B fixture in which the pair were widely tipped to appear.

Unquestionably, the addition of Peter Withe was pivotal. He wasn't so much the last piece of the jigsaw but the glue that bound tightly the various bits. David Geddis, after his occasional successful cameos, could feel justifiably hard done to at being left out of the side. But Saunders wanted his best XI whenever possible, and that included Withe. Allan Evans described Withe's arrival as exactly 'the tonic signing we needed'.

Always working the opposition defenders, ever an aerial threat, Withe was the ideal spearhead. His gift for holding up the ball, laying it off and linking the play perfectly suited the way the Villa team was set up. With him in the line-up, Villa functioned at their very best. 'An absolute dream to play with,' was how Gordon Cowans described his team-mate.

Years later, Withe revealed that when Saunders was selling the club to the big Scouser, he told Withe he envisaged him teaming up with Brian Little as the two main strikers, with Shaw more on the fringes coming in when required. It was a prospect which excited the then-Newcastle United forward. It wasn't to be, of course. Withe and Little only turned out together once in Villa colours – for Little's testimonial match versus an England XI; a fixture in which Little scored a hat-trick.

As it was, the combination of Withe and Shaw proved irresistible. In the words of football commentator Gerald Sinstadt, they 'went together like bacon and eggs, and they sizzled'. About their chemistry, Withe told the *News of the World*, 'It's like a sixth sense. You know where they are going to run, how they will react, without looking.' His young strike partner's reflexes, Withe said, were 'superb' and '[he] snaps up just half a chance'. Shaw was already 'a better all-round player' than Tony Woodcock in Withe's view.

Like Andy Gray before him, Shaw was voted Young Player of the Year by the PFA. Unlike Gray, Shaw was allowed to attend the awards ceremony. The only Birmingham-born player in the Villa team, Shaw said that playing for 'my favourite club was beyond my wildest dreams'. Now regarded as the country's most gifted young forward, the golden boy from Kingshurst inevitably became the side's pin-up, yet his feet were firmly fixed to the floor. 'How would you spend a million pounds?' the ex-Holte Ender was asked in *The Sun Soccer Annual 1981*. 'Very carefully,' was Shaw's answer. When the same question was posed to Andy Gray, by then a Wolves player, Gray replied, 'Very quickly.'

Fragmented by the loss of Gray and Gidman, Villa were now a cohesive unit. 'This is the third team I have built in my time at Aston Villa,' Saunders said, 'and this is the first year it has been together.' Proud of each and every one of them, he envisaged the side staying together for three or four years at least. 'This team of mine are young enough and good enough to improve even further,' he said. 'I believe our potential is enormous.'

The day after Highbury, on a wet and windy Sunday, that lunchtime celebration went ahead after all. Winding their way from the Aston Villa Leisure Centre, the victorious team and staff took to the streets in a celebratory open-top bus tour of the Second City. Fittingly, Brian Little, a recent recipient of the Midlands Soccer Writers' Merit award, was on board. Braving the freezing cold, fans flocked to pay homage to their returning heroes. 'When Villa brought the famous old trophy home,' Gerald Sinstadt recorded, 'long and loud and massive were the scenes of rejoicing.'

It was a day of high emotion. Fresh from attending a civic reception at Birmingham Council House, the players appeared on the building's balcony. Then, Ron Saunders accepted the championship trophy from Birmingham City chairman Jack Wiseman (a cue for even more heightened joy) and, in a lovely moment of self-awareness, announced to those gathered below in Victoria Square, 'I will now smile!'

'Laugh-a-minute Saunders' – as one sarcastic wit labelled him – quizzed by ATV's Gary Newbon a few hours after the Arsenal game about why he seldom had a smile on his face, had responded, 'Well, you know, life's not just about laughing. Football is a serious business, because it's your job.'

Now, even Saunders allowed himself the luxury. The crowd chanted his name. Feted by thousands, it couldn't have been a farther cry from a year-and-a-half previously when the bitter boardroom battle had seen his tenure under threat. 'My biggest ambition is to have a long holiday and come back looking and feeling ten years younger,' he told reporters afterwards. He was still smiling as he said so.

Two days later, Villa were playing in Joe Gallagher's testimonial at St Andrew's, running out 6-3 winners against a Blues XI. Winning the title was, as Ian Johnson put it, 'no longer a cobwebbed memory' yet there was little time for reflection. 'We will not be sitting back and looking at the championship trophy,' Ron Bendall promised. 'We intend to build on this.'

According to the *Birmingham Post*, Saunders had already been given the green light to move ahead and strengthen the squad.

Competing in Europe's premier tournament was a thrilling prospect. 'No one can say we are not qualified to represent England in the European Cup,' Saunders said. 'I see no reason why we shouldn't play to the strengths we have shown this season, which have been built on good, honest teamwork, to bring us success on foreign fields.'

In the manner of Liverpool, it was, Saunders believed, merely a question of tinkering with the existing successful formula. 'I think our current set-up is good enough for us to do what Nottingham Forest and Liverpool have done,' he said, 'and by that I mean winning the European Cup.' For a manager not given to forecasts, it was quite an extravagant claim.

The Architect

IN a *Daily Telegraph* article published shortly after the title triumph, Ron Saunders' journalist namesake Donald hailed the Aston Villa manager as its 'architect', the man who 'has built the team by carefully nurturing homegrown talent, buying wisely and blending skilfully'. For the second time in his reign, Saunders was named Bell's Scotch Whisky Manager of the Year. Given Bobby Robson's far more genial and appealing public face, the award was perhaps a surprise.

Sympathy for Ipswich, though, Donald Saunders wrote, 'should not be allowed to minimise the importance or merit of Villa's accomplishment'. The voters agreed. Robson was rewarded – receiving a salver and cheque in recognition of his season's achievements – but the top prize (the money rising from £1,000 to £2,500 since he first received a cheque from Eric Morecambe) deservedly went to Saunders. 'Only 18 months after warring factions within the boardroom had threatened to destroy the club,' Donald Saunders noted, 'he has guided them to the greatest success in their history.'

On his departure in 1970, Tommy Docherty said of himself and assistant Arthur Cox, 'In the future we shall be able to look at what Villa have achieved and take satisfaction from the knowledge we started it.' Docherty and Cox had indubitably been a springboard for all that followed. Vic Crowe – like Saunders, 'a very strong character' according to Peter Withe – could also take huge credit. But it was the man whom Donald Saunders termed a 'thoroughly iron-willed realistic Merseysider' who'd 'done more than anyone else to take the championship back to Villa Park for the first time since the leisurely, relatively uncompetitive Edwardian era'.

Building a football team is like 'constructing an enormous and highly complex jigsaw puzzle', writes Colin Shindler in *Manchester United*

Ruined My Life. Even Doug Ellis would later say that, while Crowe had largely laid out all the pieces, Saunders was the one 'who finally put the jigsaw together'. His shaping had involved much diligence, courage and perceptiveness. More than once Saunders' hand had been forced. Which other manager lost so many players to career-ending injuries or, in John Robson's case, illness? Now, after seven years, he'd assembled it in exactly the right order. The signing of Withe – 'the bargain of the season', Donald Saunders called it – highlighted just what a shrewd operator he was. Saunders sensed how vital an addition Withe would be and, as the player himself said, he 'was right on with his convictions'. If Saunders was, as Alex Cropley called him, 'a lucky manager' then it was mostly of his own making.

The full extent of Tony Barton's influence couldn't be dismissed. Barton, Dennis Mortimer said, 'was the man who did Ron's scouting, so in some way it was Tony's recommendations on players that also brought us all together'. Indeed, in possibly the last interview he gave before his untimely death from a heart attack in 1993, Barton told Dave Woodhall there were several players he'd scouted who became essential components in Villa's success. Such was Barton's integrity, though, he asked Woodhall that no names be published; at the time of their scouting, Barton wasn't officially employed by the club. Rimmer, Swain, Gibson, McNaught, Withe, Bremner and Morley were all said to have been targeted after Barton's initial suggestion.

All the same, it was Saunders' capacity for getting the very best out of individuals that was his foremost strength. In that respect, he had proven he had few equals. 'He has persuaded them to play for each other,' stated Donald Saunders, 'to stand firmly together in adversity and to rise to the heights when the occasion demands it.'

Saunders' methods of persuasion were many. Much was made of what the *News of the World* journalist Reg Drury termed the manager's 'rugged kind of style' but, Drury believed, Saunders was adept at the delicate balancing act every boss had to perform and knew just 'when to praise, when to criticise'. Frank Carrodus agreed. 'By the time he [Saunders] was at Villa, he had learnt that you can't treat all players the same,' Carrodus told the *City 'til I Die* website in 2004. 'Some need discipline; some need a gentle word every now and then.' Saunders realised where he'd gone wrong at Maine Road, the midfielder reckoned. 'Certainly his man-management was much better at Villa,' Carrodus said.

Just as the Charlton brothers differed in their views of what made players want to play for Sir Alf Ramsey – Jack feeling it was through the respect they had for him, Bobby believing that it was more out of fear – opinions about Saunders' motivational tools fluctuated wildly. Whereas Ramsey struck a headmasterly pose, Saunders to some was more the school bully whose chief weapon was intimidation. Brian Little, for one, found his style 'strange' and believed that all the Villa bosses he'd played under – Docherty, Crowe and Saunders – had erroneously 'held the philosophy that they had a certain plan that was going to work on anybody and everybody'.

A 'one size fits all' approach wasn't, Little felt, the most productive. There were any number of egos within every dressing room. Boxing gloves were used on a few when kid gloves were required. The Villa manager, Alex Cropley argued in *Crops*, was 'a dour and serious man who I don't think really knew how to handle people', and 'would often castigate a player in front of others, when perhaps it would have been better done in private'.

Little couldn't see the point of any manager yelling at him – it wasn't as if he was deliberately making mistakes. 'Some players go out on the field scared, and they come back the same way, and quite often they have good reason to feel that way,' George Cohen wrote in his autobiography. 'But the manager doesn't help anyone by shouting and screaming. All he does, in fact, is diminish his own position.' A similar accusation of ruling by fear was levelled at Brian Clough. 'Fear?' wrote Clough in *Cloughie: Walking on Water*. 'If I ruled with anything, it was relaxation!' Nonetheless, Clough acknowledged there was a line a manager could easily cross. 'If you seem to be belittling people,' he said in an interview with Hugh McIlvanney in 1979, 'however good your ultimate motives may be, there is a danger that they think you will have ceased to be loyal to them.'

While some grew tired of the constant prods at their psyche, others took it on the chin and set out to impress. 'We went out every game to prove him wrong,' said Tony Morley. Saunders was 'very, very hard', the winger said. 'If you did the business for him, he'd look after you. If you didn't, he'd cut your throat.' Morley, according to Kenny Swain, was one of those players who 'knew he had to please him [Saunders] otherwise the manager would drag him off the field'. Aware that you had two or three chances but, after that, you were out, 'there was a bit of fear in a way', Morley said.

In Cowans, Shaw and Morley, Villa possessed three of the country's finest young talents and idols that schoolboys wanted to emulate on the playground. Saunders said there was nothing he enjoyed more than watching the accelerated development of youngsters. But he was adamant that once they'd achieved their breakthrough they didn't start believing they'd already made it. 'I think he thought we had a bit more "something" that could give a bit extra to the team,' Morley said, 'and by being on top of us, he would get the best out of us.'

Saunders pushed them perhaps even harder than the more senior members of the side. 'He did and said things to the young players to keep them on their toes,' said Peter Withe, 'and encourage them to strive to be better than their last game.' The attention wasn't always appreciated. 'A few of us young players thought he was a bit hard on us,' Cowans reflected. 'He forever seemed to be getting on at us and knocking us down.' To the extravagantly skilful midfielder, a player whom Morley said 'could effortlessly land a ball on a sixpence from 40 yards', Saunders' routine line was, 'You couldn't pass water.'

Cowans, in Saunders' view, showed 'all the signs of going to the top', but still had plenty to learn. There were always, for example, five or ten minutes somewhere in a game where Cowans wasn't involved as much as he should be. Highlighting shortcomings or where he might improve, Saunders – 'an expert at gamesmanship', Cowans called him – kept chipping away. Eventually, the youngster got his head down and realised that his manager was correct. 'He brought us up in the right way, making sure nobody got big-headed or started thinking they were better than they were,' Cowans said. 'At the same time, he knew when to compliment you and put his arm around you and have a word with you. His ways were probably a lot more beneficial to us than if we'd had a manager who was a lot easier on us and was letting us get away with things we shouldn't have been doing.'

For another of Villa's home-produced starlets, Shaw, inconsistency was an issue. 'The boss kept on telling me to buck my ideas up and not lose concentration,' Shaw said at the season's end. The striker was told he was too flash. What Shaw later called Saunders' clever ploy of 'winding us up' reaped rich dividends. 'Whether that was by leaving us out or not praising individual performances,' Shaw said, 'he had a knack.' With a confidence player like Morley, in particular, Saunders – 'a total one-off' who 'had fantastic man-management skills', the player said – pressed exactly the right buttons and pressed them hard. Saunders may have beaten Morley with a stick more than he dangled a carrot before him, but the transformation of the ex-Burnley winger into a game-changing performer demonstrated the effectiveness of Saunders' cruel-to-be-kind thinking. 'He was ruthless,' Morley remarked, 'but always for the right reasons.'

It wasn't just Villa's young flair players who were exposed to the manager's mind games. Neither Colin Gibson nor Gary Williams were spared. Taking the defenders into his office one at a time, the Villa boss informed Williams of his superior defensive qualities that made him Saunders' number one choice, then told the speedy Gibson he was the better forward-playing defender and would be Saunders' first pick for left-back. The two defenders weren't fooled; they were friends as well as team-mates, so knew exactly what was behind Saunders' methodology. They accepted it as the manager's way of geeing them up.

No one was mollycoddled or cosseted. 'There were no big-time players at the club, players who thought they were better than anyone else,' reflected Cowans. 'Ron made sure it stayed that way and the players he brought to the club complemented those who were already there.' Saunders, as one journalist described him, was 'a manager who puts maximum value on a pat on the back'. It was another trick: when you did get one, you knew you'd earned it.

Underpinning it all was a 'no man is greater than the whole' ethic. You could enjoy a starring role on a Saturday but wouldn't get a mention on the Monday. Even during games, Saunders held back from praise. 'At half-time, you may have scored the goal of the season,' said Tony Morley, 'but he'd say, "You only made six tackles."' Just to reinforce his point, Saunders would have apprentices on the bench assigned to counting them. 'If Ron ever said you played well, you must have been f**king brilliant,' John Gregory said in *Geoff Twentyman: Secret Diary of a Liverpool Scout*. 'If ever he gave you a compliment or pulled you to one side and said, "You did well today, son," it was the ultimate accolade. He was a tough man to please.'

Speaking to the *Birmingham Mail* in 2007, Saunders explained his parsimony. 'If we scored a goal, my feeling was that that player was on the field to do that – so why should I go around telling him what a great player he was? I scored a lot of goals. I can't ever remember someone jumping on top of me and making a big fuss.'

The philosophy was eminently straightforward. 'I am a simple person who says what he thinks and knows what he wants,' Saunders explained to Donald Saunders. 'Football is a simple game – and we try to keep it simple.' In a short feature specially commissioned by the *Daily Mail* in the season's run-in, his captain outlined the manager's policy. 'He sees his job as sending out 11 players who will do their job honestly,' Dennis Mortimer wrote. 'He's a guy with no frills; he doesn't go in for fancy talk or ideas.'

What Saunders couldn't excuse was anything less than maximum endeavour. 'All he asks from you is that you give 100 per cent every game,' said Mortimer. 'If you do that, he won't have a go at you, even if you play badly. But he will blow his top if you try to cheat him.' Players were to stand up and be counted at all times. One of the crucial things that made great sides, Eamon Dunphy wrote in *Only a Game?*, was 'people being willing to make mistakes when they know how bad they look'. It was what football was all about, 'Seeing a challenge and accepting it. And accepting the risk of failure.' So far as Saunders was concerned, there was no hiding place on the football field. Anyone not giving total commitment – 'ducking out of the action', he called it – was made fully aware.

It wasn't only 100 per cent that Saunders demanded. The call for 110 per cent effort that concluded his programme notes was repeated because Saunders was someone, wrote Ray Matts, who 'always expects more than he knows he can get'. In his interview with McIlvanney, Clough told the writer, 'One of the worst crimes you can commit in life, not just in football but in life, is to ask people to deliver something they haven't got. That destroys them totally.' Saunders always wanted footballers to go that extra yard. The ingredients for success could be summed up, he said, 'in three little words: hard work…dedication'. But, Allan Evans insisted, he 'put out a team he knew could play together. He knew their strengths and didn't ask any player to do what they weren't capable of doing.'

Saunders drilled into everybody their individual jobs and what they needed to be doing at any given time. Heads weren't filled with complicated systems. Instead, Saunders instilled in his players the belief that they were capable of beating anyone. 'He'd say, "Get out there and play our way and we'll win,"' said Gordon Cowans. 'He wasn't a fantastic tactician, but his style wasn't to worry too much about the opposition.' Gordon Smith agrees. 'We didn't discuss the opposition much, if at all,' he says, 'and he would simply tell us that we were good enough to beat whoever we faced.'

Villa's opponents were dismissed with a ploy that Saunders picked up from Shankly. 'Whenever he got the oppo's teamsheet,' John Gregory told Simon Hughes, 'Ron would walk into the dressing room, look at everyone and screw the paper up and throw it in the bin. "They're f**king s**t," he'd say. There was a little bit of arrogance in him that made him successful.' Pre-match, Saunders simply reminded the players what *they* were capable of. 'He just used to say, "Do exactly what you all did last week and we will be okay,"' Dennis Mortimer told *The Observer*'s Tim Adams in 2006. 'More often than not, we were.'

The desire to work and chase for each other was immense. If Swain pushed forward, Des Bremner would drop back and cover. When Evans went up for a corner, McNaught remained marshalling the defence. 'All players with ability need a platform from which to express themselves,' said Saunders. 'At Aston Villa we have the best platform in the world – the team.' It was the canvas on which the more elaborate brushstrokes could be made. 'If the team doesn't work well,' Dennis Mortimer said, 'individuals don't always shine as they might.'

Saunders, of course, put great store by physical fitness. But the emphasis on improving bodily condition was, Mortimer thought, overblown by outsiders. Arriving at the club, Mortimer, warned by Coventry team-mate David Cross (a player under Saunders at Norwich) that the Villa manager 'will work you hard in training', found the routines surprisingly easy compared with what he was used to. The sole focus wasn't on developing stamina, either – perfecting ball skills was as much a priority. 'We were a very, very fit team full of natural athletes,' Mortimer recollected years later, 'but our training wasn't geared to fitness; it was geared to playing football. There wasn't hard running every day.'

Billy Bremner once said of Revie that he 'must die a thousand deaths every match', such was the intensity of the manager's emotions during a game. If Saunders suffered similar agonies, he rarely showed it. The implacable Liverpudlian gave the impression of existing almost entirely on a diet of starch. Saunders, Reg Drury testified, could 'wrap his tongue around a few choice adjectives if he regarded a defeat as an injustice', but fans didn't need to see overt demonstrations or touchline histrionics to know the manager cared passionately.

Behind the austere appearance Saunders cultivated, there was often tenderness. One of his players, Eamonn Deacy, was so modest he didn't even feel he warranted a championship medal after playing what he considered only a bit part in the side's success. Nothing could have been further from the truth, Saunders told him, and, when the team were at the City Hall to show the trophy to a packed Victoria Square, the manager gave Deacy his medal. Deacy responded by bursting into tears. Yet there still had to be a cut-off point. 'He always had that dividing line between himself and the players,' said John Gregory. 'He'd have a laugh and a joke at times but always knew when to step back.'

Kipling's famous poem, 'If', urges a grounded stoicism in the face of life's ups and downs. Saunders was very much 'a Man, my son!' – he met with both Triumph and Disaster and treated those two impostors just the same. He was more steely-eyed than stiff upper lip but refused to yield to either the highs of victory or lows of defeat.

'The main thing I took from him,' said Gregory, 'was never to get too excited about anything. You can never get carried away in management because one day you're the bee's knees and the next day you're a zero.' Football was a game, Saunders wrote in *Ron Saunders' Aston Villa Scrapbook* that summer, that has 'given me the emotion of glorious victories and kicked me viciously in the teeth', one which has 'probably moulded my character'. It was also a game, he'd put in his own testimonial programme, that 'has taught me many things' and 'I thank football as a whole and all the people I have met, even those I didn't get on with, because you learn something from everyone.'

What Saunders had probably learned most of all, though, and what would become evident in the following months was that, even after the greatest success or failure, football was a game in which nothing could ever be taken for granted.

A Beginning, Not the End

THE Monday after Highbury, the *Daily Mail*'s regular cartoon, Jon's Sporting Types, featured an illustration of a middle-aged man, on a day off from work, proudly sporting an Aston Villa scarf and a satisfied smirk, turning towards his somewhat disbelieving wife who is saying, 'You mean it's a Bank Holiday because Villa are champions?'

Seventy-one years had been a long wait. Now, having, as Donald Saunders put it, 'decided to wake up and resume the leadership of English football', the Midlanders wanted to establish themselves as a much-feared team not just on home soil but throughout Europe. That, at least, was the hope. The climax of seven years' hard work in bringing the title to Villa Park was, Saunders insisted, just the first step. 'This is the beginning of an era,' he said, 'not the end of one.' A side that already had enough ability and character was, he felt, capable of improving even further. 'Providing everyone at the club is prepared to work that little bit harder to achieve more success,' Saunders said, 'I have every confidence we can do just that.'

While supporters evidenced their own optimism – takings from ticket sales neared a club record £1m mark – the bookies quoted Villa at only 8/1 for the title. 'There may still be one or two people who are not sure about us,' Saunders said, 'but I know that if we get the right start to the season we could come close to being an exceptional side.'

Predictably, Liverpool were once again the outright favourites, their deposing as champions seen as only a brief aberration. Form was temporary but class was permanent. The Merseysiders, fifth-placed finishers in the First Division, had still won the League Cup before going on in the spring of 1981 to claim their third European Cup, an Alan Kennedy goal defeating Real Madrid 1-0 at Paris's Parc des Princes. Paisley's team, Saunders said, were 'one of the best-equipped outfits in the world, never mind the First Division or Europe'.

If the 'Everest' to which Saunders had referred in his very first programme notes had been reached, the European Cup presented a whole new summit. Emulating the feats of the previous five years of the Anfield club and Forest demanded a different oxygen. Yet Saunders didn't see why it couldn't happen. 'We have instilled basic principles into our players over a long period and these should stand them in good stead,' he said. 'Obviously we don't have players tried and tested in Europe like Liverpool have but, like them, we can only gain that experience by competing at the top – and staying there.'

In a knockout competition Villa would have to acclimatise straightaway. Their manager welcomed the challenge. 'We have got to live by experience at the highest level of competition,' Saunders said, 'and by doing that we will become an even more battle-hardened crew.' Scottish sports writer David Leggat had every faith they could prosper. 'Villa, always assuming the absence of plague, pestilence or a Russian pre-emptive strike,' Leggat wrote, 'can go into Europe's top tournament at the start of next season and try to turn the clock back' to the days when Celtic and Manchester United ruled the continental roost with their swift and swashbuckling football. Villa's 'inbred urge to attack' and capacity for playing 'the game at a pace not suitable to the tip-tap stuff of foreign defensive formations', Leggat said, could only be to the benefit of the European novices.

Pre-season, a rejuvenated Villa Park looked impressive: the club offices held a new position, the whole ground had been given a fresh lick of paint, and the pitch looked immaculate. Villa would even be sporting a brand new kit, designed by French company le Coq Sportif. 'It all adds up to a promising future,' one journalist wrote, 'for a side that Ron Saunders has modelled on no other.' The players, themselves, were ambitious. Dennis Mortimer spoke of scaling the same heights as the season before. 'With the same application and dedication we could do it again,' he said. 'But if we think it's going to be easy, we could fall flat on our faces.' Even if they couldn't win the championship this time, Gordon Cowans felt, 'We should be a better side [because] we would have had an extra year's experience.'

Andy Blair, the Kirkcaldy-born midfielder signed from Coventry City for a fee of £300,000, was the one new face. The 21-year-old, who'd joined the Highfield Road club as an apprentice before making his first team bow in October 1978 in a 2-1 win against Birmingham City, arrived declaring he hadn't signed 'just to play in the reserves'. For another Scottish ballplayer who had been consigned to second team football, however, there was no future at the club. A three-game spell on loan at Newcastle United during the previous campaign had given Alex Cropley a brief taste of First Division action but the terrible misfortunes that had befallen the player had, Saunders decided, stripped Cropley of the qualities that once made him so special. Unable to force his way back into the first team after fighting so valiantly to regain fitness, Cropley was informed he would be released if he could find a new club.

His goodbye from Saunders typified their relationship. When Cropley asked if he could keep his club car – 'a very nice Audi' – Saunders questioned why he should be allowed to. Cropley replied, 'For services rendered.' The Villa manager, albeit reluctantly, eventually complied with the player's request. As fearless as they came, Cropley was unafraid of ruffling the feathers of even the toughest of birds, his ferocious tackling earning him the affectionate nickname of 'Studs' from Andy Gray and the love of the Villa Park terraces. Yet as Gray, Cropley's close friend, wrote in the foreword to the midfielder's autobiography, 'The way he [Cropley] launched into tackles against people twice his size cost him dearly.' He couldn't have played the game any differently but, ultimately, the man who had the distinction of having his ankle broken by none other than Alex Ferguson while playing for Hibernian against Falkirk had paid the highest price.

Villa's warm-up games gave little by way of a form guide. During a mini-tour to France and Spain, they lost 4-0 to Nantes and defeated Real Valladolid. A flying visit to Greece yielded a 2-2 draw with AEK Athens. Though after a 4-2 win at Villa Park – Peter Withe scoring twice – against the East German national side, even Saunders was moved to observe that his team looked 'really tremendous'.

On 22 August, when Villa took on FA Cup winners Spurs in the annual showpiece, the Charity Shield, it was another opportunity to further furnish the trophy haul rather than any indication of the side's prospects. On a warm afternoon in the capital, with a 92,500-strong crowd packed into Wembley Stadium, much interest centred on Tottenham's new signing, Ray Clemence. The England goalkeeper, for so long integral to Liverpool's success, was making his debut for the Londoners following a £300,000 move. It proved to be an inauspicious baptism.

With Geddis in for Shaw and Gibson replacing Williams, Villa were largely on the back foot in the early stages, but on the half-hour mark they took the lead. And they had Clemence to thank. Going up, unchallenged, to catch a Tony Morley corner, the experienced keeper completely fumbled the ball, dropping it at the feet of Withe who had the simple task of putting it into the roof of an empty net. Thankfully for Clemence, Mark Falco soon spared his blushes. Two minutes before the interval, the 21-year-old, swivelling on the spot just outside the penalty area, hit a cracking right-footed drive past Jimmy Rimmer's athletic dive. Then, three minutes into the second period, the same player – only partnering Scottish international Steve Archibald because of a cartilage injury to Garth Crooks – put Spurs ahead, firing powerfully home, this time with his left, after Galvin's wing play had set him up inside the box. Villa's response was swift. Within four minutes Withe had matched Falco's feat. After a weaving run from Gibson, Morley's looping cross evaded Clemence but not the head of the tall Liverpudlian who made it 2-2. With no penalty shoot-out, the shield was shared for the first time since 1977.

While pleased that Withe was 'still knocking them in', Saunders was disappointed overall. 'We didn't perform anything like the level we are capable of,' he said. It was to be a familiar complaint. With Gary Shaw facing a lay-off with a jarred instep suffered in the friendly in Athens, the Villa manager was keen to increase his attacking options. Asked post-match about Falco, Saunders quipped, 'We've just bought him!' Two days later, though, he made a genuine bid – for Trevor Francis. The first £1m player's career at the City Ground had never really taken off, an Achilles injury plaguing Francis's time there. Still, it was something of a surprise that Clough was willing to get rid. However, when Saunders failed to meet Clough's asking price, a Forest manager eager to recoup at least the money he'd forked out to Birmingham rejected the offer. The following month Francis moved to John Bond's Manchester City for £1.2m.

Aston Villa were the last English champions under the two-points-for-a-win system. In the summer of 1980, a report titled *Soccer – the Fight for Survival* was put out by the Secretaries, Coaches and Managers Association, which comprised the findings of a specially selected think-tank. One member of that group was Ron Saunders. Along with fellow managers or ex-managers such as Bill Nicholson, Harry Haslam, Terry Venables, Graham Taylor and Alan Dicks, Saunders put forth a number of suggestions – scrapping the offside laws, having America style shoot-outs at the end of drawn matches – on how to improve the game's rotting image and get the fans flooding back through the turnstiles.

At the Football League's AGM on 9 February 1981, while the majority of these ideas were ignored completely, the proposal to introduce a new system of three points for a win was one to which chairmen and managers gave a thumbs-up. The old system had operated since the Football League's formation in 1888/89.

Villa began their title defence with a home game against Notts County, promoted under the management of wily Scot Jimmy Sirrel and guidance of captain Don Masson. Prior to kick-off, the freshly won Charity Shield (Villa and Spurs keeping it for six months apiece) along with the championship and Manager of the Year trophies were paraded before the 31,978 crowd. By the end of the 90 minutes the afternoon's lustre was completely lost.

After 24 minutes of their first fixture in the First Division for 55 years, County took the lead, Iain McCulloch heading in Paul Hooks' in-swinging corner, and despite concerted Villa pressure – Morley going closest late on when a scintillating dribble culminated in a shot against the bar – the visitors stoutly repelled any advances to go away with a surprising 1-0 win. Interviewed afterwards by Hugh Johns, Saunders didn't pull any punches. 'We never got started,' he complained. 'We gave about ten per cent and, at the end of the match, got what we deserved.' The glass of white wine in Saunders' hand may well have been to calm his anger.

The following Tuesday evening, when Villa lost again, 2-1 at Sunderland, if they wanted to confirm suspicions that the title win was a fluke, they could scarcely have made a better job of it. A quick re-match with Spurs saw Villa run out 3-1 winners at White Hart Lane to claim their very first three-point haul, Terry Donovan adding two more goals to the one he'd netted at Roker Park, but the promise came to little.

Villa embarked on an unbeaten run of 14 league and cup games but within that was a club record sequence of six league draws in a row that left them with only nine points from nine games and in the table's lower half. After a 1-1 draw at home to Manchester United – a game in which, when one Villa fan shouted 'Saunders for England!' the Villa manager responded, 'Do you want me to go?' – Villa went into their next fixture, with Liverpool at Anfield, with Saunders adamant, 'It's early days yet. I said a fortnight ago that I'd settle for finishing as far ahead of Liverpool as we did last season, and nothing has happened since to change my mind.'

In a hard-fought goalless draw in which Liverpool's Ray Kennedy, provoked into taking a swing at Allan Evans, was dismissed eight minutes from the end by referee George Tyson, Villa displayed all the battling qualities that Saunders demanded. But two further stalemates against Stoke and Birmingham City suggested that even at this embryonic stage the crown was already slipping from the champions' head. Villa's failure to convert draws into wins was costing them. The introduction of the new points system was, in Saunders' view, having little effect on how teams played. Yet it did mean, 'The difference in points between the bottom teams and the top teams is beginning to look frightening.'

For their next game, at Elland Road, to give the wingman 'a kick up the backside', Saunders dropped Morley, accommodating Blair in a four-man midfield. Like his team-mates, Morley had struggled for consistency since the season's start. In his absence, however, Villa once more could only muster a 1-1 draw when, according to Saunders, 'It looked as if we might get three or four goals in the first half-hour.' The manager maintained, 'I don't think we have thrown the championship away yet, but we are not half making it hard for ourselves.' When Villa were held yet again, 1-1 at Coventry City, retaining their title seemed a near-impossible ask. They were 16th and, Dennis Mortimer said, 'There must be a question mark against the attitude of some of our players in some departments.'

In the week before the game with Leeds, Bill Shankly died, following two heart attacks within three days. He was 68 years old. It was a loss felt deeply by the football world. As Villa faced United, it was hard to imagine that not so long ago Liverpool and Leeds had fought many a battle with one another as the two top teams in English and, arguably, European football. The Merseyside club had gone from strength to strength but Leeds' decline since the days of Revie was to reach its nadir at the end of the season when, under former goalscoring legend Allan Clarke, they would finish 20th and were relegated to the Second Division.

Over the years, both Leeds and Liverpool had inevitably had to suffer the expectations of supporters used to glory. After the heights of league title wins or FA Cup victories any comparative failure was deemed unacceptable by an ever-demanding public. Finish runners-up in the table and you were perceived to be heading downhill. As Revie famously said, 'You get nowt for being second.' Whether a team was at the top, in the middle or at the bottom of the table, all managers were subjected to what Ian St John termed 'advice by the armchair managers'. The Scottish forward, who played under Shankly until 1971, witnessed first-hand the effects that such criticism had upon his boss. 'Sometimes, I feel sure, a manager must want to scream from the housetops and tell everyone just how hard he is trying to solve the problems, whatever they may be,' said St John.

Villa's failure to replicate their dynamic form of the previous campaign was bringing Saunders his own share of 'advice'. In late September, John Wile, in a newspaper article, wrote, 'Now that opponents know what to expect from them, Villa will need to become more subtle if they are to maintain their success.' If they were to achieve the development, Wile opined, Gordon Cowans was the key. The West Brom skipper, in a thinly veiled jibe, felt that Villa's title triumph 'came through an extreme direct, uncomplicated style of play based just on getting the ball from the back to the front as quickly as possible' and, as a consequence, Cowans – 'an excellent distributor' and 'the sort of player who likes to put his foot on the ball and dictate the pace of the game' – had suffered. Cowans himself refuted the suggestion. 'I'm lucky to play in a Villa side that can express itself,' he said. 'We're an attacking team and that suits my style.'

Even Cowans, though, accepted that during the title campaign he wasn't always at his best, yet, even while the supporters had had a go at him, Saunders had refused to drop the midfielder 'because he said my work-rate added to the team'. Cowans' ability to decide a game with a single slide-rule pass brought a vital element of inventiveness to the Villa side. Hugh McIlvanney, however, was another who put the blame for Cowans' dip in form on Villa's football. 'Their forceful directness often by-passes some of the more subtle and entertaining aspects of the game,' McIlvanney wrote, 'and there can be no doubt that this tendency reduced whatever chances Cowans had of rising above his profoundly moderate form of recent months and re-establishing himself as their most creative midfield player.' Whether Saunders shared the sentiments of what he called 'the uninformed critics' was doubtful.

Given Villa's modest displays there was perhaps a degree of wisdom in Wile's opinion; opponents were certainly wiser to Villa's ways and had sussed them out. Teams were rolling up their sleeves a bit higher when facing the champions. Injuries were another mitigating factor. The perceived fortuity Saunders enjoyed in 1980/81 deserted him almost instantly. Ken McNaught was substituted ten minutes into the first-day fixture and, like Gary Shaw, had missed many of the opening matches. The teamsheet that had written itself was now adorned with regular crossings out. For all Dennis Mortimer's insistence that 'we have been working hard behind the scenes to put things right', and 'have spent a lot of time analysing our faults', it didn't mean that 'there aren't problems still to be solved'.

When Villa won their next game, 3-2 at home to West Ham – David Geddis notching a rare goal to end the Hammers' 27-match unbeaten league run – the skipper felt, 'This could prove to be a turning point for Villa.' It wasn't. Although Wolves were swept aside convincingly (Shaw again showing his liking for Molineux with a double-strike in a 3-0 win), Villa then lost five of their next seven First Division fixtures.

Following a Halloween nightmare on 31 October when a ninth-minute Russell Osman goal gave Ipswich another win at Villa Park, Saunders wasn't mincing his words. 'We had 85 per cent of the play but didn't give their goalkeeper a shot to save,' he said afterwards. While Bobby Robson's men, keeping in close touch with leaders Manchester United, had maintained their place near the top of the class, Villa were clearly struggling to keep up.

Only the European Cup had provided a ray of sunshine. Dipping their toes into the waters of Europe's biggest competition for the first time, an unseeded Villa warmed to it immediately. Icelandic champions FC Valur of Reykjavik – with a teacher, economist and radio commentator among their amateur numbers – were hardly the most demanding opposition but Villa responded to Saunders' request to go 'flat out for four or five goals' and they managed just that. After Morley opened the scoring, Withe and Donovan grabbed a pair apiece, and the home side cruised to a resounding 5-0 win, their biggest for three years. *The Times* described Valur's efforts as a 'frail challenge'. That was being kind.

Two weeks later, on an appalling pitch at the Laugardalsvollur stadium, Villa battled icy gales and a fishy stench in the air to complete the formality of the second leg; Gary Shaw, returning to action for a season's first outing, bagged a brace either side of half-time without reply to seal a routine passage to the next round. The professional manner with which his side had negotiated their opening hurdle left Saunders extremely pleased.

A trip behind the Iron Curtain was the prize. Preparing to confront Dynamo Berlin – later proven to be the favoured team of the East German secret police, the Stasi – Saunders acknowledged that the second-round tie would dictate the shape of Villa's season. 'If we reach the quarter-finals,' he told the *Daily Mail*'s Jeff Farmer, 'we will, in seven years, have progressed from being a Second Division nonentity to an established First Division team in the last eight of the best club competition in the world.' A victory over Dynamo 'would also guarantee that our season stays nicely alive', he said, and 'take the pressure off the players in domestic football'. If Saunders was looking for the same kind of attitude that had won the title, in Berlin he got it. None more so than from Tony Morley.

His backside duly kicked, the 27-year-old proved the difference on a memorable night. Leading 1-0 after only five minutes through Morley's superb volley from outside the box, Villa looked to be in for a long fight to stay level when Riediger, heading in from a left-wing free kick, equalised five minutes after the break. They nearly lost it, too. Six minutes from time, Ivor Linton, a 67th-minute substitute for the injured Gary Williams, conceded a penalty, bringing down Netz in the area. It was the former West Bromwich schoolboy's first touch. Artur Ulrich's spot-kick, though, smacked the right-hand post before Rimmer reacted, miraculously tipping Ulrich's follow-up over the bar, and Morley made the Berliners pay. From the resultant corner, scampering away from inside his own half after Villa's defence cleared, the winger outpaced the chasing defenders before firing past the advancing Rudweilet's outstretched arm.

The value of Morley's solo effort – 'a wonderful goal befitting a stirring performance', *The Times*' Norman Fox wrote – was only emphasised two weeks later on the Wednesday after the Ipswich defeat. Stunned by a 15th-minute Frank Terletzki low-range shot which gave Dynamo the lead at Villa Park, Villa walked along the precipice on a nervy night that put their supporters through the wringer and, despite Peter Withe's best efforts (two first-half chances were cleared off the line), were eventually grateful for Jimmy Rimmer pushing a late Riediger shot on to the post to see them through on away goals. Saunders described it as 'a major breakthrough for everyone at the club'.

Their stumbling league progress went on, however. On a cold afternoon at Villa Park an ineffectual home side drew a blank as Arsenal ran out 2-0 winners. 'The players have to look at their application,' Saunders berated. 'One hears people talk incessantly about skill and, though that is important, there has to be application, too. You have to earn the right to demonstrate your skill.' His patience was plainly wearing thinner. 'The time for talking is over,' he said. 'We must provide the sort of action which will pay dividends.'

In their next fixture, after 21 years without a win at Middlesbrough's Ayresome Park, Villa's hoodoo continued. Pegged back after leading 3-1, the 3-3 draw left Saunders ruing that 'we have thrown two points away' in a 'game we should have won comfortably'. A year earlier, they might well have done. 'The difference between now and last season,' Jimmy Rimmer said, 'is that we had a team then. Now we have got 11 players.'

Still, Saunders insisted that Villa were 'not far away from being the side we were' and it 'will come flooding back if we win three or four games in a row'. When Forest were beaten 3-1 at Villa Park in the next match, Des Bremner grabbing a rare double, it was, in the manager's eyes, 'The first time this season we've played so well here for sustained periods.'

But, again, the lights quickly dimmed. A 1-0 reverse at Manchester City (Dennis Tueart scoring from a quickly taken free kick as the Villa players protested over its award, and Saunders claiming post-match that 'the referee shouldn't have allowed the goal because the play had stopped'), a 2-1 defeat at Swansea City (that left the Welsh team, competing in the First Division for the first time, as surprising league leaders), and another loss, 2-0 at Everton (now under player-manager Howard Kendall), left Villa 17th in the table, just two points outside the relegation zone. As the *Argus* exclaimed after the Goodison game, 'Oh Villa! Champs Face a Bleak Christmas'. The coffin lid had long come down on any successful title defence and even an end-of-year gritty 1-0 victory at the Goldstone Ground thanks to a Tony Morley goal couldn't stop the nation's football writers hammering in the nails.

In the week before the Everton clash, Saunders had called for 'more effort' from his players. A lack of endeavour, though, wasn't the sole reason for Villa's failings. Villa's stuttering start was, Saunders told Jeff Farmer, down to the 'completely new challenge' of European competition. 'They won't admit it, but the European Cup has been at the back of their minds all season,' he said. 'We haven't applied ourselves consistently; it's as simple as that.'

The pieces that had slotted together so well the season before were now looking distinctly disjointed. Saunders wanted to add to the picture: Leeds' centre-half Paul Hart, Doncaster's 18-year-old midfielder Ian Snodin and Fulham's Welsh striker Gordon Davies were all reportedly on the Villa manager's radar. But whispers of interest proved to be no more than that.

A bid of £100,000 for 20-year-old wideman Mark Chamberlain was rejected by Port Vale. West Brom's Gary Owen was another name supposedly in the Villa hat. Meanwhile, increasing disgruntlement was rumoured among Villa's existing ranks. Andy Blair was considering asking for a transfer only a few months after arriving from Coventry. Following talks with Saunders, Blair was told he could go if Villa received a 'substantial offer'.

Derby were linked with Terry Donovan. David Geddis, fed up with acting as back-up, was also looking to leave. On 17 December Saunders even had to dismiss reports that Dennis Mortimer was on his way to Everton. Ivor Linton and Noel Blake, against Swansea and Everton respectively, had both played their last games for the club. Villa evidently was no longer a happy ship.

If any two fixtures typified the patchy nature of Villa's season, it was the first two games of 1982. On 5 January, Saunders took his side to Meadow Lane for an FA Cup third-round tie with Notts County. Possibly determined to exorcise the ghost of the opening day defeat, Villa completely outplayed their hosts, finding the net six times without reply. Geddis, partnering Shaw up front in place of Withe, hit the hat-trick trail for the first time in a Villa shirt.

Despite his goals, Geddis reiterated his desire for a move. 'At 23, I should be in my prime,' said the striker, 'but I have too much ambition to enjoy it at Villa if I'm not in the side.' Geddis admitted his future was in the balance. 'Ron Saunders holds all the cards,' he said.

Eleven days later, with Geddis once again left on the sidelines, Villa returned to Meadow Lane for a First Division game. But, Withe or not, any hopes that the FA Cup victory might ignite an upsurge in league form were sunk again. On an icy pitch – condemned as unfit by Saunders – Villa skated to defeat before a paltry 9,597, failing to capitalise on numerous goalscoring chances before falling victim to a late Trevor Christie winner as County recorded a repeat of the August scoreline. Villa's two performances in the East Midlands were virtually unrecognisable from one another.

Still alleviating the general gloom were their displays in the cup competitions. Aside from the FA Cup win, Villa had been making steady progress in the League Cup (now renamed the Milk Cup). After a 5-3 aggregate victory in the second round over cash-strapped Wolves (Andy Gray's sending-off in a stormy first leg for a wild lunge at Dennis Mortimer leaving the Villa Park fans celebrating like their team had scored a last-minute winner), narrow wins over Leicester (after a replay) and Wigan Athletic at Springfield Park had set up a quarter-final tie with West Bromwich Albion. On a damp Wednesday night on 20 January, 35,197, including Ron Greenwood, packed into Villa Park for the game.

If the England manager was running another rule over Morley, to whom he'd handed a first cap as a second-half substitute in a 1-0 home win over Hungary in November, he'd only get to do so for 45 minutes. Behind to an early Albion goal, Villa pressed hard for an equaliser, with Morley particularly prominent. But as the teams left the pitch for half-time Morley argued with referee Ray Chadwick and was dismissed.

Morley – only ever booked once in his Villa career and 'normally a player who wouldn't say boo to a goose,' Saunders said – had been stuck in a pre-match traffic jam and struggled to get to the stadium on time. When the wideman had three or four penalty appeals turned down, plus some too-close attention from the visitors' defenders, his frustration boiled over. Morley's manager had little sympathy, but still felt, 'It is sad that you can go over the top to someone and only get booked. He opened his mouth and was sent off.' In the second half, Villa's ten men were unable to find a leveller – Shaw snatching at a gilt-edged chance – and a potential Wembley date was erased from Saunders' diary.

Villa recovered promptly from the disappointment. Three days later, a trip to Second Division Bristol City in the FA Cup fourth round resulted in a narrow win, Shaw driving home a 78th-minute decider after Gordon Cowans' cross wasn't cleared. But the revival was brief. The following Saturday, unable to combat an on-form Liverpool, Villa's weaknesses were ruthlessly exposed as two goals by Terry McDermott and another by Ian Rush saw the Reds record a 3-0 win at Villa Park. Despite 'strong words' at half-time, Villa were well beaten. 'On this showing, anyone who beats Liverpool deserves to take the championship,' was the Villa manager's rather predictable assessment. While the Merseysiders had returned to their default setting, the wiring of Saunders' side appeared badly in need of repair.

The table made for painful reading. Villa started February in 17th place, level on points with Stoke and only three ahead of Birmingham City and Wolves, managerless after John Barnwell's resignation. North-eastern rivals Sunderland and Middlesbrough were propping up the division, with Boro, on only 12 points from 20 games, seemingly already doomed.

On Tuesday 2 February, Villa entertained Sunderland. With McNaught, Evans, Morley and Shaw all missing through injury or suspension, an unfamiliar line-up had Blair and Ormsby in the number four and five shirts, while Gary Shelton was offered a rare start. It was to be the ex-Walsall man's final appearance before moving to Sheffield Wednesday in March. Villa's makeshift XI struggled to overcome the lowly Rokerites, only a 52nd-minute goal by Geddis separating the sides.

As minimal as the allure of a midweek match on a chilly winter night was, a crowd of only 19,916 was clearly indicative that the Villa supporters had accepted their team's fate. They'd known for a while that the title dream was over. What no one in the ground that night – or in the entire football world, for that matter – could have known, though, was that they had just witnessed an Aston Villa team at Villa Park for the very last time under Ron Saunders. And Saunders himself had overseen the last victory of his reign as Aston Villa manager.

An Office Boy

ON Tuesday 21 October 1980, elected at the club's AGM after Harry Kartz relinquished the post, Ron Bendall became the fourth different chairman Ron Saunders had served under at Aston Villa. Kartz, Sir William Dugdale's successor, had rarely felt comfortable in the role. 'I was chairman for two years,' he would say, 'but I wasn't a good one – I hated the publicity.' The disagreement with Saunders over Mick Ferguson was another factor in Kartz's moving aside.

Bendall, 72 years old, now headed a four-man board comprising his 29-year-old son, Donald, Kartz, who remained as vice-chairman, and estate agent and auctioneer Trevor Gill, club president since Pat Matthews' resignation. After a steady accumulation of shares, the Bendalls between them had netted a 43 per cent stake in the club. Bendall Snr had, in all but name, been controlling club affairs since his victorious power struggle with Doug Ellis. The natural supposition was that Donald would one day assume the reins from his father.

When taking over, Ron Bendall declared that he would be 'striving for peace and tranquillity'. Throughout the 1980/81 campaign, it seemed as if he'd achieved that aim. The new chairman backed his manager on the issue of bonus payments. When reports surfaced that a trimming of the Villa playing staff might be necessary to balance costs, the Villa fans' fears were assuaged by Bendall's statement that 'selling is up to the manager'.

To all intents and purposes, Bendall and Saunders were singing from the same hymn sheet. On the cusp of glory at Highbury, Bendall gave a rare interview. 'If we win the title,' he said, 'it will be because of our faith in the manager, peace in the boardroom and the right incentives for the players.' The implication was obvious: without Ellis, an atmosphere of common purpose existed within the club that had nourished the seeds of success. The Villa board had always maintained, Bendall emphasised,

'The manager must be given the freedom to do the job. Continual interference would only mean that we had the wrong man.'

On Friday 5 February 1982, Ron Saunders received an official letter from Aston Villa informing him that his existing 'roll-on' agreement with the club was being cancelled and altered to a new, straightforward three-year deal. The unique 'roll-on' deal guaranteed that, effectively, Saunders began a new three-year term every day and would always be entitled to three years' compensation upon the event of his dismissal. No more. In Ron Bendall's words, 'A certain clause has been invoked and notice has been given; the contract now has three years to run.'

In practice, three years from that day, Saunders would have to renegotiate new terms. With an estimated salary of £40,000 per annum, Saunders wasn't the highest-paid top-flight manager but he was financially secure should he and Villa go their separate ways. The 'roll-on' contract wasn't just economically rewarding but a symbol of stability, one which Saunders felt was important to build a successful football team. 'Players need to know that their manager is on a long-term contract,' he once said, 'because that helps to engender confidence throughout the club.' Now, with the modified deal – the story first broken in the *Birmingham Mail* – it seemed the rug had suddenly been pulled from under him.

Quite why the Villa board had made the decision, and at that particular time, wasn't revealed. Ron Bendall was non-committal, denying that financial reasons were behind the change, yet stating that economies had to be made. 'Obviously we have been thinking about our results this season, because we are always reminded of them by our fans,' Bendall said. 'But I stress, this is in no way a vote of no confidence.' Saunders clearly didn't agree. Asked how the new situation might affect his long-term future, he replied, 'I have always said that I wanted to spend the rest of my life with Villa. But the present situation means that the odds of this happening are stacked against me.' It didn't take much to read between the lines.

The day afterwards, Saunders took his struggling side to Old Trafford for a daunting fixture against a Manchester United team second-placed behind leaders Southampton. Before the kick-off Villa shared in a tribute to players and friends lost 24 years earlier in the Munich air disaster. Then, matching the bright, breezy Manchester weather, Villa opened well, a 21st-minute goal from David Geddis putting them ahead.

But Ron Atkinson's side, with John Gidman firmly established at number two following his move from Everton, were 17 points ahead of

Villa in the First Division standings and their obvious superiority told. Irish centre-half Kevin Moran equalised just before half-time then second-half goals by Bryan Robson, Coppell and Moran, again, saw the home side storm to a 4-1 win. Villa's early fire, as so often during the season, soon petered out.

After the game, Peter Withe told reporters, 'Anyone looking at the result would think we got hammered, but we could have murdered them in the first half.' Villa's centre-forward was adamant, 'We have just hit a bad patch.' The heavy reverse had, however, again highlighted the lack of depth and quality available to Saunders. If Villa were to compete again with the clubs at the table's top, the squad, he conceded, needed at least two or three new faces. But what about Villa's reported £1m overdraft and the lack of funds for new signings? 'You win some, you lose some,' was Saunders' somewhat flippant response. His mind appeared to be still very much on other matters.

The following Tuesday at Bodymoor Heath, the players' morning warm-ups concluded, Saunders emerged from his office, as he normally did, to take an hour or so's training session. There was nothing normal about him that cold February day.

With his charges watching on, Saunders – looking 'a little under the weather' according to Peter Withe – was making his way across the training field when he suddenly collapsed on all fours, suffering a prolonged coughing fit. After the club physio took him inside, the next the players saw of their manager, he was driving off in his Mercedes, leaving Roy MacLaren to oversee the remaining routines. Apparently stricken with the effects of flu, Saunders would never again put them through their paces. Later that evening, a story came out that left English football recoiling in astonishment: Ron Saunders had resigned as manager of Aston Villa.

Word spread rapidly. Interviewed on TV that night at Anfield after Ipswich had held Liverpool to a 2-2 draw in the Milk Cup semi-final second leg, Bobby Robson declared himself shocked at the news. He wasn't the only one. The next morning the revelation claimed both back- and front-page headlines. In the *Daily Mirror*, Dave Horridge reported that it 'follows weeks of wrangling with chairman Ron Bendall'. Evidently, it was New Year's Eve when Saunders had first been told by the board they were withdrawing the 'roll-on' clause. He'd persuaded them to change their minds, only for them to go through with it anyway.

'If I'm going to manage then I want to be a manager, not an office boy,' Saunders told a hastily convened press conference. It was an enigmatic comment. TV reports maintained that he'd quit over the terms of his contract, but Saunders refused to go into specifics. 'I was well aware that when this [alteration] happened, they [the board] were taking the security away from me,' he told a Central Television reporter, 'which I feel the manager's got to have. Which I felt that I deserved. And I felt that I owed them nothing.' The interview continued:

Reporter: Did you feel that you were not allowed to be the manager any more?

Saunders: Things were beginning to look that way, yes.

Reporter: You used a phrase that was quoted in the papers where you said that you felt like an office boy.

Saunders: No, I didn't. I said, if I'm getting paid as a manager, I expect to be able to manage, not to be an office boy.

Reporter: Last May you won the league title for Aston Villa and were named Manager of the Year. Has what happened today made you wonder about the state of football?

Saunders: No different to what I was thinking yesterday or last week. The state of football is a little bit serious at the moment, and there's a lot of things got to be done. But I'm out of football and I'm unemployed at the moment, and, you know, I'll just have a rest and then we'll see whether we come back into football or whether we come back into some other business.

A statement expressing surprise at Saunders' sudden resignation was quickly issued by the Villa board. It totally refuted a suggestion that Saunders was no longer able to run team affairs without interference, with Bendall insistent that the manager always had total autonomy in that department. 'The directors, contrary to some reports, have never attempted to select the team,' Bendall said, 'and differences arose when the manager wanted to be responsible for the complete control of the club, to which the board could not agree.'

The chairman also expressed upset at an interview Saunders had given shortly before resigning in which the Villa manager intimated he was being forced to sell existing players before he could add any new ones. Saunders, Bendall claimed, was guilty of broadcasting confidential club information to the press. Any such statement, Saunders countered, was 'completely misleading'. He had told the press of the difficulty of buying players merely to keep supporters abreast of the current transfer situation at Villa Park.

The allegation that he had craved a greater say in all club affairs was also denied. Following the title success, Saunders' reward – Jeff Farmer reported in the *Daily Mail* – was a possible promotion to a pioneer role as the First Division's first salaried managing director. In October 1980, when a new ruling allowing clubs to pay board members was first being mooted at FA headquarters, Saunders was supposed to be an interested party. 'If the right offer came along, naturally I would consider it,' he said at the time.

The prospect of not having to look constantly over his shoulder will certainly have appealed. Although he personally was against such a move – 'because it could lead to certain abuses' – Bendall had said that promoting Saunders 'would be a different matter'. But, he'd added, 'Whatever happens, I will remain in charge at Aston Villa.' Nothing materialised. Now, Saunders emphasised that he had had no desire whatsoever in the position. It was, in fact, a role that Donald Bendall was rumoured to be far keener on filling. About his resignation Saunders simply told reporters he was 'sorry it had to happen', but he could either let things carry on or stand up and be counted. He'd chosen the latter.

The story went that, after a heated telephone exchange with Bendall, Saunders informed the chairman that he was terminating his contract. He'd apparently penned his resignation letter propped up in his sickbed (before notifying club secretary Steve Stride). Bendall later said that the phone conversation ended with Saunders 'ranting and raving and claiming I was undermining his management'. In his *Mirror* article, Dave Horridge wrote of 'disagreements between manager and chairman over the running of the club'. Whether they concerned football or money matters or both was still hazy.

Rumours were rife of financial wrongdoings connected with the building work taking place at Villa Park during the time leading up to Saunders' exit. There were, it was said, irregularities over the financing of the North Stand. In a 2006 article for the *Birmingham Post*, Pat Murphy wrote, 'In subsequent chats I had with him [Saunders], he used to hint darkly about certain aspects of Villa's financial dealings that appalled him.' Another theory forthcoming was that Saunders had got wind of an imminent return to the club of Doug Ellis. Someone even speculated that it was a fall-out over a trifling matter – his parking space at the ground – that led to Saunders walking out.

Claim and counterclaim kept treading on each other's heels. They only threw up further questions. How was Saunders' management being undermined? What did Bendall mean by Saunders seeking 'complete control'? Horridge stated that Saunders had become 'increasingly frustrated at having no money to spend because of an £800,000 overdraft'.

The lack of investment – except in the acquisition of Andy Blair – had created ongoing tensions and played a role in what was to follow. If Bendall, as understood, was unhappy about the commitment on the field of play, why then didn't he back Saunders with further funding to allow the manager to strengthen his squad? Despite Villa's poor showing in the league – only 25 points from 23 games, given the new system, was a very disappointing return – they hadn't become a bad side overnight.

After a league-winning campaign that had reportedly cost the club £1,026,329 in wages, Bendall, by profession an insolvency specialist, was definitely keeping a tighter hold on the purse strings. But surely Saunders deserved a budget for new players, especially after having made do with only 14 the season before? Bendall himself had expressed how he wanted Villa to become a genuine force, at home and abroad.

There were whispers now that Saunders' 'roll-on' deal wasn't as lucrative as many thought, a feeling too that its' scrapping was more politically motivated rather than for economic reasons. Upon announcing the modified contract, Bendall had stressed that Saunders was a good manager who had done a fine job and that the board would be willing to renegotiate when the present deal expired. His timing, though, seemed incomprehensible. It was bound to have a knock-on effect.

Just how disruptive it proved was perhaps Bendall's precise intention. 'I see myself as a steadying influence. I have no wish to exert any so-called power,' Bendall had said on joining the Villa board in 1975. 'But if things aren't going as they should, then I'm prepared to jump on people's backs.' Was it Saunders' back that Bendall had been deliberately jumping on? Harry Kartz would, years later, reveal that Bendall, just a few weeks into his chairmanship, had declared his intention to goad Saunders into resigning. Although Bendall changed his mind shortly after, Kartz realised then that the working relationship between Bendall and Saunders was all but doomed.

If Bendall's act of revising Saunders' deal was an undervaluing of all the manager had achieved, it wasn't the first. In May 1981, when Manchester United, trophy-less for four seasons, were seeking someone to fill their hot-seat following the 30 April sacking of Dave Sexton, Saunders, along with Lawrie McMenemy and Bobby Robson, was one of the possible replacements. With Sexton's position precarious since the New Year and Saunders' prestige boosted by Villa's standing in the table, United had already courted Saunders' services for many weeks and finally made an approach.

At a board meeting at which Saunders was present, his availability was enquired after and, rather than refuse United permission, Bendall simply handed the phone to his manager. 'At that stage I was turning down the earth, if you like,' he recollected to the *Birmingham Mail*, 'and Mr Bendall gave them permission to speak to me – in front of anyone.'

Martin Edwards, then chairman of United, said in a 2011 interview with Matt Lawton of the *Daily Mail* that advances for Saunders 'never really amounted to anything' (fourth choice, West Brom's Ron Atkinson eventually landed the job), and whether he would have been a hit at Old Trafford is anyone's guess. One journalist some years later suggested that 'he would probably have been a disaster at Manchester United, as he was at Manchester City, because their players grow up under a regime of big money and a commitment to flowing football' whereas 'Saunders emphasises discipline and the long ball', methods and tactics that went against the grain of the two Manchester clubs. It was only conjecture. Saunders passed up the opportunity, but in Bendall's willingness to entertain an offer from a rival club, the Villa manager perceived an act of disloyalty that was, in Saunders' view, as good as an insult.

When the Liverpool board went behind Bill Shankly's back in 1962 and sold Johnny Morrissey to Everton, it took Shankly's ally Matt Busby to stop him from quitting the Anfield club. 'Never give them the satisfaction,' Busby told his friend. It was a manager's duty to flout any authority. But Saunders had had no one to put on the brakes. It's likely their words would have been wasted anyway. A 'gut-reaction thing', Saunders told *Birmingham Mail* reporter Mat Kendrick in 2006, was something he'd lived with since the day he was born. Given that Saunders 'had already quit at Norwich on a matter of principle', his abrupt departure from Villa Park perhaps shouldn't have been so astonishing.

For the players, however, it was totally unexpected. Kenny Swain summed up the feelings of his team-mates when he told reporters they were 'shocked' by Saunders quitting, though he himself was not entirely surprised. Saunders had become 'fed up', Swain believed, with confrontations with the board. The players were aware there were problems but not to what extent. 'Nobody had any idea he was about to leave,' Tony Morley would say later. 'There was a lot of politics going on behind the scenes that we didn't know about.'

Even the night before he resigned, Saunders had phoned Dennis Mortimer at his home and insisted to the Villa captain that although 'there was a big fight going on between himself and the Bendalls', there was no way he would be leaving the job. The following morning, Mortimer was being woken by his phone ringing – with people asking his thoughts on Saunders going.

From out of nowhere, Saunders was coming into Bodymoor Heath to say his farewells. 'It was a very emotional occasion,' Swain wrote in his autobiography. That evening, with Tony Barton handed temporary charge, Villa played host to Southampton. The south-coast side were enjoying a fantastic season and, as they arrived in the Midlands, they headed the division, a point clear of Manchester United. Prior to the match, Saunders would only say that he was 'satisfied' with his achievements at Villa. He hoped the game with the Saints would 'sum up everything that had happened during his management' in the Midlands.

It was an entertaining clash. Villa, with Ken McNaught making his first start since September, did well to focus on matters in hand and, though a goal down to a Kevin Keegan strike just before the break, a Withe leveller on 71 minutes earned them a deserved point. The game over, sitting in their usual post-match watering hole, there was a solemn mood as the still-disbelieving players struggled to come to terms with the events that had unfolded and, as Swain wrote, 'We sought to make some kind of sense from a situation that had none.'

If Saunders quitting was a bombshell, nowhere were the reverberations felt more strongly than among the Villa support. Veterans of years of boardroom upheaval, they were experiencing a horrible sense of déjà vu. On a tense Wednesday evening the cold wind blowing around Villa Park did nothing to quell the heat of genuine anger from the fans towards the club's chairman. A terrace song to the tune of 'The Red Flag' got straight to the point, 'We won the league, we won the cup, now Ronnie Bendall has f**ked it up!'

With only vague explanations why Saunders had vacated his post, the Villa faithful had drawn their own conclusions: the contractual shock and lack of money for rebuilding were the last straws and had pushed out Saunders. Throughout the 90 minutes the claret and blue contingent among the 24,287 were vocal in their backing of the departed boss, continually chanting Saunders' name. At the full-time whistle, four fans ran on to the pitch with a banner calling for his reinstatement. A small demonstration took place outside the ground's main gates. 'The fans have been fantastic to me,' Saunders had said, 'and I am sad to be leaving them.' The sentiment was mutual. For many supporters it was their JFK moment. Few would ever forget exactly where they were when they heard that Ron Saunders had quit.

In the days that followed, local newspaper columns were taken up with letters proclaiming their support for the departed manager. A meeting of protestors at a Birmingham pub, the Royal Oak in Sparkbrook, drew a large crowd and spawned the new Aston Villa Democracy Group, its aim: to get a fan elected to the board and for fans to have a greater say in the running of the club. Primarily, though, they wanted Saunders back. A week after the bolt from the blue, as Villa faced Spurs for the second time in four days, leaflets were handed out at Villa Park and a petition gathered signatures. The hope was that sufficient weight of numbers might persuade the Villa board to ask Saunders to return. Events, however, had taken an even more unforeseen twist.

Two days earlier, on Monday 15 February, after a dire run of just one win since the start of October had left them hovering close to the basement, Birmingham City had sacked Jim Smith. The press immediately linked Saunders with the vacancy. As outrageous as it seemed, it was wholly feasible: Saunders was available, he lived in the city and, from a City perspective, they would be getting on board a title-winning manager into the bargain. It wasn't long before Saunders was actually installed as the hot favourite for the job.

Tony Barton would later claim that Saunders had contacted him shortly after his resignation to say that he believed he would be reinstated in a few days. It was never even an option. As far as Aston Villa was concerned, Saunders had been consigned to history. Saunders' car park space had already been painted over. A cursory note in the corner of the first page of the Spurs matchday programme encapsulated the club's attitude. 'On Tuesday 9 February, Ron Saunders terminated his contract with Aston Villa FC and left the club,' it read. 'The chairman and board of directors wish to place on record their appreciation of Mr Saunders' service to the club over the past seven years.' The terseness couldn't have been more telling.

The following morning, the forlorn hopes of the pro-Saunders campaigners were crushed: Saunders was confirmed as Birmingham's new boss. Just nine days after leaving Villa Park he'd pitched up at their near-neighbours, becoming the first-ever former Villa manager to take over at the Blues. The fates had obviously been following events closely; the next fixture for both, scheduled for the Saturday, was the local derby encounter against each other.

City issued a statement that read, 'The final formalities were in the hands of solicitors and accountants and, subject to completion of the details,' Saunders would be taking over formally at the club on the Monday after the match, with Norman Bodell acting as manager until then. It was, given the circumstances, the wise thing to do.

The news left supporters of both sides stunned. City followers, though largely welcoming, were still gobsmacked by the reality of who would now be occupying the manager's chair. A club director, comedian Jasper Carrott, even resigned, not so much in protest at Saunders' arrival but at not being consulted about the dismissal of the popular Smith, a manager whose sides always produced attractive football.

For the Villa fans, still feeling the effects of the fall-out from Saunders leaving, there were even stronger shockwaves to now face. Hadn't Saunders only recently suggested that he intended to take a sabbatical from the game? A return to management in due course was inevitable. They accepted that. But so soon! And at St Andrew's! Outrage with Bendall turned to outright hatred towards their ex-manager. Saunders, once seen as the innocent party, was swiftly recast in the role of traitor and castigated for an incomprehensible act of betrayal. Rumours that Saunders was already in negotiations with City before he left Villa Park, though bearing all the hallmarks of malicious gossip, only stirred up the pot even further.

'As far as I am concerned, what has happened this week is irrelevant,' said Barton, prior to the match at St Andrew's. 'It is just another derby – we want to beat them and they want to beat us.' But a fixture already loaded with extra spice had been given a hefty helping of poison.

The atmosphere was extremely fraught. There were reports of fighting breaking out between the two sets of fans both before and after the final whistle. With Saunders watching on from the home side's directors' box, the Villa fans in the kop end left him in no doubt about their feelings. 'You must be f**king mad, Saunders,' they chanted, 'you must be f**king mad.' Another ditty aimed at their erstwhile hero, 'We don't need you anymore,' perfectly put in a nutshell how, in the space of just over a week, love and affection had become an altogether different emotion.

Amid all the bitterness, Peter Withe's goal was the one sweet moment that gave Villa victory, but the real story was about the man waiting in the wings as his new club took on the one he'd just abandoned.

Was Saunders joining Villa's deadliest foes a two-fingered gesture at Bendall? Had he taken up City's offer merely as an act of retribution? Taking over at St Andrew's, Saunders was offered the security he sought, on a wage of £40,000 per annum with the 'roll-on' contract he so desired. Only four other First Division managers – Manchester City's John Bond (£45,000), Liverpool's Paisley and Lawrie McMenemy of Southampton (£50,000), plus the top earner Clough (£60,000) – commanded a higher salary. It was never about the money in Saunders' eyes, though. The England job with which his name was linked several times towards the end of the 1980/81 season would have been much higher waged but, amid the speculation, Saunders stated, 'I have never sought the position and don't want it.'

The move, Saunders later said, was designed to keep his family happy. Effectively, to stay where he was. 'Ever since we had been married with kids we had moved,' he told Mat Kendrick. 'To move far away from the Midlands would have broken us up. They had had a lot to put up with.'

As Birmingham City boss, Saunders was able to remain in the suburban Solihull home he and wife, Breda, and their four children had occupied since first joining Villa. For a pragmatic man, one who'd said he'd never endured any sleepless nights with any club he'd managed, there was little over which to agonise. His two-and-a-half-mile hike across the city made perfect sense.

The cloud under which Ron Saunders left Aston Villa, however, has never cleared. Why the 49-year-old Merseysider who, just ten months earlier, announced his intention to spend the rest of his career with the club had vacated Villa Park was and still is, as Dave Woodhall termed it, 'one of the greatest mysteries of modern football'. It is one likely to stay unsolved. In subsequent years, Saunders kept his counsel, his reluctance to reveal the real reasons behind his resignation remaining as keen as ever. 'No doubt,' wrote Pat Murphy in the *Birmingham Post* in 2006, 'he'll take those secrets to the grave.'

What Saunders did say shed no clear light on the subject. 'Everyone thinks I resigned from Villa in 1982 but it was more like a sacking,' he told the *Sunday Mercury*'s Tony Larner in 2001. 'But I am not prepared to go into details.' Even an interview given in 2007 failed to lift the cloak of ambiguity. 'I left Villa because they showed a complete lack of respect for me and a complete lack of trust in my ability,' Saunders recalled. 'It wasn't that I "felt" it – it was happening.'

Disgusted by being 'treated like a bad office boy', Saunders 'just ran out of patience'. The Villa board, he believed, 'were so obsessed with the European Cup that they felt there was no way I would do anything about it.' They were very mistaken.

Behind all the ambiguity, one thing was explicit: the book had been closed on the story of Ron Saunders' reign at Aston Villa. His quitting, wrote Dave Horridge, 'adds yet another chapter to the club's turbulent history'. With that one decision, the tale of the man with his hands so recently on the championship trophy seemed now like a work of the strangest fiction and, with his puzzling exit, all the joys of the previous May had become little but a footnote on its pages.

A Nice Guy

TWO days before Ron Saunders walked out on Aston Villa, a wandering gypsy woman showed up on the doorstep of Tony Barton's house in Sutton Coldfield. Barton's wife Rosina, declining to hold out her palm to the fortune-telling Romany nor look into her crystal ball, chose instead to purchase a delicate piece of lacework on offer. The gypsy turned away, saying, 'In the next few months your husband will be successful. He will take a step up in his job, and the future looks rosy for you and your family.' On 26 May 1982, that 'lucky' lace was in Rotterdam, Rosina Barton secretly slipping it into the pocket of the claret jacket her husband wore as he watched his Aston Villa side claim the most prestigious prize in European club football.

On the day of Saunders' resignation, Barton was away on a scouting mission. The news about his ex-Portsmouth team-mate quitting only reached him via the car radio while heading home that evening. Alerted by Rosina that he'd had a message from a flustered Ron Bendall, Barton returned the call to discover that the Villa chairman wanted him to take charge of the team for the following night's game against Southampton. It was to be the start of a mesmerising few months in the life of the 45-year-old.

Thrust into the limelight, Barton had little choice but to accept that attention, welcome or not, would come his way. With feelings among fans running high in the immediate aftermath of Saunders' departure, Barton was even subjected to abuse from certain sections of the unhappy home support. When, three days after they'd drawn against Southampton, Villa exited the FA Cup, 1-0 at Tottenham (Mark Falco again finding the back of Jimmy Rimmer's net), doubts about Barton's appointment hadn't gone away.

Yet despite their last hope of domestic cup glory disappearing, Villa's fighting performance on the day showed a strong desire to pump fresh blood back into the club. Tony Morley, under the impression from Saunders he'd only be used for certain matches, had announced his desire to leave the club for 'professional and personal reasons'. Earlier in the campaign, Spurs and Manchester United were interested in signing him. On the day that Morley had actually spoken to Ron Atkinson, the winger went to see Saunders in his office. 'He told me there'd been two clubs asking about me,' Morley told the *Sunday Mercury*. 'I acted surprised and said, "Who are they?" He replied, "Halifax and Rochdale. Now realise how lucky you are to be here and get out!"' With Saunders gone, Morley declared himself 'happy to stay' and the transfer request was withdrawn.

Before Villa hosted Spurs in the league just four days after the cup defeat, Barton was composing the manager's programme notes for the first time. 'You can be assured that every single person at the club is striving to keep Aston Villa at the pinnacle which has been reached over the last four or five years,' he wrote. The first job was to restore some unity following a fragmented few days. Barton, in tandem with Roy MacLaren, set out to lift the players' spirits. 'We had to get their heads up,' MacLaren said, 'and we worked on that more than anything.'

An unknown to all but the staunchest of supporters and only occupying the hotseat by default, Barton was also aware of a personal need to gain the fans' seal of approval. Saunders' defection to Birmingham City certainly helped ease Barton's passage into their affections. But it was the 1-0 victory at St Andrew's that really won them over. That game was, in many ways, the moment that reality finally kicked in for those supporters struggling to overcome their disbelief at Saunders' exit. Forced to accept that Saunders wasn't coming back and, even worse, had joined the enemy, they were now, in the main, willing to rally behind the new man.

A popular figure with the players, Barton set about managing them in his quiet, unassuming manner. Barton was, in Dennis Mortimer's description, 'A nice guy who never shot his mouth off, but just got on with the job.' It was bound to be a period of transition. And while, initially, it took Villa's senior pros some time to adjust to treating Barton as 'the gaffer' rather than just a familiar face they were used to seeing around Villa Park, their new boss was soon establishing his credentials.

Barton, while an unexpected choice of manager, was a wise one. Few outside Aston Villa might have recognised him but Barton knew the club inside out; he was acutely aware of its heritage. While there were rumours that Robson, McMenemy and even Clough were in the running, Harry Kartz advised Ron Bendall that Barton was a much better fit. A new manager from another club, Kartz told the chairman, would most likely make wholesale changes, bring in his own players and staff, and alter the entire Villa set-up.

For Bendall, the kind of man Len Shackleton had in mind when he included in his autobiography a chapter headed 'The Average Director's Knowledge of Football' and left it as a single blank page, Barton might have been an easy option. But, fortunately for Bendall, he got lucky. Kartz was right.

In spite of his lack of managerial experience, Barton was intelligent enough not to tinker too much with the existing format. They did change the style a bit but it was a positive shift. 'Tony didn't have Ron's discipline or strength of character,' said Gordon Cowans, but 'he would encourage you to try things whereas Ron would just tell you to play it simple and not get carried away.' The main course was still relatively modest, but Cowans and co. were now allowed to add a little more salt and pepper. The good habits the players had learned under Saunders hadn't been lost. It was more a matter of letting them perform and trusting that those habits would return.

Barton was right to do so. Ken Shellito, taking over at Chelsea following the surprise resignation of Eddie McCreadie in 1977/78, firmly believed, 'The most important people in the club are the players and all you do, if they are good players, is steer the boat.' While Villa's boat was not exactly floundering on the rocks in the wake of Saunders leaving, it had certainly hit a sizeable boulder. With Barton at the helm, it was soon on an even keel again. The players' self-belief returned. There was a bounce in their step and a bite to their football once more. Before long, the side was looking back to its title-winning best.

The derby victory marked the first of a four match unbeaten run, including three victories, that saw Villa slowly ascending the First Division ladder. Just three weeks into Barton's reign, Villa faced another trip to the Eastern bloc, with Soviet champions Dynamo Kiev waiting in the European Cup quarter-finals. Handed arguably the toughest of the four ties that pitted East and West Europe, Villa not only had to contend with a redoubtable Kiev side that boasted several Russian internationals including former European Footballer of the Year Oleg Blokhin, but also the Russians' blatant pre-match gamesmanship.

With Kiev's stadium frozen over and the pitch unplayable, the fixture was switched to the Crimean city of Simferopol, a Black Sea coastal resort 300 miles south. Hotel arrangements were changed at the last minute, leaving Villa's players confronted with staying in a dilapidated 1940s relic with rock-hard beds and paint stripping off the walls. Cowans found a dead cockroach inside a breaded snack. Kiev even moved the kick-off forward two hours to accommodate local TV.

Barton declared it 'shocking' that the opposition should stoop to such ploys. Yet by the end of the 90 minutes, Kiev's underhand tactics had had little effect. Told by Barton to 'smile and bubble', Villa, though riding their luck at times – Blokhin hit a post and was culpable of missing two clear opportunities, while Yevtushenko had a late goal ruled out for a foul on Bremner – gave what Barton termed an 'excellent, professional performance' that ultimately earned a deserved goalless draw. 'All 11 were a credit,' a delighted Barton said of his players.

Two weeks later, 38,579, the biggest home crowd of the season so far, filled Villa Park to see Villa complete the task in hand. On a pudding of a pitch that was more sand than grass after the wettest March on record in Birmingham, the home side got off to a flyer, Gary Shaw's shot sneaking past Viktor Chanov at the keeper's near post to give them a sixth-minute lead. Then, when, just before half-time, Chanov flapped at Cowans' corner, Ken McNaught rose to head into an empty net and assure Villa's comfortable path to the semi-finals.

As defending cup holders Liverpool were undone by an extra-time goal from Bulgaria's CSKA Sofia and the chance of an all-English final died, Villa – and Barton – had passed another test with aplomb. 'A job like manager of Aston Villa does not just fall into your lap,' Barton told reporters. 'You have to earn it.' The Surrey-born Barton was proving he was more than worthy of the role he'd been handed.

Even the Villa board, when questioned about potential new managers, said they 'had no one else in mind'. By the start of April, Villa had lost only three games in the 12 under Barton's tutelage. On Thursday 1 April, two days after a 2-1 home win over West Brom, Barton was offered a three-year, £20,000-per-annum contract to take over as manager on a permanent basis (with Roy MacLaren as his full-time assistant). He accepted. The fact that his appointment was confirmed on such a date was not lost on those still unforgiving towards Bendall, the man whose foolishness they felt had led to Saunders' resignation. But whatever doubts many had had about the wisdom of Barton's initial appointment were now all but vanquished.

In Barton's first game as official manager, Villa came up against RSC Anderlecht, the last obstacle to navigate on the road to Rotterdam, the venue for the European Cup Final. For the first leg in Birmingham, Anderlecht, who'd shocked Juventus in the second round and knocked out Red Star Belgrade in the quarter-finals, made their defensive intentions perfectly clear, dropping top scorer Willy Guerts. The result was a predictably tight encounter with Villa frustrated for much of the match by the Belgians' strict offside trap. It took a 27th-minute Tony Morley strike following a nifty counter-attack to scupper the visitors' plans for a draw and perfectly set up the return leg.

Barton wasn't just optimistic Villa's slender lead would prove enough but that even better things lay ahead. 'I really believe we can win the trophy,' he declared. 'What's more, my players believe they are good enough to carry on the tradition established by Liverpool and Forest over the past four years.'

Two weeks later, expecting an onslaught in Brussels, Villa – easily 'the better side' in Barton's opinion – were rarely troubled. Anderlecht, despite the prompting of their young Spanish midfielder Juan Lozano, were timid in attack and, although Villa deserved victory on the night, the 0-0 draw was enough to see out the job. 'This is one of the greatest achievements in the club's history,' Barton enthused afterwards.

What was an accomplished showing on the pitch, however, was soured by ugly scenes off it. In a volatile atmosphere, violent skirmishes between the Villa and Anderlecht fans broke out at one end of the ground and saw the game halted for eight first-half minutes. One spectator (later discovered to be an army soldier on leave from his barracks in West Germany) had stumbled on to the playing surface in what appeared to be a drunken stupor and, in doing so, obstructed Anderlecht's Kenneth Larsen just as he was about to take a shot at Rimmer's goal. Afterwards, the Belgian side protested strongly, citing the 'psychological harm' that their players had suffered from the incident as just cause for the game to be replayed.

The normally softly-spoken Barton couldn't mask his anger. 'We won fair and square and definitely deserve to be in the final,' he insisted. With concerns in the Villa camp that the club could even be thrown out of Europe – 'It would be a tragedy if we were excluded from the competition,' Barton said – the news that Anderlecht's appeal had been rejected and the result stood came as a monumental relief. Villa were fined £14,500 and would have to play their next European home game behind closed doors. It wasn't the happiest outcome, but at least all minds could now focus on 26 May.

In the league, through April, confident and in good form, Villa strung together a three-match winning streak, including a 3-0 victory at The Dell that saw title-chasing Southampton almost arrogantly dispatched. Barton – once labelled 'the least-known manager in the First Division'

– was announced as the Bell's Scotch Whisky Manager of the Month. One-time Villan Danny Blanchflower's belief that Barton – 'a nice guy with decent values and a sensible attitude' – would 'restore unity to Aston Villa' was right. The calming influence of a man who, according to his wife, had only lost his temper once in 25 years, had a profound effect on Villa's fortunes. Yet Barton wasn't one to blow his own trumpet. 'If you stick your neck out,' he said, 'someone is likely to cut off your head.'

With any possibility of relegation having disappeared, Villa played out their remaining league fixtures and, despite winning only two of the last seven – a Pat Heard strike giving them a 1-0 triumph at The Hawthorns and goals from Morley, Withe, and Bremner seeing off Swansea City 3-0 at Villa Park in the season's last game – they finished 11th in the First Division. The boat that might have sunk in February was safely harboured in mid-table. Villa's points tally of 57 was a full 30 behind champions Liverpool, who reclaimed their crown, with second-placed Ipswich, in Bobby Robson's last season with the club before being wooed by the England job, the bridesmaids once more, trailing Paisley's side by four points despite a late dash for the title.

Had the old two-points-for-a-win system still been in place, Villa would have ended with 42 points, their lowest total since the 39 earned in 1975/76. Given the season's troubles, however, few around Villa Park were complaining. Villa were still the highest-placed Midlands club, with Clough's Forest one spot beneath them. Birmingham City, under Ron Saunders, finished 16th.

Pinpointing the exact reason for Villa's early season failings was still hard. 'I can't explain why,' Kenny Swain wrote in his autobiography, 'other than to highlight the expectation surrounding the quest for European success.' The pressure on Villa to keep the trophy in England undoubtedly weighed heavily and 'as the domestic season wore on and we became less and less capable of clawing our way back into the top three or four,' Swain wrote, 'the European Cup became more central to our focus.'

If Villa's players, distracted by Europe, took their eye off the ball under Saunders, their attentions unquestionably sharpened with Barton in charge and, somewhat perversely, their league form improved the closer they got to reaching the final. Villa certainly weren't the first team to experience domestic tribulations the year after a title-winning campaign. In 1974/75, on the back of three West German championships in a row and following the first of their three successive European Cup triumphs, Bayern Munich slumped badly, finishing only tenth in the Bundesliga. And it was with Bayern that Villa had a date.

While nowhere near as strong as the mid-70s team, Bayern still possessed a daunting array of talents: international defender Klaus Augenthaler, World Cup-winner Paul Breitner captaining in midfield, and one of the most feared frontmen in Europe, European Footballer of the Year Karl-Heinz Rummenigge were just three momentous names in a highly experienced line-up. The West German club were unbeaten in their 12 previous European finals. Despite some erratic form – they'd lost 4-3 at CSKA Sofia in the first leg of their European Cup semi-final, by the same score to Hamburg in a Bundesliga game, and had been trailing Nuremberg 2-0 before battling back to win the West German Cup 4-2 – the Bavarian powerhouses had the odds heavily stacked in their favour.

Tony Barton was determined to upset them. 'People keep talking about Breitner and Rummenigge,' he said, 'and we know they are world-class players. But we have plenty of players for them to worry about.' Barton was convinced that Villa were 'a better all-round team'. Ironically, neither of Bayern's two main stars were underestimating their English opponents. 'I think they [Villa] will be harder to beat than Liverpool,' said Breitner. 'Villa don't play English football as we know it. They have a more modern style.' Rummenigge felt, 'Villa have a good mixture of youth and experience, and I don't see why we should be such strong favourites.' Tony Morley agreed. 'People see us as a team of workers,' he said, 'but I feel we have the class to win the cup.'

And on a bright, humid evening in Feyenoord's De Kuip stadium, while there might have been very little class on show, Villa produced a display of courage, guts and doggedness and did indeed win the cup. A crowd of 39,776 watched what *The Guardian*'s David Lacey described as 'a final which, while the quality of the football was at times less than distinguished, turned out to be one of the most eventful and exciting matches of its kind in recent seasons'.

Overcoming the confidence-shaking loss of Jimmy Rimmer after only nine minutes to a cricked neck he'd suffered in training on Tuesday of that week, Villa refused to panic, and rose magnificently to the challenge. None more so than Rimmer's replacement, Nigel Spink. In just his second senior game, the 23-year-old understudy played a hero's part in Villa's triumph. Unaware beforehand of Rimmer's injury, and far from being overawed, Spink performed like a veteran, thwarting the Bavarians' attacks with a series of vital saves. Spink's flawless European debut – 'a fairytale' he later called it – broke German hearts. 'Storybooks make fortunes out of such tales,' penned the *Birmingham Mail*'s Leon Hickman in his match report. 'Here it was coming true in front of us.' Rummenigge was denied by a blockading spread of Spink's body; Dürnberger had a low drive stopped by a full-stretch, reflex save; a courageous plunge at the feet of Hoeness kept out the Bayern number nine.

With Villa unable to wrest the game from their opponents, Bayern poured forward more and more. Rummenigge's acrobatic overhead kick from 15 yards went narrowly wide; a goalbound Augenthaler header was cleared coolly off the line by Swain; Bayern's top scorer Hoeness arrived unmarked in the goalmouth, only to miss the ball completely from five yards out. The heart-stopping apprehension for the claret and blue multitude in the three-quarters-full stadium was almost relentless.

But in 'a match which – the longer it went on – seemed to be theirs for the taking', in David Lacey's view, the Germans couldn't make the breakthrough. Villa, to a man, dug in deep, defended resolutely and resisted the barrage. For all the pressure Bayern inflicted, Villa were equal to it. And in the 67th minute, the underdogs bit.

A dormant threat throughout, the 'mosquito-bite dangerous' Tony Morley (as Hickman called him) at last had a chance to go at the full-back. Latching on to a lovely through-pass from Gary Shaw and finding space on the left, the Villa wideman advanced into the Bayern box and 'taking the path with a disco-dancer's hip wiggle' (Hickman), twisted and turned Augenthaler before squaring a perfect, low, skidding cross across the face of the goal to the feet of Peter Withe. Barely a yard out, with certain immortality at his mercy, the big centre-forward almost made a hash of it, the ball bundling in off Withe's shin and ankle before hitting a post, beating Manfred Muller in the Bayern goal and finally, as *The Guardian*'s Charles Burgess put it, 'thrashing about in the net like a landed pike'.

After surviving a German onslaught, Villa were ahead. The state of screeching pandemonium among their fans showed they didn't care one jot how. 'The football which surrounded that 67th minute of giddy achievement may not have been so profound as much of that played in the recent past by Liverpool, or even Forest,' wrote the *Daily Mail*'s Jeff Powell. 'But this time the occasion scaled higher peaks of excitement.' Withe's miskick – 'it bobbled at the last second', he said afterwards – prompted a memorable commentary from ITV's Brian Moore, 'Shaw... Williams prepared to adventure down the left...there's a good ball in for Tony Morley...Oh, it must be, and it is! Peter Withe!'

It also proved to be the match-winner. In a nerve-racking last 20 minutes, though Bayern pressed for an elusive equaliser, in truth they couldn't replicate their previous incisive play and rarely threatened.

The dying minutes provided one last heart-in-the-mouth moment, however: Bernhard Dürnberger – the one player remaining from the 1973 friendly squad – looked to be in on goal only for Hoeness to latch on to the ball and fire it into the back of Spink's net. As the danger man wheeled away in celebration, linesman Joel Quinion raised his flag. Hoeness was correctly adjudged to have netted from an offside position.

After 43 seconds of added time, French referee Georges Konrath sounded his whistle and, as the Bayern players sank to their knees, the Villa fans caged in behind barbed wire fences on the terraces and by fear in their hearts were finally free. For the fifth time in a row, the European Cup Final was settled by a solitary goal. Aston Villa were European champions.

'It would have been impossible to invent a more appropriate end to this club's improbable season,' Jeff Powell wrote. 'The Unlikely Lads', as Powell titled them, had proved again that, as a team, they were a match for any collection of big-name players. Moments later, Dennis Mortimer climbed the stairs, shook the hand of UEFA president Artemio Franchi, then, as Leon Hickman described it, 'took hold of the high-shouldered silver European Cup and thrust it challengingly at the sky'. It was, Mortimer said afterwards, 'the greatest moment of my life'.

Villa had become, in Ian Johnson's words, 'the millionaire aristocrats of Europe' ready to 'compete with the world's football elite'. The victory was expected to net them £1m, with highly lucrative and prestigious challenges in the Super Cup and World Club Championship to come, and would also 'trumpet Aston Villa's name across the world'. Ron Bendall acknowledged, 'It means an awful lot to us.' Yet the success signified far, far more than a healthier bank balance. Aston Villa could sit proudly alongside the pantheon of Europe's greats.

Of Tony Barton, Leon Hickman wrote, 'His triumph has been expected and yet it could not go to a better man, whatever the sometimes baffling future of football may hold for him. His name is written in history now and, unassuming as he is, he will nevertheless relish that.' Barton, with typical modesty, said afterwards, 'I am really surprised to be here but not surprised for Aston Villa. It was another great team performance. We lived quite dangerously for quite a time but if you are going to win you have to be able to do that.' Barton confessed to being 'a little disappointed' that the official match programme made no mention of his name – Roy MacLaren was down as the team manager – but perhaps it was a measure of just how unobtrusively Barton had guided the club since those disquieting days when he was first handed the reins.

While accepting that Ron Saunders deserved a share of the credit, Barton declared himself 'delighted for everyone concerned with Aston Villa, after a mediocre season. It's happened so quickly!' Missing from the programme or not, after only 56 days at the helm, the man the press had dubbed 'Tony Who?' had now imprinted his moniker indelibly in the football history books, joining his far more illustrious compatriots Busby, Paisley and Clough as a manager of a European Cup-winning team.

Ron Bendall was unreserved in his praise for Barton. 'Tony is a very clever chap,' he said. 'He knows his stuff and has made me a very proud man.' The gamble to give Barton a contract had been won. 'There is an entirely new atmosphere at the club,' Bendall said. 'Players are working harder for each other and what we are seeing is an entirely new Aston Villa.'

The 'new' Aston Villa, though, had been schooled in the old ways of their former boss. 'Whatever the current feeling about him at Villa Park,' Leon Hickman wrote about Saunders the day following the final, 'it would be churlish to deny that he created this team. No one can tell whether they would have won this trophy for him, but the habits and discipline that were tested and proved last night were his.'

The players, Mortimer would later say, 'didn't make any kind of pact to go and win it for Ron, but I always call it Ron's team'. Saunders was quoted as saying that the side he'd built was so well-drilled and professional that it could run itself for 18 months, regardless of who they put in charge. Mortimer agreed. A manager was there essentially as a frontman. 'If you've got enough quality and experience in a side then a manager, to me, is there just to keep things ticking over,' Mortimer said. 'The side was playing so well that it didn't need stimulus.'

When Barton took over, however, Villa weren't playing well. In difficult circumstances, Barton kept the focus of an out-of-sorts team and, most importantly, maintaining the spirit of what Saunders had created, he didn't try to fix what wasn't broken. 'He left a well-oiled machine to run itself,' said Kenny Swain. The continuity was so instrumental in Villa's success. Barton said later that the European Cup win 'was the moment we had all dreamed of'. For all that that night was the culmination of Saunders' work, it was Barton who ensured that the dream came true.

Boy, I've Got the Birmingham Blues!

BY the end of 1981/82, Birmingham City's form was sufficient to see them remain in the top flight in a relatively comfortable 16th place, albeit only two points clear of Leeds United who went down along with Wolves and Middlesbrough. They won just one of their first ten league games under Ron Saunders, but a 3-3 draw at Elland Road then a 1-0 win at Coventry in their last two fixtures eventually saw them safe.

At St Andrew's, as was his wont, Saunders found himself in a quarrel with a number of experienced players. Archie Gemmill, Colin Todd and Frank Worthington, the foot soldiers brought in by Jim Smith to a side labelled 'Dad's Army', were deemed unfit for active service and soon shipped out.

Unlike at Maine Road, there was no wholesale revolt within the senior ranks. Saunders had, effectively, been given carte blanche by City chairman Keith Coombs and the freedom, compromised Saunders felt by outside forces at Villa, was his. 'I think that a manager should be allowed to manage,' Saunders said on taking up his new position. 'If that means having a finger in every pie, I do not believe that should be a bad thing.'

Dennis Shaw, a *Birmingham Mail* journalist until 1978 and by 1982 the commercial manager with the Blues, found Saunders' style the complete reverse of Smith, who was 'mutually supportive, full of enthusiasm, acutely aware of the need for all concerned to pull in the same direction and ready to share a laugh or two when the pressure was off'. Shaw endured an unhappy 12-month stay during Saunders' City reign and felt that Saunders, with his free hand, was more determined than ever to exert a tight grip on all club affairs.

Any commercial matters had to be first referred to the City boss rather than Shaw. Saunders insisted on extensive lists of club sponsors and executive box holders. He cut a shirt sponsorship deal with a local brewery – for, in Shaw's view, the 'ludicrously low' figure of £35,000 – and also ordered a huge quantity of towels bearing the Birmingham City logo to be stocked in the club shop, an item in which Shaw knew the home supporters would have little or no interest. Saunders wanted a cuddly toy as the new 'lucky mascot' to be placed in the City dressing room.

His eccentricities became more exaggerated. One matchday, a woman Saunders believed had 'a direct line to poppa' was entertained by the manager with her favourite tipple, a bottle of vodka. The supposed curse on St Andrew's, imposed since City's first game at the ground on Boxing Day 1906 by a group of disgruntled gypsies infuriated at being evicted to make way for the football club, was too much for a man with Saunders' superstitious nature to ignore. He sent for an exorcist to lift the curse, had crucifixes placed on each floodlight pylon and the soles of the players' boots painted red. Unsurprisingly, it had little effect on the club's fortunes.

In the 1982/83 season, City's escape from the drop was even narrower and couldn't have been secured in more dramatic fashion. In the relegation places for the best part of the campaign – the one real high spot being a 3-0 home humiliation of Villa at Christmas in a match held up for two minutes after missiles were thrown on to the pitch – when City were beaten 3-1 at Luton Town on 12 April, they were bottom and six points from safety with six games to go. But 1-0 wins over Coventry and Everton, a 2-1 victory at Sunderland, a 1-1 home draw with Brighton then a 2-0 defeat of Spurs set up a final-day clash at Southampton, with City needing a win at The Dell to survive.

They duly obliged. In the 87th minute, Mick Harford popped up with the only goal of the game and Saunders' side were 17th, safe by one point, Luton's 1-0 win at Manchester City condemning the Maine Road club to the Second Division together with Brighton and Swansea City.

The bleeding had been stopped but the wound didn't heal. The following season, one of six Midlands clubs in the bottom six, City finished 20th and lost their top-flight place in the company of Notts County and Wolves, the latter suffering an immediate return to the second tier a year after promotion.

Few were sad to see City go. Long before the media tagged Dave Beasant's Wimbledon with it, the 'Crazy Gang' label aptly captured Saunders' squad of characters with a penchant for extremely physical football and off-field fun. Harford was just one – Tony Coton, Pat Van

Den Hauwe, Mark Dennis, Noel Blake and Robert Hopkins were others – in a team that thrived upon the on-field battle and were, purportedly, rather fond of the bottle, too. 'Saunders didn't care if you drank all night so long as you trained properly,' Robert Hopkins told the *Sunday Mercury* in 1998. 'Once we were on the training ground we worked our socks off,' said Harford. 'We trained hard and lived hard.'

No match typified that toughness more than a clash at a rain-lashed Villa Park on 15 October 1983, on a day when Villa were hardly the innocents. Described as one of the most bad-tempered derbies ever – and headlined 'The Horror Show' in the following morning's *Mercury* – an utterly bad-tempered encounter was littered throughout with clattering tackles, off-the-ball incidents and free kicks. It took a minor miracle (and the referee's blind eye) that at its conclusion – the spiteful contest settled by a scrappy Peter Withe winner after 29 minutes – just six players were booked and only Colin Gibson received his marching orders.

Noel Blake, who had a goal controversially disallowed, also missed a penalty for the visitors but, as the clash ended, appeared to be more accurate with a headbutt on Villa's Steve McMahon. It was the final act on an afternoon that the *Birmingham Mail* dubbed 'Brum's day of shame'.

'There's a circus in the town, Ronnie Saunders is a clown,' sang the Holte End. 'And Birmingham are going down.' It was a prescient ending to the chant. For all their fight, Saunders' bunch of bargain basement buys couldn't lift the club from the canvas. The cruel irony was that their relegation sucker-punch was delivered by not only one of their own players but the player Saunders had coveted for Villa before acknowledging that Peter Withe was a better bet.

After an unsuccessful spell at Goodison Park under Howard Kendall, Mick Ferguson had ended up at St Andrew's, initially on loan – top-scoring with eight league goals in 1982/83 – before making the move to the Midlands permanent. But Saunders, after finally getting the chance to manage Ferguson, had loaned the forward back to his old club, Coventry City. On 12 May, as Birmingham could only play out a goalless draw at home to Southampton, Ferguson grabbed one of the goals in the Sky Blues' 2-1 home win over Norwich – and Coventry stayed up. Saunders' men didn't.

Ferguson left for Brighton shortly after. Coton, Van Den Hauwe and Blake soon followed through the exit door. The ex-Liverpool forward Howard Gayle, whose one-time romantic link with Saunders' daughter led to an unsavoury brawl between boss and player, was another on his way out before long. With City strapped for cash and his hands tied financially,

Saunders assembled a squad of old heads – Ray Ranson, Brian Roberts and Gerry Daly among them – who'd already been there, done that and got several t-shirts to show for it, and decent but unremarkable youngsters, with ex-Wolves forward Wayne Clarke, Allan's younger brother, the stand-out individual.

In September 1984, Des Bremner rejoined his former Villa manager. Three months later, David Geddis did so, too, signing from Second Division Barnsley, replacing the Luton-bound Harford. Even Tony Morley, having moved to West Brom, enjoyed a brief four-game loan spell under his old boss's charge. Although winning few admirers with their football, City earned promotion back to the First Division at the first attempt, finishing runners-up two points behind Oxford United, managed by Jim Smith. Some would actually insist that it was Saunders' finest managerial moment, one few others could have succeeded in realising.

Nevertheless, it was a feat tainted by tragedy. On 11 May 1985, the final day of the 1984/85 season and the same afternoon as the tragic fire at Valley Parade in Bradford, the club's reputation was tarnished even further by its notorious hooligan element. Rioting between rival supporters at the end of the Blues' home game with Leeds led to the death of a 15-year-old Leeds fan. When police pushed the Leeds supporters away from the pitch a 12ft wall collapsed under the pressure of the crowd, and the youngster, believed to be sheltering from the trouble, was left fatally injured. Still a schoolboy, Ian Hambridge had been watching his first game. What should have been a celebration instead resulted in ugly scenes of appalling violence, equated by Justice Popplewell in the subsequent investigation to more like 'the Battle of Agincourt than a football match'.

Birmingham's rendezvous with First Division life began well. By mid-September, they had won five of their first nine. But a 2-1 home victory over Leicester City on 21 September was the last league triumph they enjoyed under Saunders. A nightmarish 17-match winless sequence, including 15 defeats, left City near the table's basement and on 16 January 1986, two days after an ignominious FA Cup third-round home defeat to non-league Altrincham, Saunders resigned. 'I walked out in protest at a new director,' Saunders told Mat Kendrick. 'It was the principle and I wasn't going to put up with it.'

The new director was Ken Wheldon, the former scrap metal merchant who, just weeks earlier, had relinquished his interest in Walsall and bought Birmingham City from its owners the Coombs family for the princely sum of 25p in return for taking on responsibility for the club's £3m debts. When Wheldon made it known from the start that money for team strengthening was unavailable, Saunders jumped ship. Of all people, it was John Bond, having failed at both Burnley and Swansea City after his Maine Road stay, who replaced him.

Dennis Shaw termed Saunders' spell at St Andrew's 'a disaster with few redeeming features', yet he wasn't long out of work. The following month, fellow strugglers West Brom, replacing Nobby Stiles, who'd filled the caretaker role following the resignation of Johnny Giles (the Irishman quitting the Baggies for a second time), made Saunders their new manager. Ironically, Stiles' third and last game in temporary command saw West Brom complete a double over Birmingham City in Bond's first home match as the new Blues boss. The Baggies had endured an abject campaign, an opening day draw with top-flight new boys Oxford United preceding nine losses on the trot. It got decidedly worse and, by the time Saunders, with ex-England World Cup legend Stiles as his assistant, was entrusted with the task of picking up the pieces, Albion were bottom with only three wins to their name.

Despite chairman Sid Lucas's optimism that 'the appointment of Ron Saunders, with his long managerial experience and track record, is most likely to put Albion back on course for a more successful future', staving off relegation looked nigh-on impossible. Saunders, appointed on Valentine's Day, made no attempt to romance the West Brom support. 'It will not be the end of the world if we go down,' he told reporters. It sounded like he'd already accepted the inevitable. In their final 13 games, Albion won only once, collecting just five out of a possible 39 points and were left isolated at the table's foot. At St Andrew's, Bond fared little better, City winning just twice more by the season's end and unable to avert what would be a 16-year absence from the top flight.

Albion's demotion was confirmed at QPR with a month of the season still to go, a game in which future England international Steve Bull came on as sub to make his only appearance before Saunders dispatched him to goalscoring fame at then-Fourth Division Wolves, allegedly asserting that Bull 'had no first touch'. If selling Andy Gray to Wolves was considered a clanger by many, flogging Bull to the Black Country club was reckoned possibly the biggest of Saunders' career.

Another wrong step, some felt, was the boss's immediate demand that all players live within 25 miles of The Hawthorns or leave. Too much time, Saunders believed, was spent commuting rather than training. Experienced midfielders Gary Owen, Mickey Thomas and Steve Hunt (finding himself out of favour with Saunders once more) never featured again for the first team. Tony Grealish didn't start another Albion game.

Long-serving keeper Tony Godden was another casualty, replaced by Saunders' first recruit, Lincoln's Stuart Naylor. Faith was placed in honest graft more than genuine class but with minimal effect; Albion's demise was already on the cards.

In the Second Division for the first time since 1949, they showed no signs of leaving in a hurry. Upwards, at least. Tumbling down the table, home attendances fell with them, the average dropping below 10,000 for the first time since 1910. From mid-December Albion recorded a dismal single victory in their next 15 league games.

By February 1987 there was already press speculation about Saunders' position. With the West Brom board increasingly concerned about the team's strength despite Saunders being involved in no less than 20 transfer deals since he took over and former favourite Ron Atkinson available after his sacking at Old Trafford, the temptation for a change at the top was reportedly very strong.

The board resisted, but only temporarily. Staring down the barrel of the relegation gun, Albion eventually dodged the bullet, two 1-0 victories in the last week of April over Millwall then Portsmouth – the latter secured by a goal from Robert Hopkins, playing under Saunders at a third club – proving crucial. After a winless final three games, Albion ended 15th, clear of the drop but only by three points.

For Saunders, though, it was a brief stay of execution. On 2 September 1987, with West Brom bottom on only one point from four games of the following season – a goalless draw against Oldham Athletic and defeats to Blackburn, Swindon and Leeds – the Baggies' board announced that their manager had been dismissed. A month later, as expected, they brought back Atkinson for a second crack of the whip.

Overseen by Saunders, Albion lost 34 of the 67 games they played. Factoring in his spell at St Andrew's, conspiracy theorists among City and West Brom supporters might have been forgiven for thinking that Saunders was, as a writer on Albion's official website put it, 'a double agent, sent out by Aston Villa to wreak havoc among its neighbours'. His career as a top-flight manager had ended with an extraordinary run of just one win in 30 games, and that unwanted record of effectively taking the two sides down in 1985/86 would ensure Saunders' place in many a pub quiz and an even more revered place in the hearts of Villa's fans.

Saunders was, Reg Drury said, a man who 'seldom regards football as a joking matter', so what was unquestionably a career nadir would have filled him with less mirth than usual. However, Tony Morley, who'd signed permanently for Albion before the 1987/88 season, had sensed a perceptible change in his manager's relationship with football. 'When I played for him at West Brom, I knew that he was beginning to lose interest in the game,' Morley told the *Birmingham Post*. 'I think he'd had enough by 1987, he really had.'

There was, Morley observed, little of Saunders' old fire left. Five-a-sides, competitive low-scoring affairs at Villa, were instead matches finishing 11-9. 'He wasn't as fierce, the discipline had gone, the players weren't frightened of him anymore,' said Morley. 'Things like that made me realise he couldn't do it anymore.'

Dennis Mortimer, playing for Brighton against West Brom, recognised a difference, too. 'I'd never seen him look so ill. He looked pale, drawn. I just thought, "The game's getting to you."' Towards the very end of his reign, prevented by the Albion directors from travelling on the team bus, Saunders had to drive to a game in his car. 'It was a disgraceful way to treat someone of his integrity and experience,' Morley told *The Observer*'s Tim Adams. 'On the Monday at training he came in and said he was finished with it all. "Football these days is run by morons," he said.'

The Sergeant Major and Parish Priest!

RON Saunders' 14-month tenure at The Hawthorns was the last role in his 20-year managerial career. To date, he remains the only man to have taken charge of Aston Villa, Birmingham City and West Bromwich Albion. At every football club he ran, Saunders polarised opinion like perhaps no other manager of the period. The gulf could not have been starker between those who railed so forcefully against what they considered Saunders' draconian ways and those who, though they may not have followed him blindly, had total faith in him to lead them. Nowhere was it better illustrated than in Saunders' relationships with two of the club's goalkeepers at St Andrew's.

Jeff Wealands, demoted to third or fourth team football and subsequently suspended for two weeks by Saunders for making sarcastic remarks to reporters upon an emergency first team recall – 'I told the local press it was nice of him to remember that I was alive,' Wealands said, 'that I'd thought I must have had bubonic plague or something' – declared, 'Saunders is the only man I've ever hated.'

David Seaman, conversely, was glowing in his praise of a manager who 'knew everything about football' and 'all about the art of goalkeeping'. Seaman, signed from Peterborough in October 1984, had never had a real goalkeeping coach. 'He was telling me all about the position of my hands, when to catch, when to deflect,' Seaman said. 'He was a great, great help.' The drills Saunders taught Seaman were ones used by the future England number one throughout his career.

Wealands, meanwhile, sold by Saunders to Manchester United, was to derive great personal satisfaction when he next encountered his former boss; Wealands was keeping goal for the Altrincham side that became only the second non-league club to eliminate a top-flight team on their own ground, winning 2-1 at St Andrew's in Saunders' last game in charge of City. 'You could say that the man had got his comeuppance,' Wealands told *The Northern Echo* in 2012.

Centre-forwards seemed to benefit most from Saunders' know-how. Having himself been very much an old-style number 9 – a story went that he'd once broken a bone in his neck only to discover the injury a couple of decades later – Saunders was wise to how best to handle oneself on the field, to 'aspects of self-preservation' as Andy Gray called them. That knowledge proved invaluable.

'I was a better centre-forward when I left Blues than when I arrived,' said Mick Harford. 'He got the best out of me and taught me to look after myself physically on the park.' Wayne Clarke was quoted as saying that Saunders helped him 'toughen up' as a player. David Cross, at Norwich, hailed Saunders as the one who really showed him how to play as a striker, how to battle hard for the team even if he wasn't playing that well individually. 'I had to be difficult to play against,' Cross told the *My Time In Football* website. 'Whoever we were playing, I wanted their centre-backs to be thinking: "F**king hell, I've got to play against that nuisance on Saturday." Ron Saunders taught me that.'

Even Andy Gray graciously conceded that Saunders' helpful lessons – teaching the striker to be less static or to attack the near post as often as he could – had brought him a lot of goals.

In a feature in the 1975 *Shoot* annual about the essential ingredients of a manager, what is required, it states, is 'Not only a first-rate knowledge of football, but also an ability to understand and handle men – in an odd sort of cross between sergeant major and parish priest!'

Most would contend that Saunders leaned far more to one camp than the other. He never pretended not to have foibles but nonetheless remained convinced that his methods provided overwhelming evidence of his ability to get the best out of players. His successes make it hard to argue otherwise. 'He knew what he wanted and he knew how to get it,' wrote Brian Little in his 1996 book *Return of the Little Villan*. The forward, with whom 'Ron used to fall out for fun', ultimately realised that his manager was only 'doing things for the best'.

Little admitted even adopting some of Saunders' footballing ethos into his own management style. Saunders' notion that a hard side to beat was one heading in the right direction, for one. 'There are so many things he did that I would never do,' Little, managing Tranmere Rovers at the time, told *The Independent*'s Brian Viner in 2004. 'But some of his techniques I use. I find myself saying, "We're 1-0 up, so let's win 1-0." When I was a player I disagreed with that. He's had a bigger influence on me than I ever would have imagined.'

Managers, by nature, are nonconformists. 'Brian Clough, Bob Paisley, Don Revie and Ron Saunders are as different as chalk, cheese, chutney and chopsticks,' write Andrew Ward and John Williams in *Football Nation: Sixty Years of the Beautiful Game*. Clough, for all his brashness, though, needed a partner in Peter Taylor with whom he could both spar and who would temper his own extravagances. In their often uneasy relationship (once described by Bob Paisley as 'like an Agatha Christie mystery'), Taylor it was, Clough acknowledged, who was the judge of talent. He, Clough, was the one who made sure the player delivered it.

As Paisley had proved so profitably, you didn't need to be an outgoing individual to have straightforward views and convey them in the clearest fashion. But he did have the help of a dedicated boot room staff who toiled tirelessly at Melwood, Liverpool's training ground, on every possible aspect that might enhance a player's performance. Shankly, too, had relied heavily on Paisley's meticulously detailed logs about players' mental and physical make-ups. Saunders ploughed a particularly lone furrow.

A self-confessed antisocial who, he admitted, 'made few real friends in football', (though he cited Paisley, Shankly, Bill Nicholson, Jim Smith and Bobby Robson as 'my kind of people' with whom he got on well), Saunders emphasised no one major influence. 'I've listened and learned,' he wrote in *Ron Saunders' Aston Villa Scrapbook*, 'but finally been big enough to do my own thing.' He always knew what he was doing, he once said, 'because I am doing it my way'.

The contribution made by Roy MacLaren couldn't be underestimated. Andy Gray, for one, credited MacLaren with working on the forward's weaknesses and spending long afternoons practising ball control which ultimately made Gray a better footballer. Jimmy Rimmer undoubtedly benefited from the guidance of the ex-keeper. MacLaren worked with the players on a day-to-day basis but soon learned that he wouldn't really be party to any major decision-making. While any coach should be progressive in his thinking and have his own ideas, his basic responsibility, MacLaren recognised, was 'to pass on the boss's ideas and thoughts to the players'. A coach's job, in MacLaren's view, was 'to back him [the boss] to the hilt' and, although one should throw in one's personal suggestions, the manager is the one who counts at the end of the day'.

Rightly so, felt Harry Kartz. 'It is the manager who runs a club,' he said, 'and he [Saunders] did that very, very well.' There was no director of football overseeing his every move, no coterie of staff to surround him. Saunders would have been appalled by the idea. 'He decreed everything,' said Ken McNaught, 'from what brand the tea lady would brew to who played for the first team.' Dennis Shaw took a different view. 'Saunders was beyond question the best and most successful team manager the club ever had,' Shaw wrote in *A Game of Three Halves*. 'I emphasise the word "team". As a "club" manager I feel that he had man-management problems to put it mildly. Had he stuck to his strength, namely turning out teams that were fighting fit, bursting with stamina and clear-eyed about their duties on the field, Villa could have built on their championship/European Cup success.'

Management, Saunders once said, was a vocation akin to the priesthood. Unlike Shankly for whom the game was a drug and who, even in retirement, remained addicted to it – 'I'm running every bloody club in the country,' he once said after various clubs benefited from his vast experience post-Liverpool – Saunders didn't eat, sleep and drink football. Shankly might have believed that football wasn't just a matter of life and death but 'much more important', but Saunders took a far more romantic view of the game. His players 'put Villa and their own mates second only to their wives and sweethearts', he'd said in a *Shoot* interview during the title season. 'That's the way it should be.'

Saunders made a vow to never return to the game – and he kept it. The moment he left West Brom, he put football behind him, he said. He'd promised himself that, come 55, he'd be out anyway. 'I started in football when I was 16 and left when I was 55. That's a lot of years,' *The Independent*'s Jon Culley was told in 1993. The way Saunders simply severed his ties was perhaps not so surprising. During Norwich's promotion season of 1971/72, interviewed after the side had made a winning start to the campaign, Saunders told *Goal* magazine, 'Even if we don't go up next May, it won't break our hearts. Nothing in this life ought to do that.' Even at that stage, for all his fierce ambition, Saunders appeared to have a clear perspective on football's place in the general scheme of things.

Retirement was divided between the garden, the golf course and grandchildren, 'Doing the things I always wanted to do but never had enough time for when I was working.' Religion played an increasing role in his life. Interviews were rare. Firmly ensconced in family life and shunning all publicity, Saunders earned a new label: that of shy recluse.

In 2001, a VIP invitation to attend a dinner to mark the 20th anniversary of Villa's title triumph was declined. Saunders accused the club of cold-shouldering *him* for the previous 20 years. 'I have hardly received a phone call from Aston Villa since I left,' the 69-year-old said at the time, 'so I don't see why I should make the effort now.'

Certainly Aston Villa gave little recognition to Saunders' accomplishments in the years following his departure. Dennis Mortimer, who led a campaign to get it rectified, attributed that to Doug Ellis. At Villa's AGM in October 1982, it was revealed that the club were £1.6m in debt, a financial burden exacerbated by escalating wages and building costs, including the construction of the North Stand. The following month, Ron Bendall declared his intention to sell his controlling interest in the club. Neither Harry Kartz nor Trevor Gill was in the running. Both had been removed from Bendall's Christmas card list when the pair were prominent in initiating police investigations into the new stand's financing.

Prior to the European Cup Final, a story had surfaced that thousands of pounds had gone missing in connection with work carried out on offices being added to the new stand. An internal report by a design consultancy commissioned by the club concluded that invoices totalling over £700,000 could not be accounted for from a total bill of £1.3m. There was evidence that duplication of charges had occurred on costs of work that had been completed on the club's behalf. The new offices were built under the auspices of a company part-owned by Villa stadium manager Terry Rutter.

Another report, by the club's auditors, Deloitte, Haskins and Sells, called into question the position of Rutter being both the employers' representative and the site engineer for the work. On Monday 27 September 1982, while the Villa team and officials were on their way to the second leg of a European Cup tie with Besiktas, Villa Park received a visit from the police. Kartz and Gill had taken the initiative in calling them in. Three years later, at Birmingham Crown Court, Terry Rutter and his partner Harry Marsden, who had been the North Stand's architect, faced fraud-related charges, including conspiring with Bendall to obtain money by deception, and were both handed 12-month suspended jail sentences.

The man reported to be the likely buyer of Bendall's shareholding was Harry Parkes, widely regarded as one of Aston Villa's most popular players of all time. But with the deal seemingly assured, Parkes made a fatal hesitation. Having elected to bring in accountants and a solicitor, too much time passed and Parkes' opportunity was lost. Instead, a new announcement was made: Bendall had sold his 42 per cent stake to none other than Doug Ellis. After apparently flying out to the Isle of Man to seal the deal, Ellis paid approximately £465,000 for the privilege.

On 30 November 1982 both Ron and Donald Bendall resigned from the board. Just why Ron Bendall went back on his agreement with Parkes and sold his holding 'for a pittance to a man he despised', as Harry Kartz described it, was unknown. Sensing the encroaching shadow of legal action, did Bendall want out quickly and sell to the highest bidder? Or was it a more sinister act? In selling to Ellis, was Bendall hoping to get some revenge on Kartz and Gill?

A plausible theory had it that Ellis and Bendall had an agreement that whoever lost in November 1979 would have first chance of buying back the club when the time came. Whatever his motive, Ron Bendall took it to the grave. The following year the man who'd occupied the Aston Villa chair during the club's finest achievements of the modern era died. Had it not been for his death, the judge, when sentencing Rutter in 1985, made it clear that Bendall would also have been in the dock for his part in the making of fraudulent claims.

Six months after Peter Withe's goal against Bayern Munich, Doug Ellis was Aston Villa chairman for a third time, his shareholding making his position as secure as it could possibly be. Back in the seat of power, his enemies on the board and in the dugout conquered, Ellis had everything he'd always wanted. Yet he would never be fully loved – and that is maybe what he desired most of all. Ellis didn't even witness the win in Rotterdam, his flight to Holland getting cancelled with Ellis stuck on a plane diverted to Shannon Airport in Ireland because of industrial action.

With his return, Villa, in Dennis Mortimer's view, 'became Doug Ellis FC', a club synonymous with their personal glory-seeking chairman who revelled in the moniker, 'Deadly'. Hostile towards any reminders of just how successful Villa were while he was out of the boardroom, Ellis, Mortimer believed, was eager to eradicate all traces of both Saunders' and Barton's achievements. 'He wasn't there and he just parked that history,' said Mortimer.

In 2006, however, shortly after Ellis sold the club to American billionaire Randy Lerner for £62.6m, Saunders accepted an offer from the new chairman to be guest of honour at the match between Villa and Manchester United. On 23 December, before the home side's 3-0 defeat, Saunders was introduced to the 42,551 crowd and a chance for the Villa fans to say a long-overdue thank you to him fostered an emotional response. Saunders received a rapturous reception. Finding that Villa had not forgotten him, he admitted he was taken aback.

Dwelling on the past had never been Saunders' habit. 'I don't particularly look back on what I achieved with Aston Villa, as that was then and this is now,' he'd told the *Sunday Mercury* in 2001. Neither was he a man with regrets. 'I can honestly say there is nothing that ever happened in my life which, if I had my life over again with all the strengths and weaknesses I have got, I wouldn't do exactly the same,' he informed Mat Kendrick five years later.

The 'unfortunate circumstances', as Tony Morley called them, of Saunders leaving, though, arguably robbed Aston Villa of even greater glories. Had Saunders remained at Villa Park for the long term, could the club really have cemented their standing and ultimately challenged Liverpool's place at the top of the pecking order? The players thought so. 'I am adamant that if Ron had stayed on and had been given a new, longer contract,' said Morley, 'Villa would have been the team, definitely in England, if not Europe.' Not becoming the side of the 1980s, Morley felt, was an opportunity missed. 'Instead, it was Everton who dominated in the years straight after,' Morley told the *Sunday Mercury*, 'and a lot of our FA Youth Cup team never came through.'

All that Saunders had laboured over was 'broken up too soon' in Mortimer's opinion. 'Ron was good at putting good teams together, and this one had the legs to go on another couple of seasons,' he said, 'and with Ron's experience good players would have been brought in to continue the success.'

Even without Saunders, the European crown could have been the catalyst for Villa to establish itself as a major force but, rather than kicking on, the club tripped over its own bootlaces. Liverpool in the post-Paisley period would celebrate sustained success for another six or seven years, with Paisley himself continuing at Anfield in a boardroom role until 1992. Paisley passed away in February 1996 and to this day remains the club's most successful manager.

For Villa, however, the stay at the very peak was all too ephemeral. Tony Barton, after the final, had insisted, 'This has always been a great club. Now we are doing great things. The future holds exciting things for us.'

That future never materialised. The foundations were there for an era of domination but they were built on sand. Any designs on establishing a Liverpool-like empire quickly went to ruin and within five short years the club had sunk to its knees again.

The starting XI that beat Bayern – Rimmer, Swain, Williams, Evans, McNaught, Mortimer, Bremner, Shaw, Withe, Cowans and Morley – had first played together in a goalless local derby with West Brom on 8 November 1980. The European final was the very last time they did so. By 1986/87, only five players – Spink, Williams, Evans, Blair (who'd returned to the club from Sheffield Wednesday) and Shaw – remained from either the league or European Cup-winning sides.

In early September 1983, Shaw, on the threshold of a glittering international career, received a serious knee injury at Forest's City Ground that would eventually require six operations in four years and effectively hamper the rest of his playing career. When players left, their experience went with them. 'I do not think that we used the players to pass on their knowledge to the new generation,' said Peter Withe. The villain of the piece, in Morley's eyes, was definitely Ellis who 'changed everything and got rid of the likes of myself and Dennis Mortimer'. What could have been a conveyor belt of medals was stopped dead.

In December, with Ellis in place once more, Villa ventured to Tokyo for the money-spinning World Club Championship match versus Uruguayan champions Peñarol. Despite acquitting themselves well against the South Americans, a 2-0 defeat made for a long trip home. Early in the New Year, Barton's men faced Barcelona (holders of the European Cup Winners' Cup) in the two-legged Super Cup Final. Having lost 1-0 in the Nou Camp, a brutal return leg definitely not for the timid was won 3-0 and Barton's standing was enhanced even further. But that was as good as it got.

In March 1983, after seeing off the Turkish champions Besiktas then Dynamo Bucharest of Romania, Villa surrendered their hold on the European Cup, losing in the quarter-final to a Juventus side containing French captain Michel Platini, Polish ace Zbigniew Boniek and no less than six of the Azzurri's victorious 1982 World Cup team. Just over a year later, after 'results were simply not good enough for a big club like Villa' Ellis said, Tony Barton was dismissed. He never again managed in the top flight.

The appointments of, first, Shrewsbury Town's Graham Turner, at 36 Villa's youngest-ever manager, as Barton's successor, then Manchester City's 46-year-old ex-Lisbon Lion Billy McNeill, both proved exceptionally poor judgment on Ellis's part. Neither possessed the know-how nor, it appeared, the heart to stop the rot. Results nosedived year on year and on 4 May 1987 (a game played on the 30th anniversary of Villa's last FA Cup win), a 2-1 home defeat to Sheffield Wednesday ended a season-long nightmare as the Midlanders were officially relegated from the First Division. Four days later, McNeill, whom Villa secretary Steve Stride believed was 'never really committed to the club', was on his way. When Villa lost their last match of a catastrophic campaign, 3-1 at Old Trafford, they were at the very bottom of the pile.

The post-mortem on Villa's decline inevitably resulted in accusing fingers pointing in Ellis's direction. His sympathisers believed that he took the right approach. The large debts built up by the previous regime's incompetence had almost forced the sale of Villa Park. It was only Ellis, they felt, who stopped that happening. Ellis's so-called penny-pinching made perfect business sense. To his detractors, Ellis was, as he had always been, a miserly man more concerned with balancing the books than the pursuit of honours. Because of him, they were convinced, the shine that the league and European Cup wins brought was far-too-quickly dulled.

Ultimately it was only Aston Villa Football Club who lost out. They were practically starting over from the very point at which Saunders had arrived 13 years before. Saunders certainly wasn't exempt from blame. To draw a veil over his abdication from the club is to forget how it left them in the lurch at such a vital time. The vitriol engendered by Saunders pitching up at St Andrew's only days later was significantly softened by Villa's European Cup glory but still took a long time to fade. Ignoring the fact that, throughout his Villa years, Saunders had many doubters would also be hypocritical. Sales were queried, tactics questioned, the manager's judgement – and, occasionally, his sanity – came under severe scrutiny.

The likelihood is that, even if Saunders had stayed on, his Villa Park tenure would have only been prolonged a little while longer. Ellis was so determined to get his feet back under the table he was, Dave Woodhall wrote, 'no doubt working out ways of returning even as his Rolls-Royce was pulling out of the car park' following his resignation. His return would have guaranteed Saunders' departure. If Ellis didn't sack him, Saunders would in all probability have quit anyway. Despite Saunders' generous assessment of their relationship – 'We had some classic confrontations, but by and large we got on,' he said – a happy marriage was impossible.

Even Ellis, though, the perceived arch nemesis, accepted Saunders' value to Villa. 'He did a good job for the club, no doubt about that,' he said. Another ex-chairman Harry Kartz cranked up the superlatives much higher. Saunders, he said, ranked 'right up there with Bill Shankly and Brian Clough for what he did at Villa'.

Whereas Shankly and Clough are hailed as giants of the game, however, alongside these two towering figures, Ron Saunders has been almost completely dwarfed. Possibly, that was of his own making. 'He was never interested in the media hoopla,' wrote Pat Murphy in the *Birmingham Post* in 2006. 'Of all the managers who have won the championship in recent decades, only Bertie Mee in 1971 had a lower profile.' Love Clough or loathe him, you couldn't ignore him. In comparison, Saunders was virtually invisible. 'A club is always judged on its results at the end of the day,' he argued, 'and not on how loudly individuals can shoot off their mouth.' Likewise, a manager.

That the national press portrayed Saunders as a dour introvert was no surprise. There was little attempt to remove the mask. Managers, Brian Scovell wrote, 'come from very different moulds via different routes' but the one thing they each have in common is 'vulnerability'. Saunders refused to let that vulnerability show. 'He was hell-bent on not showing a softer side to anyone,' said Brian Little. 'But he had a softer side and when I had to retire he was brilliant to me and made sure that I was looked after.' Gordon Smith was also witness to it. 'No doubt he had his insecurities and limitations, and masked these with his persona and expressions,' reflects the Scottish full-back, 'but I saw and experienced his warmth, generosity and humour as well.'

As forbidding as an Easter Island statue as he often looked, Saunders got great pleasure from producing a wisecrack, at press conferences with certain local journalists or in the dressing room. That they didn't always raise a laugh was, Pat Murphy said, down to 'his downbeat, wry Scouse humour [which] escaped many of his players, never mind reporters'. In *The Heart of the Game* by Jimmy Greaves, the famous England striker relates a story in which, at a club Christmas party, Saunders is approached by the wife of one of the Villa players who attempts to engage him in conversation. She informs Saunders that her husband (an unnamed player) says, 'He will buy me a new car if I can talk to you and get more than two words out of you.' Saunders' clever and witty reply is, 'You lose.'

The people who knew him, Saunders said, realised he was 'a very gentle man, especially when dealing with genuine people'. During the title-winning campaign, Dennis Mortimer tried to shoot down what he saw as the myth about his manager's persona. 'It's about time someone said that the real Ron Saunders doesn't resemble his cold, unsmiling reputation,' argued the Villa captain. Saunders, he said, 'doesn't suffer fools in football', but 'he will listen to anyone's problems and help solve them. He knows how to laugh and allows his players a bit of leeway to keep things bright.' To Jimmy Rimmer, the manager was more teddy bear than tough guy. 'I don't understand how Ron got his iron-man image,' Rimmer told Ray Matts. 'He's one of the best bosses I've worked for and they include Sir Matt Busby and Bertie Mee.' Saunders, he said, was 'helpful, tolerant, prepared to listen to any ideas'.

Saunders' regard for the Villa supporters was always sincere. Ironically, it was precisely Saunders' authoritarian air that inspired most belief in the bulk of them. 'Growing up, having him as Villa manager, almost felt like your dad was in charge,' wrote one on an online fan site. 'The best way I could sum up Ron Saunders,' expressed another, 'is to say that you had total trust in the man.'

The long coat, the fixed stare, and the lack of nonsense were symbols of a proper, hard-boiled, 'old school' manager, one whom players crossed at their peril. 'You got the distinct impression that if we played bad in the first half, Ron would lay into them,' was another comment. He was a man 'whose word was law' and you'd better abide by it.

Many experienced the flesh and blood beneath the hard exterior. 'Many thanks for the interview you gave my mate and I for our school newspaper in 1979,' wrote one fan on an online Villa forum, 'I won't forget you gave us the chance of a cuppa and a fruit Club biscuit with the players afterwards.' Another debt of gratitude was paid, 'Thanks for giving me and my husband the tickets for the 1977 League Cup Final,' the poster put. 'We had booked our wedding before we won the semi-final but then couldn't get tickets for the final. You came to our rescue. Thanks Ron.' They were heartfelt messages to a man who'd provided them, one more said, with 'some of the best days of our lives'.

Saunders, Brian Little writes in *Return of the Little Villan*, was 'difficult to fathom out, to say the least'. If he was 'hewn from purest granite,' wrote Richard Whitehead in *The Soul of Aston Villa in 50 Moments*, 'why, I have always wondered, did he feel it necessary on winter afternoons to watch the game under a paisley picnic rug?', huddled in the dugout with 'the rug that he frequently arranged rather fussily over his lap like a pensioner determined to ignore the chill of an April afternoon at the seaside.' Saunders' 'hard man' effect might have been somewhat marred but his habit caught on: the Trinity Road stand at Villa Park would often be awash with tartan blankets whenever the temperatures dropped!

Is Saunders unlucky not to be included in a list of all-time managerial greats? There's a case for both yes and no. His critics might highlight the fact that, unlike Clough who moved to Derby's bitterest rivals, Forest, and attained even greater heights, Saunders' post-Villa years yielded little but controversy. But then, replicating Clough's feat – leading two different clubs to the league championship – was something only three others, Tom Watson, Herbert Chapman and Kenny Dalglish, have ever managed.

Then again, could Clough, had he been handed the Villa job in 1974, have achieved what Saunders did, in such a relatively short space of time, and against a backdrop of almost relentless boardroom turmoil? Clough's revolutionising took two East Midlands clubs to unimaginable heights. Villa, a fallen football giant, had already reached the stars. Saunders allowed them to touch them again.

To paraphrase Clough himself, Saunders wasn't the best Aston Villa manager in the business. But he was in the top one. 'Saunders found himself out of work at the time the Villa were looking for a new manager,' wrote Dennis Shaw. 'Such timing was either coincidence or fate.'

Whichever it was, the story of Aston Villa is richer for Ron Saunders, and vice versa. In tandem they authored one of the club's most memorable chapters. Saunders' subsequent failures after leaving Villa Park have only confirmed the Villa fans' feeling that their club was his club, a spiritual home at which he was almost destined to succeed. The Midlanders and the manager seemed a precise fit.

'We have always tried to seek perfection,' Saunders once said during his time with Aston Villa. And, do you know what, just for a moment, they really did find it.

Bibliography

Armfield, Jimmy (ed.), *All Stars Football Book*, World Distributors, 1970

Shipley, John, *Aston Villa Champions 1980/81*, Tempus Publishing Ltd, 2005

Woodhall, Dave, *The Aston Villa Miscellany*, Vision Sports Publishing, 2008

Woodhall, Dave, *McMullan to O'Leary: Claret and Blue Managers*, Heroes Publishing, 2003

Articles

McIlvanney, Hugh, *Motivation!, The Observer*, 18 November 1979

Jawad, Hyder, *2-2 ...and I scored them all; Villa legend Chris Nicholl recounts his double dose of embarrassment to Hyder Jawad 30 years after the match, The Birmingham Post*, 18 March 2013

Websites

www.astonvilla.vitalfootball.co.uk

www.avfc.co.uk, *Little at 60: "Everyman" Brian always on the road to glory,* feature by Paul Brown, 2013

www.avfc.co.uk, *Villan on the Spot* series, interviews with ex-stars conducted by Colin Abbott, 2015

www.citytilidie.com, *An interview with Frank Carrodus,* by Gary James, first published in the Manchester City programme 11 September 2004

www.eafa.org.uk/catalogue/118592 *Promotion to 1st Division for City:* Anglia Television sports report including interviews with manager Ron Saunders and Norwich City Football players.

www.europeancuphistory.com

www.heroesandvillains.net

www.letstalk24.co.uk, *Best of enemies*, posted on 22 August 2013

www.mightyleeds.co.uk

www.myoldmansaid.com

www.playupliverpool.com

www.thevillablog.co.uk

Other sources

Villa Park Centenary: The Aston Villa Story 1897-1997 [VHS], 1997

Aston Villa: 1980/1981 Season Review – Champions [DVD], 2012